Austrian Cavalry of the Revolutionary and Napoleonic Wars, 1792–1815

Enrico Acerbi, András K. Molnár
Illustrations by Bruno Mugnai

Helion & Company

Helion & Company Limited
Unit 8 Amherst Business Centre
Budbrooke Road
Warwick
CV34 5WE
England
Tel. 01926 499 619
Email: info@helion.co.uk
Website: www.helion.co.uk
Twitter: @helionbooks
Visit our blog http://blog.helion.co.uk/

Published by Helion & Company 2021
Designed and typeset by Serena Jones
Cover designed by Paul Hewitt, Battlefield Design (www.battlefield-design.co.uk)

Cover: *Gemeiner* in service dress, 1805–1809, Husaren Regiment Nr. 3, Erzherzog Ferdinand Carl. By Bruno Mugnai © Helion & Company 2021

ISBN 978-1-913336-56-1

British Library Cataloguing-in-Publication Data.
A catalogue record for this book is available from the British Library.

For details of other military history titles published by Helion & Company Limited, contact the above address, or visit our website: http://www.helion.co.uk

We always welcome receiving book proposals from prospective authors.

Contents

Acknowledgements

The authors and illustrator of this book would like to thank those who helped them in their work. Special thanks to Paolo Coturri, Samuele Rocca, Herb Metzler and Terry Hooker for their contribution on the topic. Very special thanks go to Yves Martin for his invaluable help in the search of the iconographic sources.

1

The Imperial–Royal Army Before and After the French Revolution

Austria was the most implacable of Napoleon's Continental enemies after Britain. Austrian involvement appears particularly relevant if compared in terms of active belligerence; Austria was at war with France for 108 months; Prussia faced France for 58 months, and Russia 55 months. Furthermore, over the following 26 years after 1789, the Austrian army would wage six wars against Revolutionary and Napoleonic France. Also the geostrategic involvement appears relevant, considering that the Austrian army fought in no fewer than 264 engagements from the Low Countries to Italy, from the Swiss Alps to the hills of Moravia, an extent unequalled by any other European state. However, by analysing the political and economic dynamics in greater detail, it appears that the Austrian army was constantly in an emergency state, and in need of tactical reforms.

The considerable effort of the House of Austria in supporting the army was constantly subject to a search for the financial means to enable it to face the growing French military power.

The Austrian unpreparedness had its roots in the years before 1789. In the 1780s, the army Emperor Joseph II had bequeathed was not as capable as that which he had inherited from his parents. Scholars outline that Joseph's ceaseless meddling and obsession with state control had demoralised the army as much as it had all the sectors of Austrian society.[1] The new emperor, Leopold II, appeared to usher in a period of domestic calm, free from foreign adventure. He lowered the temperature with his considerable understanding and intelligence. Unfortunately, this enlightened ruler reigned for two years before succumbing to illness, but in those two brief years he achieved much, calming the state which under his predecessor had bridled at so

1 Karl Gutkas, *Kaiser Joseph II. Eine Biographie* (Vienna-Darmstadt: Zsolnay, 1989), pp.445–446.

Austrian Habsburg Domains in 1792.

many indigestible reforms. With regard to the army, Leopold's reign offered a welcome respite of stability after the frenetic changes that had occurred in recent years. Leopold devoted relatively little of his energy to military reform; earlier, in Tuscany, he had nearly disbanded the army and navy. As a result, the Imperial Austrian army which was to face Revolutionary France was largely that bequeathed by Joseph II. Following the peace of Svitšov in August 1791, Leopold II had sensibly reduced the army to 215,478 men, a

To the right, Emperor Joseph II (1741–1790), and to left his successor and brother Leopold II (1747–1792), portrayed by Pompeo Batoni in 1769. The Austrian military's unpreparedness had its root in the years before 1789. As a consequence of his action as reformer, Joseph II considerably reduced the resources of the army. The new emperor, Leopold II, calmed the state which under his predecessor had bridled at so many indigestible reforms, but he devoted little time to the Imperial military machine. Furthermore, earlier as Grand Duke of Tuscany, Leopold had nearly disbanded the army and navy. He had died after only a short illness on 1st March 1792, leaving his 24-year-old son Franz, not yet crowned emperor, to deal with the inevitable war against Revolutionary France. (Kunsthistorisches Museum, Vienna)

formidable force yet but well below the peacetime establishment of 1787, when Austria had 313,804 men under arms.[2]

Even from the point of view of the distribution of costs for supporting the army, the state of the Habsburgs showed a very unequal scenario. Despite the economic potential of the Austrian monarchy being considerable, with many agriculturally rich areas, substantial mineral resources, a good supply of skilled craftsmen and manufacturing enterprises, the financing of the army had always represented a serious task for Vienna. Throughout the eighteenth century Austria had financed the wars by foreign loans and by issuing paper money. Even so, the Emperor did not go far enough and there remained numerous restraints on military policy. The fragmented nature of the Habsburgs' domains was the cause of major problems. The Habsburgs ruled by virtue of separate titles over territories that had little or nothing

2 Michael Hochedlinger, *Austria's War of Emergence. War, State and Society in the Habsburg Monarchy, 1683–1797* (London and New York: Routledge, 2013), p.300.

Emperor Franz II, later Franz I of Austria in 1805 (1768–1835), whose complete name was Franz Joseph Carl Johan. Portrayed here by Joseph Kreutzinger in 1814. During his reign, Franz went through the long cycle of wars against Revolutionary and Napoleonic France. Despite having held leadership roles in the army, his contribution was far from positive. In particular, historians blame him for his schizophrenic attitude towards his brother Archduke Carl, and his attempts to reform the House of Austria's military machine. (Neue Galerie am Universalmuseum Joanneum of Graz, Austria)

in common and their military posture was weakened by the lack of uniformity in these matters. Some provinces retained anachronistic privileges and the local estates were ready to use the law to oppose the Emperor. The Tyrol, for instance, preserved the ancient privilege to raise a burgher–peasant militia for its own defence and to limit the recruiting for the standing army. Also the Italian domains as well as the Low Countries, because of their distance from Vienna, were largely excluded by military financing. In 1789, the attempt of Emperor Joseph II to enforce reforms in the Low Countries turned into open revolt and the endeavour had to be suspended. Also Hungary had provided little support in military affairs.

In 1722 the Hungarian Parliament had finally accepted the principles of a permanent Royal Army under the strategic control of Vienna, definitively shelving the exemption from taxation in return for military service in the obsolete feudal levy: the *Insurrectio*. Although this system remained in use for assembling the local militia, Hungary entered the Habsburg military, but retained control over recruitment and supply. Even after this agreement, disagreements and problems continued. The Diet convoked in 1764 to raise the provinces' contribution to army finances, and to convert the service obligations of the local aristocracy into a cash subsidy for the army, refused to act.[3] Because of this uncertain financial situation, payment on debts and current expenditure pushed the monarchy into a deficit of about 9,600,000 florins annually. In 1790 the deficit climbed to 27 million, then grew to 23 million the next year, and after Leopold II reduced the army it reached a low of four million florins in 1792.

Although the army strength remained considerable, the strategic centre of gravity was shifted in different directions. Before 20 April 1792, the day that opened the long series of conflicts against France, with the Paris' Legislative Assembly's declaration of war to 'the King of Hungary and Bohemia',[4]

3 Gunther Rothenberg, *Napoleon's Great Adversary. Archduke Carl and the Austrian Army 1792–1814* (Bloomington: Indiana University Press, 1982), p.20.

4 This was neither a mistake not a deliberate breach of etiquette. In fact, Leopold II had died after only a short illness on 1 March 1792, leaving his 24-year-old son Franz, not yet crowned Emperor, to deal with the now inevitable war. The *interregnum* provided an ideal and diplomatically correct opportunity for France to keep the *Reich* out of the war and to concentrate solely on Austria.

Austria's major concerns were in the south-eastern and northern borders. In addition to the *Erbfeind* (the Ottomans as hereditary enemy), Vienna had faced a possible war against Prussia in Bohemia. The military effort was then concentrated to the region far from the Western boundary, because since 1752 France had been the first Austrian ally and nothing seemed to modify this scenario before 14 July 1789. Anyway, in 1792 the strategic situation could even get worse for Vienna, because close to the precepts of traditional anti-Austrian foreign policy, Friedrich Wilhelm II was obstinately courted by France, Prussia being the natural enemy of Austria.[5]

Prince Albert Casimir of Saxony, Duke of Teschen (1738–1822), by an unknown artist. A humanist and fine arts collector, the Prince was appointed as Governor of the Austrian Low Countries in 1782. Ten years later he achieved poor results holding military command in the province during the first campaign of war against France. (Albertina Collection, Vienna)

Towards the end of April 1792, the French declaration of war had not yet reached Vienna, but French troops invaded Belgium in a three-pronged surprise offensive. The reduction of the army strength in 1791 delayed the Habsburg reaction in the Low Countries. In the face of the mounting tensions with France, the 31,000 Austrian troops in the Low Countries had been put on alert in late 1791. However, this force was hardly sufficient to ward off French aggression, let alone launch any large-scale expeditions against France itself. In addition, the Austrian governor Prince Albert of Sachsen-Teschen,[6] who held military command in the province, was probably not the better choice available.

Vienna hoped that firm diplomacy supported by some sabre-rattling would be sufficient to intimidate the enemy, but when the war escalation accelerated, alongside the troops in the Low Countries the other significant military presence was in Anterior Austria, which numbered approximately 50,000 men, increased by a further 12,000 only at the beginning of 1793.

It was only in May 1792 that a plan of operations was agreed between Austria and some German states including Prussia. The military support was very minimal. With Prussia, only Hessen-Kassel, Mainz, Anhalt-Zerbst and Würzburg contributed with some contingents, while the Imperial circles mobilised their force exclusively for defensive tasks, showing a disconcerting reluctance to participate. Effectively this was no multinational crusade

5 Jordan R. Hayworth, *Revolutionary France's War of Conquest in the Rhineland. Conquering the Natural Frontier, 1792–1797* (Cambridge University Press: Cambridge, 2019), pp.39–40.

6 Prince Albert Casimir of Saxony, Duke of Teschen (1738–1822) was a prince from the Electoral House of Wettin who married into the Habsburg Imperial family. His military career proceeded quickly punctuated by the appointments to the Austrian and Hungarian offices, soon becoming *Feldmarschall* in 1765. He was the royal governor of Hungary until 1781, then appointed as governor of the Austrian Low Countries. In Brussels he built a palace in Laeken (the present-day home of the Belgian royal family) as his residence. There he assembled the beginnings of his vast art collection, which he took with him when the couple had to flee from Brussels to Vienna in 1793, due to the military defeat by French invasion forces in 1792. He became a notable art collector and founded the Albertina Collection in Vienna.

The battle of Valmy, after Horace Vernet (authors' archive). The "battle" was actually an artillery exchange which occurred on 20 September 1792, and to which the Austrians arrived too late to take part in the action. The episode marks the beginning of the military transformation that occurred after 1789. The main actor of this new warfare was the French army, heated by the social changes brought about by the Revolution. Military change was directly triggered by social transformation, with the removal of feudal social barriers, the expansion of national consciousness, and economic conditions being the main drivers. In other European countries this reform was typically carried out from above, from the direction of the ruler, leaving society untouched on the surface, so that for a long time it could not be really effective against the French. In this regard, the military power of the Habsburg monarchy underwent the most spectacular and thorough change. However, this was not due to internal development and evolution of the army, but to external coercive forces.

against Revolutionary France, but a Prussian–Austrian invasion. There were also 20,000 French *émigrés* who took part in the operations, but their presence was a dangerous and misleading signal for Vienna. Austria in particular had no intention to re-establish the *Ancien Régime*, but intended to support a constitutional monarchy that would disable France as a European power, thereby permanently relieving the Habsburgs from their nightmare of French–Prussian cooperation. Unfortunately the Austrian plan was destroyed even before the first allied soldier had set foot on French soil, when on 25 July the Duke of Brunswick issued his manifesto declaring the stabilisation of the French monarchy.

The plan entrusted the major offensive task to the army under Duke Carl Wilhelm Ferdinand of Brunswick, who would have to invade France by marching through Luxembourg, while the Austrians had to support the advance with two flanking operations from north and south. The Austrian army in the Low Countries had to perform an important part covering the Brunswick's right flank by advancing along the Meuse, while the troops in Anterior Austria received the easier task of protecting the left flank of Brunswick's army. In the event, Austria's contribution was to prove smaller than anticipated. The army in the Austrian Low Countries, in particular, was considered much too weak to face the enemy in the open field, and its involvement in the domestic insurrection prevented the Austrian commanders from effectively supporting the Duke of Brunswick. Just 14,000 men were ultimately dispatched from Brussels, while from Anterior Austria no more than 15,000 troops marched across the Rhine to take care of the strong French fortress of Thionville.

Successive events are well noted, as well as that the Austrians arrived too late to take part in what was just an artillery exchange at Valmy. The allies could hardly risk a further advance towards Paris and Brunswick chose to beat a hasty, and finally costly, retreat. Dysentery and difficulties of supply more than battle losses had dramatically thinned the allies' ranks. Further north, as a result of the uncoordinated allied offensive, Sachsen-Teschen was forced to abandon the siege of Lille at the beginning of October. After the retreat, the Austrians had withdrawn to a defensive position near Mons. The Austrian commander could deploy only a quarter of the Austrian troops in Belgium, the rest being scattered over the country in accordance with the traditional defensive cordon system. Consequently, at Jemappes, the field army under Sachsen-Teschen, no more than 13,000 men in all, was attacked and defeated by superior French forces on 6 November.[7] Within a few days the Habsburgs' rule in the Low Countries collapsed, and the country, with the exception of Luxembourg, was occupied by the French.

To repair the setbacks of the first campaign, Austria mobilised on a large scale for 1793. About 55,000 men were to be concentrated on the Lower Rhine, a further 30,000 covered Trier and Luxembourg, 40,000 supported the Prussians on the Middle Rhine, while 25,000 protected the Upper Rhine. Despite these considerable means, in mid February 1793 the French again took the offensive by invading the Dutch Republic. However the 40,000 Austrians under *Feldmarschall* Friedrich Josias Duke of Sachsen-Coburg-Saalfeld[8]

7 The same day in which the young Archduke Carl received his first baptism of fire commanding the Austrian right wing. Despite its modest numbers, the Austrian army performed fine, and though outnumbered nearly four to one, it fought for six hours before falling back in disciplined order, inflicting heavy casualties on its opponents. Although 13,000 Austrians faced 43,000 French, they inflicted more than 2,000 casualties. Austrian losses were 304.

8 Friedrich Josias Duke of Sachsen-Coburg-Saalfeld (1737–1815) was the youngest son of Duke Franz Josias and Princess Anna Sophie of Schwarzburg-Rudolstadt. He was the great-uncle of King Leopold I of Belgium, and the great-great-uncle of Queen Victoria of the United Kingdom. Josias joined the Habsburg army as colonel in 1759, participated in the Seven Years' War, and rose to the rank of *Feldmarschall-Lieutenant* by 1773. In the Russian–Ottoman–Austrian war of 1788 he commanded an corps under Laudon, occupying Moldavia and sharing in Aleksandr Suvorov's victory at Focşani on 1 August 1789. Having beaten the main Ottoman army under Grand Vizier Koca Yusuf Pasha in the Battle of Rymnik, he captured the greater part of Wallachia, including Bucharest, being welcomed by the population after the flight of Prince Nicholas Mavrogenes, and soon after became a *Feldmarschall*. In 1793 and 1794 he commanded the army in the Austrian Low Countires during the Flanders campaign. Due to his victory in the French Revolutionary Wars at Neerwinden in March 1793, he returned the region to Austrian control. Entering France he took Condé, Valenciennes, Quesnoy and Landrecies. However, due to unfortunate positioning, partly due to disunity amongst the allies and their forces, he suffered a string of minor setbacks in front of the French on the Sambre followed by the decisive defeat at Fleurus on 26 June 1794. He thereupon abandoned the Austrian Low Countries, which Habsburg diplomacy had already decided to give up. Angered by this, and openly criticising the policies of Austrian diplomacy, the Duke resigned as a commander, replaced by the Count of Clerfayt, and retired to his estates. He never joined the Austrian army.

Friedrich Josias, Duke of Sachsen-Coburg-Saalfeld (1737–1815). An aged veteran of the Seven Years' War, the Duke replaced Prince Albert of Sachsen-Teschen in the Austrian Low Countries, and after his victory at Neerwinden in March 1793 he returned the region to Habsburg control. Entering France he seized Condé, Valenciennes, Quesnoy and Landrecies. However, as a consequence of unfortunate positioning, partly due to disunity amongst the allies and their forces, he suffered a string of minor setbacks in front of the French on the Sambre River, followed by the decisive defeat at Fleurus on 26 June 1794, which caused the definitive loss of the Austrian Low Countries. (Engraving by unknown artist. Authors' archive)

started a counter-offensive from their base behind the Roer, and defeated the French at Aldenhoven on 1 March 1793. The campaign continued with a long series of Austrian and Prussian strategic gains on the Rhine, but this success was undermined by economic concerns. Prussian enthusiasm for the war had long since waned. Berlin's treasury was now all but empty, and soon an increasingly strong peace party in the court and military circles advocated a rapid withdrawal from the expansive but unprofitable war in the west, while in November Prussia tried to extort massive subsidies from Austria, the *Reich*, and finally Britain and the Dutch Republic, by threatening to leave the coalition. The Prussian passivity deprived the Austrian offensive in Alsace of flank cover. In November 1793, after the Austrian storming of the Lines of Weissenburg on the River Lauter and the conquest of Strasbourg in October, the French had liberated Alsace once more.

The deteriorating relations between Austria and Prussia inevitably drew Vienna's attention towards developments in the east, which were taken very seriously. As early as 1793 Austria had asked Russia to put military pressure on Prussia to remain in the coalition. Even open hostilities were no longer excluded between the two allies.

In 1794 Austria resumed the war, assembling on paper a gigantic reserve army of 144,000 men. Initially 70,000 men were destined to reinforce the army for the Low Countries and a further 50,000 for the Rhine, but the unsettled strategic scenario reduced the latter to 4,500 infantry and 3,000 cavalry in all.[9] It now seemed much more important that Bohemia and Moravia were covered again from any possible Prussian threat and the Ottoman border, it was felt, could not be neglected either.

Superficially, this decision appears to confirm the view, expressed by both contemporaries and later historians, that Austrian geostrategy was not really determined to retain the Low Countries with all the available forces. Actually, it is a popular myth, because from April 1794 onwards Emperor Franz II served in the theatre of war personally. Austrian plans were indeed ambitious, to provide an 87,000-man force to be dispatched against the French in the Low Countries. A further 85,000 would protect the Lower Rhine and 40,000 were to support the Sardinians in Piedmont. Unfortunately these figures existed only

9 Hochedlinger, *Austria's War of Emergence*, p.413.

on paper, but the initial phase of the campaign promised well. At the end of April 1794 Landrecies on the Sambre was seized, but soon the French repulsed the allies from Flanders to Luxembourg and utterly defeated them at Tourcoing on 18 May. Shortages of supply and poor staff work worsened the situation. On 26 June, at Fleurus, the coalition army under Sachsen-Coburg was defeated again. In 15 hours of struggle – described by the later French Marshal Soult, then a young lieutenant, as 'the most desperate fighting I ever witnessed' – the Austrian and Dutch troops, supported by the Duke of York, fought doggedly, inflicting heavy casualties on their opponents.[10] Compared to 208 allied losses, more than 5,000 Frenchmen were left dead or dying on the battlefield. But the French forces prevailed thanks to Jourdan's skill and tenacity in marshalling his troops.[11] The Austrian soldiers had fought well, on the whole, but they were facing a new style of warfare with techniques that were novel and unfamiliar. A new way of waging war was about to burst in on the unsuspecting generals of the anti-French coalition. The Habsburg army was able to withstand these assaults thanks to the abilities and personality of Emperor Franz's brother, Archduke Carl, who served under Sachsen-Coburg.

The war continued for a further three years and concluded with a substantial Austrian defeat on all fronts. During much of the time the army had fought with only little support. Compared with France or Prussia, where centralised institutions produced higher revenues and more coherent military establishment, the Habsburg state suffered a considerable disadvantage. However, despite the unpreparedness and the emergency climate that had plagued the operations, the Austrian soldiers performed well on several occasions and victory often vanished due to the aforementioned negative background. The fact that the army behaved positively may appear as a significant result, considering that just one year before the war with France broke out, Carl Mack von Leiberich,[12] then a promising young staff officer,

10 Michael Glover, 'Jourdan: The True Patriot', in D. Chandler (ed.), *Napoleon's Marshals* (New York: Macmillan, 1987), p.162.

11 Anti-French relations of the battle insist that Jourdan was helped by the first known use of aerial surveillance, thanks to the intrepid balloonists of his newly formed French Aerostatic Corps. They manned *L'Entreprenant*, giving Jourdan exact details of the movements of Coburg's five columns. *L'Entreprenant*'s sister balloon *L'Intrépide* was captured at the Battle of Würzburg in 1796 and is still on display in the Austrian Military Museum of Vienna.

12 Carl Mack von Leiberich (1752–1828), native of Ansbach, is best remembered as the commander of the Austrian forces that capitulated to Napoleon's Grande Armée after the Battle of Ulm in 1805. In 1770 he joined an Austrian cavalry regiment, in which his uncle was a squadron commander, becoming an officer seven years later. During the brief War of the Bavarian Succession he was selected for service on the staff of Count Kinsky, under whom, and subsequently under the commander-in-chief *Feldmarschall* Count Lacy, he did excellent work. He was promoted first lieutenant in 1778, and captain on the quartermaster-general's staff in 1783. Count Lacy retained the highest opinion of his young assistant. In 1785, he was ennobled under the name of Mack von Leiberich after his wedding with an Austrian noblewoman. In the Ottoman War of 1788–91, Mack was employed on the headquarters staff, becoming in 1788 major and personal aide-de-camp to the emperor, Joseph II, and in 1789 was promoted to lieutenant colonel. He distinguished himself at the storming of Belgrade in 1789. Shortly after this, disagreements between Mack and Ernst Gideon von Laudon, now commander-in-chief, led to the former demanding a court martial. Mack left the front but received a colonelcy and the Order of Maria Theresa. In 1790 Laudon and Mack, reconciled, were again on the field together. During these campaigns Mack received a severe head injury from which he never fully recovered. In 1793 he was made quartermaster-general to

commented that 'lack of unity, conflicting jurisdictions, and large distances make the Austrian military system far more complex than others'.[13]

After the Campoformio settlement, signed on 17 October 1797, a large faction in Vienna regarded this treaty as little more than an armistice. Febrile activity engaged the Aulic War Council in the preparation of ambitious but unrealistic plans. On 4 February 1798 Franz II ordered his brother Carl to bring the army as fast as possible into a war establishment. However, pressed by a nightmare economic scenario, the country and the army needed time to recuperate and therefore the Archduke warned his Imperial brother against undertaking ambitious reorganisation and reform.[14] There were divisions in Vienna regarding the army reform. The major duality materialised in the two

---

Prince Josias of Sachsen-Coburg, commanding in the Austrian Low Countries and he enhanced his reputation by the ensuing campaign. The young Archduke Carl of Habsburg, who achieved his own first success in the action of 1 March 1793, wrote after the battle, 'Above all we have to thank Colonel Mack for these laurels.' Mack distinguished himself again at Neerwinden and had a leading part in the negotiations between Sachsen-Coburg and French general Dumouriez. While he continued to serve as quartermaster-general, Mack became *inhaber* of a cuirassier regiment. He received a wound at Famars, but in 1794 was once more engaged in active service, having at last been made a *General Wachtmeister*. But the failure of the coalition allies, due though it was to political and military factors and ideas, over which Mack had no control, was ascribed to him, as their successes of March–April 1793 had been, and he subsequently fell into disfavour in military circles. However, the Emperor Franz II remained his supporter and in 1797 Mack was promoted *Feldmarschall-Lieutenant*. In the following year he accepted, at the Emperor's personal request, the command of the Neapolitan army. However, he could do nothing with the unpromising material of his new command against the French troops, and before long, being in actual danger of being murdered by his men, he took refuge in the French camp. Initially he was promised a free pass to his own country, but Napoleon ordered that he should be sent to France as a prisoner of war. Two years later he escaped from Paris in disguise. Mack was not employed for some years, but in 1804, when the war party in the Austrian court needed a general to oppose the peace policy of the Archduke Carl, Mack was made quartermaster-general of the army, with instructions to prepare for a war with France. He did all that was possible within the available time to reform the army, and on the opening of the war of 1805 he became commander-in-chief in Germany; the Archduke Ferdinand Carl Joseph of Austria-Este, who was himself inexperienced in military command was his second. Consequently, Mack was the real responsible commander of the army that faced Napoleon in Bavaria, but his position was ill-defined and his authority treated with minimal respect by the other general officers. Furthermore, the reform of the Habsburg army had been incomplete; Mack chose to initiate some of Archduke Carl's innovations, while ignoring others. His own insecurities and vagaries did not encourage the confidence of the staff; in the campaign that led up to the Battle of Ulm, Mack's frequent reversals of Viennese policy, and even his own decisions, further undermined an already fragile command structure. At Ulm, in October 1805, he surrendered the entire army to Napoleon. A few of his officers, including the Prince of Schwarzenberg, broke through the French defences in a massed cavalry charge and escaped, but most of the Austrian high command was captured with 25,000 men, 18 generals, 65 guns, and 40 standards. The general officers received a parole that required them to abstain from combat with France, removing the bulk of Habsburg commanders from the possibility of service in the upcoming campaign of the Upper Danube. After Austerlitz Mack was convicted of cowardice by a court martial. He was deprived of his rank, his regiment, and his honours, including the Order of Maria Theresa, and imprisoned for two years. Upon his release in 1808 he lived in relative obscurity until 1819, when the ultimate victory of the allies had obliterated the memory of earlier disasters. He was, at the request of Prince Schwarzenberg, reinstated in the army as *Feldmarschall-Lieutenant*, and a member of the Order of Maria Theresa.

13 Rothenberg, *Napoleon's Great Adversary*, p.21.

14 The Archduke wrote that 'if the war break out, before such changes have been completed for some time, the army will be in disarray and there will be disaster'. Rothenberg, *Napoleon's Great Adversary*, p.66.

centres of command operating in March 1798, when the army headquarter under Carl was in Prague, and the Emperor and his military advisors were in Vienna. Despite Carl's warning, on 8 March 1798 Franz II appointed *Feldzeugmeister* József Alvinczi de Borberek[15] to the chair of the *Militär-Hof-Commission* in order to direct the reorganisation and perfection of the Imperial–Royal army. The office had to deal with organisation, weaponry, tactics, supply, the medical service, and overall to restore the army's morale. Alvinczi availed himself of prominent senior commanders, among these veterans such as Bellegarde, Unterberger, Vincent, Zach, and even the president of the Aulic War Council Ferdinand von Tige, while Archduke Carl remained excluded. Alvinczi pointed out on the need to improve discipline, subordination, *esprit de corps* and confidence in the officers, and called for expert testimony from officers of the field army. However, the commission achieved a poor result, notwithstanding its work produced a great number of documents. A worrying scenario emerged and the proposals to remedy inefficiency and incompetence were divergent. Some members focused on the apathy of the officer corps, due to the surfeit of regulations introduced since the Seven Years War, which left little to individual initiative, while others deplored the growing civilian influence on the army and feared that the civilians might use the present circumstances of an unlucky war to reach for control.[16] According to some relations, there

15 An ethnic Magyar, József Alvinczi (or Alvinczy) de Borberek (1735–1810) was born in Transylvania and spent his boyhood in the household of Count Ferenc Gyulai before joining his regiment as a *Fähnrich* aged 14. By 1753 he had risen to *Hauptmann*. During the Seven Years' War, Alvinczi distinguished himself leading a grenadier company in the battles of Torgau and Teplitz, where his courageous leadership won him a promotion to second major. At the end of the war he worked extensively on the implementation of Franz Moritz von Lacy's new regulations throughout the army. Promoted to *Oberst* commanding an infantry regiment in 1774, he served during the War of the Bavarian Succession, where he seized the city of Habelschwerdt and captured the Prussian Commander Prince Hessen-Philippsthal, a feat which won Alvinczi promotion to *General Wachtmeister* and award of the Order of Maria Theresa. Alvinczi fought under Ernst Gideon von Laudon in the Ottoman War of 1787–91, but did not accomplish his mission of capturing Belgrade. After a short period instructing the future Emperor, Archduke Franz, he returned to command his regiment. After being promoted to *Feldmarschall-Lieutenant* he was transferred to the Austrian Low Countries in 1790 to suppress the United States of Belgium, until a fall from his horse forced him to retire from active service. Alvinczi commanded a division, steadying his demoralised men at a key stage of the victorious battle of Neerwinden in 1793, leading his soldiers forward to capture the village; for this exploit he was awarded the Commander's Cross of the Order of Maria Theresa. He took command of an auxiliary army which supported the British under the Duke of York and Albany, fighting at Landrecy and in the Battle of Fleurus, before being wounded at Mariolles. On his recovery and promotion to *Feldzeugmeiste*r, Alvinczi advised William VI of Orange at the successful relief of Charleroi in June 1793, losing two horses under him in the process, and earning a new reward. Briefly commander of the army of the Upper Rhine, he was recalled to Vienna to serve on the Aulic War Council in 1795. In late 1796 he took over command of the army that was fighting Napoleon Bonaparte in the north of the Italian Peninsula. After organising the Tyrolean militia to face the threat of the French advance in 1796, he was tasked with the third relief of the siege of Mantua. Alvinczi's army was largely composed of new recruits with few experienced officers, however he defeated Bonaparte at Bassano on 6 November and Caldiero on 12 November. Ultimately, Bonaparte won the hard-fought victory over Alvinczi at the Battle of the Bridge of Arcole on 15–17 November 1796. Despite deteriorating health, Alvinczi regrouped and tried again. He suffered a severe defeat at the Battle of Rivoli on 14–15 January 1797. Mantua surrendered soon afterwards. After serving in the court's military commission, he was appointed as military governor of Hungary, and promoted to *Feldmarschall* in 1808.

16 Oskar Criste, *Erzherzog Carl von Österreich* (Vienna-Leipzig, 1912), vol. II, pp.11–12.

A single trooper of the Szekler Grenz-Husaren regiment engages a group of French cavalrymen during the 1796 campaign in Germany, from a print after Johann Baptist Seele. The wars engaged in the 1790s concluded with a substantial Austrian defeat on all fronts. Despite unpreparedness and the emergency climate that had plagued the operations, the Austrian cavalry performed well on several occasions, and when victory vanished it was often due to poor leadership, and Napoleon's talent of course. Note the infantry canteen model, and the sabre suspended from the right wrist on the leather strap. (Authors' archive)

existed a deplorable lack of interest in the military career among the officer class, composed mainly of noble cadets who entered the army because they were excluded from inheritance, and whose focus therefore was only pay, emoluments, decorations and occasional drill.[17] Furthermore, colonels, major and captains neither knew nor valued their soldiers, and in return they were neither loved nor trusted.

Further controversies arose regarding the field army organisation, which had to adopt the corps system, but the opposition of Archduke Carl and the lack of time to introduce such radical changes resolved in nothing being done.

The commission introduced new weapons and new kinds of units, such as the light infantry battalions and the *Leichte Dragoner*, and some branches augmented their numbers, such as the cuirassiers, which deployed 12 regiments. Together with further newly raised units, the overall strength of the army had risen to 438,000 men and 102,700 horses on paper, but the actual number was far less, about 300,000 men including garrisons and services. Worst of all, shortage of transport hampered Austrian operations throughout the war campaigns. In June 1799 the field army consisted of 250,000 men. Of this force, 92,000 were stationed in Italy, 92,000 on the Upper Rhine, 8,500 in Dalmatia, 5,500 in other places. Additionally 8,000 arrived from hospitals after recovering from their wounds, and 14,000 arrived as recruits. There were also 30,000 as exchanged prisoners.

Defeats suffered in the Second Coalition War once again demonstrated the urgency for reform of the Austrian military machine and in the following three years, Archduke Carl acted as the main actor to implement changes despite the opposition of strong interest and the suspicious of his brother

17 Rothenberg, *Napoleon's Great Adversary*, p.66.

and Emperor Franz. Moreover, the emergency scenario persisted, and when, against Carl's desires, Austria declared war to France in 1805, the army still was understrength, ill-equipped, poorly trained, and with too many inadequate officers. Much of the cause of this deplorable scenario has been attributed to the result of the work of Carl Mack von Leiberich, who became an instrument of reactionary factions at court and in the army. Historians have long deplored the choice of Franz II to exclude his brother from the post of commander-in-chief by appointing Mack in his place, whose nefarious work was the principal cause of the failure of 1805.Although officially it was the Italian front, to which Carl was destined, that constituted the main strategic theatre, Mack's appointment seemed a disavowal of the Archduke's reforming ideas.

A Hungarian from Transylvania, József Alvinczi (or Alvinczy) de Borberek (1735–1810), was a veteran of the Seven Years' War, who entered the Austrian army as a *Fähnrich* aged 14. Alvinczi gained a reputation also as theorist, when in the 1760s he worked extensively on the new army regulations introduced by Franz Moritz von Lacy. In late 1796 he took over command of the Austrian army in the north of the Italian Peninsula. His army was largely composed of new recruits with few experienced officers, however he defeated Napoleon at Caldiero on 12 November. Ultimately, General Bonaparte won a hard-fought victory over Alvinczi at the Battle of the Bridge of Arcole on 15–17 November 1796. (Engraving by unknown artist. Authors' archive)

It is remarkable to see how, even in the absence of decisive political support, Carl never gave up on his intention to modernise the army of the House of Austria. Although the results were intermittent, the Archduke was able to reform the military administration and to create an actual war ministry. Its authority extended over the Aulic War Council, in order to have a clearly defined duty in matters of recruitment, pay and pensions, equipment, observance of regulations and military training. Historians have criticised Carl for his emphasis on administration and bookkeeping, but this must be considered in the overall context of state finances. With the monarchy bankrupt, the army budget had been cut from 87 million florins in 1801 to 34.5 million in 1804. It was still larger than the military budget of 1792–96 but now it was necessary to keep the troops deployed at all times. Cantonments, barracks, new fortifications and war material were also required. At the same time there was an increase in the number of regimental cadets and volunteers, as well as new promotion from the ranks in order to motivate the officers in their duty. However, officer competence and knowledge continued to be a major concern. The poor training and limited prospects of the officers further depressed the level of proficiency of the units. A detailed plan of instructions was created, including basic addition, subtraction, and division for junior officers, because as stated in the reports only a few had graduated from the academies while the majority were totally ignorant.[18] Alongside the improvement of officer quality Carl limited the use of corporal punishment,

18 Criste, *Erzherzog Carl*, pp.17–18.

The hero's death of corporal Georg Zuchtrigl of the Levenehr Leichte Dragoner (Regiment Nr. 14), occurred on 11 June 1799 at Fenestrelle (engraving by Bartsch and Kininger). The reform of the army in 1798 introduced new weapons and new kinds of units, like the light infantry battalions and the *Leichte Dragoner*. Together with further newly raised units, the overall strength of the army had on paper risen to 438,000 men and 102,700 horses, but the actual number was far less, about 300,000 men including garrisons and services. (Authors' archive)

which had seriously affected the *esprit de corps* within the regiments. He and his collaborators also insisted in the introduction of regular training for the troops including manoeuvres, and firing and theoretical lessons, especially in the artillery.

Certainly one of the major improvements introduced by the Archduke was the creation of a modern general staff. He elaborated this plan from the 1790s, when Mack became chief of staff of the army under Sachsen-Coburg in the Austrian Low Countries. Mack issued the *Instruktionspunkte fur die gesamte Herren Generals*, the last of the 19 points setting out the roles of staff officers, dealing with offensive and defensive operations, while helping the commander-in-chief. In 1796 Carl augmented these instructions with his own *Observationspunkte*, writing of the chief of staff: 'he is duty bound to consider all possibilities related to operations and not view himself as merely carrying out those instructions'.[19] The Archduke persuaded his brother to modify the tasks of the officers of this corps and requested it maintain a permanent cadre

19 *Österreichische Militärische Zeitschrift* (Vienna, 1860), III, pp.229–233.

of 21 staff officers ranked above *Major* alongside 16 captains and 12 junior officers. The new general staff acted under a *General Quartiermeister* 'engaged with his staff in making plans covering long periods and the entire campaign, and that he would not merely implement the commander's plan in practice, but act his proper and well-prepared advisor to examine intelligence and projects of all kinds'.[20] However, the army commander retained the final decision. On 20 March 1801 *Feldmarschall-Lieutenant* Peter Duka von Kádár became the world's first peacetime *General Quartiermeister* at the head of the staff, and the wartime role of the chief of staff was now focused on planning and operations to assist the commander. Archduke Carl produced a new *Dienstvorschrift* (service regulation) on 1 September 1805, which divided the staff into three branches: 1) political correspondence; 2) direction of operations, dealing with planning and intelligence; 3) the direction of military service, dealing with administration, supply and military justice. The Archduke set out the position of a modern chief of staff: 'The Chief of Staff stands at the side of the Commander-in-Chief and is completely at his disposal. His sphere of work connects him with no specific unit'.[21] Now each commander would dispose of his staff, whose chief was responsible for directing operations and executing the overall headquarters plan. The new arrangements remained largely on paper until 1805, but the *General Quartiermeister* did work out plans for the commander and generally supervised the operations of the staffs with the armies in Italy and Germany. However, an actual general staff did not function until late in 1809.[22]

In terms of strength, the Austrian army progressed less. Although the Austro-Russian treaty of November 1804 obliged the Emperor to gather 275,000 field troops against Napoleon, nobody at court had a clear picture of the military resources of the monarchy. The report produced by the *General Quartiermeisterstab* pointed out that the army was not prepared for war. The overall theoretical force was about 300,000 men, but over 33,000 men were lacking in the regiments. Moreover, the available forces included 11,455 invalids still registered in the muster rolls. The remount situation was unsatisfactory: only 23,000 remounts were available. Altogether, even after the mobilisation, the Austrian army would number 60,000 infantry and 20,000 cavalry fewer than in 1799.

After the disaster of Ulm and Napoleon's masterwork at Austerlitz, Archduke Carl resumed his efforts to overhaul the Austrian military establishment. Before military reforms could become effective the emerging

---

20 Kurt Peball, 'Zum Kriegsbild der österreichischen Armee und seiner geschichtlichen Bedeutung in den Kriegengegen die Französischen Revolution und Napoleon I, in den Jahren von 1792 bis 1815', in W. von Groote and K.J. Müller (eds), *Napoleon I und das Militärwesen seiner Zeit* (Freiburg, 1968), pp.145–146.

21 'The Commander-in-Chief decides what should happen and how; his chief assistant works out these decisions, so that each subordinate understands his allotted task.' Now each commander had a staff, whose chief was responsible for directing operations and executing the overall headquarters plan. See in Oskar Regele, *Generalstabschefs aus vier Jahrhunderten das Amt des Chefs des Generalstabes in der Donaumonarchie, seine Träger und Organe von 1529 bis 1918* (Vienna–Munich: Herold, 1966), p.55.

22 Rothenberg, *Napoleon's Great Adversary*, p.92.

Dagobert Sigismund von Würmser (1724–1797). A veteran of the Seven Years' War, and an early member of one of the Josephinian lodges, Würmser became *General der Cavallerie* in 1787 and mounted several successful campaigns in the Rhineland in the initial years of the French Revolutionary Wars. His most significant achievement was the seizing of the Lines of Lauterburg and Weissenburg in October 1793. Promoted to *Feldmarschall*, from August 1795 Würmser commanded the Army of the Upper Rhine and then received a command in Northern Italy in 1796, in his 74th year. After his successes against the French in Germany, he was expected to make light work of the French Armée d'Italie. Because the Italian marshy terrain was considered unsuitable for cavalry, Würmser had only one regiment of uhlans and a few squadrons of hussars. Furthermore he had lost much of his talent and the campaign closed with the loss of the key fortress of Mantua. Today Würmser is most remembered for his unsuccessful actions against Bonaparte, but the defeat suffered in Italy did not diminish the lustre of his service and he was granted another appointment immediately. The portrait shows with good detail the bearskin headdress with cloth bag reserved for hussar field officers before 1799. (From *Histoire de la Revolution Francaise* by Louis Blanc, Paris, 1857. Authors' archive)

scenario had to be resolved, and in this regard a thorough reform of the Austrian society and state was required, but neither the Archduke nor his opponents were willing to engage this challenge. Although some improvements in the military administration and in the effectiveness of regular training under experienced officers had given initial results, the aim was much narrower. Unfortunately even in this limited objective Emperor Franz II feared, like most Habsburg rulers before him, the concentration of power in one person. Waving the spectre of Wallenstein, his advisors persuaded him not to fully support his brother, and instead instigate intrigues against him and his projects. However, the debacle of 1805 posed a mandatory challenge to the whole Austrian military and political system and foremost to the army supreme command. The response, unfortunately, was inadequate and despite the recent bitter lesson, the Emperor and the Archduke, together with their retinue of courtiers, politicians and senior officers, did not abandon their ambitions and at once resumed the struggle for personal power and influence that had frustrated the reforms of 1804–1805. Although he was not without fault, Carl did have good reason to worry about the state of the army. One of the main effective features of the French army in 1805 had been its mobility; while compared to its enemy, the Austrian army appeared like a slow and excessively cautious instrument of war. Unfortunately economic shortages persisted as usual, and remounts and draft horses were in short supply and the trains inadequate and poorly directed. Some field equipment, especially pontoons, had failed to arrive. No army appeared less ready to fight than the Austrian one.

A much more critical problem was the hasty last-minute introduction of new higher field units. Although in 1798 and 1805 the Archduke had opposed adoption of the French-like organisation, on August 1808, with the Emperor's approval, corps were activated in the field army. The introduction of a new organisational structure could not however ignore the ability of the commanders to take advantage of this new tactical tool. The negative experience of 1805 confirmed that the Austrian command and control structure was defective. High-ranking officers, including army commanders, were selected by seniority and

Detail from 'The Capitulation of Ulm' on 20 October 1805, by René Théodore Berthon. The painting depicts *Feldmarschall* Carl Mack von Leiberich with his staff, as he surrenders the entire Austrian army to Napoleon. Ulm marks the worst Austrian army performance of the age. The result was even more disappointing because it occurred after the reforms introduced to remedy the defeats suffered in previous wars against France. The responsibility for the failure was attributed to Mack von Leiberich. Though he introduced some of Archduke Carl's innovations, Mack ignored others, while his own insecurities and vagaries did not encourage the confidence of the staff. Moreover, Mack's frequent reversals of Viennese policy, and even his own decisions, further undermined an already fragile command structure. The painting correctly shows the uniforms of the Austrian generals and officers between 1801 and 1805. Most of them are wearing the 'full uniform' in white cloth with ponceau red breeches and just a couple have the field coat in *hechtgrau*. Three generals wear the Hungarian uniform in red. It is possible to identify some of the officers portrayed assuming their rank in 1805. The first officer in grey, close to Mack, could be *Oberst* Alois von Liechtenstein. The officers in Hungarian uniform probably are Prince Maurice von Liechtenstein, the Landgrave of Hessen-Homburg and Ignatz Gyulai. Two other officers are dressed in green, suggesting that they belong to the *General Stab*, and could be *Feldmarschall Lieutenant* Stipsicz, and *General Wachtmeister* Richter. Among the officers in white uniform, there are generals Riesch, Klenau Gottesheim, Auersperg, Hicker and Gehnedegg. (Château de Versailles)

birth rather than by merit and experience. In early 1809 the scenario was still unchanged. Archduke Johann held command in Inner Austria, while under Carl there were two further archdukes: Ludwig and Ferdinand. Other command posts were entrusted to three princes: Hohenzollern, Orsini-Rosenberg, and Liechtenstein. Only one post belonged to a veteran soldier, Johann von Hiller. None of the high aristocracy officers had any experience or schooling in operating under the corps system and this increased demands on their staff, which was not always capable of managing the new organisation. The personnel of the *Generalsstab* were still trained in mapping, mathematical computations, horsemanship, drawing and writing. Many were talented officers and capable of elaborating plans for moving the troops effectively on paper. The new system created much confusion and the Austrian general staff lacked a common doctrine and manuals of procedure. Despite some inevitable drawbacks, which led to its dismissal, the corps system was reinstituted in 1813, though the term officially used for designating the 'corps' was *Armee Abteilung*.

Despite the unsolved problems, the preparations for war took place in a less chaotic way. In 1809 the Austrian army was the third largest army in the world. In January 1809 it comprised 232,000 infantry (not including 44,000 frontiersmen), 32,300 cavalry (including 13,400 Hungarian hussars) and 9,000 artillerymen.[23] With engineers, staffs and other personnel, the total strength was between 250,000 and 270,000 men in peacetime, and 400,000–420,000 in wartime. The plan of operations and the overall geostrategic framework had been analysed in detail, and in fact in 1809 for the first time the Austrian army was very close to prevailing over the French, achieving the first major victory at Aspern–Essling. On the other hand, Archduke Carl found it difficult to replace lost horses and his cavalry continued the campaign understrength.

After 1809 new economies were achieved through the reduction of the size of the army, as imposed by the peace treaty, to 150,000 men. Despite these substantial reductions Austria did not fully comply with the restrictions of the peace treaty. In 1811, instead of the authorised strength, the army numbered 259,918 on the muster rolls. However, the actual strength was 171,066, including 22,444 men considered in the regiments for training and limited duties.[24] The effective number decreased further in 1812, when the overall strength in garrisons and barracks numbered 122,067 infantry and artillery and 27,787 cavalry.[25]

In 1812 Austria found itself in an awkward position. The leader of a conservative monarchy, the Austrian emperor had most consistently opposed the French revolutionaries. Repeatedly defeated by France, Austria was finally forced to seek an understanding with Napoleon. This resulted in 1810 with the marriage of Napoleon to Marie Louise of Austria. On 12 March 1812, Emperor Franz II signed the alliance with France, engaging Austria to gather a contingent of 24,000 foot and 6,000 horse for the incoming war against Russia, a traditional ally of Austria. The news provoked great sensation and some officers quit the service in protest. When Napoleon finally invaded Russia, the Emperor was forced to send his troops to the *Grande Armée*. The Austrian army corps operated on the southern front of the *Grande Armée* in Poland and then in White Russia under *General der Cavallerie* Carl Philip von Schwarzenberg.[26] The main task was the protection of the western lines

23 Österreichisches Staatsarchiv – Kriegsarchiv, Vienna: Alte Feld Akten, Stand- und Diensttabellen Karton Nr.3729. January 1809.

24 The well-informed British agent John Harcourt King sent to the Foreign Office a letter from Vienna, placing the figure even lower. 'The army has been so extremely reduced and what remains of it is so badly paid, clothed and equipped that 60,000 men would be the most that the Government could at the present employ on active service.' In Rothenberg, *Napoleon's Great Adversary*, p.223.

25 Österreichisches Staatsarchiv – Kriegsarchiv, Vienna: Alte Feld Akten, Stand- und Diensttabellen Karton Nr. 3731 January 1812.

26 Carl Philip von Schwarzenberg (1771–1820) was a member of one of the Bohemian aristocratic families who owed their rise to the great redistribution of wealth overseen by Ferdinand II, in the early years of the seventeenth century. Schwarzenberg entered the Imperial cavalry in 1788, and the next year fought under Lacy and Loudon against the Ottomans, distinguished himself by his bravery, and soon was promoted to *Major* in 1792. In the campaign against France in 1793 he served in the vanguard of the army under Prince Josias von Sachsen-Coburg, and at Le Cateau-Cambrésis

of communication for the Main Army. General Reynier and his Saxon corps were attached to the Austrians with Schwarzenberg in command.[27] Austrian resources were hard pressed to provide the troops for the Russian campaign, however Schwarzenberg never penetrated deep into Russia. On 20 June the Austrians reached Lublin and then headed for Minsk, but they were diverted south where Reynier's Saxons were facing the Russian corps under Tormassov. A battle was engaged at Gorodetshna on 12 August, resulting in an Austrian–Saxon victory. Schwarzenberg continued to pursue the Russians until early September, arresting the advance before the River Styr. Here followed a month of pause, during which Tormassov was reinforced by the Russian army of Moldavia under Admiral Tshitshagov, which forced Schwarzenberg to withdraw along the River Bug into central Poland. This was a fortunate event that allowed the Austrian corps to avoid the disastrous

---

in 1794 his charge at the head of his regiment, supported by 12 British squadrons, broke a whole corps of the French, overwhelmed the enemy infantry, and captured 32 of the enemy's guns. For this action he was immediately decorated with the Knight's Cross of the Military Order of Maria Theresa. After taking part in the battles of Amberg and Würzburg in 1796, he was appointed to the rank of *General Wachtmeister*, and in 1799 was promoted to *Feldmarschall-Lieutenant*. On 3 December 1800, at Hohenlinden, he led a division of the allied right wing. During the retreat his skill and courage saved the Austrian army from destruction, and Archduke Carl afterwards entrusted him with the command of the rearguard. In 1804, Carl Philipp was created *Fürst* (Prince) zu Schwarzenberg. In the war of 1805 he held command of a division under Mack, and when in October Napoleon surrounded Ulm, Schwarzenberg was one of the cavalrymen under Archduke Ferdinand of Habsburg-Este who cut his way through the enemy lines, avoiding capture. In the same year he received the Commander's Cross of the Order of Maria Theresa. In 1809, as ambassador to the Russian court, he had showed some diplomatic flair even though efforts to persuade the Russians to join the Austrians that year proved fruitless. He returned to Austria in time to take part in the Battle of Wagram, leading a cavalry division in the Reserve Corps and was soon afterwards promoted to *General der Cavallerie* and also awarded the Order of the Golden Fleece. After the signing of the peace treaty he was sent to Paris to negotiate the 1810 marriage between Napoleon and the Archduchess Marie Louise of Austria. The Prince gave a ball in honour of the bride on 1 July 1810, which ended in a fire that killed many of the guests, including his own sister-in-law, wife of his older brother, Joseph. Napoleon held Schwarzenberg in great esteem, and at his request the Prince took command of the Austrian auxiliary corps in the Russian campaign of 1812. The Austrian general achieved some victories against the Russians at Gorodetschna and Wolkowisk. Afterwards, under instructions from Napoleon, he remained for some months inactive at Pultusk. In 1813, when Austria took the side of the allies against Napoleon, Schwarzenberg, recently promoted to *Feldmarschall*, was appointed commander-in-chief of the Army of Bohemia. As such he was the senior of the allied generals who conducted the campaign of 1813–1814. Under his command the allied army was mauled by Napoleon at the Battle of Dresden on 26–27 August and driven back into Bohemia. However, his army defeated pursuing French forces at the Second Battle of Kulm, fought on 17 September 1813. Returning to the fray, he led the army north again and played a major role in Napoleon's decisive defeat at Leipzig on 16–18 October. On 27 February 1814, during the invasion of France, he attacked through Switzerland and beat the French at the battle of Bar-sur-Aube. He achieved an important success repelling an attack by Napoleon in the battle of Arcis-sur-Aube on 20–21 March and overcame the last barrier before Paris by winning at Fère-Champenoise on 25 March. His capture of the French capital on 31 March after the Battle of Paris resulted in the overthrow of Napoleon. The next year, during the Hundred Days, Schwarzenberg commanded the army of the Upper Rhine, formed by Austria and other German states of about 250,000 men. A stroke disabled him in 1817, and in 1820, when revisiting Leipzig, the scene of the 'Battle of the Nations' that he had directed seven years before, he suffered a second stroke. He died there on 15 October.

27 Reynier filled the difficult double role of corps commander and ranking French 'adviser' to keep an eye on the Austrians. Although they sometimes fought together, as at Gorodetschna, they more often worked as independent corps.

According to legend Archduke Carl (1771–1847), here portrayed by Johann Peter Krafft, seized the regimental colours and led the Austrian infantry to the charge. The Archduke would have been seen as the most gifted and outstanding Austrian military commander of his time and among the most significant commanders in of the whole pantheon of the Napoleonic wars. It was Carl's fate to be born into the era of Napoleon, though it was Austria's good fortune to have such an able general at its disposal during this exceptionally challenging period. Where his brother Emperor Franz was intellectually somnolent, Carl exuded ideas and theories. An epileptic, Carl was clever, vigorous, handsome and courageous, and all his portraits unfold a vivid personality. But for the accident of birth he might have proved the greatest revolutionary of them all. But as an Austrian officer and a Habsburg, his loyalty lay first and foremost to his House. Every military decision he took always had this unhesitating obedience as its subtext. Carl was also a formidable military reformer. His writings on military science, which even in the abridged version run to six volumes, reveal a remarkable synthesis of practical experience on the battlefield with the dictums of German philosophy and classical literature. Moreover, in his three-volume *Grundsätze der Strategie* (Foundations of Strategy) he developed a theory of war that is equal in every way to that of Clausewitz and is perhaps even superior to it in its inherent objectivity. Note the Archduke's saddle cover, showing the golden woven lace reserved for the rank of *Feldmarschall*. (Heeresgeschichtliches Museum, Vienna)

retreat from Moscow. However, the supply system had broken down and this provoked a couple of incidents which involved the Austrian troops in looting and arbitrary requisitions. The Austrian corps was engaged in the open field again in October but this was largely a cavalry campaign of reconnaissance, raids and skirmish. As a consequence there were numerous small actions, however sometimes they resulted in hundreds of casualties. The Austrians were concentrated at Minsk, in order to protect the French retreat from Moscow, but with the Saxons suddenly under attack, Schwarzenberg was diverted and Minsk fell into Russian hands.[28] Historians deal with the Russian campaign by describing the terrible fate of the *Grande Armée*, and little effort has been spent to consider the pains suffered by the Austrian corps. An exceptionally cold November caused the collapse of the logistics organisation in the rear, leaving Schwarzenberg's soldiers in a miserable state. According to the commander's memories: 'Men and beasts are approaching complete disintegration.'[29] In the 1812 campaign in Russia, Austrians suffered 7,000 killed in battle and 4,000 dead of disease and exposure.

Petar Duka von Kadar (1756–1822) was born in Osijek, in an ethnic Aromanian family of low condition. In 1776 he joined the 13th Wallachian-Illyrian Grenz-Regiment as a cadet. Thanks to the positive service and his remarkable talent, Duka advanced quickly in the military hierarchy: promoted in 1794 as lieutenant colonel, *General Wachtmeister* in 1798 and *Feldmarschall-Lieutenant* in 1801, later he became *Feldzeugmeister*. In 1801, under Archduke Carl, Duka became the world's first peacetime *Generalquartiermeister* at the head of a modern general staff. (Engraving of unknown artist. Authors' archive)

The French disaster in Russia changed the whole geostrategic scenario. In 1813 many Habsburg subjects felt that Austria should at once declare war on Napoleon and join the alliance with Great Britain, Russia and Prussia. Resistance to this address existed at court, and even ministers such as Metternich did not share the popular enthusiasm. He and others feared that with Austria poorly armed and financially depleted, premature action would lead to the replacement of French by Russian hegemony in Germany. However, in January 1813 the council of ministers authorised increases in effectives and in February orders were issued to assemble a strong corps of observation in Bohemia. This force became operational in April and numbered 100,000 men, though supply remained difficult. Taking advantage of neutrality, Austria continued to negotiate both with Napoleon and his enemies, now also including Sweden.[30] Doubtless, a

28 For the loss of Minsk and its valuable depots, Napoleon accused Schwarzenberg of treachery, although in the end he did not push the matter. Rothenberg, *Napoleon's Great Adversary*, p.226.

29 Rothenberg, *Napoleon's Great Adversary*, p.226.

30 Metternich offered Napoleon a 'golden bridge' to peace. In a famously stormy meeting with the *Empereur* in Dresden, he argued the merits of accommodation with Prussia and Russia but

Prince Carl Philip zu Schwarzenberg, (1771–1820) here portrayed in 1814 as *Feldmarschall*, was a member of one of the most distinguished aristocratic families of Bohemia. He entered the Imperial cavalry in 1788, and the next year fought under Lacy and Loudon against the Ottomans. Later Schwarzenberg served in the first campaigns in the Austrian Low Countries, confirming the bravery and daring attitude showed at the beginning of his career. Perhaps his best talent was to see the leadership quality in others. This made him a formidable adversary and he always surrounded himself with excellent officers. In 1813, on his appointment as commander-in-chief of the allied armies, his first move was to secure the talented Radetzky as his quartermaster general and chief of staff. (Unidentified artist; Český Krumlov Castle, Czech Republic)

major success for the allies should be represented by the intervention of a reconstituted Austrian army, but the Emperor still hesitated. In early May the corps of observation was officially designated as an army and the newly promoted *Feldmarschall* Carl von Schwarzenberg appointed as commander-in-chief, with Radetzky von Radek as his chief of staff. While the latter insisted on the mobilisation of all available forces, in Vienna there was still thought for a diplomatic accommodation to avoid the conflict and Schwarzenberg himself was supporting this line. On 14 June, the Imperial conference that met in the Austrian headquarters decided on full mobilisation, and on 22 June the Aulic War Council issued order for reservists to report to their regiments. On 6 July the *Landwehr* was also called up. Although shortages in manpower developed, forcing the lifting of exemptions and the enlistment of underage recruits, a very considerable army had gathered: 200,000 men were quartered in Bohemia; in addition, the Army of Inner Austria mustered a further 37,000 men and the army of the Danube stood at 39,000. By the end of August Austria had 479,000 men under arms, with 298,000 in the field, and would eventually mobilise a total of 568,000.[31]

Though men were available, weapons, equipment and provision were lamentably insufficient. Army headquarters continually requested muskets, uniforms, boots, shoes, and ammunition, but the Austrian treasury could only reply that the last reserve stocks had been used up in the Russian campaign and that no major deliveries could be expected until autumn. When hostilities opened, the Austrian army was the worst equipped among the allies.[32]

After the failure at Dresden, the allied successes at Kulm and Dennewitz turned the campaigns in the hoped-for direction. As Schwarzenberg advanced with 60,000 men along the right bank of the Elbe, Napoleon's right flank became vulnerable. Less than a fortnight later Napoleon began concentrating his forces around Leipzig, where he awaited the advance of the vast enemy

discreetly left Austria out of this equation. Napoleon reacted, hurling his hat across the room and accusing Metternich of not knowing how to 'die for France'. Metternich responded by quietly opening the shutters so that the 'soldiers below' could hear how 'they should all die for France'.

31 Rothenberg, *Napoleon's Great Adversary*, p.228.

32 See Edmund Glaise von Horstenau, *Die Tage von Dresden 1813* (Leipzig: Edlinger, 1911), p.31.

Austrian cavalry on campaign, 1812–14, by Johann Cotta. The victory of Leipzig opened the way to Paris, but the triumphal march usually narrated was another very hard campaign for the Austrian army. In October 1813, *Feldmarschall* Schwarzenberg could deploy about 200,000 men between Basle and Mannheim. The troops were in a miserable state, the ranks decimated by disease made worse by the lack of winter clothing. (Authors' archive)

The battle of Hanau, fought on 30 October 1813 between the Austrian–Bavarians under Carl Philipp von Wrede against Napoleon's army of Germany, by Wilhelm von Kobell. The Battle of Hanau was a minor battle, but in Austria and Bavaria was celebrated as a success and took an important places in the history of the Austrian cavalry. Following the successful skirmishing against the French rearguard in the morning early, General Wrede began to deploy his forces to face the main French force of 20,000 men. On 30 October Wrede placed his centre with the River Kinzig behind it, and his right wing to its south in an isolated position with only a single bridge linking it with the main force. Napoleon had only 17,000 troops including Marshal MacDonald's infantry and General Sébastiani's cavalry to face the enemy forces blocking them. Due to dense forests to the east of Wrede's positions, the French were able to advance and make close contact with the allies almost unseen. Napoleon decided to attack the allies' left with all available troops. By midday Marshal Victor and MacDonald had cleared the forest in front of the allies' centre. Soon after, General Drouot found a track in the forest towards Wrede's left on which cannon could be moved. Hours later grenadiers of the Old Guard had cleared the area. French cavalry attacked the Austrians on their left flank, then attacked Wrede's centre. The allies started to fall back, skirting the banks of the Kinzig River and suffering heavy casualties. On the right wing, Austrian–Bavarian forces tried to cross the single bridge over the Kinzig River to reinforce the centre, but many drowned in the attempt. Thanks to the Austrian–Bavarian cavalry's countercharge, Wrede was successful in rallying his troops to form a defensive line running from the river to the town of Hanau. Wrede suffered 9,000 casualties, Napoleon suffered fewer, but some 10,000 French stragglers became prisoners between 28 and 31 October. However, the battle was a significant French strategic victory allowing Napoleon to retreat the army onto French soil to recover and face the invasion of France. (Neue Pinakothek Munich)

force. The long campaign of 1813 was now drawing to its inexorable climax. The victory of Leipzig opened the way to Paris, but the triumphal march usually narrated was another very hard campaign for the Austrian army. In October 1813 the main army under Schwarzenberg was deployed between Basle and Mannheim. The troops were in poor shape: the ranks decimated by disease made worse by the lack of winter clothing. Schwarzenberg had about 200,000 able men under his command,[33] not including the corps of Klenau[34] which was detached to besiege Dresden, held by the French until 11 November. Schwarzenberg, in true Austrian style, was reluctant to risk his army even when he was commanding vastly superior forces. This was particularly the case when facing Napoleon. Under Schwarzenberg the Austrian troops performed less well than under Archduke Carl in 1809, and seemed to be in danger of reverting to their old ways. Thus at Arcis-sur-Aube 80,000 Austrians faced 28,000 hastily conscripted French but were so cautiously deployed that the French held out until dark before making good their retreat and destroying the bridge. In the course of the action they had inflicted far more casualties on the Austrians than they had incurred, but neither time nor numbers were on the French side.

Meanwhile, in the south, the relatively strong Army of Inner Austria under *Feldzeugmeister* Hillier seized the Croatian provinces but was repulsed by Eugene in Northern Italy. The offensive resumed under *General der Cavallerie* Heinrich von Bellegarde,[35] who achieved better results until

33 Schwarzenberg's main army included also Russian, Prussian and Bavarian troops.

34 Johann von Klenau (1758–1819) belonged to an ancient Bohemian noble family which provided the Austrian army with several officers. He joined the Habsburg military as a teenager in the War of Bavarian Succession against Prussia, and served in the Ottoman War of 1788–91. In the early years of the French Revolutionary Wars Klenau distinguished himself at the Lines of Weissenburg, and led a battle-winning charge at Handschuhsheim in 1795. As commander of the Coalition's left flank in the Adige campaign in northern Italy in 1799, he was instrumental in isolating the French-held fortresses on the River Po by organising and supporting a peasant uprising in the countryside. Afterwards, Klenau became the youngest *Feldmarschall-Lieutenant* in the history of the Habsburg military. As a corps commander, Klenau led key elements of the Austrian army at Aspern–Esslingen and Wagram, where his troops covered the retreat of the main Austrian force. He commanded IV Corps at the 1813 battle of Dresden and again at Leipzig, where he prevented the French from outflanking the main Austrian force on the first day of the engagement. After Leipzig, Klenau organised and implemented the successful Dresden blockade and negotiated the French capitulation there. In the 1814–15 campaign he commanded the corps the army of Italy. After the war in 1815 he was appointed commanding general in Moravia and Silesia. He is considered one of the best cavalry tacticians of the Austrian army.

35 Heinrich von Bellegarde (1756–1845) was born in Dresden in the Electorate of Saxony; his family stemmed from an old line from Savoy. His father was the Saxon General Johann Franz von Bellegarde. Bellegarde first served in the Saxon army, receiving a commission as a *Fähnrich* (ensign). Transferring his services to Austria in 1771, Bellegarde distinguished himself in the War of the Bavarian Succession. In 1781 Joseph II named him *Major* of the Savoy dragoons, and four years later he was colonel of a dragoon regiment. After his participation in the Ottoman war of 1787–91 he was appointed a *General Wachtmeister* and fought in the War of the First Coalition in the Austrian Low Countries campaigns of 1793–1794, under Prince Hohenlohe. After promotion to *Feldmarschall-Lieutenant*, in 1795 Bellegarde served on the staff of Archduke Carl in Germany. He accompanied the Archduke to Italy in the following year, gaining the esteem of the senior officer and becoming one of his main collaborators. In 1799 Bellegarde fought in Switzerland and finally joined the Archduke in northern Italy. He conducted the siege of the citadel of Alessandria, and was present at the decisive Battle of Novi. After the Austrian defeat at Marengo, Emperor

the final armistice signed on 12 April 1814, when the Austrian strength in Northern Italy had increased to 70,000 men.

The struggle was not yet finished. The Hundred Days saw the Austrian army engaged in minor actions, because Napoleon was defeated before Schwarzenberg could gather his army in Germany. However, in Italy, where Murat followed his dream to become the ruler of the whole Peninsula, the Austrians intervened with greater urgency. In April 1815 11,000 Austrians under *Feldmarschall Lieutenant* Frederick von Bianchi[36] advanced along the Adriatic route to engage the Neapolitan army of King Gioacchino. Further troops from Italy entered southern France in June, but encountered little opposition and sustained only minor skirmishes.

The balance sheet of the wars that had begun in 1792 could already be drawn up for the Austrian army in 1814. As rightly stated by Gunther Rothenberg, and contrary to often-expressed opinion, this balance came out in favour of

---

Franz II appointed Bellegarde a command in Italy with the rank of *General der Cavallerie*. On 25 December the French defeated him at the Battle of Pozzolo. In 1805, when Archduke Carl left to take command in Italy, Bellegarde became president *ad interim* of the council of war. He was, however, soon employed in the field, and at the bloody Battle of Caldiero he commanded the Austrian right. In the War of the Fifth Coalition he commanded the *I Armee Korps*. Then he supervised the *II Armee Korps*, which was also posted on the north bank of the Danube. Cut off from Archduke Carl as the result of the Battle of Eckmühl, he retreated into Bohemia, but managed to rejoin the main army before the great battles near Vienna. He held the command of the *I Korps* during the battles of Aspern–Essling and Wagram. After the 1809 war, Bellegarde became a *Feldmarschall*. From 1809 to 1813 he was governor-general of Galicia, but was often called to preside over the meetings of the Aulic War Council, especially in 1810 in connection with the reorganisation of the Austrian army. In 1813, 1814 and 1815 he served in Italy. His successes in these campaigns were diplomatic as well as military, and he ended them by crushing at Tolentino the last attempt of Joachim Murat to regain the Kingdom of Naples in 1815. Between 1815 and 1816 he was Viceroy of Lombardy-Venetia. From 1816 to 1825, when he had to retire owing to failing eyesight, he held various distinguished civil and military posts.

36 Vincenzo Federico Bianchi, Duke of Casalanza (1768–1855). Born in Vienna, he studied at the Imperial Engineering Academy in Vienna. In 1788, he was a *Unter-Lieutenant* in the Army of Slavonia and distinguished himself at the siege of Bubitza. He was appointed captain after the siege of Valenciennes in 1793. In 1796, he was staff officer under Würmser's command in Italy. He captured the aide-de-camp Joachim Murat at Brescia. While commanding at the battle of Rivoli he was taken prisoner, but released at the request of General József Alvinczi. In 1799, as an *Oberst-Lieutenant*, he was attaché to Archduke Ferdinand, who was followed by Archduke Carl during the campaign in Germany and Switzerland. He was promoted to colonel in three months, commanding the 48th Hungarian infantry Regiment. In 1804 he put down a revolt at Cattaro, on the Dalmatian coast. General Adjutant after the campaign in Germany, Bianchi commanded his regiment during the campaign and 1807 he was made *General Wachtmeister*. In June 1809 he confronted the French Marshal Davout, denying him the bridgehead over the Danube near Pressburg, and was awarded the Military Cross of Maria Theresa. He was then promoted to *Feldmarschall-Lieutenant* and inspector of infantry in Hungary. In 1812 he commanded the 1st Division of the army of Carl Philip of Schwarzenberg, taking part in the Russian campaign. In 1813 he distinguished himself at the Freyburg gate of Dresden, which he had tried to assault until he was attacked by Napoleon. Bianchi performed with valour at Leipzig and afterwards he was awarded the Cross of Saint-Georges by Tsar Alexander I of Russia. In 1814 he commanded an army corps which participated in the French campaign engaging the French at Moret-sur-Loing. He was then sent to Dijon to halt Marshal Augereau, but was defeated on 11 March 1814. In 1815, now promoted to *Feldzeugmeister*, Bianchi was dispatched to Italy with a 20,000-strong force, to prevent Joachim Murat from conquering Italy in the Neapolitan War. He gained a decisive victory against Murat at the Battle of Tolentino, which earned him the title of Duke of Casalanza from Ferdinand I of the Two Sicilies, and then a promotion to *Feldmarschall*.

the army.[37] Though the Habsburgs army remained a dynastic force, relying on its 'old regime' spirit, it represented the actual and perhaps only 'national' organisation in the multicultural Austrian Empire. In purely military terms, it is evident that neither the Austrian generals nor the troops ever equalled the French at their best, however they fought much better than could be expected from an army that always managed in a long-lasting emergency.

The *Reichsarmee*

The German Holy Roman Empire – the *Reich* – was a very particular confederation. In the eighteenth century, the word most often used to describe the old Empire in its final phase is 'morsch' (brittle).[38] Contemporary critics too often described the *Reich* as aged or 'gothic'; Schiller famously referred in 1802 to the 'gothic ruins of an old and barbaric constitution'. That it proved impossible to reform the *Reich* is undeniable, though an extensive literature continued to make proposals for that throughout the last years of its existence. However, more problematic from the point of view of the arguments that emphasise the allegedly terminal decline of the *Reich*, is the fact that during the 1790s the German Empire and its institutions underwent a notable revival, especially in military matters.

From 1792 the war against France transformed the *Reich*'s scenario. Although the Emperor was at war, this did not mean that the 300-odd states, principalities, duchies, and others were automatically at war too. The Imperial dignity was elective and executive power was exercised by the Imperial Diet. Each state had the right to conduct its own foreign policy and make its own alliance, provided that these were not directed against the Emperor or the Empire. The *Reich* had established its own military force calculating the extension of the states divided into 10 *Kreise* (circles): Austria and Bohemia, Franconia, Swabia, Bourgogne, Bavaria, Lower Rhine-Westphalia, Upper Rhine, Rhine-Electoral, Lower Saxony, Upper Saxony. This formula had been introduced in the sixteenth century, and the last modification, which still represented the basis for the military organisation of the Empire, had been voted in 1681. Each circle had to gather its contingent and to economically support it on campaign. Although on paper the collective force came to over 100,000 soldiers as for the *triplum* of the basic quota, the actual strength was always lower. Austria and Bohemia, both Habsburg domains, were exempted because the Emperor already fielded his own regiments for the *Reichsarmee*, which usually assembled on the Rhine. Moreover, Bavaria, Prussia and Electoral Saxony had not formed their contingents for the circles for over a century and a half, except for minor contingents. Other states, such as Hessen-Kassel and the bishop-electors of Mainz, Trier and Cologne did not join their troops within the *Reichsarmee*, declaring them as *Haustruppen* exempted from Imperial service. Hannover, ruled by the King of England,

37 Rothenberg, *Napoleon's Great Adversary*, p.242.

38 Joachim Whaley, *Germany and the Holy Roman Empire. Volume II: The Peace of Westphalia to the Dissolution of the Reich, 1648–1806* (New York: Oxford University Press, 2012), p.560.

Johann von Klenau, Baron of Janowitz (1758–1819) portrayed by Johann Heinrich Schmidt. Reputed as an excellent cavalry commander, Klenau took part on the campaigns on the Rhine and northern Italy in the early years of the French Revolutionary Wars, and in 1800 became the youngest *Feldmarschall-Lieutenant* of the Austrian army. In 1809 he led key elements of the army at Aspern–Esslingen and Wagram, when in the latter engagement his troops covered the retreat of the main Austrian force. Klenau later commanded IV Corps at Dresden and again at Leipzig, where he prevented the French from outflanking the main Austrian force on the first day of the decisive battle. (Heeresgeschichtliches Museum, Vienna)

was also exempted from participating in the gathering of the army.

In September 1792, the reverses following Valmy caused alarm amongst the German princes, who saw immediately that it would result in increased pressure from Austria and Prussia. Maximilian Franz, Prince-Bishop of Cologne-Münster, himself a Habsburg prince and uncle of Emperor Franz II, commented that 'each prince in Germany fears the French less than these two powers', and that their advocacy of war represented a 'cure worse than the malady'.[39] Pamphleteers complained that Austria and Prussia had reduced Germany to a 'shadow empire', but the growing French threat convinced the princes of the inevitability of war in Germany. It had proved impossible to prevent a Franco-Habsburg great power struggle from spilling over into the *Reich*.[40]

Since the armies of the combatants were already over their frontiers, the lesser territories felt that only by participating could they have any say in the future course of the conflict. Hanover led the response to Austria's call for financial assistance by demanding full mobilisation instead, and in November 1792 the Imperial Diet sanctioned a triple quota of soldiers as a defensive measure. Three months later the request for further funds was scaled down to the sum to be paid into the *Reichs Operations Kasse* (Imperial Operations Fund), while finally, on 23 March, the assembled representatives declared the existing struggle to be a *Reichskrieg*. However, full mobilisation was delayed.

As early as September 1792 the French concentrated a small corps around the fortress of Landau (a French enclave in the Palatinate), and fell upon almost neutral *Reich* territory. After this event, the Imperial Diet at Regensburg finally converted the de facto state of war with France into a formal *Reichskrieg*, which, however, did not prevent individual German princes and free cities from declaring their neutrality. In addition to the traditional purpose of restoring the Westphalian Settlement of 1648, the new *Reichskrieg* was intended to secure reparation of all costs since the start of the conflict. The second aim was imposed on the Reich by Austria and Prussia to legitimise their expansionist objectives of securing territorial compensation from France and as such committed the other territories to an

39 Peter Wilson, *German Armies, War and German politics,1648–1806* (London: UCL Press, 1998), p.307.

40 Whaley, *Germany and the Holy Roman Empire*, pp.569–570.

offensive war. This tension between the defensive concerns of the majority and the annexationist designs of the two allied powers coincided with incipient fragmentation of their rapprochement in the face of the mounting impossibility of any gains in the west. On 31 March 1793 the Diet empowered Franz II to name a commander, and he selected the veteran *Feldmarschall* Josias of Coburg-Saalfeld. Though Coburg was a popular choice, a German and Protestant,[41] the Empire remained passive and only British subsidy payment stirred a few states from their lethargy. Many of the more important German states sent their troops to join either the Prussians or the Austrian forces, others preferred to buy themselves out by means of subsidies to both major powers. The French resumed the offensive in summer 1793, forcing the Germans back over the Rhine and recovering control of the left bank territories. Another offensive the following year shattered the Austrians at Fleurus on 26 June and secured permanent possession over the Austrian Low Countries. The Austrian failures were magnified by Prussian successes, as Friedrich Wilhelm II satisfied Hohenzollern ambitions through the Second Partition of Poland in January 1793. Prussia now lost interest in continuing the war in the west, particularly as it became embroiled in suppressing a Polish revolt from spring 1794, until the third and final partition removed the kingdom from the European map in 1795. Austrian isolation was increased by Russia's initial refusal to support the war against France, leaving it increasingly reliant on what help it could extract from the *Reich*. The gradual shift in Habsburg policy was furthered by a change in the Austrian government, which also coincided with the *Reichskrieg*. Baron Johan Amadeus von Thugut, the former ambassador to Constantinople, became the new foreign minister on 27 March 1795 and began implementing a new hard-line attitude towards the princes, with the intention of seizing control over German military potential as compensation for flagging Prussian support.

As a result, conflicts for the commander-in-chief's post resumed. Prussia had responded to Coburg's appointment by mobilising the Diet to back its campaign to exert influence on the military executive. The Emperor was compelled to nominate the Prussian general, Prince Heinrich August von Hohenlohe-Ingelfingen, as second Imperial *Feldmarschall* in 1794, but the Prussian success was frustrated by his death two years later. Though the Diet did demonstrate its autonomy by rejecting the Habsburg candidate, Würmser, for a new appointment in 1796, it accepted the Habsburg Archduke Carl as an Imperial *Feldmarschall* even though, as a Catholic, he was technically not eligible for a vacant Protestant post.

The mastership of the general staff was a primary objective. Its control offered not only access to the *Reichsarmee* and direction of operations on the field, but also opened the control of territorial manpower by continuing the practice of the controlling entities assigning contingents directly to their own armies. No less important was the management of the cash contributions to the *Reich*'s operations fund. A further advantage in controlling the general

41 This could not obscure the fact that, like other senior officers, he held the rank of general in the Austrian army. His successor in 1794, Albert von Sachsen-Teschen, was Franz II's uncle and also a member of the Habsburg clientele.

staff lay in the reforms to strengthen powers to tap territorial resources either centrally or through the *Kreis* structure, while the final issue was the question of a *Volksbewaffnung* (mass popular mobilisation) to counter the growth in French forces. Austria enjoyed distinct advantages in controlling the general staff of the *Reichsarmee*, thanks to its entrenched influence in selection and appointment procedures. Only a single Prussian was among the eight officers who were active generals in 1793. The success of the Habsburg monopoly of the high command was undermined by an inability to control the contingents.

Mobilisation in 1793 produced different categories of troops. The first were the *Kreistruppen*, who traditionally formed the backbone of the *Reichsarmee*. However, this time only three of the 10*Kreise* formed integrated contingents and of these only Swabia mobilised in full. Württemberg opposition to the war was weakened by Carl Eugen's death on 24 October 1793, and the Duchy was overruled by the Catholic pro-Habsburg majority in the *Kreis* Assembly. With Württemberg participation, Swabian mobilisation was significant. Already in 1792, 4,400 men had been assembled on the Rhine as a defensive measure. These rose to 6,800 by 1793, and following later increases to a nominal 18,500, 11,330 were actually present by September 1795. This represented seven times the region's basic quota, and collectively the Swabians accounted for 65 percent of the total *Kreistruppen* in the *Reichsarmee*.[42] Though Prussia did field five cavalry squadrons in place of the traditional Ansbach-Bayreuth contingent, Franconian participation was reduced by the separate service of Würzburg and Bamberg's troops as Austrian auxiliaries since 1790, leaving 1,569 men from the smaller territories as the only integrated *Kreistruppen* in 1793–1795. Similarly, Upper Rhine forces were reduced to two weak infantry regiments by the decision of the two Hessian landgraves not to combine their troops with those of the other members. The absence of the Electoral Rhine was due to losses suffered in 1792, which saw the disbanding of the Mainz troops after the battle of Speyer on 30 September and subsequent siege of the city. Trier and Cologne also suffered casualties, and French occupation of most of their territory by 1794 prevented all three electorates from reconstituting their military forces. Though never amounting to much more than 15,000 men, the *Kreistruppen* represented a considerable effort on the part of those lesser territories that provided them. They were insufficient to constitute a fully autonomous force but their presence in the *Reichsarmee* indicated the determination of the lesser territories to maintain their autonomy. Attempts by the Austrian-dominated Imperial general staff to subordinate the troops to direct Habsburg control were resisted vigorously, despite threats in March 1795 to arrest *General-Lieutenant* Stain, the Swabian commander.

A further category of troops was represented by the aforementioned *Haustruppen* who joined the allies separately. Saxony and Hessen-Kassel sent their troops to the Prussian army, while Anhalt-Zerbst, Würzburg, Bamberg, Hesse-Darmstadt, Salzburg, Nurnberg and many others sent their contingents to the Austrians. Competition mounted after 1793 and both powers sought to tie these forces closer to their own troops. The Prussians refused to let the

42 Peter Wilson, *German Armies*, p.310.

Saxons act as an autonomous contingent and kept them firmly attached to their own corps on the Middle Rhine, also persuading Hesse-Darmstadt to reassign its units from the Austrian command, although they later rejoined the official *Reichsarmee* further to the south. Meanwhile, the Emperor insisted that Hanover and Bavaria subordinated their forces to the Imperial command. The latter eventually sent a reduced contingent of about 2,500 soldiers, but the former refused to send any men at all on a campaign where a proper *Reichsarmee* had not been formed, and on the basis that 'the Austrians were using those units that had assembled for unconstitutional offensives'.[43]

A large number of other territories also failed to send soldiers, preferring to pay cash *Relutionen* instead.[44] Historians have interpreted this as a consequence of the general apathy and lack of concern for the *Reich*, but in fact it derived from the breakdown of the *Kreis* structure in northern Germany, and from recruiting difficulties, as well as from the desire to avoid direct involvement in a war many were opposed to politically. Some of the funds went to hire substitutes provided by some principalities like Hesse-Darmstadt, which provided 2,400 men from September 1793.[45] Other payments were used to subsidise the *émigré* regiments operating on the Rhine. Paderborn and Wolfenbüttel hired the 1,800 strong Corps Rohan until 1795, when it transferred into the Austrian army, while the princes of Hohenlohe-Bartenstein and Hohenlohe-Schillingsfurst collaborated with the Condé and Mirabeau legions on a private counter-revolutionary venture in which they sank most of their own resources.[46] The bulk of the *Relutionen* went directly to Austria and Prussia through bilateral agreements with individual territories. Prussia drew sums equivalent to 10,000 men, mainly from the weaker north German lordships, whilst Austria had arrangements with about 60 territories, including Gotha, Weimar, Cologne, Mecklenburg and Lippe to substitute for the quota of 12,000 *Kreistruppen* assigned to them. The total value of these sums was comparatively small, amounting to only two million florins by 1797, but their political importance was considerable, since they reinforced the general dependency on the two major German powers.

Independent auxiliaries formed the last category of German military involvement, but unlike previous wars payments from the maritime powers were slow in coming and did not increase the bargaining power of the medium princes. Some units were already serving the Dutch under agreements made before the war with Stadtholder William V, but the chaotic conditions within the Republic precluded further arrangements and most were withdrawn following the French invasion in 1795. Britain initially refused to pay

43 Wilson, *German Armies*, p.310.

44 The Diet of 15 September 1681 permitted states to replace their *Kreis* contingent by paying cash contributions called *Relutionen*, that could be used to hire substitutes either indirectly via the Imperial War Treasury, or directly by separate agreements with a local armed prince. The final piece of legislation on 16 March 1682 concluded the financial arrangements by confirming that territorial subjects were to assist in paying for these forces.

45 Wilson, *German Armies*, p.310.

46 Wilson, *German Armies*, p.311. In 1793 the Condé and Bourbon regiments comprised 329 well-paid officers, but only 1,125 other ranks.

The Saxon-born Heinrich von Bellegarde (1756–1845) was one of the prominent cavalry commanders of the Austrian army. In 1795 he served on the staff of Archduke Carl in Germany, and the following year he accompanied him to Italy. Here he gained the esteem of the senior officer, becoming one of his main collaborators. (Engraving after A. Mansfeld, Bildarchiv der Österreichischen Nationalbibliothek, Vienna)

subsidies, believing victory could be achieved without their expense, but signed a number of agreements from March 1793 for German troops to reinforce its own corps with the Austrians in the Low Countries. As in earlier conflicts, these treaties pulled the best troops away from service with the *Reichsarmee*, but it is unlikely that the contributory territories would otherwise have had the resources to have deployed them all on the Rhine. Service with the maritime powers kept these troops out of the reach of Austria and Prussia, but any chance that their service might enhance their princes' political position was removed by the complete allied military collapse in the Low Countries in 1795.

Circumstances forced a change of tack, and already in January 1794 Austria realised this policy was counterproductive at a time when the war was going badly and Prussia was proving increasingly unreliable. However, support for the *Reichskrieg* was growing as many German princes appreciated that this was now a truly defensive war against French aggression. Baron Thugut sought to exploit renewed calls for reform in order to strengthen central authority and thereby gain greater direct access to German resources. Punishment for those who defaulted on their obligations to the Empire was to be taken out of the hands of the *Kreis* executive and entrusted to the Imperial, namely Austrian, general staff, who were to be allowed to proceed directly by occupying the territory without a prior court hearing. In a further, highly controversial suggestion, defaulters were to lose their political rights within the Imperial constitution, leaving them open to further exploitation. The *Reichstag* was to authorise new and additional contingents for the *Reichsarmee* to legitimise Austria's extraction of greater material and manpower resources from the weaker territories. The *Relutionen* system was to be abolished in a move intended more to deprive Prussia of income and influence than to augment the actual strength of the *Reichsarmee*. New methods of fundraising were to be introduced. Direct negotiations behind the scenes met with mounting opposition from princes who feared that the enhanced executive powers were merely a device to annex Bavaria and much of south Germany as compensation for Austria's military effort.[47]

47 These measures would have gone a long way towards implementing the monarchical solution to the old question of defence reform, and it is testimony to the continuing strength of the *Reich* that

Many German princes also opposed the attempted reforms, preferring instead to keep arrangements deliberately vague to deny Austria the chance to accuse them of defaulting. As occurred several times in its history, the *Reich*sacrificed military efficiency for the sake of preserving its traditional political structure, this time by blocking military reforms altogether.[48]

Vincenzo Federico Bianchi, (1768–1855). He was the elder son of an Italian nobleman from Como who moved to Vienna in the 1760s. Having studied engineering, Bianchi entered the Austrian army in 1788 as *Unter-Lieutenant*. He was considered a skilled technician and a daring commander. In 1812 he participated in the campaign of Russia as Austrian attaché to the French General Staff. (Print of the engraving by Blas Hoffel after Louis René Latronne. Authors' archive)

Proposals were submitted in the Diet in May 1794 to raise the formal strength of the *Reichsarmee* to a *Quintuplum* for 200,000 men in all. These met with a favourable response, as many believed that only by establishing a truly autonomous force could they escape Austro-Prussian domination. Again, Austria manipulated these concerns to pursue its own objectives. Vienna knew that most territories were completely incapable of fielding five times their basic quota, since they could not even muster the existing quota, and intended to use the increased requirements to extort more money, despite the official Austrian demand that *Relutionen* were to be abolished. Prussia voted in favour but publicly announced that it would not provide any extra soldiers. Nonetheless, many responded positively once the measure had been passed on 9 October 1794. Saxony increased its contribution from 4,704 men in 1794 to 9,706 by the following year,[49] while Bavaria and others also augmented their contingents.[50] More significantly, many territories that had previously paid *Relutionen* now took steps to send soldiers instead, seizing the opportunity to terminate their agreements with the two great powers. Both Lippe and Schaumburg-Lippe raised contingents, although the latter at least did not manage to join the *Reichsarmee.*[51] Nonetheless, the Westphalian Circle now sent 2,434 soldiers, while Münster also provided 1,200 infantrymen.[52] Despite Prussian interference, the Upper Saxon Circle mobilised with contributions from Weimar, Gotha, Reuss, Schwarzburg, and Nordhausen, all of which

Austria refrained from tabling them for open discussion at the Reichstag. See Karl Härter, *Reichstag und Revolution* (Munich: Akademie der Wissenschaften, 1991), pp.414–422 and 430–435.

48 Wilson, *German Armies*, p.314.

49 O. Schuster, F.A. Franke, *Geschichte der Sächsischen Armee von deren Errichtung bis auf die neueste Zeit* (Dresden: 1885), vol. II, pp.202, 210, 214.

50 Wilson, *German Armies*, p.319.

51 Christian U. von Ulmenstein, *Die Offiziere des Schaumburg-Lippischen Truppenkorps, 1648–1857* (Berlin: Verl. f. Standesamtswesen 1940), p.14.

52 Klemens von Bönninghausen, *Die kriegerische Tätigkeit der münsterschen Truppen, 1651–1800* (Coesfeld: privately printed, 1978), p.189.

had previously paid cash instead, and Würzburg rejoined the Franconian organisation and fielded its *Kreistruppen*.[53]

Further plans did not come to fruition. Margrave Carl Friedrich of Baden, Landgrave Wilhelm IX of Hessen-Kassel and the Nassau minister, Botzheim, met at Wilhelmsbad in September–October 1794 and concocted a plan for a new alliance entirely free of Prussian interference. The proposed league was thrown open to medium princes to establish a common force of 40,000 men underwritten by a loan of 24 million florins. The response was hardly overwhelming. Mainz and Wolfenbüttel did join but refused to provide troops, while Palatinate-Bavaria, Mecklenburg-Schwerin, and Württemberg remained lukewarm and Hesse-Darmstadt refused outright. Only Franz Ludwig von Erthal, Bishop of Würzburg and Bamberg, was truly enthusiastic, promising no less than 10,000 men.[54] This was highly embarrassing, since he had only been invited for form's sake, as Baden and Hessen-Kassel were secretly planning secularisation as compensation for their war effort. With 16,866 regular troops, Hessen-Kassel was the only member with significant forces, and Wilhelm IX intended his involvement should bring him an electoral title. In the end, despite support from Catherine II of Russia, the league folded after it was publicly opposed by the Emperor in November: 'the Viennese court did not recognise a third party, only vassals', and its reaction was an overhasty instinctive response that regarded all such projects as inherently anti-Habsburg.[55] It would have been difficult to embrace the Wilhelmsbad group as a means of rallying *Reich* support given its members' ulterior motives, but outright rejection was certainly a mistake and constituted the first push forcing the princes into the arms of France. Mainz broke the deadlock by tabling a set of peace proposals on 13 October 1794, four days after the Diet had sanctioned the *Quintuplum* contingent.

The members of the Wilhelmsbad alliance aimed to restore the territorial status quo to that of 1792, establishing a mutual guarantee of non-interference in internal affairs, in return for which the *Reich* would recognise the regicide French Republic as a full member of the international community. Vienna stalled, arguing that France was still governed by criminals who came and went with such rapidity that no one could be sure that any treaty signed with one group would be respected by the next. However, Austria could not prevent the Diet formally requesting on 22 December that the Emperor negotiate peace on the basis of the Westphalian Settlement of 1648. Austria continued to delay matters, deflecting the peace initiative by a prolonged

53 Wilson, *German Armies*, p.320: 'Many began to see greater exertions not as an attempt to defeat France but as a basis to negotiate peace from a position of strength. A number of proposals were floated for a revived *Fürstenbund* to enhance princely bargaining power both in respect of Austria and Prussia and in possible negotiations with France, which, since the fall of Robespierre in July 1794, seemed a more reasonable and stable country. Some projects were completely unrealistic. Mainz suggested an electoral alliance of itself, Cologne, Trier and Palatinate-Bavaria to raise an army of 79,000 men, yet at the time only Bavaria was not occupied by French troops!'

54 Whaley, *Germany and the Holy Roman Empire*, p.575.

55 Karl Aretin, *Heiliges Römisches Reich 1776–1806: Reichsverfassung und Staatssouveränität* (Wiesbaden: Franz Steiner Verlag, 1967), vol. I, p.369.

debate on the formation of an Imperial deputation to conduct the talks.[56] This refusal to take the initiative quickly revealed itself to be a serious miscalculation, as Prussia broke ranks and signed a separate peace with France at Basel on 5 April 1795. The war was becoming unpopular amongst the Berlin elite, which viewed with alarm the worsening situation in Poland, where revolt had broken out a year before. The *Pax Borussica* was to last until a final peace settlement, effectively restricting *Reich* involvement in the war to areas south of the neutrality zone. Separate secret articles agreed that if a final treaty endorsed French annexation of Prussian territory west of the Rhine, compensation was to be found at other princes' expense to the east. These arrangements represented the first formal French sponsorship of German annexations and so heralded the reorganisation of the *Reich* that was to be affected by Napoleon.[57] Some German princes defended Prussia's action as the necessary first step toward a general peace, accusing Austria of continuing the war for its own interests. Already under Prussian pressure to abandon the war, the Saxons finally pulled out on 21 July, depleting the Austrians' northern, right, wing by 10,000 men. The whole of Upper Saxony, including the Ernestine duchies, was sucked into the neutrality zone. However, most condemned Prussia for abandoning the *Reich* in its hour of need in a treacherous break of faith and responsibility, with a few going so far as to argue that only a strengthening of executive power and unquestioning submission to Imperial authority could save the Empire. This was precisely what Austrian ministers wanted to hear and they lost no time in capitalising on the admittedly dire situation.[58] However, suspicion of Austria remained and the Prussians mistakenly believed the Emperor was already negotiating with France over a Low Countries–Bavaria exchange. Meanwhile, the strategic situation had altered significantly to Prussia's disadvantage with the allied collapse in Flanders in July 1794. The French subsequently drove into the Dutch Republic, conquering the country after a short campaign.[59]

The war was becoming unpopular in the Rhine territories too. Austrian generals were empowered to take whatever action they felt necessary, and on 21 November Würmser seized Mannheim to prevent the local authorities surrendering it to the French. Two Bavarian ministers were arrested on grounds of treason and the unfortunate inhabitants forced to contribute 400,000 florins to the Imperial war effort. The protests of the *Reichstag* were ignored, and this deliberate show of force was intended to intimidate the southern Germans into continuing to support Habsburg policy.[60] After 1795 Austria became

56 Wilson, *German Armies*, p.322.

57 Whaley, *Germany and the Holy Roman Empire*, p.589.

58 Generally the Austrian viewpoint has been the accepted interpretation of the Peace of Basel, although recently some historians have argued that Prussia's action was a perfectly rational move, in keeping with its general strategy since 1740 of avoiding protracted and unprofitable wars. See Wilson, *German Armies*, p.323.

59 Wilson, *German Armies*, p.322: 'Westphalia was now the front line, placing France in a position to threaten Prussia's north German sphere of influence for the first time directly.'

60 Wilson, *German Armies*, p.323: 'The change in attitude in 1795 is graphically illustrated by a breakdown in payments from the Palatine civil and estates' treasuries for military requisitioning. Money extorted by France amounted to over 335,470 florin. Spread fairly evenly across the period

Four depictions of soldiers from *Kreis-Cavallerie* regiments from the circles of Franconia and Swabia in late 1780, after the *Nachricht von den Fränkischen Kraistruppen nebst einem Angang von den schwäbischen Kreisregimentern*. Empire troops played a marginal role in the war campaigns from 1792–1800, however, contrary to popular mythology, Reich soldiers did not desert in droves. Although 734 men absconded from the Swabian *Kreistruppen* in 1795 without the corps ever coming into action, this was still only just over six percent of the total and probably lower than the rates suffered by the Austrian army, where hard discipline and poorer supply arrangements made desertion both easier and more compelling. (Authors' archive)

Würtenbergiſches Dragoner
Regiment.
Würtenberg.

Hohenzolleriſches Curaſier
Regiment.
Hohenzollern.

increasingly high-handed towards the lesser territories' contingents. Prussian neutrality had caught Münster's soldiers still with the *Reichsarmee*, but when Maximilian Franz tried to withdraw them, the Austrian generals refused to release them and they were obliged to cooperate with Habsburg forces until 1801.Moreover, Vienna reordered its strategic priorities at the *Reich*'s expense to concentrate on combating the inroads the French had made into Habsburg possessions in northern Italy since 1795. Taking advantage of a brief armistice on the Rhine in May 1796, Würmser with 25,000 men was switched south over the Alps, cutting the two Austrian armies in Germany to about 140,000 in total. When these forces proved insufficient to prevent Moreau and Jordan with 157,000 French from crossing the Rhine, the Imperial *Feldmarschall* Archduke Carl made a strategic withdrawal, abandoning most of south-west Germany and pulling back to a central position closer to the Danube.[61] While this made sense given the indefensibility of the Rhine, it proved politically disastrous. Meanwhile, the situation for the southern territories in Swabia became desperate, as they were now the next French goal. Württemberg withdrew its *Kreistruppen* from the Swabian corps on 1 July 1796 and opened negotiations with the French, signing an armistice on 17 July, agreeing to deliver huge quantities of food, horses and boots to the invaders as well as cash. Baden followed suit on 25 July, with the other Swabian states agreeing to pay war contributions to Paris, depleting the numerous ecclesiastical properties in the region. Also defenceless, the Franconian states offered cash and war materials. The Austrians naturally regarded this as nothing short of treachery, and at thc crack of dawn on 29 July 8,000 of their men burst into the camp of the remaining 3,000 Swabian soldiers, disarming them and impounding their weapons. Nonetheless, the defection of the southern medium states was highly significant, representing both recognition of the futility of traditional reliance on Habsburg protection and patronage and acknowledgement that a middle course was no longer possible. In any event, matters were being decided in the south where Napoleon Bonaparte led a revitalised French Army of Italy in a winter campaign across the Alps into southern Austria, forcing the Emperor to abandon the war by the preliminary Peace of Leoben of 18 April 1797, which included a six-month truce for the Germany. The Habsburg position continued to deteriorate after April, while the French consolidated their hold over northern Italy, forcing the Austrian negotiators into greater concessions in the Treaty of Campoformio of 18 October. Austria now acknowledged the

---

1792–9, and while that paid to Austria came to only just over half this figure (164,856 fl.), all but 4,328 florin fell in the period.'

61 However, Archduke Carl's strategy worked well, and, having drawn the French deep into Germany he turned and inflicted a series of defeats on their overextended forces, driving them back over the Rhine by October. See also Wilson, *German Armies*, pp. 324–325: 'In the light of this success, many later writers have followed the official Austrian line and argued that the south German withdrawal from the war was a mistake, resulting from political short sightedness and a lack of enthusiasm for the common cause. Instead of paying the huge sums to the French, the German states should have invested the money in their own war effort. However, the southern Germans had no way of predicting that Charles's withdrawal was a piece of strategic brilliance rather than a hasty retreat. More importantly, they sensed correctly that the *Reichskrieg* could not be won given the loss of the left bank and the neutrality of the north.'

principle of secularisation as the basis of compensation, effectively abdicating its responsibilities to the *Reich* in order to save its territorial empire. Effectively, Franz II had signed in his capacity as Habsburg ruler rather than as Emperor and now had to negotiate a full settlement on behalf of the *Reich*. Austria was increasingly isolated in Germany, and suspicion surrounding the true terms of Campoformio appeared to be confirmed when its troops handed the Mainz fortress to the French in December. Habsburg ministers took steps to prevent the complete evaporation of their influence, especially as Vienna now appreciated the value of the *Reich* as a buffer against both France and Prussia. The Habsburg emperors had always struggled to exclude the *Reich* from international negotiations, but Franz II now welcomed its involvement. The Deputation, appointed by the Reichstag following the initial peace initiative in 1795, was permitted to represent the *Reich* at the peace conference that opened at Rastatt in November 1797. The German princes were left with little choice but to deal directly with France and also Russia, which now resumed its earlier role of protecting German client dynasties. France made new treaties with Bavaria, Baden, Württemberg, Prussia, Hesse-Darmstadt and Mainz between July 1801 and May 1802, which, with the exception of Mainz, were followed by the movement of these territories' troops into the lands of their neighbours.

The political scenario that materialised after 1801 had swept away the old *Reich*, although it nominally remained in existence until 1806. While key elements of the traditional structure were retained, including elective emperorship, the Diet, the Imperial residences, circles and Imperial knights, the *Reich* military structure had been disbanded. Moreover, the traditional association of the *Reich* with Catholicism had been broken by the destruction of the *Reichskirche*, giving the Protestants a majority for the first time. The *Reich* was clearly moving inexorably towards a federation of sovereign princes before Franz II definitively abdicated on 6 August 1806. Franz II's abdication marked the formal extinction of a multi-state organisation which had spanned much of central and western Europe for more than a millennium. Already in 1804, he assumed a hereditary Austrian Imperial title as Franz I to counter the one Napoleon had created for himself in France. The new title symbolised Austria's disengagement from traditional Imperial politics and announced its determination to concentrate on preserving its own domains.

2

The Austrian Cavalry

On the eve of the First Coalition War against France, the Austrian Empire incorporated 5.6 million Germans, 5.3 million Hungarians and Slovaks, 4.4 million Czechs and Moravians, 2.1 million Flemings and Walloons, 1.8 million Italians, 1.6 million Croats and Serbs, 1.6 million Romanians and 3.4 million Poles, Ruthenians and Ukrainians, as well as a number of smaller ethnic groups. As with every multicultural empire, this scenario reverberated in the composition of the army. The Austrian cavalry comprised cuirassiers, dragoons, chevauxlegers, *Jäger zu Pferde* (horse chasseurs), hussars and uhlans. Each specialty reflected the different parts of the Habsburg's domains. Cuirassiers, dragoons, chevauxlegers, and *Jäger zu Pferde* were considered 'German cavalry' because their recruitment interested the provinces belonging to the Holy German–Roman Empire, namely Austria, Bohemia and Moravia, while the *uhlanen* regiments were composed of Poles, Ruthenians and Ukrainians from Galicia. In 1798, seven of the 12 regiments of hussars were entirely formed by native Hungarians, two more from Slovakia, one from Croatia, and two with recruits from Transylvania, which all were part of Royal Hungary.

The Austrian heavy cavalrymen were reputed as excellent swordsman: well-trained and well-mounted horsemen who usually enjoyed great esteem among their contemporaries since the late seventeenth century.[1] At the beginning of the wars against France, Austrian commanders considered their heavy horsemen as the best of Europe, notwithstanding the alternate results achieved against the Ottomans in 1788–1791. Furthermore, the Poles and Hungarians were also highly considered as excellent light cavalrymen, and several contemporary commenters recognised their valour. Dezydery Chlapowski, an officer of Napoleon's Old Guard Lancers commented that he 'was of the opinion then, as I am still today, that the Austrian light horse is the best trained in this kind of warfare (skirmishing and reconnaissance). The

1 'The Armies of Europe', in *Putnam's Monthly*, No. XXXII, 1855: 'The (Austrian) cavalry is excellent. The heavy or German cavalry, consisting of Germans and Bohemians is well horsed, well armed, and always efficient ...'

Austrian cavalry at Marengo, 14 June 1800, in the scene celebrating the courage of the French artilleryman Bareiller, depicted by Alphonse Lalauze (Print after the oil painting exhibited at the "Salon de Paris" in 1910). Concerning the uniforms, the artist turned to several specialists, and the result was very good. Note the cuirassier officer still wearing the older pre-1798 uniform, as a historically correct feature, because officers could tailor the new uniform within two years. The cavalry was considered the best element of the Austrian army, but rarely played a decisive role in the field. Not only were many of the troops inexperienced, but the quality of some of the officers was mixed. The years of Josephinian change had exacted a toll. The new political climate also affected morale. As one authoritative commenter, General Franz Joseph von Dietrichstein, wrote in the 1790s: "The officers especially argue rather a lot, are politicised and give vent to improper and reprehensible views in front of the men. The generals set the example. From where does this come? Well in part from our misfortunes but above all from the poor selection of officers; too many soldiers of fortune, over-promoted NCOs. Moreover the ruinous system of promotion by seniority means we do not have any generals and few colonels of ability … this stifles talent, discourages merit and removes all boldness. We do not have anyone who is inventive among our highest in rank."

Jäger zu Pferd, after Richard Knötel, from the *Grosse Uniformenkunde*, published in 1908–12. Compared to the coeval source, the version of Knötel differs by the green piping on the breeches. The newly raised regiment of *Jäger zu Pferd* followed the experiment to form a 'German' light cavalry, but like occurred for the *Leichte Dragoner*, the project was abandoned and after three years this regiment was disbanded.

Austrians are always the most skilled at placing outposts to guard their army'.[2]

According to several commenters, the Hungarian hussars were reputed the most renowned of the House of Austria's cavalrymen since the age of Empress Maria Theresa. Someone put their skill down to the fact that 'most Hungarians learned to ride in childhood and when out riding soon acquired a natural sense of direction, making them the ideal recruits for light cavalry duties'.[3] Given this premise, readers should expect noteworthy enterprise, instead people interested in the Napoleonic wars will surely have noticed that the Austrian cavalry seems to have played a secondary role in the battles fought between 1792 and 1815. No action carried out by the Austrian horsemen seems to rival those carried out by the French or even by their Russian and British allies. Of course there are several explanations, which we will try to expose in this book, without thinking, however, that these are the only possible ones.

Certainly, economic aspects influenced the cavalry's role on the field. As outlined by several scholars, the Austrian commanders were reluctant to use their horsemen *en masse*, because these troops represented a high economic value to preserve.[4] There was also a lack of large-scale exercises for the cavalry. As a result, the single regiments and brigades of Austrian cavalry were often outnumbered and defeated by French brigades and divisions. According to popular myth, this attitude derived also from the low cavalry ratio of the Austrian army. Effectively, with the exception of the Danube Valley and the Hungarian *Puszta*, the Austrian domains were mountainous and poorly suited to horse breeding. For this reason Austria could only deploy a lower percentage of cavalry compared to her enemies. However, this statement is not completely acceptable. The Austrian army, used to facing the Ottomans in a long series of wars in the seventeenth and eighteenth century, had always deployed a significant mounted force.[5] Austria was an Alpine country, but Bohemia and Moravia had a significant expanse of flat ground, and the same environmental conditions existed in the Low Countries. Moreover, compared to its allies, in 1801 the Austrian army had one horseman for every 6.5 infantry; more than Britain and Prussia and a little less than France, which could deploy one for

2 Chlapowski Dezydery, transl. Tim Simmons, *Memoirs of a Polish Lancer: The Pamietniki Of Dezydery Chlapowski* (Chicago, IL: Emperor's Press, 2002), p.15.

3 Antoine Fortuné de Brack, cited in 'The Armies of Europe', *Putnam's Monthly*, No. XXXII, 1855.

4 John R. Elting, *Swords around a Throne* (Cambridge MA: Da Capo Press, 1987), pp.221–222, and Rory Muir, *Tactics and the Experience of Battle in the Age of Napoleon* (New Haven and London: Yale University Press, 1998), p.101.

5 David G. Chandler, *The Art of Warfare in the Age of Marlborough* (New York: Hippocrene Books, 1976), p.30.

every six. Only Russia was able to gather a major force with a ratio of one to five.

After 1801, the comments on the Austrian cavalry continue to be positive both from allies and from enemies.[6] Nevertheless, Austria suffered a long series of defeats. Hampered by the inherent conservatism of the hierarchy, the Austrians had to fight the most modern army in Europe. Before 1809, the Austrian command did not offer particularly effective innovation concerning the tactical role of the cavalry.[7] Some scholars try to explain this failure by focusing on the variety on nationalities in the army.[8] Contemporary commenters described the great confusion of nationalities as a serious evil: 'In the British army, every man can at least speak English, but with the Austrians, even the NCOs of the non-German regiments can scarcely speak German.'[9] Other explanations for the defeats at the hands of the French army include poor administration and staff work, incompetent generals and antiquated tactics.[10] Despite a certain amount of experimentation and organisational, tactical and strategic change, the Austrian army underwent no radical modification in its character and remained essentially a typical eighteenth-century dynastic organisation. The reason for this conservatism stems from the preoccupation of its rulers and the very nature of the Habsburg Empire, with its diverse political institutional and nationalities all inhibiting radical changes.

However, after 1809 this old-fashioned army gave a good account of itself. The individual regiments performed well and were usually considered solid. The Austrian regulars, as well as

Feldmarschall Friedrich Moritz von Nostitz-Rieneck (1728–1796). A veteran of the Seven Years' War, he was appointed as president of the Aulic War Council and held this position from May 1796 until his death later that year. He was among the supporters who claimed the reform of the cavalry as well as the whole Austrian army. (Engraving by unknown artist. Authors' archive)

6 For French cavalry officer de Brack, the Hungarian hussars were some of 'the best European cavalry'. More or less in the same period, Sir Robert Wilson wrote that 'both (Austrian) cuirassiers and hussars are superb'. Another British observer described their cuirassiers in 1814 in Paris as 'outstanding'.

7 According to George Nafziger, *Imperial Bayonets: Tactics of the Napoleonic Battery, Battalion and Brigade As Found in Contemporary Regulations* (London: Greenhill Books, 1997): '... the Austrian 1805 Regulation is a miserable document which devotes more time to church services, payrolls and musters than it does to military manoeuvres. The only truly 'military' matter it contains is found in the plates at the back. It provides no illustrations of regimental manoeuvres, but limits itself to those of divisions (division = 2 squadrons) and squadrons.'

8 Philip J. Haythornthwaite: *Napoleonic Cavalry* (London: Cassell & Co, 2002), p.9.

9 Sir Robert Thomas Wilson (ed. Rev. Herbert Randolph, 1861), *Private Diary of Travels, Personal Services, and Public Events, During Mission and Employment with the European Armies in the Campaigns of 1812 and 1813*, (London, 1814), p.334.

10 Of this, Archduke Carl remarked: 'The generals are a weakness in our army. It robbed the rank and file of success they deserved.' In Rothenberg, *Napoleon's Great Adversary*, p.93.

irregular frontiersmen, performed with discipline in several occasions, and the Habsburg soldiers played a central part in the coalitions against France, from the campaigns in the 1790s to the Austerlitz campaign of 1805, the closely-balanced campaign of 1809, and the final victorious campaigns of 1813–1814. Undoubtedly, the Austrian cavalry remained one of Napoleon's most redoubtable enemies in term of time and size.[11]

Recruiting

The army played a significant role in the lives of the citizens of the Austrian Empire. Prior to 1802 a soldier's term of service was for life, although he was not necessarily on active duty for the entire period. There were basically only two types of recruits: those who opted to serve on a voluntary basis and those who had been forced by the state. But the oaths were the same for both. In 1769 the *Dienst* (service) regulation laid the primary emphasis on taking the oath of loyalty, obedience and devotion to the sovereign as the most important obligation of every soldier.

In 1771 Austria introduced general conscription, but exemptions were granted to some free towns and provinces, as well as to several professions. However, for the first time in the Habsburgs' domains, military conscription was applied also to Jews.[12] Not only were they now eligible to be called up, but their houses, like everyone else's, were numbered and their villages catalogued and delineated. Emperor Joseph II, who introduced conscription, understood the importance of the 'small men' and his recruiting machine not only conscripted frontline soldiers but hairdressers, footmen, bakers and candlestick makers, widening the cultural make-up of the army. An authoritarian bureaucracy administered a microcosm of the Empire which reflected its social diversity, though the officer class came to be dominated increasingly by the aristocracy. The experiment was not a success everywhere. Conscription in Hungary almost triggered a revolution. Its imposition in Tyrol was so unpopular among the fiercely independent male inhabitants of those valleys that shortly before his death Joseph II had to rescind all forms of conscription there.

11 'The Austrian army was the largest force continually engaged against the French Revolution and Napoleon and carried most of the burden of the war on land … Repeatedly crushed by superior forces and superior generalship, it always managed to find the strength to rise and fight again, and in the end it contributed the major contingent in the defeat of Napoleon.' – Gunther E. Rothenberg, *The Art of Warfare in the Age of Napoleon* (Bloomington: Indiana University Press, 1980), p.166. The author mentions also Cyrill Falls' statement, that: '[the Austrian army was] the most formidable army which the French had to face in the last years of the eighteenth century and the first few years of the nineteenth century.'

12 Joseph II was the principal instigator of the reform, notwithstanding Maria Theresa had always opposed this, observing acidly that 'here the frontiers of tolerance are reached', and that the question of Jews serving in the army was unmentionable. Initially Jews had only been allowed to serve in logistics and support functions and only in Galicia, but in 1789, under the pressure of the new Ottoman war, this was extended to all branches of the military services. See Marc Saperstein, 'In Praise of an Anti-Jewish Empress', in *Shofar*, vol. 6, n. 1 (Purdue University Press, 1987), pp.20–25.

Despite these setbacks, in 1781 the recruitment system was finally completed and took the name *Werb-Bezirks-System*, which lasted until 1862. The areas under conscription were divided into regimental districts for the German regiments. Tyrol, Hungary, with Croatia, the Low Countries and northern Italy remained excluded by this system. These areas relied on free recruiting while Hungary filled the ranks on a voluntary basis or through local officials according to the quotas of recruits agreed by the Hungarian Diet.

After 1781 the 37 German infantry regiments received permanent *Werb-Bezirke* (levy districts), while the German cavalry regiments, with the exception of the Dragoner Regiment D'Arberg Nr.25, which continued to recruit in the Austrian Low Countries, were referred to an area of recruitment.[13] Each levy district had to provide the necessary recruits for the completion of the cavalry regiments through volunteers as well as through conscription. However, as happened in the infantry, each regiment retained the permission to enlist volunteers not only in the hereditary domains but also in the *Reichs-Werbung*, the German Empire districts. After the incorporation of Galicia some areas were subjected to the cavalry recruitment, and therefore, every German cavalry regiment also included a certain percentage of men coming from this region of Poland. During the Napoleonic Wars Austria lost but also acquired new territories. When the recruitment districts were disbanded with their regiments, others were reconstituted with a new *Werb-Bezirke*. The low point in recruitment was reached in 1810, after the Peace of Vienna and the campaign of 1809, which imposed severe restriction regarding the size of the army.

A significant exception regarding recruitment were the two carabinier regiments, formed with recruits from the German hereditary domains, with the exception of the peripheral regions of Krain, Gorizia and Gradisca, by direct order of the Aulic War Council.

The hussar regiments recruited in the same Hungarian infantry districts and in the neighbouring border regions in Croatia and Transylvania. Effectively, In Hungary there was neither a conscription nor a mandatory statement *ex officio* in order to acquire new recruits. Finally the uhlans, organised in stable regiment-sized units in 1788, recruited exclusively in Galicia. The only subjects exempted from military service were the clergy, the nobility, some government officials, and workers employed in mining, iron production, and necessary agricultural occupations. This affected recruitment, especially in Hungary, where the local parliament did not favour the loss of manpower for the army, and introduced several restrictions through the years. In 1802, Husaren Regiment Nr.2 was allowed to recruit 400 men from 17 towns of Transylvania, and the recruitment parties were permitted to enlist only on Sunday.

Very unusually for the time period, one aspect of Austrian military life was the absence of segregation and discrimination against non–Roman-Catholic religious groups. Protestants, Orthodox Christians, and also Jews

13 After the evacuation of 1794 and the definitive loss of the Austrian Low Countries, the Latour Regiment recruited in the German provinces.

served alongside the Catholic majority in the army. Soldiers from each group retained the same rights of military membership and there were many non-Catholics who held high positions in the Austrian military.

Originally military service was, as in the infantry, lifelong; only foreigners could ask for a limitation, but only after serving in the army not less than 10 years. In 1802 lifelong service was abolished in the provinces subject to conscription, and for the cavalry the service was fixed at 12 years. In 1811, in order to avoid unequal treatment, it was fixed at 14 years as for the infantry. The 14-year period remained until 1845, when it was drastically reduced to eight years. The recruit's joining salary was three florins. In Hungary, where there was no conscription until 1828, the Emperor paid five florins. Recruits received also two ducats when transferred to another unit. Recruiting was largely a major problem for the infantry; although cavalry units were supposed to accept only men who had already completed basic training with the infantry, but this could be secondary. Cavalry regiments, specially the Hungarian ones, had little difficulty in attracting recruits able to ride horses. Hussar recruits were to be not less than 18- nor more than 30-years-old;[14] grey hair was considered an automatic bar, and preferably the recruits had to be over five *Füss* and four *Zoll* (1.68m) tall. Cuirassiers were selected from among the tallest recruits, followed by dragoons, who usually could be transferred from the infantry regiments as a prize for their positive service.

People who enrolled as volunteers in the hussars would sign a capitulation to serve from two to three years or, during wartime, for the duration of hostilities. As occurred in several European armies, volunteers retained a better position and in Austria entered the privileged category of *Primaplanisten*.[15] These soldiers held the same privileges as the non-commissioned officers, including higher wages and better equipment and clothing compared to the ordinary troopers. On parade, the *Primaplana* members marched at the head of the columns and could usually aspire to an appointment as NCO. There was also a secondary or *lessere Primaplana*, which comprised the actual NCOs. Company officers, *Primaplanisten* and NCOs held the privilege of voluntarily dismissing themselves from the army as, and when, they wanted.

In order to provide recruits in a shorter time, an army reserve was reorganised with the1 September 1812 circular. Each district organised its own reserve office and managed the recruitment stations located in the province. The office acted under a district officer, with a small staff formed by a military physician, employees and staff personnel. There was a different treatment for the reservists recruited into the infantry and those destined for cavalry and other corps. The infantry recruits agreed to the service, and after the oath they were immediately assigned to line infantry and *Jäger* regiments' depots and served for a training period of four weeks. They successively had to serve for a

14 As expressed in the contemporary documents: 'the young people are too weak for military duties and the recruits over 30 are too stiff and awkward', in D. Hollins and Darko Pavlovic, *Hungarian Hussars, 1756–1815* (Oxford: Ospery Publishing, Warrior Series, 2003), p.8.

15 The term *Primaplana* derives from Latin and means 'the first sheet'. Since the sixteenth century, in the Imperial army the *Primaplana* indicated officers and NCOs enlisted on a voluntary basis, whose names were written first in the company or squadron register

three-week period every year and only 14 days for a *Jäger*. The cavalry reserve, like the artillery and other reserve troops, were released immediately after the agreement, assignment and oath, and did not receive training; so they were added only in case of need. The reservists who had reached 40 years old were dismissed from the army with a discharge certificate.

The Army (and Cavalry) Regimental System

By coincidence Napoleon's date of birth is inscribed even in the history of the Austrian army, because 8 August 1769 coincides with the first systematic numbering of infantry and cavalry regiments introduced in Austria. Before 1769, the regiment followed the ancient tradition of identifying the regiments by the names of their *Oberst Inhaber* (colonel proprietors) or after their recruitment areas.[16] Any numeration before this date is improper, although it was sometimes applied. However, it was obvious to identify any regiment operating before 1769 as 'later regiment Nr. X', and this could help in awareness, as it was difficult to follow the regiment's history using only the colonel proprietors' names. Nevertheless, even after 1798 when the ancient denominations were replaced by the new numbering system, regiments continued to be identified in the order of battle with the colonel proprietor's name.

There was a numbering schema in use before 1769, but it lacked a system. For instance, the two carabinier regiments, established in 1768, were described as Erstes and Zweites Carabinier-Regiment (first and second regiment of carabiniers). A similar method of situational numbers existed for the *Grenzer* troops:[17] (Erstes, Zweites Székler Gränz-Infanterie-Regiment etc.), or for the garrison regiments.[18]

The new numbering system of regiments was one of the reforms introduced by Emperor Joseph II, when he took over military administration in 1765. The original description of regiments by their proprietors' names was a very variable attribute, limited by the change of proprietor (mostly after

16 In the cavalry there were the Szekler and Croatisch-Slavonisches hussar regiments, which retained the territorial origin for their denomination, however it is necessary to accept with caution an interpretation of this fact as an expression of the national origin of the regiments. The same caution has to be held for later territorial attributes used as an indication in the Army Scheme Almanacs (*Schematismus*). It is also necessary to respect the multinational character of the Habsburg monarchy and the local amalgamation of particular nationalities. Some units preserved their particular name, especially the ones formed by French *émigrés*, and some units continued to be identified for tradition by the name of some great commander or personality, such as the dragoon regiment *Savoyen* or the cuirassier *Kaiser*.

17 Southern and south-eastern regions under Habsburg rule close to the Ottoman Empire or its vassals formed special military districts, known as *Militärgrenze* (military borders). The military units belonging to the *Militärgrenze* were identified with the attribute *Gränitz*, later *Gränz* or *Grenz*, for *Grenz-Infanterie-Regiment* or *Grenz-Husaren Regiment*. After the introduction of the numbering system *Grenz* regiments represented an exception, because their original denomination remained in the official title of both units.

18 The two garrison regiments – Nr.5 and Nr.6 – were created with the elder soldiers or soldiers who were unable to carry out regular duties due to their age or to injuries, and who were stationed in some of the invalid house units. In wartime these regiments were never assigned to the field armies, but performed garrison duties as happened in peacetime.

Top: Austrian hussars marching with baggage, sutleresses and servants in the late eighteenth century, in a print after Albrecht Jebald. (Authors' archive)

Below: A closer view of details from above, and elsewhere in the print, Note the troopers still wearing the old uniform established in the 1769 regulation, as well as the trumpeters dressed in the aulic 'western' fashion. Speaking of Austrian hussars is probably improper, since they were mostly recruited in the territories of the Kingdom of Hungary, and Hungarian was their language and the ranks also retained the double German and Hungarian denomination within the regiment. Hungarian was also their famous battle cry *Rajta*! (Come on! Attack!)

his death, and less often by resigning or losing the position).[19] Theoretically, the number created a possibility of reliability, which was more useful in the infantry than in the cavalry.

The number was now added to the regiment's title, with the following description scheme applied for all the regiments:

a) The prefix k.k. (*kaiserlich–königlich* – Imperial–Royal) introductory form used since 1745
b) The military branch of service (infantry, cuirassiers, dragoons etc.), often shortened as IR, CR or DR
c) The colonel proprietor's name, if any
d) The progressive number of the regiment

However, there were some relevant discrepancies, such as historical denominations introduced for some regiments after 1888, such as the elimination of the proprietor's name during the First World War, but this traditional form lasted until the fall of the Habsburg Empire in 1918.

From a general point of view, the numbering was a useful system (even today), because it simplifies the identification of the unit's history within the army. However, even after the introduction of systematised numbering, the scenario might not be always clear. Some confusion came from several different regiments listed with the same number, as occurred often in the cavalry, where this event was even more complicated after the reform of units in new or different specialties. Moreover some 'numbers' might have been unoccupied (after a regiment's disbanding, recruitment districts under enemy rule etc.) and therefore the numbering did not always create a consecutive sequence; while an unused number could be have allocated later to different regiment. There even existed the possibility of renumbering a regiment, without changing its category.

In 1769, infantry and cavalry regiments were numbered in an ascending order, which would have followed the descending order of the colonel's social rank (starting from the Emperor downwards). Initially the infantry and cavalry had all their regiments numbered in sequence without regard of their category. The last regular infantry regiments had the number 59, while number 60 was the first *Grenzer* infantry regiment; however, with this act emerged two completely different situations.[20]

19 Before 1769, when the proprietor's name was the only way to identify the regiment, the units maintained the colonel's name even in periods of *interregnum*, namely when a new proprietor was missing or waiting to be appointed because of the death or resignation from the position of the previous *Oberst Inhaber* (colonel proprietor). In this case, the regiment was identified as vacant alongside the name of the last proprietor.

20 In the infantry, the four lowest numbers were allocated to the so-called *Haus-Regimenter*, namely regiments whose proprietors belonged to the Imperial family. For instance number '1' belonged to the Infantry regiment of the Emperor Joseph II, and successively to Leopold II and later to his son Franz II (Franz I in 1805). After these four regiments followed the garrison regiments, with numbers 5 and 6. The reason for placing these regiments, without colonel proprietor, in the first positions, was that the colonel's prerogatives were assumed by the supreme Imperial military office – the *Hofkriegsrat* (Aulic War Council). Numbers 7 to 59 were assigned to the regiments whose proprietors were Austrian or Hungarian generals or colonels. Finally there followed the aforementioned *Grenzer* regiments with numbers from 60 to 76, which were almost all without an actual colonel proprietor.

Walloon dragoon regiment Latour (Nr.25), 1792–98, after Richard Knötel's *Grosse Uniformenkunde*. This regiment retained some particularities, even when the Habsburgs lost the Low Countries' provinces. As a result, the regiment was completed with recruits from Bohemia, but continued to enlist foreigners too. Another particularity consisted in the ensign, which did not change the two pointed shape and dark green background colour with gold embroideries and fringes, issued to the regiment from the Empress Maria Theresia, and continuing to use this type of standard until the summer of 1915.

A different scenario could be seen in the cavalry although the numbering followed the same principles. For instance, the proprietor of the Chevauxlegers Regiment Nr.1 was the Emperor Joseph II, who also owned the Husaren Regiment Nr.2. In 1769, seven *Reiter-Gattung* (cavalry specialties, or branches) were established: *Karabinieren*, *Cuirassieren*, *Dragoner*, *Chevauxlegers*, *Husaren*, *Grenz-Husaren* (frontier hussars) and *Grenz-Dragoner* (frontier dragoons). By ignoring the specialties, the branches became shuffled. Therefore regiment Nr.1

Number 77 sometimes indicated the *Grenzer Tzajkisten* battalion. However, after 1780 a third garrison battalion appeared and was awarded the number 77, leaving the *Tzajkisten* without their number. In the early 1790s, the third garrison regiment was still indicated as number 77 but in some orders of battle it was registered without a number. This system remained in use until the reform of 1798, when *Grenzer* regiments finally had their own numbers, from 1 to 17, and therefore the infantry sequence changed. In 1798 the term *Linien-Infanterie Regiment* was also officially introduced, which replaced the previous denomination *Infanterie Regiment*.

were chevauxlegers, Nr.2 hussars, Nr.3 and Nr.4 cuirassiers, Nr.5 carabiniers, Nr.6 and Nr.7 dragoons etc. At the end of the list there were the *Grenz* regiments without a colonel proprietor. After the cavalry reduction occurred in the 1770s, the regiments were again renumbered. In 1780, in the new sequence remained eight unoccupied numbers, because of disbanded regiments: Nr.6 (dragoons), Nr.8, 22 and 23 (cuirassiers), Nr.24 (hussars), Nr.25 (cuirassiers), Nr.36 (hussars) and Nr.45 (*Grenz-Dragoner*). The adjustment consisted in moving numbers over the sequence, eliminating intervals, so they created a continuous sequence from 1 to 37 (for the first five regiments the numbers remained unchanged, but dragoon regiment Nr.7 became Nr.6; regiment Nr.9 received the number 7 etc.). Furthermore, almost all the *Grenz-Husaren* regiments were disbanded from Nr.33 until 36 (former Nr.40 to 43 in 1769). After these drastic reductions, which left just two squadrons per regiment, the border hussars were distributed to the Grenzer infantry regiments, where they served until 1786.

In 1789, further changes were introduced. Most of the cavalry regiments returned to the state as in 1769. The only exception was the Karabinier Regiment (Nr.15 in 1769, but Nr.13 in 1780), which was appointed as Nr.6, and in 1795 retook its original 1769 number, namely Nr.15. Until the breakout of the Coalition Wars, some minor changes occurred again. In 1790 the regiment of the Stab-Dragoner (Staff Dragoons) was established, but without number and later reformed as *Leichte Dragoner*. Finally, in 1791, the *Uhlanen* regiments were created but without a number, while a new dragoon regiment was appointed as Nr.31.

In 1792, at the beginning of the Coalition Wars, the Austrian cavalry numbered the regiments from 1 to 44. The numbers 8, 15, 22, 23, 24, 25, 36, 40, 41, 42 and 43 remained unassigned. Then, in 1798 the different specialties of cavalry received their own numbering sequence. Even after 1769 cavalry regiments were described by their speciality, by colonel's name and finally by their number according to either category, however, this identification system became mandatory after 1798, when there always were several cavalry regiments with the same number. In 1792 there were two carabinier regiments (Nr.5 and Nr.6), which deployed a larger strength of four tactical divisions.[21] Both regiments changed to cuirassiers in 1798, becoming the new Cuirassieren Regiment Nr.1 and Nr.3, with the usual three divisions each, while the *Karabinier* speciality was abolished. In 1792 the cavalry deployed nine cuirassier regiments numbered as 4, 10, 12, 14, 20, 21, 27, 29 and 33. When in 1798 both former carabinier regiments became cuirassiers, and the former *émigré* regiment Royal-Allemand Dragoner became a new cuirassier regiment, the overall number of cuirassier regiments increased to 12, now numbered 1–12. Cuirassiers after 1798:

Nr.1 (former Karabinieren Regiment Nr.2 and old Nr.15)
Nr.2 (former Cuirassieren Regiment Nr.29)

21 Divisions were the tactical unit of Austrian cavalry, usually formed by two squadrons, and commanded by a field officer, who gave the name to the division under him.

Nr.3 (former Karabinieren Regiment Nr.1, and old Nr.5)
Nr.4 (former Cuirassieren Regiment Nr.27)
Nr.5 (former Cuirassieren Regiment Nr.10)
Nr.6 (former *émigré* Royal-Allemand Dragoner)
Nr.7 (former Cuirassieren Regiment Nr.21)
Nr.8 (former Cuirassieren Regiment Nr.4)
Nr.9 (former Cuirassieren Regiment Nr.14)
Nr.10 (former Cuirassieren Regiment Nr.20)
Nr.11 (former Cuirassieren Regiment Nr.33)
Nr.12 (former Cuirassieren Regiment Nr.12)

In 1801 cuirassier regiments Nr.4, 5 and 11 were disbanded, and regiment Nr.6 transformed into a dragoon unit. In 1802 the surviving eight cuirassier regiments were renumbered as follows:

1792	1798	1801–1802	(1867)
1. Karabinieren Nr.5	Cuirassieren Nr.3	Cuirassieren Nr.3	Dragoner Nr.3
2. Karabinieren Nr.13	Cuirassieren Nr.1	Cuirassieren Nr.1	Dragoner Nr.1
Cuirassieren Nr.29	Cuirassieren Nr.2	Cuirassieren Nr.2	Dragoner Nr.2
Cuirassieren Nr.21	Cuirassieren Nr.7	Cuirassieren Nr.7	Dragoner Nr.7
Cuirassieren Nr.4	Cuirassieren Nr.8	Cuirassieren Nr.8	Dragoner Nr.8

Note: regiments Nr.1, 2, 3, 7 and 8 maintained their original number. In the last column appears the regiment that assumed the history and tradition of the old unit after the reform introduced in 1867

Regiment Nr.12 received Nr.4, regiment Nr.9 received Nr.5, and regiment Nr.10 took Nr.6.[22]

1792	1798	1801–1802	(1867)
Cuirassieren Nr.12	Cuirassieren Nr.12	Cuirassieren Nr.4	Dragoner Nr.4
Cuirassieren Nr.14	Cuirassieren Nr.9	Cuirassieren Nr.5	Dragoner Nr.5
Cuirassieren Nr.20	Cuirassieren Nr.10	Cuirassieren Nr.6	Dragoner Nr.6

Disbanded or Reformed Regiments:

1792	1798	1801–1802	(1867)
Cuirassieren Nr.27	Cuirassieren Nr.4	Disbanded	-
Cuirassieren Nr.10	Cuirassieren Nr.5	Disbanded	-
Cuirassieren Nr.33	Cuirassieren Nr.11	Disbanded	-
Royal Allemand Dragoner	Cuirassieren Nr.6	Dragoner Nr.6	Dragoner Nr.12

22 Until 1860, the situation remained unaltered when cuirassier regiments were augmented by transforming the actual dragoon regiments Nr.1, 2, 3 and 6, which now received numbers 9 to 12. In 1867, after the *Ausgleich*, the new *K.u.K. Armee* abolished the cuirassiers, and all 12 regiments were transformed into dragoons.

As for the German cavalry, the history of the light cavalry too is particularly complex, especially when the dragoons became *Leichte Dragoner*. In 1792, there were six dragoon regiments numbered 3, 9, 26, 37, 38 and 39, the Stabsdragoner Regiment without number,[23] and seven chevauxlegers regiments numbered as regiment 1, 7, 13, 18, 19, 28 and 31. Dragoons and chevauxlegers deployed six squadrons and three tactical *Divisionen*. The year 1798 brought some significant changes. Both categories were joined in single one described first as *Leichte Dragoner*. However, as there was not any other category of *Dragoner*, the word '*Leichte*' (light) was abolished before the end of the year. Nevertheless, the denomination *Leichte Dragoner* remained in use and could be seen even in official documents dated after 1798. Therefore, since 1798, the Austrians had 15 (light) dragoon regiments, numbered from Nr.1 to Nr.15. For their establishment, the Aulic War Council used the six former dragoon regiments, the former Stabsdragoner Regiment (shortly before its transformation into a chevauxlegers regiment), and the seven chevauxlegers regiments (with a newly created one). The combination of *Dragoner* and *Chevauxlegers* was as follows:

Leichte Dragoner Regiment Nr.1 (former Chevauxlegers Regiment Nr.1)
Leichte Dragoner Regiment Nr.2 (former Dragoner Regiment Nr.3)
Leichte Dragoner Regiment Nr.3 (former Dragoner Regiment Nr.26)
Leichte Dragoner Regiment Nr.4 (former Chevauxlegers Regiment Nr.18)
Leichte Dragoner Regiment Nr.5 (former Chevauxlegers Regiment Nr.13)
Leichte Dragoner Regiment Nr.6 (former Dragoner Regiment Nr.37)
Leichte Dragoner Regiment Nr.7 (former Dragoner Regiment Nr.39)
Leichte Dragoner Regiment Nr.8 (former Dragoner Regiment Nr.38)
Leichte Dragoner Regiment Nr.9 (former Stabsdragoner Regiment)
Leichte Dragoner Regiment Nr.10 (former Chevauxlegers Regiment Nr.28)
Leichte Dragoner Regiment Nr.11 (former Chevauxlegers Regiment Nr.31)
Leichte Dragoner Regiment Nr.12 (former Chevauxlegers Regiment Nr.7)
Leichte Dragoner Regiment Nr.13 (newly established)
Leichte Dragoner Regiment Nr.14 (former Chevauxlegers Regiment Nr.19)
Leichte Dragoner Regiment Nr.15 (former Dragoner Regiment Nr.9)

However, after a few years reformd again confused the recently simplified matter. Indeed, after 1801, the regiments Nr.2, 5, 6 and 9 were disbanded. The remaining 11 regiments were (once again) divided in dragoons and chevauxlegers, while one dragoon regiment was formed from the disbanded Cuirassieren Regiment Nr.6. In the intentions of the high command, these new dragoon regiments were an intermediate speciality between light and heavy cavalry. They received the white uniforms, and trained as actual dragoons able to fight dismounted, while the chevauxlegers (with hussars and uhlans) continued to serve as light cavalry.

The regiments were numbered in 1802 as follows:

23 Besides this unit, in 1797 were raised also three independent squadrons of *Stabsdragoner*.

Dragoner Regiment Nr.1 (former Leichte Dragoner Regiment Nr.3)
Dragoner Regiment Nr.2 (former Leichte Dragoner Regiment Nr.7)
Dragoner Regiment Nr.3 (former Leichte Dragoner Regiment Nr.8)
Dragoner Regiment Nr.4 (former Leichte Dragoner Regiment Nr.14)
Dragoner Regiment Nr.5 (former Leichte Dragoner Regiment Nr.15)
Dragoner Regiment Nr.6 (former Cuirassieren Regt. Nr.6)
Chevauxlegers Regiment Nr.1 (former Leichte Dragoner Regiment Nr.1)
Chevauxlegers Regiment Nr.2 (former Leichte Dragoner Regiment Nr.4)
Chevauxlegers Regiment Nr.3 (former Leichte Dragoner Regiment Nr.10)
Chevauxlegers Regiment Nr.4 (former Leichte Dragoner Regiment Nr.11)
Chevauxlegers Regiment Nr.5 (former Leichte Dragoner Regiment Nr.12)
Chevauxlegers Regiment Nr.6 (former Leichte Dragoner Regiment Nr.13)

Further modifications happened in 1814 when a former Italian cavalry regiment of Napoleon's Kingdom of Italy became Chevauxlegers Regiment Nr.7 (later Uhlanen Regiment Nr.11).[24]

1792	1798	1801–1802	(1867)
Dragoner Nr.3	Leichte Dragoner Nr.2	Disbanded	-
Dragoner Nr.9	Leichte Dragoner Nr.15	Dragoner Regt. Nr.5	Dragoner Regt. Nr.13
Dragoner Nr.26	Leichte Dragoner Nr.3	Dragoner Regt. Nr.1*	Dragoner Regt. Nr.9
Dragoner Nr.37	Leichte Dragoner Nr.6	Disbanded	-
Dragoner Nr.38	Leichte Dragoner Nr.8	Dragoner Regt. Nr.3	Dragoner Regt. Nr.11
Dragoner Nr.39	Leichte Dragoner Nr.7	Dragoner Regt. Nr.2	Husaren Regt. Nr.15
Stabsdragoner	Leichte Dragoner Nr.9	Disbanded	-
-	Leichte Dragoner Nr.13	Chevauxlegers Regt. Nr.6	Husaren Regt. Nr.16
-	Cuirassieren Nr.6	Dragoner Regt. Nr.6	Dragoner Regt. Nr.12
Chevauxlegers Nr.1	Leichte Dragoner Nr.1	Chevauxlegers Regt. Nr.1	Uhlanen Regt. Nr.6
Chevauxlegers Nr.7	Leichte Dragoner Nr.12	Chevauxlegers Regt. Nr.5	Dragoner Regt. Nr.10
Chevauxlegers Nr.13	Leichte Dragoner Nr.5	Disbanded	-
Chevauxlegers Nr.18	Leichte Dragoner Nr.4	Chevauxlegers Regt. Nr.2	Uhlanen Regt. Nr.7
Chevauxlegers Nr.19	Leichte Dragoner Nr.14	Dragoner Regt. Nr.4*	Disbanded 1860
Chevauxlegers Nr.28	Leichte Dragoner Nr.10	Chevauxlegers Regt. Nr.3	Uhlanen Regt. Nr.8
Chevauxlegers Nr.31	Leichte Dragoner Nr.11	Chevauxlegers Nr.4	Dragoner Regt. Nr.14

*Regiments Nr.1 and Nr.4 were the first dragoon units to receive the white uniforms in 1802, notwithstanding before 1805 they were allowed to use both colours: green for *Chevauxlegers* and white for *Dragoners*.

24 The chevauxlegers existed until 1851 when this speciality was abolished. Regiments Nr.1, 2, 3, 5, 6 and 7 were transformed into uhlans and numbered 6–11, Regiment Nr.4 became dragoon regiment Nr.7.

Concerning the actual light cavalry, in 1792 there were nine hussar regiments numbered 2, 11, 16, 17, 30, 32, 34, 35 and 44 (the last was originally a *Grenz-Husaren* regiment). In 1798, the hussars were identified with their own numbers, 1–12, after that three regiments were newly established, but only one was 'regular' because two were formed with *Grenzer* troopers, originally raised in 1793 for the Husaren Division of Würmser's Volunteer Corps. This corps changed its denomination becoming Grenz-Freikorps in 1795. Unlike the infantry, there was not a separate numbering for the *Grenzer* troops, but these regiments were placed at the end of the sequence. The renumbering resulted as follows:

Husaren Regiment Nr.1 (former Cavallerie Regiment Nr.2)
Husaren Regiment Nr.2 (former Cavallerie Regiment Nr.17)
Husaren Regiment Nr.3 (former Cavallerie Regiment Nr.32)
Husaren Regiment Nr.4 (former Cavallerie Regiment Nr.34)
Husaren Regiment Nr.5 (newly established)
Husaren Regiment Nr.6 (former Cavallerie Regiment Nr.16)
Husaren Regiment Nr.7 (newly established)
Husaren Regiment Nr.8 (former Cavallerie Regiment Nr.30)
Husaren Regiment Nr.9 (former Cavallerie Regiment Nr.11)
Husaren Regiment Nr.10 (former Cavallerie Regiment Nr.35)
Grenz-Husaren Regiment Nr.11 (former Cavallerie Regiment Nr.44-Székler Grenz-Husaren)
Grenz-Husaren Regiment Nr.12 (former Croatisch-Slavonisches Grenz-Husaren Regiment)

In 1800 another regiment was established, and took the name of Palatinal-Husaren Regiment, because the proprietor was the Hungarian Palatine, namely the Hungarian Governor Archduke Joseph Anton; however it was without number. In 1801 Husaren Regiment Nr.12 was disbanded, and in 1802 the number 12 was finally appointed to the Palatinal Hussars.

1792	1798	1801–1802	(1867)
Husaren Nr.2	Husaren Nr.1	Husaren Regt. Nr.1	Husaren Rgt. Nr.1
Husaren Nr.17	Husaren Nr.2	Husaren Regt. Nr.2	Husaren Rgt. Nr.2
Husaren Nr.32	Husaren Nr.3	Husaren Regt. Nr.3	Husaren Rgt. Nr.3
Husaren Nr.34	Husaren Nr.4	Husaren Regt. Nr.4	Husaren Rgt. Nr.4
-	Husaren Nr.5	Husaren Regt. Nr.5	Husaren Rgt. Nr.5
Husaren Nr.16	Husaren Nr.6	Husaren Regt. Nr.6	Husaren Rgt. Nr.6
-	Husaren Nr.7	Husaren Regt. Nr.7	Husaren Rgt. Nr.7
Husaren Nr.30	Husaren Nr.8	Husaren Regt. Nr.8	Husaren Rgt. Nr.8
Husaren Nr.11	Husaren Nr.9	Husaren Regt. Nr.9	Husaren Rgt. Nr.9
Husaren Nr.35	Husaren Nr.10	Husaren Regt. Nr.10	Husaren Rgt. Nr.10
Székler Husaren Nr.44	Grenz-Husaren Nr.11	Grenz-HusarenNr.11	Husaren Rgt. Nr.11
-	Grenz-Husaren Nr.12	-	-
-	-	Palatinal-Husaren Nr.12	-

The uhlans belonged to the most recent categories of the Austrian cavalry. In order to favour a voluntary enlistment of Poles, Emperor Joseph II authorised the formation of a corps or *Pułk* composed half by nobles *Towarzis* armed with lance and for the other half by *Pocztowy* recruits trained to use firearms. In 1784 was raised the first *Uhlanen pulks* (corps) in Galicia and Lodomeria. In peacetime their strength was established at two *Divisionen*. During the war against the Ottomans of 1788–1791, the corps increased with four more squadrons, then in 1791 this regiment-sized corps was disbanded and one squadrons of uhlans was assigned to each of six regiments of chevauxlegers, in order to form a special tactical unit.

Shortly before, in January 1790, due to the Prussian threat to Bohemia, *Major* Carl O'Donnell received permission to raise in Galicia two divisions as *Freiwilligen Corps* (volunteer corps),[25] which were separated from the original uhlan corps by a decree of 20 April 1791, and provided with their own staffs.[26] In 1790, a third division was raised in order to form a further independent Uhlanen Freiwilligen Corps and was later named after its commandants, the first of which was Major Degelmann.[27] Before the end of 1791 the uhlan corps O'Donnell was finally established into a regular regiment under *Feldmarschall-Lieutenant* Janos Mészáros, becoming Uhlanen Regiment Nr.1 in 1798. A second regiment was raised shortly after joining the Freiwilligen Corps with the uhlan companies assigned to the chevauxlegers regiments Kaiser, Karaiczay and Lobkowitz.[28] A third uhlan division followed a few years later. In 1798 the regiment assumed the denomination Uhlanen Regiment Nr.2. In 1800 the regiment was assigned to *Feldmarschall-Lieutenant* Carl Philipp von Schwarzenberg.[29]

During the wars against Napoleon another two uhlan regiments were raised: Nr.3 in 1801 in Cracow with rank and file coming from Uhlanen Regiment Nr.1 and Leichte Dragoner Nr.12 and Nr.15, and finally Uhlanen Regiment Nr.4 in 1814 with the enlistment of new recruits merged into the rank and file from the other three regiments of uhlans.

The *Jäger zu Pferd* (horse chasseurs) appeared in the Austrian army for the first (and last) time during the wars against France. The Jäger-Regiment zu Pferd was established in 1797, and being the only one existing it received no number. This regiment was formed with four squadrons of the volunteer cavalry corps recruited in 1795 by the bishops of Paderborn and Hildesheim for the short-lived Westphalian Circle's contingent. In 1797, the squadrons increased to six

25 Alphons Freiherrn von Wrede and Anton Semek, *Geschichte der K. und K. Wehrmacht. Die Regimenter, Corps, Branchen und Anstaltenvon 1618 bis Ende des XIX. Jahrhunderts* (Vienna, 1901), vol. II, p.443. The *Kaiserlich Patent*, dated 19 January 1790, authorised O'Donnell to form a mixed corps of light infantry and cavalry for 1,200 men overall.

26 Wrede and Semek, *Geschichte der K. und K. Wehrmacht*, vol. III, part one, p.74.

27 The command of the Uhlanen Freiwilligen Corps was later assigned to *Oberst-Lieutenant* Carl Philipp von Schwarzenberg, who held the position until 1794, replaced by *Oberst-Lieutenant* Johann von Keglevich until 1796, then *Oberst-Lieutenant* Anton Vogl until 1797 and finally *Oberst-Lieutenant* Joseph von Motschlitz until 1798. Wrede and Semek, *Geschichte der K. und K. Wehrmacht*, vol. III, part one, p.325.

28 Wrede and Semek, *Geschichte der K. und K. Wehrmacht*, vol. III, part one, p.319.

29 Wrede and Semek, *Geschichte der K. und K. Wehrmacht*, vol. III, part one, p.74 and p.325.

and in March entered the Habsburgs' service. In 1798, the regiment was fully established to eight squadrons joining the foreign rank and file coming from the disbanded French *émigré* mounted units of the Austrian army. The regiment was known also as Bussy Jägers and in 1800 add two further squadrons,[30] but in 1801 was disbanded. Officers and troopers were dismissed, and only a small percentage were assigned to the newly established Uhlanen Regiment Nr.3.

Usually each cavalry regiment had a depot, which also quartered the training unit in peacetime.

Organisation of the Austrian Cavalry

The privileges deriving from the command of a regiment had diminished considerably during the eighteenth century, however the system whereby the *Obrist* (or *Oberst*) *Inhaber* (colonel proprietor) had so much control over the affairs of the regiment was equally applicable in the cavalry as in the infantry, all the regiment's commissions being a colonel's matter. By the mid eighteenth century, it had become common to attribute the rank of colonel proprietor to members of the high aristocracy or court personalities (Emperor Franz I was colonel of four cavalry regiments and one of infantry). They retained this rank just as honorific title, because a second colonel proprietor was added, and he actually dealt with the regiment's management. As for the infantry, differences existed between regiments formed in the 'German' and 'Hungarian' areas of the empire. The first included all non-Hungarians, such as Walloons and Italians, and the latter also comprised Croatians, Slovaks and others. Without exception, the Hungarian cavalry was formed only by hussar light cavalry, while all the other regiments were classified as heavy or medium cavalry. Only the chevauxlegers were regarded as the light horsemen of the German cavalry, though in effect they were more similar to the medium cavalry dragoons. The uhlans from Galicia conformed to this classification, forming a separate group of national light cavalry, which included Poles, Ruthenians, Ukrainians and other minorities.

As a result of the extra time required to train a cavalryman, theoretically there existed only minor differences between a unit's wartime and peacetime establishments. Usually, but depending from the economic scenario, surplus officers and NCOs were maintained in service to enable the formation of a reserve division in wartime. Furthermore, according to the order issued by the Aulic War Council, each cavalry regiment had to kept their numbers as close as possible to full strength, but effectively this result was rarely achieved and the actual strength of cavalry regiments in peacetime never exceeded 60–70 percent.[31]

1792–1798

At the outbreak of the French Revolutionary wars the cavalry was involved in a process of reorganisation. In 1790 the overall balanced strength was 40,058

30 Wrede and Semek, *Geschichte der K. und K. Wehrmacht*, vol. III, part two, p.741.

31 Hochedlinger, *Austria's Wars of Emergence*, p.301.

horsemen, and according to the balanced strength of the cavalry, in the early 1790s the fighting force comprised 9,531 *Cuirassieren*, 2,936 *Karabinieren*, 8,097 *Dragoner*, 7,038 *Chevauxlegers*, 12,456 *Husaren*. This force was divided into two *Karabinieren*, nine *Cuirassieren*, six *Dragoner*, seven *Chevauxlegers*, one *Stabsdragoner* (staff dragoon), two *Husaren*, and one *Grenzer* hussar regiments. In 1791 a further two *Uhlanen* regiments were added with a paper strength of 3,680 horsemen.[32]

The main tactical unit for all branches was the *Division*, commanded by a field officer, which comprised two squadrons. A carabinier or cuirassier squadron numbered 150 men of all ranks, with between 170 and 180 men for a squadron of dragoons or light cavalry. The two carabinier regiments comprised four divisions for eight squadrons in all; the cuirassiers deployed three divisions, the hussars had five, the uhlans four. Dragoons and chevauxlegers had six squadrons, except for the Coburg Dragoons and Latour Chevauxlegers, which deployed eight squadrons and four tactical divisions. Ranks in the cavalry were similar to the infantry, although the rank of *Hauptleute* (senior lieutenant, or captain) of the infantry, was the *Rittmeister* in the cavalry. Further differences concerned the senior NCO rank known as *Wachtmeister* (sergeant).

In 1792 the cavalry regiments were still organised as established in 1769 with the *Exercier-und-Dienst Vorschriften* issued under the Aulic War Council's president Franz Moritz von Lacy. Each squadron was formed by two companies, divided in two *Flügel* (wings), in turn divided into two *Züge* (platoons) of two *Corporalshaften*.[33] Minor changes occurred in the following years, and in 1771 this regulation was confirmed, at least for the cavalry.

The basic administrative unit was the company, and 12 companies formed the regiment. The *Rittmeister* was the company commander and usually he assumed the command of the squadron on the field, being the *Ersten-Rittmeister* his deputy, the *Zweiten-Rittmeister*, retained the command of the second company in the squadron, while the first company passed to the *Capitain-Lieutenant*. However, the squadron had lost its original tactical role, being the *Division*, formed by two squadrons, the principal field unit in all the Austrian cavalry. Usually a regiment of 12 companies deployed six squadrons for three *Divisionen* in all. On the field, each division took the name of the Field Officer, namely *Oberst-Division* or *Leib-Division*, *Oberstlieutenants-Division*, and *Majors-Division*. Carabinier regiments, which had a strength of 16 companies, deployed a fourth division, known as *Zweite Majors-Division* (or, *2. Majors Division*). In peacetime each squadron did not serve with horses, for all rank and file and usually six or 10 horsemen served dismounted. In wartime each regiment formed a reserve squadron with these troopers. Moreover, in the carabinier regiments the actual heavy companies were just the first 12, the remaining companies consisting of *Chevauxlegers*.

Until 1798 each cuirassier and carabinier squadron deployed a regular strength of 174 rank and file, including officers and staff. In detail:

32 Wrede and Semek, *Geschichte der K. und K. Wehrmacht*, vol. III, part one, p.108.

33 Wrede and Semek, *Geschichte der K. und K. Wehrmacht*, vol. II, part one, p.19.

2 *Rittmeister*	Company Officers	Primaplana
1 *Capitain-Lieutenant*		
2 *Oberlieutenants*		
2 *Unterlieutenants*		
1 *Estandarte Führer* (per *Division*)	NCOs	
2 *Wachtmeister*		
1 *Fourier*		
1 *Feldscherer* (surgeon)		
1 *Trompeter*		
1 *Schmied*		
1 *Sattler*		
3 *Corporale*		
2 *Vice-Corporale*		
145 *Gemeinen* (troopers)		
6 *Supernumerari*		

Alongside the company staff should be included also the *Privat Cadetten*, in variable numbers. Each cuirassier regiment deployed a fighting force of 1,044.

Karabinieren regiments had two further squadrons of *Chevauxlegers* with the same staff, but with 170 *Gemeinen*. Therefore, the overall strength of a *Karabinieren* regiment totalled 1,448 horsemen.

Finally, each cuirassier and carabinier regiment had its own *Regimentsstab* with field officers, adjutants and other personnel. In detail:

1 *Oberst* (or *Regiments Commandant*)	Field Officers	*Gross Regimentsstab*
1 *Oberstlieutenant*		
1 *Major* (2 in the carabinier regiments)		
1 *Regiments Auditor*		
1 *Regiments Kaplan* or *Regiments Pater*		
1 *Regiments Rechnungsführer* (Accountant)		*Klein Regimentsstab**
1 *Regiments Estandarteführer*		
1 *Stabs Trompeter*		
2 *Stabs-Fourieren*		
1 *Stabs-Arzt*		
1 Ober-Schmied		
1 *Profoss*		
3 or 4 *Fourierschützen*		
5 *Privatdiener* (officers' servants)		

* All this rank were mounted, except *Stabs-Fourieren*, *Ober-Schmied*, *Profoss*, *Fourierschützen*, *Stabs-Arzt* and *Privatdiener*, who served dismounted.

Dragoons had the same *Regimentsstab*, but the squadron deployed its strength as the *Chevauxlegers* with 193 troopers, NCOs and officers, plus six *Supernumerari*. Each regiment of dragoons and chevauxlegers deployed six squadrons with 1,158 horsemen in all.

Hussars formed a *Regimentsstab* as for the cuirassiers but with one *Zweites Mayor*, two *Ober-Schmiede*, one *Unter-Schmied*, one *Riemer* (leather craftsman) and one *Schneider* (tailor). The squadron deployed the same staff except for the *Schmied*, decreasing the number to 22 men, and 170 *Gemeinen*, plus 10 *Supernumerari*. Each regiment fielded eight squadrons for 1,536 horsemen overall.

Uhlans were regimented like the hussars.

In 1792 the regiments were quartered in the domains as follows:

	Karabinieren	*Cuirassieren*	*Dragoner*	*Chevauxlegers*	*Husaren*	*Uhlanen*	TOTAL
Lower Austria		2	2	2			5 regts
Upper Austria		1	1				2 regts
Bohemia		4	2	2			8 regts
Moravia		2	1	2			5 regts
Hungary and Transylvania					11		11 regts
Galicia						2	2 regts
Low Countries			1				1 regts
Milan				1			1 regts
German Empire	2						2 regts
TOTAL	2	9	7	7	11	2	

Each regiment disposed of its own train to the extent of one two-horse wagon for the *Regimentsstab*, and one four-horse wagon for each squadron.[34]

In wartime, some changes were applied to increase strength and staff. In the *Karabinieren* regiments each *Chevauxlegers* squadron added 10 *Gemeinen*, while the *Regimentsstab* received one *Stabs-Feldscherer* and one *Schneider*. The *Cuirassieren* augmented the *Regimentsstab* with two *Stabs-Feldscherer* and one *Schneider*. The same occurred in the *Dragoner* and *Chevauxlegers* regiments, while each squadron increased to 180 *Gemeinen*. The *Husaren* and *Uhlanen* added 10 *Gemeinen* for each squadron. Furthermore, a reserve squadron was formed in each cavalry regiment, with the staff of a regular field squadron and 145 *Gemeinen* for *Karabinieren* and *Husaren*, and 114 for

34 Hermann Günther von Meynert, *Geschichte des Kriegswesens und der Heeresverfassung in der Österreichischen Monarchie vom Tode des Kaisers Leopold I bis auf die gegenwärtige Zeit* (Vienna: Gerold in Komm., 1854), vol. IV, p.83.

the other branches.[35] On campaign were also added *one Ober-Tierarzt* and one *Unter-Tierarzt* (veterinarian) for each regiment.[36]

These figures, resulting from a regulation established on the economic balance and therefore entirely theoretical, obviously did not reflect reality; particularly in the regiments of cuirassiers and in the two new uhlan regiments, the differences in strength between the units remained relevant for a long time.

1799–1801

As discussed before, the Aulic War Council transferred some matters concerning the army to the *Hof-Militär Committee*, formed in 1791. This was initially chaired by Archduke Franz, later Emperor Franz II, and then by Friedrich Moritz Nostitz-Rieneck.[37] In November 1795 the Committee proposed a series of major modifications regarding the cavalry organisation, including an accurate examination of the actual force. The committee reformed the separation between German and Hungarian cavalry and called for the introduction of a German light cavalry, the *Leichte Dragoner* (light dragoons). Some malicious commenters attributed this reform as a way to dispose of a new light cavalry, due to fear of an anti-Habsburg rebellion in Hungary, which would have deprived the Austrian army of regular light horsemen. However this proposal remained on standby until 1796, when Nostitz-Rieneck became president of the Aulic War Council and this favoured the reform of the cavalry. The work begun with the aim of simplification, but the final result was barely simpler than the original. On 3 May 1798, through the Imperial *Rescript G. 3847*, the Aulic War Council issued the order for the new organisation of the cavalry. The new regulation was gradually introduced and become complete the next year. The most evident change concerned the light cavalry. *Dragoner* and *Chevauxlegers* became *Leichte Dragoner* for 15 regiments in total, each with six squadrons of three *Divisionen*. As already discussed, the old numerations changed, however the reform affected not only the number series but also the strength of the regiment. For instance, the Belgian-Walloon Chevauxlegers Regiment La Tour lost its 'Nr.31' for a new *Leichte Dragoner* 'Nr.11', and its fourth division was assigned to a newly raised regiment.

The reform dealt also with the regimental strength of other specialties. Cuirassier regiments continued to deploy 12 companies and six squadrons, but the number of rank and file diminished to 168 per squadron. The reserve

35 Meynert, *Geschichte des Kriegswesens und der Heeresverfassung in der Österreichischen Monarchie*, pp.51–52.

36 Wrede and Semek, *Geschichte der K. und K. Wehrmacht*, vol. II, part one, p.20.

37 Friedrich Moritz, *Graf* von Nostitz-Rieneck (1728–1796) was a member of an ancient noble family, and several of his brothers and uncles served the Austrian monarchs as diplomatic and military advisers. Following family tradition, he joined the military service in the 1740s. He was promoted to colonel in 1759, during the Seven Years' War. On 19 February 1766 he was promoted again, to general-major, and on 19 January 1771 to *Feldmarschall-Lieutnant*, effective on 25 February 1767. On 28 March 1785 he was promoted to *General der Cavallerie*, and on 15 May 1796 to *Feldmarschall*. He was captain of the Trabanten Lifeguard and Hofburg Watch, both honorary positions from April 1785 until May 1796. He was also appointed president of the Aulic Council, and held this position from May 1796 until his death later that year. He was also a Privy Councillor and an Imperial and Royal Chamberlain. In 1790 he received the Order of the Golden Fleece. His nephew, Johann Nepomuk von Nostitz-Rieneck, was a cavalry general officer in Habsburg service during the Napoleonic Wars.

Below: *Chevauxlegers* regiment Kaiser (Nr. 1). In 1792, there were seven dragoon regiments numbered 3, 7, 25, 26, 30, 31 and 32, the *Stabsdragoner* without number, and six *Chevauxlegers* regiments numbered as regiments 1, 6, 11, 16, 17 and 23. Dragoons and *Chevauxlegers* deployed six squadrons and three tactical *Divisionen*. (Authors' archive)

Above:: Dragoner Regiment Grossherzog von Toskana (Nr. 26), 1792, after the *Schema aller Uniformen der Kaiserl. Königl. Kriegsvölkern* (Authors' archive)

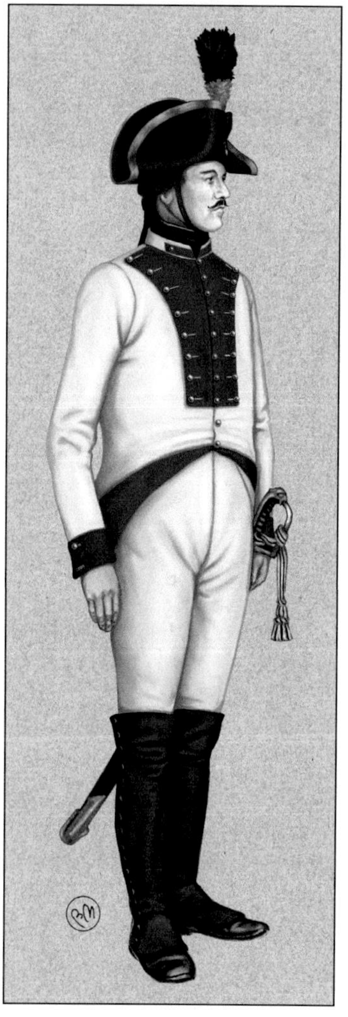

Fourier from the Cuirassieren Regiment Zeschwitz (Nr. 8), 1792–98. White coat with *dunkelgrün* facings; yellow metal buttons with yellow piped buttonholes on the lapels; black felt headdress with yellow edging lace; white breeches and black infantry gaiters. A dragoon *Fourier* wore a similar uniform except for the turn-down collar and the absence of the piping on the lapels. (Illustration by Bruno Mugnai)

squadron was established at 137 horsemen. The fighting strength of a cuirassier regiment totalled 1,145 horsemen, not including the *Regimentsstab*. The *Leichte Dragoner* had the same establishment, but each squadron numbered 203 rank and file, the same for the reserve squadron, for an overall strength of 1,421 horsemen without the *Regimentsstab*. Hussars and uhlans deployed eight squadrons each of 202 rank and file, like the reserve squadron, for 1,822 horsemen in all. The same squadron size was established for the *Jäger zu Pferd*, but with 10 squadrons and 2,224 men. The total balanced strength on paper was 63,485 horsemen, namely 13,965 cuirassiers, 21,585 light dragoons, 22,016 hussars, 3,680 uhlans, and 2,248 *Jäger zu Pferd*.[38]

Differences in arrangement continued to exist, especially for the newly raised regiments. While the first 10 hussar regiments consisted of four divisions, the Székler Husaren, now Grenz-Husaren Regiment Nr.11 had three, for 1,350 rank and file in all, and the Croatian-Slavonic hussars, now Grenz-Husaren Regiment Nr.12, deployed five divisions, for 2,246 rank and file.[39]

The *Regimentsstab* also retained some differences, like the light cavalry, which had a larger establishment, and with a third *Major* for the Croatian-Slavonic regiment.

According to the basic types of cavalry, the 1798 organisation established a balanced force of 13,956 heavy cavalry and 49,529 light cavalry. The shift in the direction of light cavalry now reached its peak after 1798. Light cavalry became three and a half times that of heavy cavalry. Despite the great expectations placed on the 1798 reform, this did not solve the problems of the cavalry in the field. The new numbering system contributed to simplify the matter, but tactical improvements were not implemented. Moreover, attempts to settle the aftermath of the war and to develop a better cavalry organisation produced ambiguous results. Though the German cavalry consisted of two branches, one heavy cavalry (cuirassiers) and one light cavalry (light dragoons), these latter did not live up to the Aulic War Council's hopes. After a brilliant beginning, the 1800s campaigns proved that this organisation was clearly unhealthy in terms of overall cavalry performance. Notwithstanding the French cavalry was still small in number and poorly equipped, the Imperial–Royal horsemen were unable to fight for decisive superiority on the battlefield. Neither in small war were they able to perform convincingly. The short-lived solution of the

38 Österreichisches Staatsarchiv – Kriegsarchiv, Vienna: Alte Feld Akten, *Stand- und Diensttabellen Karton Nr.3724*. January 1801.

39 Österreichisches Staatsarchiv – Kriegsarchiv, Vienna: Alte Feld Akten, *Stand- und Diensttabellen Karton Nr.3722*; January 1799.

Above: Husaren Regiment Erzherzog Leopold (Nr. 17), 1792. (Authors' archive)

Below: Before 1791, uhlan *Divisionen* were attached to each *Chevauxlegers* regiment; here is a uhlan from Regiment Kaiser. Note the customization of the uniform, which replicate the colours of the regiment but with Polish features. The horseman wears light cavalry boots and breeches with yellow braid piping. Note the early type of *Czapka-konfederatka* headdress, replaced after 1798 with the new model with a peak, and the saddle cover with rounded edges. (Authors' archive)

merger of dragoons and chevauxlegers is a clear indicator of the negative side of the reforms.

1802–1804

With the Treaty of Luneville, signed on 9 February 1801, Austrian holdings within the borders of the Holy Roman Empire were relinquished, and French control was extended to the left bank of the Rhine. Contested boundaries in Italy were set and Tuscany fell under French control. The outcome was another serious political failure for the Habsburgs, which followed an equally severe military defeat. After Luneville, however, it was obvious that the army would need at least a few years until another clash. This provided an opportunity to carry out the actions that were missed during 1798.

As a consequence the army underwent a new reorganisation, and the cavalry composition reduced from 42 to 35 regiments. This new organisation was officially introduced with the *Rescript* of 5 December 1801, and applied on 1 February 1802.[40] Now the Austrian cavalry deployed eight cuirassier regiments, six dragoon, six chevauxleger, 11 hussar and three uhlan regiments, plus the grenz-husaren regiment with six squadrons. Cuirassier regiments numbered 4, 5 and 11 were disbanded, Cuirassieren Nr.12 was converted to dragoons, the light dragoon regiments 2, 5, 6 and 9, the Jäger zu Pferd, were also disbanded, while Grenz-Husaren Regiment Nr.12 became the Palatinal-Husaren. All newly raised regiments had to deploy eight squadrons for four tactical *Divisionen*. The reform produced a new balanced strength – on paper – of 12,256 *Cuirassieren*, 9,192 *Dragoner*, 10,884 *Chevauxlegers*, 22,223 *Husaren*, 5,442 *Uhlanen*, for 59,997 horsemen in all. Actually, no regiment approached the prescribed number, as related in the musters registered at the opening of each year.

The regulation dealt also with the regiment organisation. Each division had now one *Ober-Feldscherer* and one *Feldscherer*. A new internal composition of the regiments was regulated by the aforementioned resolution of 5 December 1801. The regimental staff increased, with two *Fourieren*, and the medical service ranks were also reorganised. The former *Regiments-Arzt*(regiment physician) became a *Regiment Doctor*, the surgeon changed to *Ober-Chyrurgen* and one sub-chief surgeon was also added. Furthermore, in wartime one physician and one paramedic were assigned to each squadron and five *Proviantknechte* (food supply staff) were also added in each *Division*. The previous shortcomings of trained non-commissioned officers were rectified with 12 corporals and six vice-corporals, and the communication of orders by the introduction of a second trumpeter. To each squadron commander was assigned a *Fourierschütz* as ordnance lifeguard and servant, and to the other five officers a further five troopers were assigned in the same role. The peacetime strength now consisted of 144 mounted rank and file per squadron, and a further six dismounted *Supernumerari* troopers. In wartime, the reserve squadron would be formed including the dismounted

40 Text of the *Rescript* in Franz Dedekind, *Geschichte des k. k. Kaiser Franz Joseph I. Dragoner-Regimentes Nr.11, von seiner Errichtung, 20. Dezember 1688, bis 6. Mai 1879* (Vienna, published by the author, 1879), pp.317–318.

trooper joined in a single troop. The light cavalry deployed 156 rank and file per squadron with 24 dismounted troopers.

The strength of the regiment changed considerably. Cuirassier and dragoon regiments deployed a balanced force of 1,152 rank and file, and light cavalry 1,248. This reduction of strength occurred not only due to shortage of funds. Lack of troops was certainly caused by the downsizing of recruitment due to the loss of many territories. On 30 May 1801 the *Rescript* issued by the Aulic War Council ordered that all foreign volunteers enlisted in the future should be assigned to the Walloon regiments, but since this foreign quote did not satisfy the need for recruits, in 1802 another *Rescript* directed the surplus men to the former Walloon regiments with some hereditary land recruitment districts in support. As a result, the Latour Regiment was completed with recruits from Bohemia. Minor changes affected the *Regimentsstab*, which received an *Ober-Fourier* in wartime. In 1803 a *Regiments Adjutant* was also added to the *Regimentsstab*.[41]

The reform of 1802 fixed the *Regimentsstab* strength as follows:

Regimentsstab	*Cuirassieren and Dragoner*		*Chevauxlegers*		*Husaren*		*Uhlanen*	
	Nr.	horse	Nr.	horse	Nr.	horse	Nr.	horse
Oberst Inhaber	1	1	1	1	1	1	1	1
Regiments Commandant	1	1	1	1	1	1	1	1
Oberstlieutenant	1	1	1	1	1	1	1	1
Major	2	2	2	2	2	2	2	2
Kaplan	1	1	1	1	1	1	1	1
Regiments Auditor	1	1	1	1	1	1	1	1
Rechnungsführer	1	1	1	1	1	1	1	1
Regiments Adjutant	1	1	1	1	1	1	1	1
Regiments Feldarzt	1	1	1	1	1	1	1	1
Stabs Fourier	2	-	2	-	2	-	2	-
Stabstrompeter	1	1	1	1	1	1	1	1
Regt. Estandarte-Führer	4	4	4	4	4	4	4	4
Oberschmied	1	-	1	-	1	-	1	-
Ober Sattler	-	-	2	-	2	-	2	-
Schneider	-	-	-	-	2	-	-	-
Profoss	1	1	1	1	1	1	1	1
Fourierschütz	4	-	4	-	4	-	4	-
Privatdiener	5	-	5	-	5	-	5	-
TOTAL	28	16	30	16	32	16	30	16

41 Dedekind, *Geschichte des k. k. Kaiser Franz Joseph I*, pp.317–318.

Schwadronstab and division organisation was also modified:

Squadronsstab	*Cuirassieren*		*Dragoner*		*Chevauxlegers*		*Husaren and Uhlanen*	
	Nr.	horse	Nr.	horse	Nr.	horse	Nr.	horse
Ersten Rittmeister	1	1	1	1	1	1	1	1
Zweiten Rittmeister	1	1	1	1	1	1	1	1
Oberlieutenants	2	2	2	2	2	2	2	2
Unterlieutenants	2	2	2	2	2	2	2	2
Wachtmeister	2	2	2	2	2	2	2	2
Fourier	1	-	1	-	1	-	1	-
Ober Feldscherer	1	-	1	-	1	-	1	-
Feldscherer	1	-	1	-	1	-	1	-
Trompeter	2	2	2	2	2	2	2	2
Schmied	1	-	1	-	1	-	1	-
Sattler	1	-	1	-	1	-	1	-
Corporale	12	12	12	12	12	12	12	12
Vice-Corporale	6	6	6	6	6	6	6	6
Fourierschütz	1	-	1	-	1	-	1	-
Gemeinen	144	144	144	144	156	156	156	156
Supernumerari	6	-	6	-	30	-	30	-
Privatdiener	5	-	5	-	5	-	5	-
TOTAL	188	172	188	172	223	184	223	184

On paper, cuirassier and dragoon regiment strength was now 1,504 men with 1,376 horses for eight squadrons. Light cavalry regiments deployed 1,816 men with 1,488 horses in eight squadrons.[42]

Differences continued for the Székler Grenz-Husaren Regiment Nr.11, which also received its own number: in addition to the 27-man *Regimentsstab*, the squadrons deployed 158 rank and file; the regiment still consisted of six squadrons in three divisions, for a total number of 975 men and 933 horses.

Though the decrease of the overall strength had been significant, the reforms of 1801–1802 defined the organisation of cavalry until 1848. Subsequent experience has shown that this system was well balanced, affordable and sufficiently flexible. Although the strength of the regiments did not remain unchanged, the *Regimentsstab* structure and the internal organisation remained permanent. The required number of officers and NCOs in the regiment and squadron staff was still too large, but in reality

42 Österreichisches Staatsarchiv – Kriegsarchiv, Vienna: Alte Feld Akten, *Stand- und Diensttabellen Karton Nr.1351*, 1805–13-68.

the actual regimental strength, averaging 50–60 percent, solved this problem, and the regiments shrank to manageable size.[43]

The reform established new quarters and the cavalry regiments burdened the Habsburg domains as follows:

	Cuirassieren	*Dragoner*	*Chevauxlegers*	*Husaren*	*Uhlanen*	TOTAL
Lower Austria	2	1	2			5 regiments
Upper Austria	1	1				2 regiments
Bohemia	3	2	2			7 regiments
Moravia	2	2	2			6 regiments
Hungary and Transylvania				12		12 regiments
Galicia					3	3 regiments
TOTAL	8	6	6	12	3	

Compared to the previous establishment, there was an increase in the number of heavy cavalry and a decrease in the number of light cavalry, which was the main consequence of the disbanding of the light dragoons and the re-establishment of six dragoon regiments. The previous decade-long trend of light cavalry gaining ground had now been reversed. The experience of war showed that the excessive reduction of heavy troopers had a negative effect on the cavalry's performance on campaign, and it proved necessary to increase the proportion of heavy cavalry. It was an important decision that was not achieved by increasing cuirassier numbers. It proved to be decisive for the senior commanders that the dragoons could be used to support the army as reserve cavalry like the cuirassiers. Moreover, dragoons could play this role not only in the field, but could act as 'universal' cavalry able to perform several duties on campaign.

1805

Further reforms dealing with the cavalry were successively introduced by General Carl Mack von Leiberich, taking effect from April 1805. The major changes concerned the squadron strength. All regiments always fielded eight squadrons, but each with 131 rank and file in the cuirassier and dragoon regiments, and 151 in the light cavalry. These measures tried to remedy the serious shortage of troopers that affected many regiments. However, the reform proceeded slowly, forcing the regiments to delay the introduction of the new organisation, and this caused a chaotic situation, in which several regiments marched for the 1805 campaign with even fewer than 100 troopers

43 Österreichisches Staatsarchiv – Kriegsarchiv, Vienna: Alte Feld Akten, *Stand- und Diensttabellen Karton Nr.3727*, January 1805. In terms of available strength, the number of able-bodied personnel was 52 percent, and 73 percent including those unable to serve.

per squadron.[44] This contributed not a little to the defeats suffered in the year.

The *Provision* issued on 18 August 1805 imposed also a wide reduction of regimental transport in the army, cavalry included. Each cavalry regiment of eight squadrons received an established number of *Führwesenmit Geschirr* (wagons with harnesses) and draft animals as follows:[45]

1 four-horse *Deckelwagen* (wagon with cover)
4 four-horse *Leiterwagen* (open wagon)
1 two-horse wagon for the *Feldschmiede* (field smith)
1 two-horse wagon for the *Regimentsstab* (*Stabswagen*)

1806–1809

After the failures of the Third Coalition War, the dissolution of the field army was ordered on 2 January 1806, and the troops returned to quarters at the peacetime strength, but the field force of cuirassier and dragoon squadrons had greatly decreased. Meanwhile, the disbanding of reserve squadrons was ordered and their rank and file were used to replenish the regiments. As the peace was signed and the weakness of the state treasury did not allow the regiments to be replenished, the Military Committee, now transferred to Prague, worked for a new reform. The plan proposed by General Grünne for the organisation of the cavalry was approved on 25 February 1806 and issued to the regiments on 30 April. The tactical battle order of cuirassiers and dragoons formed by four divisions was abolished, and the second *Major Division* was to be disbanded in order to complete the other three *Divisionen* from it. New numbers were also established for the squadrons. The strength for the cuirassier and dragoon regiments decreased to 112 mounted troopers, and six dismounted *Supernumerari*. The light cavalry retained the four divisions establishment but with 128 mounted troopers, plus six dismounted *Supernumerari* for each squadron. These latter could act as a cadre for a reserve squadron of 60 men in the cuirassiers and dragoons, and 90 in the light cavalry.

The only exception was again the Székler Husaren Regiment Nr.11, which still consisted of three *Divisionen* with six squadrons. Based on the new regulations, the required number of ranks in the squadron was as follows:[46]

44 Rothenberg, *Napoleon's Great Adversary*, p.112.

45 *Provision für die k.k. Kavallerie* (Vienna, 1805).

46 Österreichisches Staatsarchiv – Kriegsarchiv, Vienna: *Personalunterlagen, Musterlisten und Standestabellen der k. k. Armee*; Karton Nr.6442, Kürassier Regiment Nr.1 Standestabelle 1806; Karton Nr.6897, Dragoner Regiment Nr.1, Standestabelle 1806; Karton Nr.7049, Chevauxlegers Regiment Nr.1, Standestabelle 1806; Karton Nr.7317, Husaren Regiment Nr.1, Standestabelle 1806; Karton Nr.7845,Uhlanen Regiment Nr.1, Standestabelle 1806.

Regimentsstab	*Cuirassieren and Dragoner*		*Chevauxlegers*		*Husaren*		*Uhlanen*	
	Nr.	horse	Nr.	horse	Nr.	horse	Nr.	horse
Oberst Inhaber	1	1	1	1	1	1	1	1
Regiments Commandant	1	1	1	1	1	1	1	1
Oberstlieutenant	1	1	1	1	1	1	1	1
Major	1	1	2	2	2	2	2	2
Kaplan	1	1	1	1	1	1	1	1
Regiments Auditor	1	1	1	1	1	1	1	1
Rechnungsführer	1	1	1	1	1	1	1	1
Regiments Adjutant	1	1	1	1	1	1	1	1
Regiments Feldarzt	1	1	1	1	1	1	1	1
Ober-Chyrurgen	3		4		4		4	
Unter-Chyrurgen	3		4		4		4	
Stabs Fourieren	2		2		2		2	
Stabstrompeter	1	1	1	1	1	1	1	1
Trompeter	3	3	4	4	4	4	4	4
Regt. Estandarte-Führer	3	3	4	4	4	4	4	4
Ober Schmied	1		1		1		1	
Ober Sattler			2		2			
Schneider					2		2	
Profoss	1	1	1	1	1	1	1	1
Fourierschützen	3		4		4		4	
Privatdiener	5		5		5		5	
TOTAL	34	17	42	20	44	20	42	20

As for the squadrons and divisions, the new strength was established as follows:

Schwadronsstab	*Cuirassieren*		*Dragoner*		*Chevauxlegers*		*Husaren and Uhlanen*	
	Nr.	horse	Nr	horse	Nr	horse	Nr	horse
Ersten Rittmeister	1	1	1	1	1	1	1	1
Zweiten Rittmeister	1	1	1	1	1	1	1	1
Oberlieutenants	2	2	2	2	2	2	2	2
Unterlieutenants	2	2	2	2	2	2	2	2
Wachtmeister	2	2	2	2	2	2	2	2
Fourier	1	-	1	-	1	-	1	-
Trompeter	1	1	1	1	1	1	1	1

Schmied	1	-	1	-	1	-	1	-
Sattler	1	-	1	-	1	-	1	-
Corporale	12	12	12	12	12	12	12	12
Fourierschützen	1	-	1	-	1	-	1	-
Gemeinen	112	112	112	112	128	128	128	128
Supernumerari	6	-	6	-	8	-	8	-
Privatdiener	5	-	5	-	5	-	5	-
TOTAL	148	133	148	133	165	149	165	149

Cuirassiers and dragoons now deployed a field force of 922 men with 855 horses; the light cavalry had 1,320 men with 1,212 horses. The reduction of strength resulted in a balanced strength of 41,168 cavalrymen, with 7,376 cuirassiers, 5,532 dragoons, 8,172 chevauxlegers, 15,996 hussars, 4,092 uhlans. However, in 1807 the actual available force was barely 65 percent in the 'German' cavalry, and 70 percent in the hussar and uhlan regiments.

The regulation retained the tactical repartition as in 1771, but now with a small strength. Therefore, each squadron was divided into two *Flügels* or half-squadrons, and each *Flügel* into four *Züge*. The divisions were numbered 1 to 4 consecutively and the squadrons 1 to 8 consecutively, with each *Flügel* numbered 1 and 2 within its squadron. The *Züge* were instead numbered by their rank in the tactical deployment, therefore the 1st Squadron included *Züge* 1, 3, 5 and 7, the 2nd Squadron comprised *Züge* 2, 4, 6, and 8, and so on. As for the infantry, the regiments were still identified in the order of battle after their *Inhaber*, and each division and squadron carried their commanding officer's rank. On the field, each division formed an ensign escort formed by 24 men in the cuirassiers and hussars, and 18 men in the other branches.

Each squadron of cuirassiers and uhlans had eight men armed with rifles and eight with carbines. Each squadron of dragoons, hussars and chevauxlegers had 16 men armed with carbines.

The defeat suffered in 1805 brought with it a significant drop in the number of cavalry to the level of the first half of the 1780s. However, while the strength of light and heavy cavalry was roughly the same, after 1802 the number of light cavalry shifted from the peak of the strong increase of 1798, now the one-third and two-thirds ratio became fixed as the 1806 organisation became permanent.

However, the organisation of 1806 changed once before the war of 1809. On 1 March 1807 the *Fourieren* in the squadron were transferred to the *Regimentsstab*, but the *Stabs Fourieren* decreased to one only, and this meant a decrease of three for heavy cavalry and four for light cavalry. In 1808, the *Rechnungsführer* was raised to the rank of *Rittmeister*. From the same years, each hussar regiment had to increase its horse's strength with a further 24 *Fuhrpferde* (pack horses) and nine servants, in addition to the usual establishment for the cavalry.

After a period of barely three years of peace, on 1 March 1809 mobilisation was finally ordered in preparation for the Fifth Coalition War. The squadrons mobilised their horseless troopers to provide the frame for the permanent reserve squadron to be set up. The strength of the regiments and squadrons changed again:[47]

Regimentsstab	*Cuirassieren and Dragoner*		*Chevauxlegers*		*Husaren*		*Uhlanen*	
	Nr.	horse	Nr.	horse	Nr.	horse	Nr.	horse
Oberst Inhaber	1	1	1	1	1	1	1	1
Regiments Commandant	1	1	1	1	1	1	1	1
Oberstlieutenant	1	1	1	1	1	1	1	1
Major	1	1	2	2	2	2	2	2
Kaplan	1	1	1	1	1	1	1	1
Regiments Auditor	1	1	1	1	1	1	1	1
Rechnungsführer	1	1	1	1	1	1	1	1
Regiments Adjutant	1	1	1	1	1	1	1	1
Regiments Feldarzt	1	1	1	1	1	1	1	1
Ober-Chyrurgen	3		4		4		4	
Unter-Chyrurgen	3		4		4		4	
Fourier	9	7	10	9	10	9	10	9
Stabstrompeter	1	1	1	1	1	1	1	1
Trompeter	3	3	4	4	4	4	4	4
Regt. Estandarte-Führer	3	3	4	4	4	4	4	4
Ober Schmied	1	1	1	1	1	1	1	1
Schmied	1	1	1	1	1	1	1	1
Ober Sattler			1	1	1	1	1	1
Sattler			1	1	1	1	1	1
Schneider					2	2	2	2
Profoss	1	1	1	1	1	1	1	1
Fourierschützen	3		4		4		4	
Privatdiener	5		5		5		5	
TOTAL	42	32	51	41	53	43	53	43

47 Österreichisches Staatsarchiv – Kriegsarchiv, Vienna: *Personalunterlagen, Musterlisten und Standestabellen der k. k. Armee*, Karton Nr.1470. 1809–13-89c, 89d, 89e; Karton Nr.6444. Kürassier Regiment Nr.1, Standestabelle 1809; MLST Karton Nr.6898, Dragoner Regiment Nr.1, Standestabelle 1809; MLST Karton Nr.7051, Chevauxlegers Regiment Nr.1, Standestabelle 1809; MLST Karton Nr.7320, Husaren Regiment Nr.1, Standestabelle 1809; MLST Karton Nr.7848, Uhlanen Regiment Nr.1, Standestabelle 1809.

Schwadronsstab	*Cuirassieren*		*Dragoner*		*Chevauxlegers*		*Husaren and Uhlanen*	
	Nr.	horse	Nr.	horse	Nr.	horse	Nr.	horse
Ersten Rittmeister	1	1	1	1	1	1	1	1
Zweiten Rittmeister	1	1	1	1	1	1	1	1
Oberlieutenants	2	2	2	2	2	2	2	2
Unterlieutenants	2	2	2	2	2	2	2	2
Wachtmeister	2	2	2	2	2	2	2	2
Trompeter	1	1	1	1	1	1	1	1
Schmied	1	1	1	1	-	-	-	-
Sattler	1	1	1	1	-	-	-	-
Corporale	12	12	12	12	12	12	12	12
Fourierschützen	1	-	1	-	1	-	1	-
Gemeinen	112	112	112	122	128	128	128	128
Privatdiener	5	-	5	-	5	-	5	-
TOTAL	141	135	141	135	156	151	156	151

A different strength resulted in the reserve squadrons:

Reserve *Schwadronsstab*	*Cuirassieren*		*Dragoner*		*Chevauxlegers*		*Husaren and Uhlanen*	
	Nr.	horse	Nr.	horse	Nr.	horse	Nr.	horse
Ersten Rittmeister	1	1	1	1	1	1	1	1
Zweiten Rittmeister	1	1	1	1	1	1	1	1
Oberlieutenants	2	2	2	2	2	2	2	2
Unterlieutenants	2	2	2	2	2	2	2	2
Wachtmeister	2	2	2	2	2	2	2	2
Praktikant Feldscherer	1	-	1	-	1	-	1	-
Fourier	1	-	1	-	1	-	1	-
Trompeter	1	1	1	1	1	1	1	1
Schmied	1	1	1	1	-	-	-	-
Sattler	1	1	1	1	-	-	-	-
Corporale	12	12	12	12	12	12	12	12
Fourierschützen	1	-	1	-	1	-	1	-
Gemeinen	112	112	112	112	150	150	150	150
Privatdiener	5	-	5	-	5	-	5	-
TOTAL	143	133	143	133	180	171	180	171

Prince Johann Josef I of Liechtenstein, here portrayed by Johann Baptist Lampi, was a cavalry leader highly esteemed by Archduke Carl. In 1796 he decided the battle of Würzburg with a well planned cavalry charge. In 1809 Liechtenstein was the commander of the Reserve Corps of the Archduke Carl, but after the campaign he retired. He would have been the right man for the implementation of the cavalry corps. (Princely Collection, Liechtenstein)

Cuirassier and dragoon regiments deployed six field squadrons and one reserve squadron for 999 men and 943 horses in all. Light cavalry regiments deployed eight field squadrons and one reserve squadron for 1,371 men and 1,428 horses.

The mobilisation in 1809 was not of a purely technical nature. Though squadrons and regiments filled their ranks, and most of them received the required horses, the resulting strength of the regiments was smaller than before. However, this was a tactical advantage as the smaller *Divisionen* took advantage of improved flexibility. Perhaps it is not a mere coincidence that the Austrian cavalry performed well during the war of 1809. Apparently even the fact that Archduke Carl could apply the new principles of military organisation, developed in previous years, played a decisive role, and the revised organisation favoured the cavalry's performance on campaign. The light cavalry performed well in reconnaissance and in small war action, as well as in forming an effective screen for covering the marching infantry. Also cuirassiers and dragoons, concentrated in strong reserve corps, behaved positively showing a skill that astonished the French commanders. Archduke Carl, who had already used the heavy cavalry as a decisive factor at Würzburg as early as 1796, planned a similar tactic in 1809. The situation changed to the extent that Napoleon also recognised the role of heavy cavalry and strengthened his cuirassier and dragoon regiments. Therefore in 1809 the French took the initiative, but the Austrian heavy cavalry proved to be an equal opponent. Neither at Aspern–Essling nor at Wagram could the French cavalry defeat the Austrian cuirassiers and dragoons, notwithstanding the unfavourable beginning of 21 May.[48] The heavy cavalry performed successfully during the campaign, and the fact that at Wagram the army was able to maintain its unity may be attributed to the action of the reserve cavalry. Unfortunately the problem for the Austrian heavy cavalry was the lack of skilled commanders. In fact, the Archduke did not dispose of a division commander like Nansouty, d'Hautpoul, or d'Espagne, as well as a cavalry corps commander like Murat or Bessieres, and the only above-average cavalry commander was the Prince of Liechtenstein.[49]

48 On the first day of the battle of Aspern–Essling the Austrian heavy cavalry under Liechtenstein got into trouble when it advanced in two lines and received cannon fire from the French artillery. Meanwhile, Liechtenstein received the news that enemy cavalry were sighted not far away, and ordered the charge, but the heavy cavalry proved to be ill-trained for action in large formations. The second line crashed into the first and the action failed. See also Rothenberg, *Napoleon's Great Adversary*, p.192.

49 Johann I Joseph (Johann Baptist Josef Adam Johann NepomukAloys Franz de Paula; 1760–1836) was Prince of Liechtenstein between 1805 and 1806 and again from 1814 until 1836. Liechtenstein chose a military career at age 22 and entered the army as a lieutenant in a cuirassier regiment.

Moreover, in 1809 the cavalry encountered fewer problems with supply and replenishment, because the military supply system worked well. The hussar regiments were able to set up two or three new squadrons above the required number of personnel,[50] and by the end of the war just a few regiments had fallen sharply.

1810–1812

In the months following the Peace of Pressburg the army returned to the organisation and force established at the beginning of 1809, with the limitation of 150,000 men in total imposed by Napoleon. With regard to the cavalry, in the summer of 1810 a reduction of ranks in the squadron staff was ordered. The most important decision was the abolition of the rank of *Zweiten-Hauptmann*, which entailed a one-man reduction in the number of officers serving in the squadron. The number of troopers per squadron was established at 100 for heavy cavalry and 110 for light cavalry. Overall, about 20 places remained unmanned in the squadron. The reserve squadron was also dismounted, and only the regimental staff remained unchanged.

The Székler Husaren Regiment Nr.11 also carried out the abolition of second captains and the reduction of rank, while each squadron reduced its strength to 130 horsemen and eight dismounted *Supernumerari*, and then the regiment numbered on paper 1,433 men with 1,203 horses.

The cavalry retained the same regiments as in 1809, consisting of eight *Cuirassieren*, six *Dragoner*, six *Chevauxlegers*, 12 *Husaren* and three *Uhlanen* regiments.

During the Austro-Ottoman War of 1788–1791 he earned, in rapid succession, promotion to *Major*, *Oberstlieutenant*, and *Oberst* (colonel). He acquired great renown as a good cavalry commander and was honoured with the Knight's Cross of the Military Order of Maria Theresa in 1790. During the French Revolutionary Wars he participated in an 'outstandingly effective cavalry action' at Avesnes-le-Sec on 12 September 1793, where 4,663 French troops suffered losses of 2,000 killed and wounded with the allies losing only 69 men. In addition, 2,000 soldiers and 20 artillery pieces were captured. Soon after being promoted to *General Wachtmeister* in June 1794, he fought at the battle of Fleurus. On 3 September 1796 Liechtenstein commanded a mixed cavalry–infantry brigade in Anton Sztaray's division at the Battle of Würzburg. After this action, achieved principally thanks to the cavalry charge directed by him, he was awarded the Commander's Cross of the Order of Maria Theresa.In the War of the Second Coalition Liechtenstein commanded the Austrian reserve at the battle of Trebbia. In August 1799 he received promotion to *Feldmarschall-Lieutenant*. He commanded the Austrian corps in the successful siege of Cuneo. On 3 December 1800 he led the Austrian cavalry in the Battle of Hohenlinden. At the Battle of Austerlitz he led the 4,600 cavalry of the 5th Column of the allied army. His troops fought well but he was unable to save the Austrian–Russian army from a disastrous defeat. Afterwards, he carried on the negotiations with Napoleon which concluded with the Peace of Pressburg. He earned the rank of *General der Cavallerie* in 1808. He led his cavalry and grenadiers at the battle of Eckmühl on 22 April 1809, the Battle of Aspern–Essling on 21–22 May, and the battle of Wagram on 5–6 July. He took command of the main army after Archduke Carl resigned and held this responsibility until the end of the year. Emperor Franz I promoted him *Feldmarschall* in September. He negotiated and signed the Peace of Schönbrunn. Afterwards, Liechtenstein was accused of having little diplomatic skill, and to escape criticism he resigned from the military service in 1810.

50 Gustav Amon von Treuenfest, *Geschichte des k. und k. Husaren-Regimentes Kaiser Nr.1* (Vienna: Verlag des Regimentes, 1898), pp.248–249.

Before of the end of 1810 some adjustments modified again the regiment's strength. The Aulic War Council presented the plan to the Emperor, who approved it on 2 January 1811, and definitively introduced it on 10 August 1811. Each cuirassier and dragoon regiment deployed 147 rank and file per squadron, plus 37 men in the *Regimentsstab*; a further 120 dismounted troopers brought the total to 919 in all. The chevauxlegers deployed respectively 156, 46 and 160 for 1,296 men; the hussars like the chevauxlegers, but with a *Regimentsstab* of 48 men for 1,296 men in all. The uhlans also as per the chevauxlegers.[51] In 1811, 18 troopers were officially diminished in each squadron of uhlans, bringing the regiment's strength to 1,280 men in all.

The roles of service personnel such as the *Privatdiener* were filled with aged soldiers classified in two classes, depending on their health and physical integrity, as *Halb-invaliden Privatdiener* and *Ganz-invaliden Privatdiener*.

This organisation lasted until the beginning of 1812, when Napoleon demanded Austria prepare her own contingent for the war against Russia. Two dragoon, two chevauxlegers and five hussar regiments were mobilised for the campaign in Russia. Of which, one *Division* of each regiment (the *Oberst-Lieutenant Division* for the dragoons, the *Zweiten Major* for the chevauxlegers and hussars) remained in the country as depot. The rank of second captain and other ranks were also restored. The number of troopers of the mobilised regiments was established to 150 per squadron.

1813–1815

Napoleon's defeat in Russia and the campaign in Poland and Germany in the spring of 1813 brought to Austria the role of political mediation. However, under the guise of armed neutrality the strong reinforcement of the army began as early as 1813. In the cavalry, the rank of *Zweiten Hauptmann* was restored in all the regiments, while a new recruitment campaign began. The mobilisation was decided in June 1813, in order to deploy 140 troopers in the cuirassiers and dragoons and 150 for light cavalry.

The results of the new organisation were as follows:

Regimentsstab	*Cuirassieren and Dragoner*		*Chevauxlegers*		*Husaren*		*Uhlanen*	
	Nr.	horse	Nr.	horse	Nr.	horse	Nr.	horse
Oberst Inhaber	1	1	1	1	1	1	1	1
Regiments Commandant	1	1	1	1	1	1	1	1
Oberstlieutenant	1	1	1	1	1	1	1	1
Major	1	1	2	2	2	2	2	2
Kaplan	1	1	1	1	1	1	1	1
Regiments Auditor	1	1	1	1	1	1	1	1

51 Österreichisches Staatsarchiv – Kriegsarchiv, Vienna: Alte Feld Akten: *Stand-und Diensttabellen Karton Nr.3730*, January 1811.

Rechnungsführer	1	1	1	1	1	1	1	1
Regiments Adjutant	1	1	1	1	1	1	1	1
Regiments Feldarzt	1	1	1	1	1	1	1	1
Ober-Chyrurgen	3	3	4	-	4	4	4	4
Unter-Chyrurgen	3	3	4	-	4	4	4	4
Fourier	9	3	10	4	10	4	10	4
Regt. Estandarte-Führer	3	3	4	4	4	4	4	4
Stabstrompeter	1	1	1	1	1	1	1	1
Trompeter	3	3	4	4	4	4	4	4
Ober Schmied	1	1	1	1	1	1	1	1
Schmied	1	1	1	1	1	1	1	1
Ober Sattler	-	-	1	1	1	1	1	1
Sattler	-	-	1	1	1	1	1	1
Schneider	-	-	-	-	2	2	2	2
Profoss	1	1	1	1	1	1	1	1
Fourierschützen	3	-	4	-	4	-	4	-
Privatdiener	5	-	5	-	5	-	5	-
TOTAL	42	28	51	36	53	38	53	38

Schwadronsstab	*Cuirassieren*		*Dragoner*		*Chevauxlegers*		*Husaren and Uhlanen*	
	Nr.	horse	Nr.	horse	Nr.	horse	Nr.	horse
Ersten Rittmeister	1	1	1	1	1	1	1	1
Zweiten Rittmeister	1	1	1	1	1	1	1	1
Oberlieutenants	2	2	2	2	2	2	2	2
Unterlieutenants	2	2	2	2	2	2	2	2
Wachtmeister	2	2	2	2	2	2	2	2
Trompeter	1	1	1	1	1	1	1	1
Schmied	1	1	1	1	-	-	-	-
Sattler	1	1	1	1	-	-	-	-
Corporalen	12	12	12	12	12	12	12	12
Fourierschützen	1	-	1	-	1	-	1	-
Gemeinen	140	140	140	140	150	150	150	150
Privatdiener	5	-	5	-	5	-	5	-
TOTAL	169	163	169	163	178	172	178	172

Reserve *Schwadronsstab*	*Cuirassieren*		*Dragoner*		*Chevauxlegers*		*Husaren and Uhlanen*	
	Nr.	horse	Nr.	horse	Nr.	horse	Nr.	horse
Ersten Rittmeister	1	1	1	1	1	1	1	1

Zweiten Rittmeister	1	1	1	1	1	1	1	1
Oberlieutenants	2	2	2	2	2	2	2	2
Unterlieutenants	2	2	2	2	2	2	2	2
Wachtmeister	2	2	2	2	2	2	2	2
Praktikant Feldscherer	1	-	1	-	1	-	1	-
Fourier	1	-	1	-	1	-	1	-
Trompeter	1	1	1	1	1	1	1	1
Schmied	1	-	1	1	-	-	-	-
Sattler	1	-	1	1	-	-	-	-
Corporale	12	12	12	12	12	12	12	12
Fourierschützen	1		1		1		1	
Gemeinen	180	180	180	180	240	240	240	240
Privatdiener	5		5		5		5	

Cuirassier and dragoon regiments deployed six squadrons for 1,014 rank and file and 978 horses; light cavalry regiments retained eight squadrons for 1,423 rank and file with 1,376 horses on paper.

The resulting balanced force totalled 54,145 men; in detail 10,136 cuirassiers, 7,602 dragoons, 10,470 chevauxlegers, 20,696 hussars and 5,241 uhlans.[52]

The proportions did not change despite the significant increase in the number of men, the constant two thirds–one third remained, with the light cavalry being the larger proportion.

The mobilisation against Napoleon in 1813 modified the distribution of the cavalry regiments in the domains:

	Cuirassieren	*Dragoner*	*Chevauxlegers*	*Husaren*	*Uhlanen*	TOTAL
Lower Austria	2	2	1			5 regiments
Upper Austria	1	1				2 regiments
Bohemia	2	1	3			6 regiments
Moravia	3	2	1			6 regiments
Hungary and Transylvania				12		12 regiments
Galicia			1		4	5 regiments
TOTAL	8	6	6	12	4	

The earlier trend was not broken by the 1813 mobilisation either. The only perceptible change was the relocation of the *Chevauxlegers Regiment Nr.3* to Galicia, and the formation of a fourth uhlan regiment composed of volunteers

52 Österreichisches Staatsarchiv – Kriegsarchiv, Vienna: Alte Feld Akten: *Stand- und Diensttabellen Karton Nr.3731*; 1813. August and *Stand- und Diensttabellen Karton Nr.3732*, January 1814.

and conscripts from Galicia, a province that sustained the expenses for its formation.

Another novelty concerning the cavalry strength occurred in the autumn of 1813, when a completely new type of unit was formed within the hussar regiments, the so-called *velita*, associated with the reserve squadrons. These troopers were raised from the Hungarian aristocracy on a voluntary basis. Each county and city offered a fully equipped and uniformed horsemen for the hussar regiments in order to raise a 'legion' from which eventually to appoint NCOs and junior officers for the light cavalry. Each regiment of hussars increased with two *velita* squadrons, except *Husaren Nr.1* which had three squadrons. The organisation of these squadrons was exactly the same as for the regular hussars. The *Regimentsstab* was expanded by one field officer, one chief and one paramedic, one fourier, one trumpeter, one standard bearer, and one *Fourierschütz* for each *velita* squadron.[53] These troops joined the regiments in the last months of 1813. They did not take part in any major battle, but the *velita* performed successfully in small war operations. These volunteers significantly increased the strength of the Austrian light cavalry, since the hussar regiments' strength was raised in some cases 30 or 40 percent. However, this was only a temporary benefit, because the service lasted for the duration of the war, and brought some consequences for the organisation of the cavalry.

Despite the limitation of the Peace of Pressburg in 1809, the Austrian army sought to maintain the cavalry in a good state, and this can be clearly observed in the achievements scored in 1813–14. When Austria joined the allies in the *Befreiungskrieg*, the cavalry was able to face the French army with a significant and well-trained force. Though the Austrian cavalry as well as the whole army suffered for the shortage of supplies and resources, the balance closed favourably. After the poor performance at Dresden,[54] in subsequent encounters the Austrian horsemen took the field effectively. These results may be attributed entirely to the reforms introduced after 1805 by Archduke Carl, deviating from it only minimally in the following years, and maintaining the objective of creating a more flexible structure suitable for any tactical situation. In this regard, after 1809 the organisation of cavalry regiments remained uniform, with the only significant exception of the former Székler border hussar regiment.

The number of cavalry regiments increased during 1814, as the *Chevauxlegers Regiment Nr.7* was raised from the disbanded cavalry of the Kingdom of Italy. At the beginning of the war against France, the Austrian army deployed fewer but better-organised units, which proved to be an entirely good decision. The replenishment of the reserve squadrons in the depots could therefore take place in favourable conditions, and their arrival in the war theatre filled the

53 Österreichisches Staatsarchiv – Kriegsarchiv, Vienna: Alte Feld Akten, *Karton Nr.7324. Husaren Regiment Nr.1. Standestabelle 1813*, and *Karton Nr.3732*, January 1814.

54 At Dresden, the poorly coordinated Austrian and allied assaults were easily beaten off by Saint-Cyr, and late that day Napoleon arrived with the Guard and Mortier's corps. The following morning two additional French corps arrived. Rain and lack of provisions had lowered Austrian morale and on the second day the left wing facing Murat's corps retreated and dispersed in a few hours. The casualties reveal the dimensions of the defeat. With only 32 officers and 1,132 men killed, and 142 and 5,236 wounded, 74 officers and 3,705 men were taken prisoners, while four officers and no less than 5,938 men were reported missing. Overall, the Austrians lost at Dresden 16,263 men.

void and further strengthened the cavalry.[55] In the final campaign against France, the Austrian cavalry prevailed with some regularity over their French counterparts. In contrast to the situation before 1805, this time they were able to take advantage of the numerical weakness of the French cavalry, both in small war operations as well as open field engagements, and successfully taking up the fight against the enemy, which was previously considered a formidable and skilled component of the French army, especially the heavy horsemen.

Freikorps and Foreign Units

A well-established feature of the army of the House of Austria in the eighteenth century was the creation of ad hoc units to remedy the chronic shortage of strength of the regular regiments on campaign. Entrusted to their recruiting commanders and organisers, these units were often formed of mixed cavalry and infantry specialties, and known as *Freikorps*. After 1789 this characteristic came back into use during the First and Second Coalition Wars. In most cases, these irregular formations were short-lived, however they served to form new units, as discussed for the uhlan regiments.

The first unit including cavalry was the Freikorps Carneville, raised in the Austrian Low Countries in March 1793 by the French *émigré* colonel Georges Simon de Carneville, who personally paid his soldiers, with a strength of two companies of infantry, two companies of *Jäger* and one *Division* of light cavalry. The unit fought against the Belgian insurgents until the end of 1794, and the year after was transferred to the Rhine army. The corps was finally disbanded in 1798 and merged into the Jäger zu Pferde Regiment.

Among the units comprised completely of cavalry, the most relevant was the hussar corps originally recruited between 1794 and 1795 by Prince Louis de Rohan-Montbazon. With his ambitious plan, the French noble intended to form a personal army, attracting French loyalist horsemen to join the Rohan-Étrangères infantry regiment, and to form the Legion du Prince de Rohan in British service. In the spring of 1795 the cavalry was increased by the Chasseur de Rohan-Brunswick, raised by the Duke of Brunswick as a Reichs-Kontingent.[56] However, at the end of 1796 the legion was disbanded and the cavalry entered the service of Austria on 1 May 1797 under the name Freikorps Rohan and then Rohan Husaren Regiment. The unit's strength remained considerable, deploying six and a half squadrons in January 1798.[57] Exactly one year later, the rank and file passed to the newly raised regiment of *Jäger zu Pferde*.

55 Treuenfest reports excellent data on the recruitment after 1813; see *Geschichte des k. und k. Bukowina'schen Dragoner-Regimentes General der Cavallerie Freiherr Piret de Bihain Nr.9 von seiner Errichtung 1682 bis 1892* (Vienna, Verlag des Regimentes, 1892), pp.253–254; and Treuenfest, *Geschichte des kaiserl. und königl. Husaren-Regimentes Nr.10 Friedrich Wilhelm III., König von Preussen* (Vienna, 1892), p.274.

56 Wrede and Semek, *Geschichte der K. und K. Wehrmacht*, vol. III, part two, p.924.

57 Österreichisches Staatsarchiv – Kriegsarchiv, Vienna: Alte Feld Akten: *Stand- und Diensttabellen Karton Nr. 2956*; January 1798.

Right: Illustration from Richard Knötel's *Grosse Uniformenkunde*, depicting a hussar of the Kroatish-Slavonisches Grenz-Husaren Regiment Nr. 12 in 1798–1801. The regiment was mobilised to form the cavalry corps for *Feldmarschall* Würmser, and until the dissolution occurred in 1802 deployed a higher strength compared to the other regiment of hussars. The illustration confirms that the German military artist was usually well informed, since the uniform's colours are correct, as confirmed in the contemporary print from the *Züricher Bildserie*: black shako, *hechtgrau* pelisse and dolman, *hellblau* breeches and white buttons. The substantial difference is represented by the headgear model 1769 in the Swiss source above, while Knötel represents the same subject with the new shako introduced after 1798, and the cross-belt in white leather, which instead is in black in the modern reconstruction. (Authors' archive)

An illustration showing the émigrés regiment Royal Allemand Dragoner in 1793–98, from the series of Oester (authors' archive). The uniform of this two-squadron regiment appears very different to that described in the source preserved in the Austrian Kriegsarchiv.

Overall, four French emigrant cavalry regiments and corps entered the Habsburgs' service in 1793. However, as these units could not fill their losses, it was necessary to replenish them with foreign recruits of disparate provenance, which made their maintenance superfluous. Furthermore, the *émigrés* embodied the worst characteristics of old regime armies in terms of discipline, composition and efficiency. Apart from reactionary aristocrats, few men could be persuaded to enlist in these poorly paid, ill-equipped units, and though associated with the *Reichsarmee*, the *émigrés* proved largely unwelcome guests and were not typical of the wider Imperial war effort.[58]

The Royal Allemand Dragoner, the Saxe Husaren, the Bercsényi Husaren and the Bourbon Legion (hussars), were also composed of French *émigrés*, however the Royal Allemand had a German colonel, Baron Michael von Mandell,[59] and except for the Bourbon hussars, the other units also served under German–Austrian commanders. After some years of service, in 1798 the two-squadron regiment Royal Allemand was merged with other foreign horsemen into the newly raised Cuirassieren Regiment Nr.6. A similar situation followed when the Saxe and Bercsényi Husaren, both with a strength of two squadrons, joined in 1798 with Leichte Dragoner Regiment Nr.13. As for the two squadrons forming the Legion de Bourbon, they were merged in 1798 with the regiment Bussy Jäger zu Pferde.

Further foreign units were already raised at the beginning of the 1790s. Prince August of Anhalt-Zerbst formed a mixed *Freikorps* with one cavalry squadron, as part of the *Reichsarmee* auxiliary corps in Germany. In 1791, the *Freikorps* entered the Emperor's service as mercenaries, and into Cuirassieren Regiment Nr.6.

58 Wilson, *German Armies*, p.311.

59 Wrede and Semek, *Geschichte der K. und K. Wehrmacht*, vol. III, part two, p.807. The successor also, *Oberstlieutenant* Sebastian von Speck, was a German officer.

Profoss and *Fourierschützen* of a *Leichte Dragoner* regiment, 1799–1801. Cavalry *Profoss* wore the same uniforms issued to the NCOs but without the hazel cane. As before 1798, the headdress was the black felt bicorne with 2.3cm-wide golden or silver edging lace. After 1798, the *Fourierschützen* received a new uniform issued to all the German cavalry, comprising a felt *Jäger*-style headdress, on which a brass boss with regiment's branch and number was fixed under the yellow/black plume, pike-grey coat with black collar and turnbacks, white breeches and black gaiters. (Illustration by Bruno Mugnai)

Regiments Auditor of a Hussar regiment, 1811–-1815. A specific uniform for the cavalry's *Regiments Auditor* was introduced in 1798. It comprised a *hechtgrau* single-breasted coat with tail like the one of the infantry officers, Graproth collar, cuffs and turnbacks, white waistcoat and breeches; buttons followed those of the regiment's uniform. Headgear was the felt bicorne hat with silver or yellow lace and plume. As member of the *Regiments-stab*, the rank insignia were the same of the field officers, but without sash. The hussar *Regiments Auditor* unifrom retained Hungarian features such as trousers and light boots. (Illustration by Bruno Mugnai)

Austrian Cossacks in 1809, to left an officer front and back view, and a private. According to these coeval watercolours, the Austrian Cossacks were dressed in dark blue with red facings. The officers' accessories were the same carried by the uhlans, with a bearskin headdress with red bags and gilded chain and bosses. Breeches were also dark blue with red double stripes. Note the collar with yellow-golden embroidery. As primary weapon, the Cossacks carried the lance without pennant and the hussar sabre, while inserted in a yellow/black sash were a pair of pistols. (Anne Brown University, Collection of Military Prints, Providence, USA)

The new century brought other cavalry *Freikorps* in the Austrian Army, albeit to a lesser extent than in the previous century. No unit was raised before 1809, but the variety of nationality and cavalry specialties formed up to 1813 was considerable. Following the chronological sequence, in March 1809 the Husaren-Abteilung of Freikorps Schill was raised in West Galicia with a strength of 240 horsemen. Two months after, the unit was merged with the newly raised Österreichischer Kosaken Polk, which now could deploy three squadrons. After serving with the VII Corps in Poland, in 1810 the Austrian Cossacks were quartered in Bohemia, where they were merged with Uhlanen Regiment Nr.3. Before this unit, another attempt to establish Cossacks in the Austrian army had failed in 1791. Alongside the Poles and Ukrainians from the newly acquired West Galicia, the Austrian cavalry recruited also Zaporozhe Cossacks. Initially they formed a single division, assigned in 1791 to the regular uhlan regiment of Mészáros, even if only a few Zaporozhians were still present when Mészáros was appointed as colonel. The unit was completed with other ethnic minorities settled in the area such as the Silesian Goralen.[60] Further initiatives were conducted with the emergence of the Galician Free Kazaks, in 1809–1813. Vienna authorised an Austrian-minded noblemen of the Bochnia District to recruit a mounted corps with the strength of a squadron, but he was not able to raise enough horses, except for the carriages. The French–Polish invasion of 1809 interrupted the project. The enlistment resumed in 1812, but did not yield appreciable results.

In June 1809 a further hussar corps was formed in Transylvania. The unit took the name Erzherzog Carl Siebenbürgisches Husaren-Corps, with a strength of four squadrons each of 150 horsemen. The name of the Archduke was used to attract volunteers, but ultimately this was a unit comparable to the voluntary formations spontaneously raised in the Habsburg domains on the initiative of local loyalists. The short history of the corps is indicative of its origin, in fact this unit did not engage in any war actions and in January 1810 was disbanded. The Cavallerie-Abteilung of the Fränkischen Legion, of similar origins and with an equally short life, was formed with volunteers from the neighbouring German states in the summer of 1809. They were quartered on the border of Bohemia, and strengthened with the depot of the Braunschweig-Oelschen Freikorps, which were also three squadrons of uhlans, and like the Franconian Legion were licensed in December 1809.

The wave of enthusiasm aroused by the war of 1809 again prompted the retired colonel George Simon de Carneville to recruit a free corps of hussars on his own initiative. In December 1809 he had a modest force of just 66 horsemen under his command, which was soon disbanded.

Most of these mounted formations were represented by single *Abteilungen* sections, organised alongside infantry formations, except for the regiment Neutraer Husaren. Formed in June 1809 in the Slovak district of Nyitra, with a strength of two squadrons, this unit took part with the Henther Division in the army of Hungary.[61] The regiment had a very short life, and after a few months of service was licensed in October 1809. Though the Neutraer Husaren are usually considered alongside the *Ungarische-Croatisches Insurrections*, they had been raised by the city of Nyitra on a voluntary basis in order to form a 'regular' unit.

To the same category belonged the Böhmisches Dragoner Regiment, raised in the spring of 1809 by the Count and *Feldmarschall* Philipp Josef Kinsky von Wchinitz, under the command of his nephew. The regiment had to deploy a regular force of eight squadrons, but the end of the war left the plan unresolved and the unit was disbanded.

In 1813 the 'War of Liberation' brought new enthusiasm in the Habsburg domains and this turned in a new proliferation of irregular units formed on voluntary bases. In April 1813 the *Österreichisches-deutschen Legion*

60 The Gorals (Polish: Górale; Slovak: Gorali; Cieszyn Silesian: Gorole; literally highlanders) are an ethnic group primarily found in their traditional area of southern Poland, northern Slovakia, and in the region of Cieszyn Silesia in the Czech Republic (Silesian Gorals). In the last century there was also a significant Goral diaspora in the area of Bukovina in western Ukraine and in northern Romania, as well as in the USA.

61 Wrede and Semek, *Geschichte der K. und K. Wehrmacht*, vol. III, part two, p.802.

was raised with recruits from the Austrian domains and from the German states. The legion consisted of two, later three infantry battalions, one *Jäger* battalion, and two hussar regiments. The legion assumed the name Westphälischen Legion in 1814, and was finally disbanded after the Peace of Paris. The volunteers returned to their homes, but almost all the officers were incorporated into the Austrian army.

The last 'irregular' unit formed in 1813 was the Kosaken Regiment, with a planned strength of three *Feld-Divisionen* and a further reserve division for 1,436 horsemen in all. For the formation of this unit was charged the *Major* Franz von Neuhaus de San Mauro, who had to find recruits from the licensed Cossacks of the Russian army. Information about this unit is scarce, but thanks to the muster executed some months later, is possible to know that the regiment was still incomplete, considering that in early 1814 it deployed only 460 horsemen when it joined the Army of Italy.[62]

Hired Cavalry

Though hired mercenary units should not be bracketed with the Austrian troops, their presence and subsequent disappearance marks the change in political balance in Germany and Europe. In fact, whilst in the past the Emperor had resorted to hiring regiments and whole army corps from the German and Italian states on several occasions, in the 1790s the only help in this regard came from the Prince-Bishop of Würzburg. Together with a regiment and a battalion of infantry, two squadrons of dragoons also arrived from the small state of Franconia, which took the name Würzburghische Dragoner-Division. The agreement was preliminarily signed in May 1790, and three years afterwards the contingent marched to join the Austrian army in the Low Countries. In 1796 the Würzburg Dragoons moved to the Rhine and in 1797 returned to their own country.[63]

The Reichsarmee Cavalry

Because they were the most vulnerable of the so-called *Vordere Kreise* (forward circles), since the seventeenth century only the Swabian and Franconian circles had organised permanent and regiment-sized contingents. Franconia still retained a cuirassier and a dragoon regiment raised in 1681 and 1691 in cooperation with the circle states. As a result, the Treskow Cuirassieren regiment was formed with men from 20 different territories, with Würzburg, Bamberg, Nurnberg and Ansbach-Bayreuth as major contributors. In detail: 1st company from Bayreuth; 2nd company from Bamberg; 3rd company from Würzburg; 4th company from Nurnberg; 5th company from Eichstätt, Bamberg and Henneberg-Röhmild; 6th company from Ansbach, Nurnberg and Windsheim; 7th company from Weiningen, Schleusingen, Themar, Hildburghausen, Ilmenau, Eisenach, Schwarzenberg, Wertheim and Schweinfurth, 8th company from Rothenberg, Wertheim, Schmalkalden and Castell. The *Regimentsstab* and *Schwadronsstab* comprised 28 officers, 45

62 Wrede and Semek, *Geschichte der K. und K. Wehrmacht*, vol. III, part two, p.928.

63 Wrede and Semek, *Geschichte der K. und K. Wehrmacht*, vol. III, part two, p.964.

Above: Austrian cuirassiers, possibly regiment Kaiser (Nummer 1), in 1813–14. Note the horse's fodder carried on the front of the saddle, and the shortened saddle cover for troopers introduced after 1811. (Lithography after Johann Adam Klein. Authors' archive)

Left: Cuirassier and dragoon of the Swabian cavalry in 1793–1796, by Richard Knötel. The cuirassiers still retain the white-red uniform with white metal buttons of the previous years, while the dragoon wears the new uniform issued in 1793, consisting of black felt headgear with yellow lace; dark blue coat with red lapels, cuffs and collar, gilded epaulettes; yellow lining laced of red, yellow metal buttons, white waistcoat and breeches, dark blue saddle cover and pistol holsters piped and laced in yellow.

NCOs, three surgeons, one *Regimentspauker* (timpanist), seven trumpeters, three saddlers, 246 *Gemeinen*, for 333 men in all.[64] In wartime the regiment had to deploy four squadrons, increasing the strength to 999 men, but on the eve of the *Reichskrieg* against France it could field just the half of the regular strength. Furthermore, after the reversion of his state by the last Margrave of Ansbach-Bayreuth in 1791, the regiment lost one of its contributors. Of similar composition, and poor situation, was the Ansbach-Bayreuth Dragoner Regiment, which deployed a further eight companies: 1st company from Ansbach, Schönborn and Weissenburg; 2nd company from Bamberg; 3rd company from Würzburg; 4th company from Nurnberg; 5th company from Eichstätt, Erbach, Rieneck and Lohr; 6th company from the Teutonic Order, Würzburg, and Wertheim; 7th company from Bayreuth, Limpurg and Castell; 8th company from the princes of Hohenlohe, Schwarzenberg and Castell. On paper the regiment numbered 29 officers, 50 NCOs, two surgeons, one timpanist, eight trumpeters, one drummer, 239 *Gemeinen*, for 330 men in all in peacetime and 990 in wartime.[65]

Both regiments were mobilised in the spring of 1792, and an effort to replenish their strength involved the circle's states during the year. New uniforms and equipment were also provided, but in March 1793 both regiments were disbanded and replaced as *Kreiskontingent* by five squadrons of the Frankenberg Husaren Regiment provided by Prussia. However, the regiment did not serve with the Austrian armies.

The scenario was better in the Swabian Circle, where one cuirassier and one dragoon regiment had been maintained in service throughout the years until 1792. The bulk of the circle contingent were provided by Baden and Württemberg, but also included troops from a large number of small states and Imperial cities, for example Ulm and Lindau. The cuirassiers fielded eight squadrons with a peacetime establishment of 312 men. Recruitment and maintenance involved the principalities, abbeys and free cities of Weingarten, Constanz, Salmansweiler, Überlingen, Althausen, Pfullendorf, Scheer, Trauchburg, Öttlingen, Elwangen, Eichingen, Wangen, Zwiefalten, Wettenhausen, Münchret, Kempten, the Fugger houses, Schwarzenberg, Montfort, Vaduz, Schussenricht, Buchau, St. Ullrich, Weisenau, Salingen, Augsburg, Ochsenhausen, Mindelheim, Irrsee, Wiesensteig, Heggbach, Guttenzell, Eglofs, Hechingen, Heigerloch, Wolfegg, Sigmaringen, Wurzach, Obermarchthal, Geroldseck, Justingen, Buchorn, Baden, Fürstenberg, Ursberg, Roggenburg, Rothen-Münster, Offenburg, Gengenbach, Zell am Hammersbach, Eberstein, Heiligenberg, Stühlingen, Aulendorf, Immenstadt, Mösskirch, Bondorf and Gundelsingen.

The dragoon regiment deployed in peacetime eight companies with 296 men, and was formed with recruits provided by Württemberg, Baden, Heilbronn, Kaftbeuren, Aalen, Ulm, Lindau, Ravensburg, Augsburg, Dettingen, Memmingen, Rothweil, Dinkelsbühl, Biberach, Kempten, Hall, Gmünd, Nördlingen, Singen and Bopfingen.

64 *Nachricht von den Fränkischen Kraistruppen nebst einem Angang von den schwäbischen Kreisregimentern* (Nurnberg, 1782), p.92.

65 *Nachricht von den Fränkischen Kraistruppen*, p.91.

Since 1756 the cuirassier regiment commander had been a prince of the family Hohenlohe-Sigmaringen, while the dragoons had served without interruption under a member of the Württemberg ruling house from 1687.[66] In early 1792 Duke Carl Eugen of Württemberg put his troops into the *Haustruppen*, but at the beginning of the war against the French the new duke Ludwig Wilhelm associated them again to the circle contingent. In 1793 the Swabian cavalry numbered about 1,000 troopers in all and were joined to the Austrian army on the Rhine.[67] In 1796, after the peace agreement between Württemberg and France the Duke again separated his troops from the circle contingent, but these were disarmed on 26 June by the Austrians because of unreliability. Practically, only three infantry regiments and one cuirassier regiment continued to serve with the *Reichsarmee*. On 7 December 1799 the Swabian Circle voted for the formation of a new contingent, but since Württemberg and Baden no longer participated, the attempt remained incomplete until the existing regiments were finally disbanded in 1801.

A further short-lived cavalry unit was raised in 1795 by the bishops of Paderborn and Hildesheim, as *Reichs-Contingent* for the Westphalian Circle. The four-squadron unit assumed the title Jäger-Freikorps zu Pferd, and after two years entered the Austrian service to form the aforementioned Jäger zu Pferde Regiment.

66 Georg Tessin, 'Die Inhaber der Fränkischen und Schwäbischen Kreisregimenter', in *Zeitschrift für Heereskunde*, 5–1985, pp.81–83.

67 Wilson, *German Armies*, p.309.

3

Cavalry Uniforms

The Austrian uniformology of the Napoleonic era reflects a period of transformation, with the transition from a typically eighteenth-century style to a more modern one. Although there is numerous and important research on the subject, it is not always possible to reconstruct some details of the Austrian uniforms with reasonable certainty. Unfortunately there are several contradictions and mistakes even in contemporary sources, while authoritative texts omit many important details. Furthermore, some voids on the matter exist, especially with regard to *professionisten* and specialists, such as the administrative corps. Even the differences between the ranks are a matter that not even the official regulations clarify sufficiently. This matter may be hard especially for reader with less introduction to Austrian uniforms, but this was a typical Austrian feature, effectively summarised as 'minimalist' in terms of rank insignias.[1] In this regard the Austrian army reflected the *Ancien Régime* characteristic, classifying the army as per society, with the leading class represented by the aristocracy, separated from the common people. Though the enlightened Emperor Joseph II obliged the officers to wear coats of the same colour carried by their troops, the *Monturen* (military uniforms) were still divided in two categories: that for leading people and that issued to the subjects. The officer class was in turn divided into *Stabsoffizieren* (field officers), which included the ranks belonging to the *Gross* and *Klein Regimentsstab*, and the *Ober Offizieren* (company officers). Rank and file were also divided between *Primaplana* and *Gemeine*, as discussed in chapter two. The personnel included in the *Regimentsstab* also belonged to the *Primaplana* category as well as the ranks registered in the *Klein Regimentsstab*. Within these categories, some details were used to distinguish one rank from another, but in quarters or on campaign there were practically very few differences between a *Rittmeister* and a lieutenant, or between a *Wachtmeister* and a standard bearer, if not for the wooden cane and its pommel or other minimal features.

1 The German writer Johann Wolfgang Goethe, in his *Campagne in Frankreich, 1792*, outlined the difference between Franch and Austrian uniforms: 'The French are the opposite of the Austrians. Where the Austrian uniforms were practical and simple, the French uniforms are luxurious and full of superfluous details.'

The tendency to delegate to the colonel proprietor a certain number of decisions relating to the administration and therefore to the dress issued to his soldiers has contributed to leave incomplete an actual regulation of uniforms. This characteristic survived until the beginning of the nineteenth century, in stark contrast to what happened in other armies of the time, where uniform regulations became more and more detailed. From 1765 onward the Aulic War Council issued decrees and regulations regarding uniforms, equipment and weaponry, but these could only be successively filtered for implementation and considered as barely complete only after 1771. This set of regulations, although they did not always have the official name of *Adjustierung Vorschriften*, further modified the cavalry clothing and equipment before 1792.[2]

1792–1798

Cuirassiers and Carabiniers

The *Cuirassier Gemeiner* (private cuirassier) wore the black felt tricorne hat, with a black butterfly-shaped cockade fastened on the left side of the headdress by a loop of interlaced black and yellow lace, and by a yellow metal button. Above the cockade there was a 22cm plume, the *Federbusch*. The upper two thirds of the plume was black and the lower third yellow wool. The headdress bore the rank distinctive: the corporal's hat had a 4cm (1½ *Zoll*) silver edge piping; the *Wachtmeister*, *Estandarteführer* and *Fouririeschütz* had the same golden-yellow silk.[3] Cuirassiers and carabiniers wore protective iron 'secrets' inside their hats. Alongside this protection they received a breast cuirass with only the frontal breastplate. There was a reason for not using the *Doppelkürasse*, namely a front and back protection like the French counterpart. In many German-speaking countries, popular understanding has it that the *Doppelkürasse* was abandoned for unwise ideological reasons, whereas in fact usually many cavalrymen were related to say: 'Eine brave Cavalerie dürfe dem Feinde niemals den Rückenkehren' (a good cavalry never shows its back to the enemy).[4] The Austrian cuirass was manufactured of black polished iron, with an inner lining of canvas or chamois leather, and edges trimmed with white leather. The breastplate – *Brustharnisch* – was secured with a narrow white leather waist belt and straps, which passed over the shoulders to cross at the *Kürasskreuz* belt, and were fastened to the rear of the waist belt. The frontal end of the belts were fastened to the breastplate with black (and later white) leather straps. All buckles and fittings were in white metal.

2 See the *Adjustierung Vorschrift der österreichischen Armee im Jahre 1792*.

3 During the period in which every company had a flag, this was carried by the *Fähnriche*. However when these junior officers were promoted to the rank of lieutenant, the standard bearer became a *Führer* NCO, and when these latter had to be employed as *Feldwebel* in the infantry or *Wachtmeister* in the cavalry, the task was left to another senior NCO, called the *Estandartenträger* or *Estandartenführer* for this function. Since 1769 the regimental flag-bearers were chosen between the eight *Führern* of the regular companies.

4 See Eggert Willibald von der Lühe, *Militair Conversations Lexicon*, vol. IV (Leipzig, 1834), p.443.

A fully equipped *Gemeiner Carabinier* wearing the uniform before 1798, from Rudolf von Ottenfeld and Oskar Teuber, Die Oesterreichische Armee von 1700 bis 1867. Note the cavalry musket, the overcoat folded under the pistol holsters, and the picket stake strapped to the right of the saddle, as typical of the Austrian cavalry on campaign throughout the Revolutionary and Napoleonic Wars.

The coat was the single-breasted *Rock* manufactured with white cloth and lined with coarse white fabric. The plain cuffs measured 8cm, and were closed with two buttons on the lower edge. The cavalry coat was 10.5cm shorter than the contemporary infantry one, and tailored following a different pattern. The standing collar was a narrow 2.6cm high (1 *Zoll*) strap with small button and *Paroli*, collar patch. *Paroli*, cuffs and pipings of the folded turnbacks were in the regimental facing colour, known as *Egalisierung*. Buttons could be white or yellow metal, usually tin or brass. In quarters the troopers wore the *Leibel*, consisting of a short jacket with sleeves, white or yellow metal buttons, and low standing collar without *Egalisierung*. Cuirassiers of all ranks wore white cavalry breeches with knee pads inside protecting the knees, and long boots with buckled spurs; white knee socks stood out over the boots. NCOs received gloves and *Gemeiner* only mittens.

A white leather waist belt was worn under the cuirass and over the coat, with the sword suspended on slings. The heavy cavalry's sword was the *Pallasch*, between 84 and 88cm long, with a blade 4cm wide. This kind of weapon remained the typical sword of the 'German' cavalry in the next century and continued to be distributed to the regiments with minor modifications. The trooper's hilt-basket was made of steel, that of the NCO was in brass with a grip button in form of a lion's head. According to the original 1769 model, the *Primaplana*'s scabbard was covered with black natural leather, but in the 1790s a scabbard of iron replaced the previous model. Corporals and trumpeters carried the same model of sword issued to the troopers. Equipment for all ranks included the *Pallaschkuppel* sword belt, manufactured in white leather, with two slings, each for the two rings of the iron scabbard. Generally all *Porteepee*– sword knots– were made in white painted leather with double three-cornered tips; the *Primaplana* sword knot was manufactured of yellow/black camel hair with a fringed tassel, while the corporals had the same but in *Harras* with a tassel of camel hair.[5] These dispositions concerned all the German cavalry, and did not change in the following years.

Originally some cuirassiers also had carbines (and obviously did carabiniers), carried by white leather cross belts 9cm wide. Troopers carried separate cross belts for rifle and cartridge box over the left shoulder. These were in white leather and the innermost one carried a black leather cartridge

5 *Harras* was a typical light wool ribbon coming from the city of Arras (today in France, but until 1659 in the Spanish Low Countries), known also as *Arrasch*. Sword knots were manufactured in *Kaisergelb* yellow *Harras* piped with black for NCOs.

box – *Patrontasche mit Patrontaschen riemen* – bearing the Imperial eagle and holding 18 cartridges. Further firearms consisted of the 1759 *Blunderbuss* trombone musket, which had been issued to 12 men per cuirassier squadron. In 1781 this weapon was modified and finally withdrawn in 1798. Each cuirassier and carabinier also carried two pistols in their saddle holsters.

Finally, the cane for the *Wachtmeister* and *Estandarteführer* was manufactured from *Spanische Rohr* (Spanish cane, Arundo donax). For the latter ranks, the cane had an ivory pommel on the top; corporals had a simple cane of hazel wood without a pommel 'because they could not inflict punishment'.[6]

Trumpeters wore a trooper's uniform but without cuirass. They also had a red plume on the headgear, and *pallasch*, scabbard and sword knot as for the corporal, but no hazel cane. The *Stabs-Trompeter* was uniformed like the *Wachtmeister* but with a red plume on the headdress, and no Spanish cane.

The *Carabinier Gemeiner* (private carabinier) wore the same headgear of the cuirassiers but with silver piping on the edge like the cuirassier corporals, 3.9cm (1½ *Zoll*) wide. Their cartridge box carried the Imperial eagle and cypher in brass, decorated with a 2cm-wide yellow edging . Until 1798, carabinier regiments formed a chevauxlegers division, which was uniformed and equipped like the ordinary chevauxlegers, and all armed with carbines. In early 1792 six men in every carbine-armed squadron were equipped with the Model 1789 *Kavallerie-stutzen* short-barrelled rifle.

The overcoat for the winter season was the *Roquelor* made of grey/white cloth with a 10.5cm wide collar, which replaced the old-fashioned *Randmantell* since 1765. This item become the typical Austrian cavalry greatcoat, and according to the official regulation the 1765 model was closed by six buttons on the left side, and a 63cm long and 10.5cm wide strap with six buttonholes on the right. Furthermore, a 31.5cm slit with a single button was tailored on the left side, while on the right side there was another slit 42cm long with three buttons, in order to accommodate

Another fine drawing by Rudolf von Ottenfeld, depicting the uniform of the heavy cavalry officer in 1792–98. Here is portrayed a *Stabs-Offizier*, as identified for the gilded 'arrowhead' plate on the breast armour. Junior officers' armour had the same distinctive, but shorter. Note the cane, which arked the rank of this officer, which became the symbol of is authority from the reign of Emperor Carl VI. It was to have a simple unadorned top and originated from its application with regard to punishment of soldiers.

6 Josef A. Karger, *Die Entwicklung der Adjustierung, Rüstung und Bewaffnung der österreichische-ungarischen Armee 1700–1809* (printed version of the manuscript dated 1903; Bucholz: LTR, 1998), p.48.

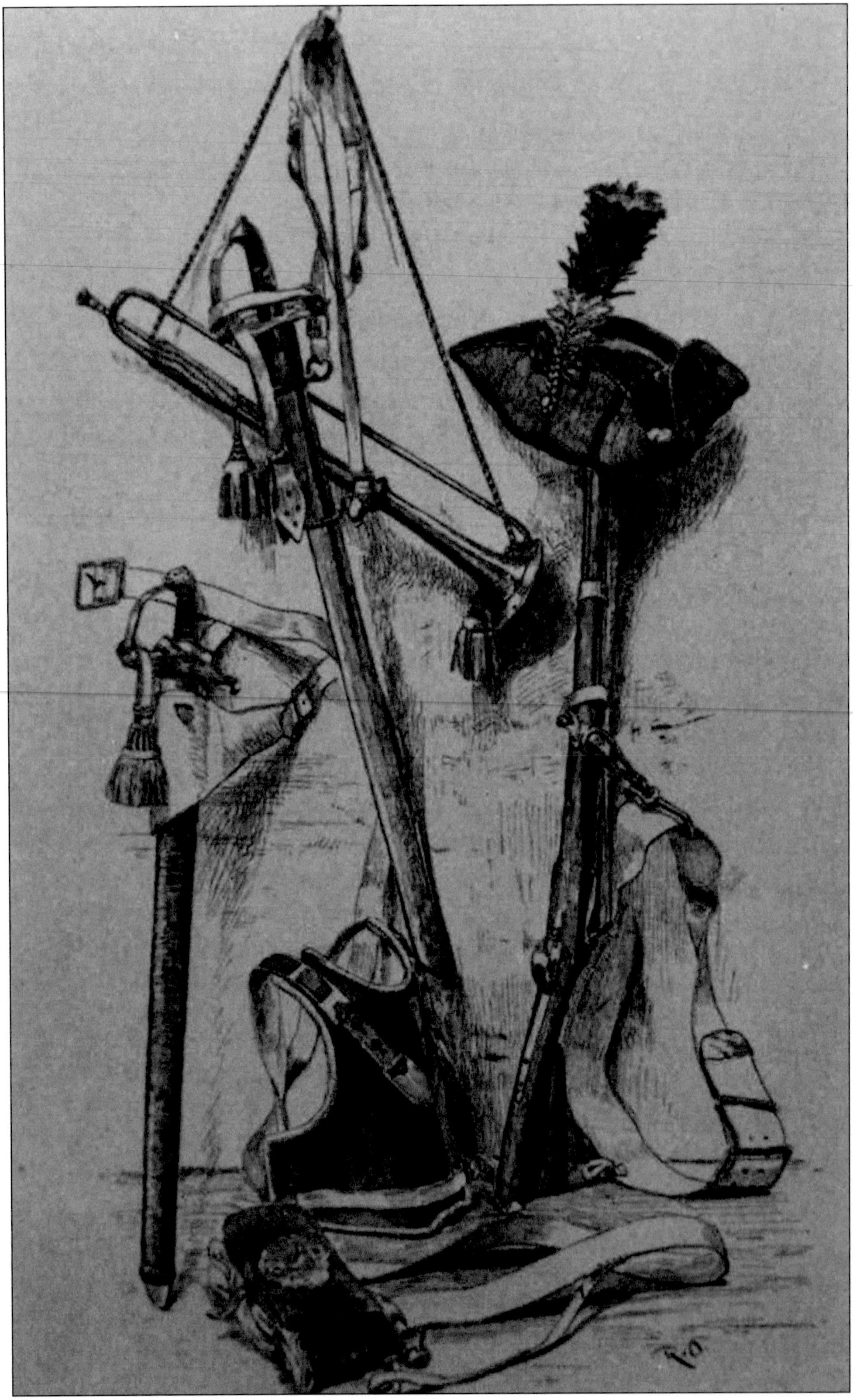

Overleaf: Cuirassier's equipment and armour, 1769–98, by Rudolf von Ottenfeld. The illustration shows trumpet and headdress with plume, a *Gemeiner's Pallasch* sword with white leather strap and 'knot' with the characteristic four holes, a *Wachtmeister's* sword with yellow and black knot and tassel and lion-head pommel, a cartridge box with brass plate with the ramrod on a strap secured to the shoulder belt and a cavalry carbine with its belt. Note the scabbard of the NCO's sword in black leather and brass fittings. The *Kürass* issued to the private cuirassier was manufactured in black polished iron, the edges lined and trimmed white leather. Only the *Brustharnisch* (breastplate) was worn, fastened with a narrow white leather waist belt and a couple of straps over the shoulders crossing at the back – forming the typical *Kürasskreuz* – and fastened to the rear of the waist belt; the tips of the straps were fastened to the breast with white metal fittings. All buckles were of white metal. It seems that in all German speaking countries the *Doppelkürasse* was unwisely abandoned for ideological reasons. Popular wisdom usually stated that, 'Eine brave Cavalerie dürfe dem Feinde niemals den Rücken kehren' (good cavalry must never show its back to the enemy).

musket or carbine when mounted.[7] Buttons were of white or yellow metal as those of the uniform. On the march, if not worn the *Roquelor* was carried under the pistol holsters of the saddle.

In field service and training, if mounted, all the German cavalry including officers wore grey overalls trousers with 12 buttons on each side.

The 1771 regulation gave more detailed information concerning the uniforms for *Professionisten* and *Proviantknecht* assigned to the regiments. The *Sattler* wore the black felt headdress without lace edging. The coat was the same issued to NCOs, but with white cuffs. Furthermore, because they did not have a cuirass, the *Kamisol* waistcoat showed the facing colours, except for the regiments with a black *Egalisierung*, which wore it in straw yellow.[8] The *Sattler's* uniform included black breeches. Similar uniform was issued to the *Schmied* but the coat cuffs were of the facing colour and the waistcoat was white. Under the waistcoat, both ranks carried a curved sword with black leather straps and iron scabbard; sword knot like the *Primaplana*. Since 1762 cavalry regiments had added one *Fourierschütz* for each officer of the *Regimentsstab* as for the infantry. This rank served on foot and could be dressed in the colonel's livery, but from that year they had to wear the regiment's uniform. The *Fourierschützen* were equipped with muskets, but after 1765 they served without firearms. Only dragoons and chevauxlegers *Fourierschützen* retained the firearms, and in addition to appropriate ammunition in the cartridge boxes, they carried the musket's bandolier.[9] *Fourierschütz* rank distinctives were like the corporal but without a cane. Also, *Privatdiener* wore the uniform of their regiment, but without weapons and equipment. Because both served dismounted, boots were replaced by black gaiters and shoes. *Fourierschützen* could serve also under the *Profoss*, who ranked as the *Wachtmeister*. His uniform was then the same established for the *Primaplana* but without a cane, and black gaiters and shoes instead boots. As for the *Proviantknecht*, his clothing would have no resemblance to the regimental uniform, and he would be dressed with a coat of undyed strong cloth provided by the colonel proprietor or regiment commander. According to contemporary descriptions, the *Proviantknecht* wore a coat

7 Karger, *Die Entwicklung der Adjustierung, Rüstung und Bewaffnung*, p.188.
8 Karger, *Die Entwicklung der Adjustierung, Rüstung und Bewaffnung*, p.194.
9 Karger, *Die Entwicklung der Adjustierung, Rüstung und Bewaffnung*, p.392.

with a turn-down collar and buttons in white or yellow as for the regiment, however the regulation prescribed a 9.3cm-wide band in the facing colour, for the left arm.[10] In this period the *Fourier* also served on foot, and the uniform comprised black felt headgear like the trooper but with the brims edged with a 2.3cm-wide silver or golden lace. The white coat had collar, cuffs and 'Swedish' lapels in the *Egalisierung* colour with piped buttonholes for cuirassiers only; buttons like the trooper, but of better quality metal. In addition, the *Fourier* wore black leather gaiters and shoes; the waistbelt under the *Kamisol* carried the infantry sword with the *Primaplana* sword knot.[11]

Also the officers' uniforms differed strongly from the private cuirassiers. Officers' headgear was manufactured in felt mixed with silk with a broad golden lace, as established in the 1777 regulation. On the left side of the headgear was fastened a small black butterfly-shaped cockade held by a loop of interlaced black and yellow lace and a black and yellow braid with button. Carabinier officers were uniformed like their cuirassier colleagues. Officers of all ranks wore the cuirass over a facing-coloured *Leibel* waistcoat,[12] and a long *Rock* coat of white cloth with facing-coloured *Parolis* collar patches and cuffs. All officers wore the breast cuirass without the back, like the troopers, but with ponceau red edgings, gilded fittings and front plate; this latter shaped like a vertical arrowhead, extending to the lower edge for field officers. Company officers had the same gilded plate but extended until half breast. Except for minor changes, the officers maintained this pattern until the 1840s, in order to identify readily their rank. Further differences between the officer and trooper uniform consisted in the quality of the cloth, which obviously was better for officers, who could tailored their own items for the *Leibes-Montur*. Breeches were white or light straw yellow, worn inside high-topped riding boots. As field sign, the officer wore the yellow/black silk sash around the waist, and had chamois or straw-yellow leather gloves with flaps. The officers' side weapon was the heavy *Pallasch* carried in a black leather scabbard with gilded accessories. Officers could provide the sword for themselves, and some retained the older *Pallasch* with gilded hilt and guard. The sword belt and straps were in red leather with white or yellow pipings on the edge. The *Portepee* sword knot consisted of golden straps with gold-fringed tassel for all the officers of the 'German Cavalry', namely carabiniers, cuirassiers, dragoons and chevauxlegers. However, the more important rank symbol for officers was the *Stock* (cane or walking stick). This was the peculiar field mark of the Austrian army since the early eighteenth century. Like the cane issued to the NCOs, this also originated from the right of punishment allowed to the senior ranks. Every officer carried the stick on and off service. According to its shape and accessories, this item continued to distinguish each rank among the officer staff, even after the introduction of other

10 Karger, *Die Entwicklung der Adjustierung, Rüstung und Bewaffnung*, p.195.

11 Karger, *Die Entwicklung der Adjustierung, Rüstung und Bewaffnung*, p.388.

12 *Leibel* is an Austrian or Bavarian term for a singlet, often sleeveless shirt, usually made of cotton and most often used as underwear for the upper part of the body.

Austrian Cuirassier, possibly Regiment Czartoryski (Nummer 21), from an unsigned series of 28 prints depicting the cavalry uniforms in 1792–98. According to the official regulation, this horsemen appears correctly uniformed, except for the golden edging lace on the headdress, a distinctive feature reserved only to ***Karabinieren***. It is difficult to know if this is a mistake or not. Official regulations are not an infallible guide, and differences could be common because of the usual delay between promulgation and implementation of a regulation. In some cases regulations seem to have been either ignored or adapted only partially. The order which specified the green coat for ***Leichte Dragoner*** in 1798, for example, seems to have had little effect, as several regiments retained the original white coats even two years after the regulation's introduction. Similarly, an element of circumspection is required with some of the coeval uniform illustrations, which in certain cases conflict with the contemporary evidence. (Author's archive)

distinctives.[13] The *Stock* was manufactured in *Spanische Rohr* (Spanish cane, Arundo donax) with an iron, silver or golden pommel on the top. *Oberst*, *Oberst-Lieutenant*, and *Major*, as well as *Rittmeister*, *Ober-Lieutenant* and *Unter-Lieutenant* carried the stick of Spanish cane. Before 1798 there was no detailed regulation about this item, and according to the existing iconography differences remained for a long time regarding shape, characteristics and accessories of the canes between one regiment and another, as established by the regiment's tradition or by the colonel proprietor.[14] As a result, the cane seems to have been used only by a few officers, because it was not considered very useful in the cavalry. The Aulic War Council *Vortrag* dated 10 July 1798 recommended that 'the Spanish cane, which until now had only been used by some officers, remained in use only for generals and field officers.'[15] The order was met through the subsequent enactment, with some changes: 'The *Stock* is carried by all generals, field officers and company officers. The cane may be of Spanish cane or grapevines with the pommel in white horn or ivory, measuring between one *Zoll* (2.6cm) or at most two *Zoll* high, very simple and rounded'.[16]

As for the other ranks in the *Regimentsstab*, the *Rechnungsführer* wore uniform like the company officers, being equivalent to the *Ober-Lieutenant*, but without cane and cuirass. *Regiments-Auditor* ranked like the field officers, but without cuirass, waist sash and cane.[17]

Concerning the medical and surgeon staff, there was no specific order relating their dress before 1802, but they were obliged to respect the order of the colonel proprietors in matters of clothing.

Dragoons

The Austrian dragoons wore the same uniform of the cuirassiers but without cuirass and no 'secret' iron defence under the headdress. As for the coat, instead of a standing collar with *Paroli* it had a turn-down collar with the regimental facing colour. The same facing colour appeared on the *Dragoner* shoulder-knot, fastened on the left shoulder. The cartridge box issued to dragoons was slightly larger than the one issued to the infantry and suitable for 30 cartridges. A brass shield with the Imperial eagle and cypher was applied on the cover of the black-leather box; the straps were of white painted leather. As a side weapon, the dragoons carried the German cavalry *Pallasch.* Like that issued to the cuirassier *Gemeiner*, the dragoon's sword knot was of white leather. The NCOs had their distinctive sword knot, as for the German cavalry. Dragoon trumpeters followed the cuirassier pattern with the red plume on the headdress.

---

13 'After the introduction of the laced coat for Senior Commanders and the laced waistcoat for Field Officers in July 1751, the cane had lost its function of rank insignia, but it remained as a symbol of dignity.' Karger, *Die Entwicklung der Adjustierung, Rüstung und Bewaffnung*, p.48.

14 In 1779 General Dagobert Sigmund von Würmser prescribed for his regiment that the stick should be provided with a white, smooth, round metal pomell, a black and yellow strap with gold and silk tassels and gilded fittings. Mem. 29 Abt., 1779,1, v. 27. Juni.

15 Karger, *Die Entwicklung der Adjustierung, Rüstung und Bewaffnung*, p.48.

16 Karger, *Die Entwicklung der Adjustierung, Rüstung und Bewaffnung*, p.49.

17 Karger, *Die Entwicklung der Adjustierung, Rüstung und Bewaffnung*, p.378.

Dragoon *Fourierschütz* and the *Professionisten* also followed the same pattern as for cuirassiers and carabiniers. *Fouriers* also wore the coat tailored as before, but with buttonholes without pipings.

Dragoon officers wore uniforms like the heavy cavalry officer but without a cuirass. They wore the field sash as their colleagues; after 1743–45 it was prescribed that they wear the *grasgrün* colour interspersed with gold or silver as for the infantry, but several evidences show that they carried the traditional yellow/black silk sash. Weapons, equipment and horse furniture was as for the German cavalry officers, but with sword belt in white leather.

Chevauxlegers

The headdress of the chevauxlegers was the Austrian *Kasket* like the one issued to the infantry in the 1770s. This headdress, measuring 23cm high and 16.5cm on the rear section, had the yellow/black cockade and plume like the cuirassiers, and yellow piping on the frontal plate: a brass oval badge with the two-headed Imperial eagle was fastened in the centre on the frontal plate.

The 1771 regulation prescribed green coats with the *Egalisierung* facing colour on the turned-down collar, cuffs and turnbacks. The buttons were in white or yellow metal. However, in the 1790s only the regiments *Kaiser* and *Karaczay* wore green coats, while the remaining four had the white *Rock*. Further differences consisted in the turnbacks of the coat, which were fully the facing colour for the regiment in green, and edged for the others.[18]

Corporals' headgear had the usual 2.3cm yellow or white lace on the frontal plate's edge: *Wachtmeister* and other *Primaplana* ranks had the same and a further lace 2.3cm wide above.

As already discussed for the German cavalry, trumpeters wore the trooper's uniform but with red plume on the headgear and rank distinctives like the corporals. However, several exceptions occurred in this period and some regiments retained the old uniforms in the reversed colours or in the colonel's livery. According to contemporary sources, during the campaigns of 1792–97 the trumpeters wore a field *Montur* comprising a *carmoisinrot* coat with dark green lapels, cuffs, shoulder knot and turnbacks.[19]

The *Leibel* fatigue jacket was in dark green or in white for all ranks; the equipment was the same issued to the dragoons. Chevauxlegers *Specialisten* and *Professionisten* were uniformed like their dragoon counterparts.

Officers wore headgear like the German cavalry, and a coat tailored as for the dragoon officers in white or green, with the usual distinctive marks reserved for the *Stabs* and *Oberoffizieren*.

Hussars

The regulations of 1767 deprived the hussar regiments of many of their traditional Hungarian features. The only items remaining of the original uniform were the tight breeches with black and yellow piping on both sides

18 *Schema aller Uniform der Kaiser. König. Kriegsvölkern, zu finden bey Artaria Comp. in Wienn* (Vienna, 1792).

19 'Krieg gegen die Französische Revolution 1792–1797', in *Kriegsgeschichtlichen Abteilung des k. und k. Kriegsarchivs, 1905*, vol. I, p.544.

Hussar's shako, late 1780s, preserved in the Hungarian Army Museum, Budapest. Although some parts, such as the cockade and the pompom appear deteriorated, this original headdress shows the extreme simplicity of the items manufactured for the private soldiers. However, the *Vitész Kötes* lanyard knot is the most elaborate accessory of the shako. (Authors' photograph)

and the trefoil knot embroidered on the thighs, known as *Vitész Kötes*.[20]

The headgear for the *Gemeiner* hussar was the felt *Tschakohaube*, painted in the regimental facing colour. This headdress was essentially a cylinder without peak bearing a yellow/black cockade with a braid loop on the front, and a black/yellow plume above a yellow woollen pompom with black centre. A cord, in the mixed yellow/black Imperial colours, was fastened around the upper edge of the headdress. On the left side, the cords terminated with two raquette-tassels.

The *Pelz* – pelisse – was trimmed with black lambskin and with 16 or 17 black/yellow loops on the breast with three buttons on each side. Buttons were yellow or white metal. The dolman, the Hungarian *Attila*, was manufactured in the regimental colour like the pelisse. The breeches could be of the same colour of pelisse and dolman, or also of different colours, with the ordinary black and yellow *Vitész Kötes* trefoil piping on the upper section. The cuffs of the dolman were decorated with a loop of lace known as 'bear claw'.

A further typical garment of the hussar was the barrelled waist sash. This was manufactured in yellow and black cord, and closed with the usual olivets and looped at the right side.

In quarters or in training, private hussars wore coarse tunics and grey/white *Loden*-cloth breeches, with buttons on both sides, as well as trouser overalls. Initially these items were made of white *halina* or *kepernek* woollen cloth, but after 1789 the hussars received the German cavalry model. However, iconographic evidences show that hussars continued to wear the older overalls until the late 1790s.

In rainy and cold weather the troopers wore a large grey/white *Mantel* cloak. This garment was very different from the German cavalry *Roquelor*, which was essentially a great coat, while the hussars' *Mantel* had no sleeves. This was essentially the traditional Hungarian *Gepernek* cloak with the flap buttoning together when in use to form a hood, which could be fastened up over the shako top to protect the head against wind and rain. The flap measured 39.5cm (15 *Zoll*). This item was manufactured of felted fabric and lined across the shoulder and to half of its length, and completed with a broad 15cm collar that could be turned up in rainy and cold weather.

The hussars' footwear was Hungarian *Czismen* boots, bordered with black and yellow piping and a *Rosette* of the same colour. The boots had fixed

20 *Vitész Kötes* in Hungarian means 'the warrior's knot' and was the traditional more or less elaborate design of twisted lace worn as part of a military uniform, usually embroidered or applied on the sleeve or breeches. The same term refers also to the headgear's flat lanyard *raquette* tassel.

Above: *Gemeiner Husar* in field dress with overall trousers prior to 1798. (Print from Teuber-Ottenfeld)

Left: Hussar trumpeter wearing the Western-style uniform of the 1769 Regulation

iron spurs. As for the German cavalry, all the *Primaplana* and corporals had yellow leather gloves, while the troopers received white mittens. Hussars wore also a *Halsflor*[21] in black wool. Sword belts and straps were in 'Russiani' red-brown leather as well as the sword knots. Troopers were equipped with a carbine.

The *Wachtmeister*'s and *Estandarteführer*'s headdress was edged at the top with two golden or silver laces: respectively 1.3cm and 2.6cm wide. The loop of the button for the cockade was also 1.3cm wide. The corporal's headdress had just a single 2.6cm lace.[22] As for the German cavalry, NCOs were exempt from carrying carbines and they had no cross belt for the firearm, but just the white leather cross belt for the cartridge box.

Trumpeters wore the German-style uniform comprising felt hat with silver or golden edging lace and red plume, the *Rock* usually of reversed colour or in the colonel's livery, and high boots with German spurs. However, there were a lot of arbitrary uniforms for the trumpeter. In the Regiment Würmser (Nr.8), the *Trompeter* wore a *galamontur* consisting of *papagei grün* single-breasted long coat in German style with falling collar closed with two buttons on each side, ponceau red facings and lining; and smooth brass buttons with yellow lanyard. Also a waistcoat of ponceau red cloth lined white, straw-yellow deerskin breeches with yellow piping, German boots and brown leather belt and straps. Horse furniture was like the German cavalry,[23] weaponry as for the German pattern. The same sources also relate the uniform for the *Professionisten*. *Schmied* and *Sattler* wore the felt hat without tassels, coat as for the trumpeter but with 'Polish'-style cuffs of parrot green; ponceau red waistcoat, dark grey trousers. The *Regiments-Schneider* wore the same uniform as the *Wachtmeister* except the headdress, which was the aforementioned felt hat without tassels. The weaponry consisted of the hussar's sabre.

Each hussar proudly brandished the Hungarian sabre inside an iron scabbard. The sabre straps and belt were of red 'Russiani' leather, sabretache in red laced in white or yellow, and the Emperor's monogram in yellow. NCOs had a sword knot like the troopers but with fringed tassel in yellow/black camel hair; corporals as before but in *Harras*.

Wachtmeister and *Estandarteführer* had pelisses trimmed with fox fur edgings. The sword knots identified the rank as for the German cavalry.

Hussar *Fourierschütz* wore the same uniform as the corporal except for the boots, replaced by the Hungarian infantry shoes and some special features established by the colonel proprietors, like the *Rosette* cockade with the colour of the colonel's livery.[24] A wide variety of uniforms existed for the *Fourier* too. In his authoritative manuscript, Johan Karger describes the *Fourier*'s uniform of the regiment Würmser (Nr.8) in 1779:

---

21 The *Halsflor* was a handkerchief wrapped around the neck, and sometimes it is a synonym of *Halsbinde*, although the two terms identified different items. The *Halsflor* could have several forms and shapes, and possibly its closer translation is 'neckband'.

22 Karger, *Die Entwicklung der Adjustierung, Rüstung und Bewaffnung*, p.232.

23 Karger, *Die Entwicklung der Adjustierung, Rüstung und Bewaffnung*, p.232.

24 Karger, *Die Entwicklung der Adjustierung, Rüstung und Bewaffnung*, p.110.

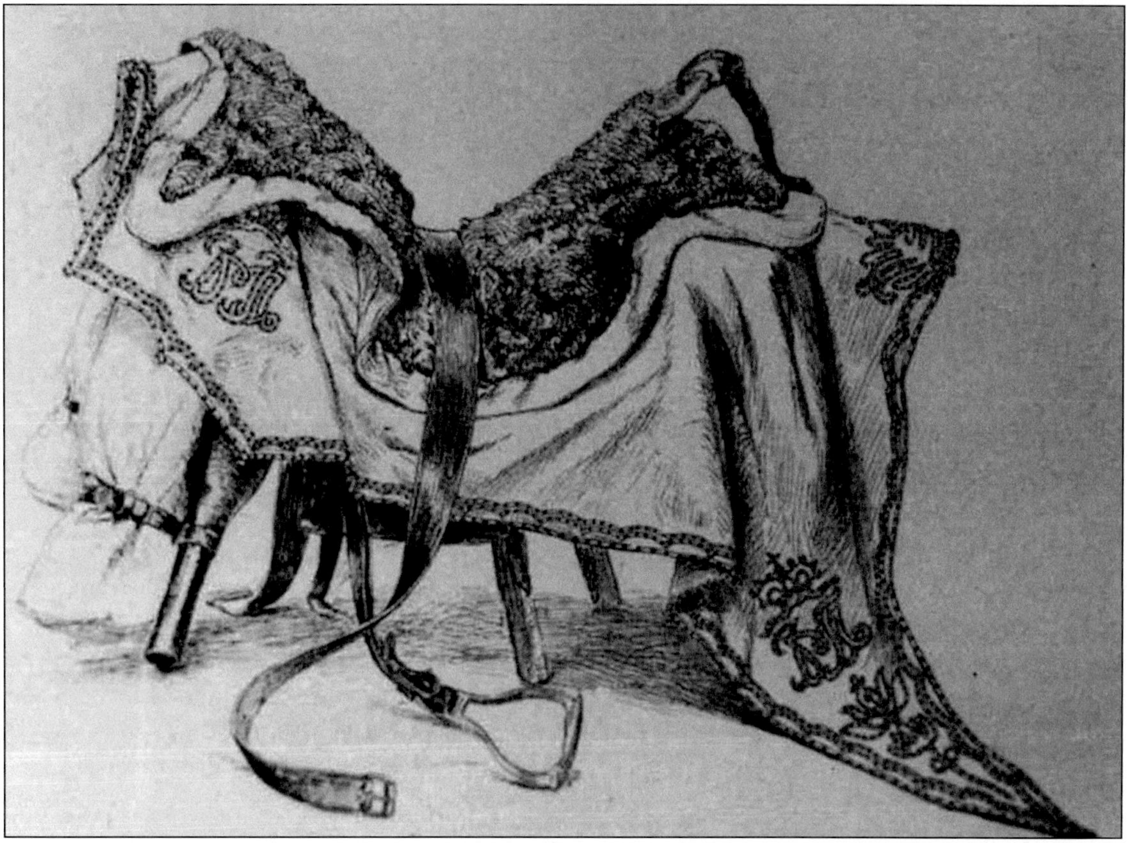

Above: Hussar horse furniture, 1769–1798, by Ottenfeld. The saddle cover bore the same lace of the German cavalry. Note the cloak rolled under the saddle cover, as for the *Roquelor* in the German cavalry.

Below: *Attila*-dolman and *Pelz*-pelisse (left), 1769–1798; *Attila*-dolman after 1814, for *Gemeiner Husar* (right), by Rudolf von Ottenfeld. Note the yellow-black braids fixed with only three buttons, instead of the five established by the regulations and normally depicted in most coeval sources.

> Headdress according to the regimental pattern, with cords and fringed tassels of yellow and black silk. *Attila* made of parrot-green cloth with round smooth buttons, ponceau-red lapels in Polish style, and ponceau-red lining. Black neckband. Ponceau-red waistcoat with little buttons. Straw-yellow breeches and light boots. Sabre with English brown leather belt.[25]

Before 1799 there are very few notices about the dress worn by the *Professionisten* and other ranks in the hussar regiment and squadron staff. Furthermore, because the evidence suggests that these personnel wore uniforms issued by the colonel, it is difficult to provide a general pattern. This happened also for the officer uniforms, which could be tailored privately. Officers' headgear was the *Pelzkalpak* bearskin cap with *Reiherbusch* heron plume. The bearskin cap was completed by a busby bag in the facing colour. When not in service, officers wore the felt bicorne hat with edging lace. The *Pelz* was lined with brown, white or black fur, embroidered with silver or gold laces. In quarters the *Pelz* was usually not worn. The cuffs were usually embroidered with a double *Vitész Kötes* Hungarian knot.

Footwear was the short *Czismen* Hungarian boots for the rank and file, made from 'Cordovan' leather, with golden knots for officer, and brass spurs. The large waist belt was made from yellow silk, with olivet buttons mottled gold and black. The curved sabre had the golden silk sword-knot with tassel as usual. Sabretaches were in leather covered with red fabric with straps of crimson leather.

The officers carried as distinctive item the cane like the one of the German cavalry. In field service and training, officers of all rank wore cloaks or alternatively the *Roquelor*, with light boots in Hungarian style.

Uhlans

The first uniform of the Austrian uhlan comprised the yellow square-topped *Czapka* as headgear. Initially lower, peakless, and closer to the Polish *konfederaka*, this headdress was a four-pointed hat fixed on a base of brown fur, and bearing a black–yellow plume on the left side. The coat for uhlans, introduced in the early 1790s, was a double-breasted dark green jacket with lapels, turn-down collar, 'German' plain cuffs, shoulder straps and turnbacks in ponceau red. Yellow metal buttons, white hussar-style breeches and *Czismen* short boots completed the uniform. The only difference between the units consisted of a dark green waistcoat for the *O'Donnell* uhlans, and *ponceaurot* for the Uhlanen Freiwilligen Corps (later respectively Uhlanen Regiment Nr.1 and Nr.2). Moreover, uhlan *Divisionen* assigned to the chevauxlegers regiments wore a coat with the same *Egalisierung* facing colour of these latter, but it also included open lapels, which showed the white or green waistcoat undress as the one worn by the chevauxlegers. In the regiments wearing white coats, the uhlans also wore a white uhlan-style jacket. Hungarian-style breeches were in white or *lichtblau* cloth, and

25 Karger, *Die Entwicklung der Adjustierung, Rüstung und Bewaffnung*, pp.388–389.

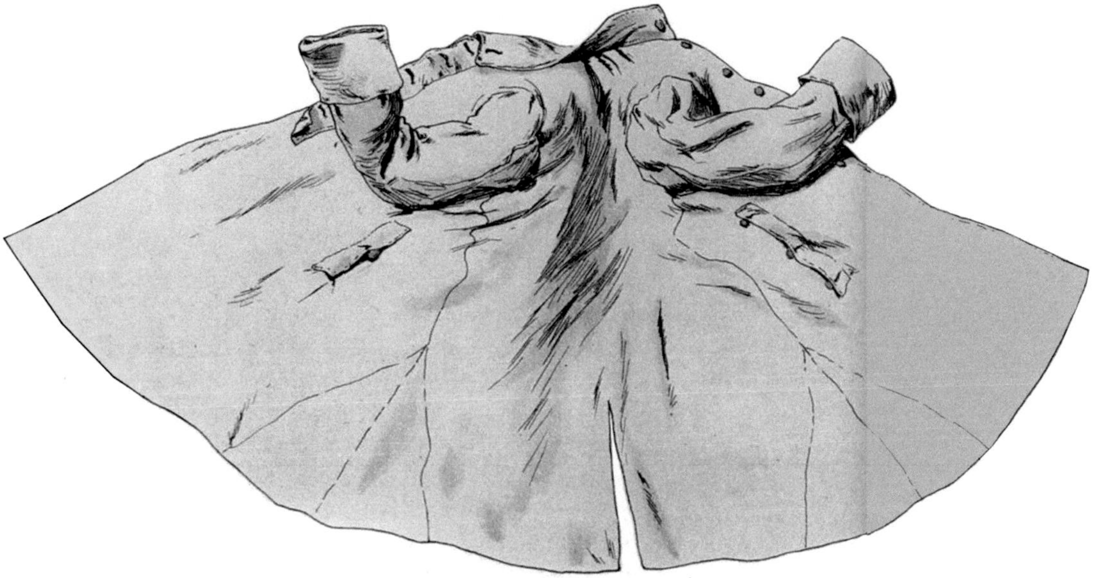

Roquelor, 1765–1798. This typical Austrian cavalry overcoat was issued to all the German cavalry and uhlans. It was manufactured from grey-white cloth with a 10.5cm-wide collar, which after 1765 replaced the old fashioned *Randmantell*. After 1798, the *Roquelor* modified its pattern adding a 6.5cm standing collar with patches according to the regimental facing colour. The patches disappeared in 1802, but were added again after 1811. On the march, the *Roquelor* was rolled beneath the pistol holster of the horse furniture. (Print after Teuber-Ottenfeld)

Czapkas were yellow for all.[26] The sword knot and other rank distinctives were as for the hussars. Trumpeters wore the uniform like the corporals, but with the usual red plume on the headdress.

The greatcoat was the *Roquelor* in grey/white cloth as for the German cavalry. As weaponry, the uhlans carried the hussar sabre, but the main weapon was the 2.5m *Lanze* (lance) carried by troopers and NCOs. The pole, painted in black, had a iron point on a small globe, and carried a black–yellow *Fähnchen* (flame, pennant) made of *Tafft* taffeta, a crisp, smooth, plain linen fabric. Before 1798 the pattern of the pennant varied considerably. Contemporary iconography shows black–yellow pennants quartered, or horizontally divided with the black above the yellow, and even vertically shaped.

The officers' headgear was the Polish *Czapka*, the white four-pointed hat fixed on a base of brown fur and a black-yellow *Federbush* plume on its left side. The *Czapka* was also decorated with embroidery on the top and gilded chain. The jacket was worn over the white cloth waistcoat reserved for the officers only. The officers' greatcoat was the German cavalry *Roquelor*. The officers' footwear was the Polish-style boot, which for parades was usually of Moroccan leather. As side weapons they carried Hungarian hussar sabres. Officers of all

26 *Schema aller Uniform der Kaiser. König. Kriegsvölkern, zu finden bey Artaria Comp. in Wienn* (Vienna, 1792).

ranks carried a 5.3cm cross-belt in black leather with golden pipings carrying the cartridge box.

Horse Equipment

Austrian cavalry had two models of horse furniture, one issued to 'German cavalry' and another to the light cavalry. Cuirassiers and carabiniers mounted on horseback with a black leather saddle positioned on a grey-white blanket four times folded. The pistol holsters were known as *Stützeln* or *Echabraque-Stützeln* and were lacquered leather with their cloth cap closed with a black leather *Halftergürtel* flap. The rectangular red saddle cover had rounded rear corners and separate pistol holster caps, decorated by a wide yellow *Harras* edge lace of 5.2cm with a 'diamond' pattern in white and black. Before 1777 the pistol holster caps and rear corners of the saddle cover carried the colonel proprietor's coat of arms, but after this date they carried the Emperor's crowned cypher 'F.II.' in yellow *Harras* with a narrow black trim. The edge of the saddle cover and pistol holster had different widths depending on rank. The edge of the saddle cover was bordered by three laces, the central one with the same design as for the *Gemeiner*, plus a further 2.6cm-wide yellow lace on both sides. The laces for the *Wachtmeister* were in camelhair and those for the *Estandarteführer* in *Harras*.[27]

The company officers' bridles and reins, from the *Rittmeister* downwards, were completely smooth without decoration and in black leather, in order to differentiate their horses from those belonging to the *Stabsoffizieren*, who could provide for their horses a richer equipment.[28]

The storage sack or sack for provisions, known as *Mantelsack*, placed behind the saddle and fixed with black leather straps, was manufactured with brown sheepskin, but late models were of red or grey cloth, being different in shape for heavy and light cavalry.

The saddle had a leather cantle and wooden structure with surcingle in *Spagat* leather, a breastplate also in *Spagat* with swing belts and collar (or leather without swing belts), stirrup straps, and unlined horse blankets. Horse equipment comprised reins and bridles as usual. All cavalry, excluding hussars, was also equipped with horse shoes and a kit of accessories. Each troopers and NCO received also two bags of black leather, carried backwards on the saddle, and a pack-sack in rough fabric for oats.

The saddle cover for hussars had the traditional pattern of pointed tails without separate caps for the pistol holsters, but edging lace and the Emperor's cypher followed the scheme as for the German cavalry. Uhlan saddle covers were similar, but with rounded rear edges.

The field equipment for a unit or single soldier included: the tents (10 for the company staff, 31 for the squadron), the field water bottles of tin (*Zeltflaschen*, literally tent bottles), a cooking kettle and a casserole, four rifle covers (tent-

27 Karger, *Die Entwicklung der Adjustierung, Rüstung und Bewaffnung*, p.193.
28 Karger, *Die Entwicklung der Adjustierung, Rüstung und Bewaffnung*, p.195.

shaped for recovering the carbines and muskets on campaign), staples and shovels, then cutters and ropes, camp banners, and the *Capellen-tent*. In addition, each trooper had to be provided with food bag, food knapsack and foraging blanket for the horse.

1792–1798 Colour Scheme

Cuirassiers and Carabiniers

Denomination	Number in 1792	Coat	Breeches	Facings	Buttons	Note
Sachsen-Teschen Karabinieren	Karabinieren Nr.5	W	W	*pompadourrot*	Y	Cuirassieren Nr.3 in 1798
Lacy Karabinieren	Karabinieren Nr.13	W	W	*pompadourrot*	W	Cuirassieren Nr.1 in 1798
Hohenzollern Cuirassieren	Cuirassieren Nr.7	W	W	*ponceaurot*	W	Cuirassieren Nr.8 in 1798
Zeschwitz Cuirassieren	Cuirassieren Nr.8	W	W	*dunkelgrün*	Y	Cuirassieren Nr.5 in 1798
Khavanagh Cuirassieren	Cuirassieren Nr.10	W	W	*dunkelgrün*	W	Cuirassieren Nr.12 in 1798
Nassau-Usingen Cuirassieren	Cuirassieren Nr.12	W	W	*lichtblau*	W	Cuirassieren Nr.9 in 1798
Jacquemin Cuirassieren	Cuirassieren Nr.18	W	W	black	Y	Cuirassieren Nr.10 in 1798
Wallisch Cuirassieren	Cuirassieren Nr.19	W	W	*dunkelblau*	W	Cuirassieren Nr.7 in 1798
Czartoryski Cuirassieren	Cuirassieren Nr.21	W	W	*carmoisinrot*	Y	Cuirassieren Nr.4 in 1798
Erzherzog Ferdinand	Cuirassieren Nr.22	W	W	black	W	Cuirassieren Nr.2 in 1798
Anspach Cuirassieren	Cuirassieren Nr.27	W	W	*apfelgrün*	W	Cuirassieren Nr.11 in 1798
Anhalt-Zerbst Cuirassieren*	-	W	W	scarlet red	W	Merged with Cuirassieren Nr.6 in 1798

*Single-squadron regiment as part of the *Anhalt-Zerbst'schen Freikorps*.

Dragoons

Denomination	Number in 1792	Coat	Breeches	Facings	Buttons	Note
Kaiser Dragoner	Dragoner Nr.3	W	W	*ponceaurot*	W	Leichte Dragoner Regt. Nr.2 in 1798
Prinz Eugen von Savoyen Dragoner	Dragoner Nr.7	W	W	black	Y	Leichte Dragoner Regt. Nr.15 in 1798
Toskana Dragoner	Dragoner Nr.20	W	W	*carmoisinrot*	W	Leichte Dragoner Regt. Nr.3 in 1798
Latour Dragoner	Dragoner Nr.25	W	W	*pompadourrot*	Y	Leichte Dragoner Regt. Nr.11 in 1798
Sachsen-Coburg Dragoner	Dragoner Nr.30	W	W	*krebsrot*	W	Leichte Dragoner Regt. Nr.6 in 1798
Württemberg Dragoner	Dragoner Nr.31	W	W	black	W	Leichte Dragoner Regt. Nr.8 in 1798
Waldeck Dragoner	Dragoner Nr.32	W	W	*dunkelgrün*	W	Leichte Dragoner Regt. Nr.7 in 1798
Royal Allemand (French Émigrés)	-	KB	W	*kornblau**	W	Merged in the Cuir. Regt. Nr.6 in 1798

*The *Adjustierung* of 1798 relates a *dunkelblau* coat with *carmoisinrot* facings. Contemporary iconographic evidences state a different uniform, which is the one represented in the colour plates. Probably in 1798 the dark blue uniform was prescribed but never issued.

Chevauxlegers

Denomination	Number in 1792	Coat	Breeches	Facings	Buttons	Note
Kaiser Chevauxlegers	Chevauxlegers Nr.1	G	W	*ponceaurot*	Y	Leichte Dragoner Regt. Nr.1 in 1798
Kinsky Chevauxlegers	Chevauxlegers Nr.6	W	W	*lichtblau*	Y	Leichte Dragoner Regt. Nr.12 in 1798
Modena Chevauxlegers	Chevauxlegers Nr.11	W	W	*dunkelblau*	W	Leichte Dragoner. Regt. Nr.5 in 1798
Karaczay Chevauxlegers	Chevauxlegers Nr.16	G	W	*ponceaurot*	W	Leichte Dragoner Regt. Nr.4 in 1798
Levener Chevauxlegers	Chevauxlegers Nr.17	W	W	*grasgrün*	Y	Leichte Dragoner Regt. Nr.14 in 1798
Lobkowitz Chevauxlegers	Chevauxlegers Nr.23	W	W	*lichtblau*	W	Leichte Dragoner Regt. Nr.10 in 1798

Hussars

Denomination	Nr. in 1792	Shako	Pelz and Attila	Breeches:	Buttons	Note
Kaiser Husaren	2	black	*dunkelblau*		Y	Husaren Regt. Nr.1 in 1798
Erdődy Husaren	11	black	*dunkelgrün*	*ponceaurot*	Y	Husaren Regt. Nr.9 in 1798
Blankenstein Husaren	16	black	*lichtblau*		Y	Husaren Regt. Nr.6 in 1798
Erzherzog Leopold Husaren	17	*ponceaurot*	*lichtblau*		Y	Husaren Regt. Nr.2 in 1798
Würmser Husaren	30	black	*papagei grün*	*ponceaurot*	Y	Husaren Regt. Nr.8 in 1798
Esterházy Husaren	32	*hechtgrau*	*dunkelblau*		Y	Husaren Regt. Nr.3 in 1798
Vécsey Husaren	34	*hellblau*	*papagei grün*	*ponceaurot*	W	Husaren Regt. Nr.4 in 1798
Barcó Husaren	35	*dunkelgrün*	*lichtblau*		Y	Husaren Regt. Nr.10 in 1798
Székler Grenz-Husaren	44	black	*dunkelblau*		W	Husaren Regt. Nr.11 in 1798
Croatisch-Slavonisches Grenz-Husaren	-	black	*hechtgrau*	*lichtblau*	W	Disbanded in 1802

Uhlans

Denomination	Nr. in 1792	Czapka	Kurtka	Breeches	Waistcoat	Buttons	Note
Mészáros Uhlanen	-	*Kaisergelb*	*dunkelgrün*	W	*dunkelgrün*	Y	Uhlanen Regt. Nr.1 in 1798
Uhlanen Frewilligen Corps	-	*Kaisergelb*	*grasgrün*	W	*ponceaurot*	Y	Uhlanen Regt. Nr.2 in 1798

Freikorps and Foreign Units

Denomination	Strength	Headgear	Coat	Facings	Waistcoat	Breeches	Buttons
Carneville Freikorps*	2 sqn	black peakless shako	dark green uhlan-style coat with lapels	black	white	dark green Hungarian-style trousers	Y

Rohan Husaren	2 sqn	azure hussar-style shako	*grasgrün* Attila and Pelz	-	-	carmine red Hungarian-style trousers	Y
Saxe Husaren	2 sqn	black hussar-style shako	*grasgrün* Attila and Pelz	-	-	carmine red Hungarian-style trousers	Y
Bercsényi Husaren	2 sqn	black hussar-style shako	*dunkelblau* Attila and Pelz	-	-	*dunkelblau* Hungarian-style trousers	W
Bourbon Husaren	2 sqn	black hussar-style shako	*dunkelblau* Attila and Pelz	-	-	*ponceaurot* Hungarian-style trousers	Y

*Equipment and weaponry as for the uhlans.

The 1798 Uniform Reform

The new regulation published on 26 October 1798 and titled *Adjustierungs-Vorschriftfür die k.k. Armee*, included five new additions for uniforms and equipment involving the whole generalship, infantry, and the weaponry for hussars, uhlans and newly formed *Jäger zu Pferd* (horse chasseurs). A previous chapter dealt with the uniforms of the cuirassiers and dragoons, which now became *Leichte Dragoner*. The *Vorschrift* introduced new patterns for coat, facings, buttons, laces and cockades, as well as a new colour scheme for the whole cavalry. The regulation became official on 26 October 1798, but the *Hofkriegsrat* began to reform the army the next year. In fact, the regulation was officially published on 1 January 1799, and had to be applied immediately to the regiments Kaiser Leichte Dragoner (Leichte Dragoner Regt. Nr.2), Erzherzog Ferdinand Husaren (Husaren Regt. Nr.3), the infantry regiments Josef and Wenzel Colloredo, Splenyi (all garrisoned in Vienna), and furthermore the new 15 battalions of light infantry. Finally, the officers had to wear the new uniform introduced from April 1797, but this term was deferred on 1 January 1800.

German Cavalry

The main modification in the uniform concerned the headdress and affected the 'German' cavalry, which received the new 1798 model *Helm*. Like infantry and *Jäger*, the German cavalry replaced the felt hats with this headdress, and the first regiments that received the helm were Bussy Jäger-zu-Pferd, Kaiser Leichte Dragoner Nr.2, Leichte Dragoner Nr.9, Cuirassieren Nr.2 and Cuirassieren Nr.9. The officers would have provided the new helm for themselves.[29] This new headgear was very similar to the one issued to infantry:

29 *Adjustierungs-Vorschrift für die k.k. Armee*, 27 October 1798.The regulation came into force from 1 January 1799, and was applied immediately to the aforementioned regiments, which were quartered in Vienna; in addition, the first battalion of each of the three infantry regiments garrisoned in the Austrian capital, as well as the infantry regiments Jordis, Neugebauer and

this headdress, which came to be named as *Raupenhelm* or *Bügelhelm* (crest helm), was manufactured with hardened boiled leather painted in black, and garnished with a triangular plate of gilded brass for staff and junior officers, or brass for *Gemeiner*, bearing the Emperor's cypher 'F.II'. The plate was placed above the peak and was 10.7cm high (4 *Zoll*, 1 *Linie*). On both sides of the helm, two 3.3cm (1 *Zoll*, 3 *Linien*) gilted brass round knobs were applied on the bottom edge, with a diameter of 5cm (1½ *Zoll*) on which were tied the chinstraps. On the helm's back, there was a neck flap 9cm (3½ *Zoll*) deep. From the upper centre of the helm, on both sides, were applied two thick flat iron wires, which improved resistance. On the officer's helm the wires were in gilded brass, while for troopers and NCOs they were painted black. The peak's outer border was edged by a similar metal sheet 6.6mm (1 *Strich*) wide, below and above, and slightly tilted the peak downwards in the helms for all ranks. On the left side of the helm, a hub-cap allowed insertion of the *Feldzeichen* for parades.

To each helm's sides, between the peak and the neck flap, were applied two leather patches (*Lappen*) 4cm long (1½ *Zoll*), to prevent rainwater dripping down the horseman's ears, and like a small gutter, both patches drove the rain backwards over the neck flap. Except during bad weather, these two flaps were always kept closed. A leather comb topped by a 17cm (6½ *Zoll*) chenille crest of black over yellow completed the headdress. The comb was frontally large at 4.5cm (1¾ *Zoll*) and it became thinner down towards the back, where there was a small funnel, intended to accommodate and fix the end of the crest. The comb mounted on the officer's helm was covered by a gilded brass plate with four open ovals on both sides. On the frontal side of the comb there was another gilded plate fixed with a screw-in form of flower. The comb was made from lacquered leather, with a crest of yellow/black silk fringes for company officers, and golden fringes for field officers.

Leather chinstraps secured the helm to the horseman's head, but in action metal *Schluppenketten* chin-scales replaced the leather ones.[30] However, they were not always permitted to button them under the chin, as this would have prevented the soldier from hearing sounds and commands. On the officers' helm, the chinstraps were decorated with two small chains of gilded brass. The regulation recommended never grabbing the helm by the two peaks, because they could break off or bend. Therefore it had to be grasped with the thumb and the forefinger by the crest front, and in this way it could be dressed or taken off.

Samuel Gyulai and the cavalry units uniformed for the first time, such as Carneville, Carl and Louis Rohan legions. The German cavalry received the new model helm and equipment, and officers had to wear the new helm if the troopers were already equipped with it. However, all cavalry officers already had to wear the new uniform from April 1797, but this term was deferred to 1 January 1800, especially for officers who had to change the colour of the uniform as in the case of *Leichte Dragoner*.

30 The helm had, on each side, above the gutter-like groove, a round stud to which a thin strip of black leather was applied, 2cm (3 *Strich*, 1 *Strich* being 3 *Linien*) wide. These *Schlachtoder Bataille-Riemen* – combat chinstraps – were long enough to close one above the other under the chin with a leather button, in order to securely fix the headdress to the soldier's head without sliding down. Chinstraps were accommodated around the back of the helm, fixing the two edges above the neck flap.

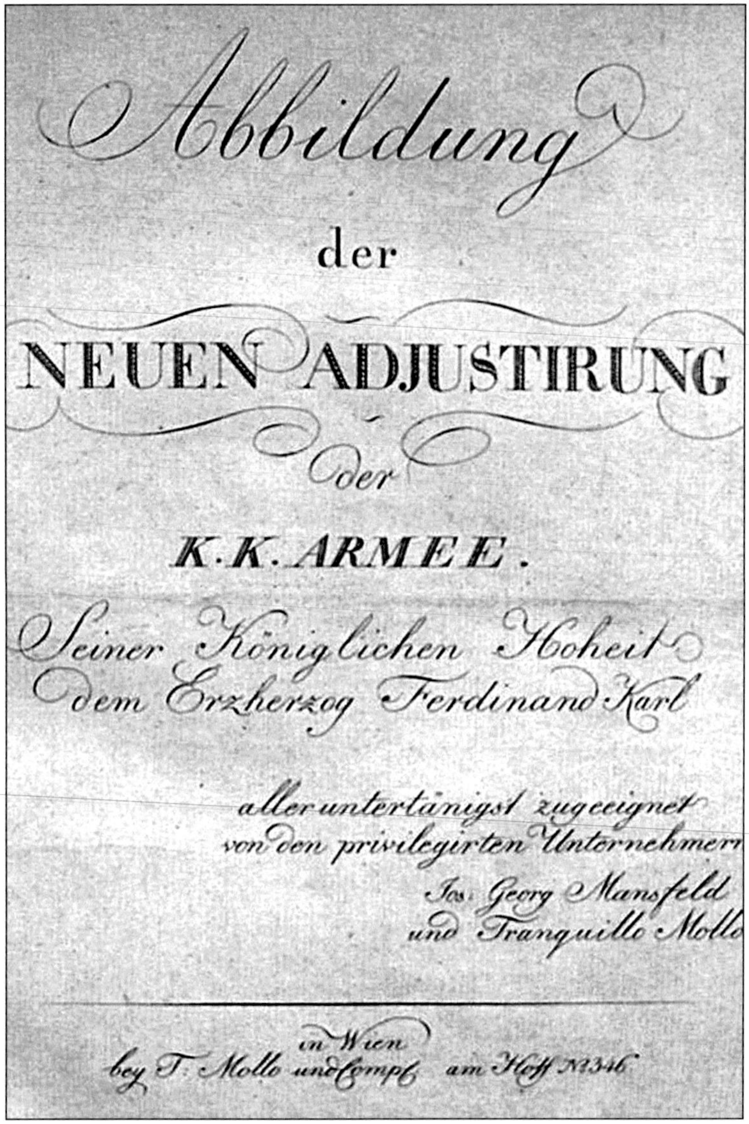

Abbildung

der

NEUEN ADJUSTIRUNG

der

K.K. ARMEE.

Seiner Königlichen Hoheit
dem Erzherzog Ferdinand Karl

alleruntertänigst zugeeignet
von den privilegirten Unternehmern
Jos. Georg Mansfeld
und Tranquillo Mollo

in Wien
bey T. Mollo und Comp. am Hoff No 346

First page of the illustrations attached to the Adjustierungsvorschrift introduced in 1798. The new regulation was a formidable document and the first actual attempt to impose a strict uniformity. The text was written in the aftermath of Napoleon's victories in Italy and was a clear attempt to breathe new life into an army fighting a modern war with an antique mentality. The language alone was remarkable. Given that it bore the Imperial imprimatur it offered neither subtlety nor nuance in its condemnation of sloppy practices which by implication had cost the Imperial House so much blood and resources in the Po Valley. The document was designed to shake the army out of its complacency and it brooked no argument. For example the tendency of officers to wear items of civilian dress was described as a 'dangerous delusion' and a practice that not only 'did not father a military spirit' but was to be systematically ausgerottet (stamped out). All luxury was to be eschewed and generals were not to appear in front of their men without their coats 'fully buttoned'. (Authors' archive)

Leather helm of a German cavalry officer, 1798–1805. (Royal Army and Military History Museum of Belgium)

On campaign both troopers and officers usually removed the chenille crest, in order to spare this item from rain and dust.

Cuirassiers and Light Dragoons

The *Gemeiner Cuirassier* maintained the traditional 1771 model cuirass in black-painted metal, now with shoulder straps of white leather and accessories in black polished or natural white metal. As occurred for all the German cavalry, a new coat replaced the older model. The new jacket – *der Röckel* – was manufactured in white cloth for the cuirassiers; the collar maintained the traditional *Paroli* patches but the standing collar increased its size, measuring now 3.2cm (2 *Zoll*, 3 *Linien*).

Compared to the previous one, the new coat reduced the size of the skirts, but held the same 10 large buttons on the breast and two at the back, with further two small buttons on each cuff, one to each pocket, and one to each turnback. A single strap of the facing colour was at the left shoulder, with another small button in order to maintain the bandoliers. In the later model, a further strap was carried to the left side at the waist level, fastened by a button, to accommodate the sword belt.

All German cavalry replaced the previous neck dresses with a black *Halsbindel* neckband for all ranks, manufactured in horsehair for troopers and NCOs and in silk for officers.

Horse furniture for the German cavalry until 1798, by Rudolf von Ottenfeld. Note the saddle cover's lace, bearing the pattern with white and black diamonds on yellow.

The breeches were white in baize cloth. Each trooper received also a pair of *Gattiehosen*, a piece of underwear which currently we call leggings, and a cotton shirt. For camp duties and on campaign they wore overall riding trousers, which were preserved under the valise or the saddle when not worn. The German cavalry maintained the fatigue jacket with sleeves – *Leibel mit Ärmel* – but now it was white for cuirassiers. Troopers received also the *Kittel*, a very simple cloth garment or frock of natural linen or cotton, without lining and cuffs, manufactured in grey/white fabric for all the cavalry specialties. In some duties, troopers are documented as wearing the *Kittel* over their regular uniform in order to preserve it from dust. Finally, each trooper had his own *Fouragiermütze* fatigue cap made, as in the past, with old coats that had exceeded the prescribed duration. Troopers and NCOs maintained mittens and gloves of the previous regulation.

The boots, now reduced to a height of 5cm (2 *Zoll*) below the knee, had spurs fixed on 2.6cm (1 *Zoll*) heels. The uniform was completed by the traditional *Roquelor* overcoat, which modified its pattern adding a 6.5cm (3 *Zoll*) standing collar with *Paroli* patches according to the regiment *Egalisierung*. New overall trousers made from grey *Zwilch* (a thick, tear-resistant, strong woollen cloth) were also distributed, replacing the old ones made from disparate cloth.

The white leather sword belt was modified in order to improve mobility when the horseman was dismounted, with the addition of one loop on the left side, to accommodate the scabbard and to raise it up away from the legs, and with a further loop for the pistol. Cuirassiers maintained their old *Pallasch*, but starting from 1800 a model with a new profile for the guard was distributed to the heavy cavalry regiments. Cuirassiers also maintained the same model of equipment and cross belts of the previous regulations, but the cartridge box cover had no brass badge, and was closed by a brass button.

The 1798 regulations also improved the horseman's equipment with a new storage sack similar to the hussars' *Mantelsack*. The equipment comprised a furry *Tornister* haversack containing the 'two-days' bread' and other items, a knapsack for grooming equipment, two *Eisentaschel* leather pouches containing two horseshoes and 30 nails in the left one, and the fatigue dress with picket ropes in the other. On campaign each horseman carried an additional haversack and a wooden canteen, like the one issued to the infantry, both carried on the right shoulder.

All German cavalry received a new *Sattelhaut* cover of lambskin in white fur for troopers and NCOs and black for officers, both with red piping on the edge. The new horse furniture comprised a new *Echabraque* saddle cover in *krebsrot* cloth, with rounded frontal section and rectangular rear corners, measuring 128cm (49 *Zoll*) long, and a two sided 60.5cm (23 *Zoll*) wide.

The saddle cover lost its elaborated diamond edge lace, replaced by a new yellow lace piped with two black pipings for troopers and NCOs. The rear corners carried the Emperor's monogram with a crown. Pistol holsters were now placed under the saddle cover. In order to extract the pistol, two slots were applied in the flaps. The new *Mantelsack* was a tubular, red cloth valise, carried under the lambskin saddle, in which could have been stored various items including two shirts, cleaning material for clothing and equipment, and shaving kit. The horse equipment included for both branches a horse blanket, but the saddle was different for *Leichte Dragoner*, who received light cavalry saddles as for hussars and uhlans. Further differences concerned girths and surcingles, as well the *Steigriemen* stirrup straps. Both the cuirassiers and light dragoons carried two pistols with brass fittings. These latter had their carbine as the shorter hussar model. Light dragoons received also a carbine socket to be used on quarter duty.

Each cuirassier squadron had now eight troopers armed with the new carbine model. They were carried in carbine sockets, though whilst on parade, in training and in action they were carried hooked. The cavalry *Stutzen–Jäger* rifles – which armed a further eight horsemen in each cuirassier squadron, were always carried hooked, because of their shortness.

NCOs wore the same uniform as for the troopers, but their helm had a gilt plate, and camel hair crests for *Wachtmeister* and *Estandarte-Führer*. Both maintained the black and yellow sword knots of the previous regulation,

Although the work of Teuber-Ottenfeld is considered an authoritative source, there are some inaccuracies and contradictions for the period 1792–1815. Here are depicted a private cuirassier of the Anhal-Zerbst regiment, and a private dragoon of the Royal-Allemand regiment (in 1798 both merged in the Cuirassieren Regiment Nr. 6). While the first horseman is correctly represented, the dragoon wears a dark blue coat with red facings that is not confirmed in the coeval iconographic sources.

and the 'Spanish reed' cane sticks, but no brass sword fittings. Corporals had woollen sword knots and hazelwood canes. Trumpeters were dressed as for the corporals and did not bear the cane, as a distinctive they had a red crest on the helm; the *Stabstrompeter* (trumpeter major) had a helm with coloured crests and plume on parade and the same distinctive as the *Wachtmeister*, cane excluded.

According to the regulation of 1798, the *Fourieren* of the German Cavalry received a uniform like the *Wachtmeister*, but instead of the helm they wore a felt bicorne hat with a silver or gold lace on the edge, straw-yellow breeches and black gaiters. As for the other *Professionisten* in the *Primaplana*, the fourier had the yellow/black sword knot like the *Wachtmeister* but did not carry the cane.[31]

The *Profoss* retained the uniform as for the *Wachtmeister* without the cane, furthermore the headdress was replaced by the black felt bicorne with 2.3cm-wide silver or golden lace as before 1798.

The *Fourierschützen* lost their colourful dress, and after 1798 they had to wear the uniform introduced throughout the German cavalry, comprising a felt *Jäger*-style headdress, on which a brass boss with the regiment's branch

31 Karger, *Die Entwicklung der Adjustierung, Rüstung und Bewaffnung*, p.389.

The illustrations published by Georg Mansfeld and Tranquillo Mollo for the Regulation of 1798 are a very useful source of knowledge concerning the Austrian uniforms. However, as for all the army regulations of this age, they show us how an army should look and not how it actually was. Here is portrayed a private cuirassier wearing the new leather helm and *Röckel* of the new uniform. Note the pistol's ramrod inserted above the cartridge box, and the saddle cover with black sheepskin. This seems to contradict the text of the regulation, which instead prescribes white sheepskin for rank and file, and black for officers only: original sources from the original regulations are not a reliable source either! (Authors' archive)

and number was fixed under a yellow/black plume; a pike-grey coat with black collar and turnbacks, white breeches and black gaiters.[32] The rank insignia was like the corporal's, but without cane. *Privatdiener* received a similar uniform, but their headdress was without a plume.

Field and company officers wore the helm, but in undress they continued to use the felt bicorne hat. Now the officers' *Röckel* was similar to the one issued to the troopers, but with longer turnback tails and no straps on the left shoulder, but with flat undecorated buttons like the troopers. Officers' dress included a tailless waistcoat of light straw-yellow cloth with a standing collar to be worn under the coat. As occurred in the infantry, the cavalry officers could

32 Karger, *Die Entwicklung der Adjustierung, Rüstung und Bewaffnung*, p.392.

Cuirassier in *Stallanzug* undress uniform, after Mansfeld and Mollo, 1798. This soldier is wearing the *Leibel* waistcoat, and the *Fouragiermütze* with the Emperor's ciphers embroidered in the facing colour. This item was common for all the German cavalry, in green for *Leichte Dragoner* and grey for *Jäger zu Pferd*. Note the cloth reinforcement on the shoulder of the waistcoat for cuirassiers only. (Authors' archive)

wear an *Überrock* greatcoat or a cloak instead of the common *Roquelor*. The *Überrock* was manufactured in grey or even white cloth, with collar and cuffs of the regimental facing colour; it also had side pockets and buttons as on the coat. This and the cloak were usually worn in winter season as city dress. In service, officers wore the grey/white *Roquelor* as the private horsemen with metal buttons. Moreover they wore yellow leather gloves with gauntlet cuffs. Field officers carried the customary distinctions: a black and golden silk crest on the helm's comb, silver or gold laces on cuff edges for coat and *Überrock*, golden silk sash, white sword belt and slings with red edging piping, golden *Portepee* sword knot with gold/black fringed tassel. The cuirass was of black polished metal with a ponceau red velvet trim on the edges 2cm wide; the cuirass maintained the 1.3cm (½ *Zoll*) brass frame on the edge and the frontal brass plate, arrowhead shaped, for identifying company officers and field officers. Cuirass belts were made from white leather; the white shoulder straps had brass fittings and red piping.

Saddle covers were in *ponceaurot* with yellow/black lace of different pattern in order to distinguish company officers from field officers. Company officers' saddle covers had an edge lace in yellow like that of troopers and NCOs but with a single and wider black piping in the centre. Another more elaborate lace was designed as a rank insignia for *Stabsoffizieren*, consisting in a wide red lace with yellow and black piping.

The 1798 regulation turned also on the uniforms of the *Regiments Auditor*, now dressed with a *hechtgrau* single-breasted coat, *graprot* collar and cuffs, white waistcoat and breeches, buttons as for the regiment. As to headgear, he now wore the felt bicorne hat with silver or yellow lace and plume. Modifications were introduced also for the *Rechnungsführer*, who retained the rank of *Ober-Lieutenant* until 1807, but he did not have cuirass and helm, this latter replaced by the felt hat without plume with silver or gold edging lace.[33]

Light dragoons received the same helm issued to cuirassiers, but their *Röckel* was in *meergrün*, a tone of colour resulting from the dyeing of a blue cloth. The coat had a 5cm (2 *Zoll*) standing collar with the facing colour, as well as the turnback edging. The *Leibel* waistcoat and forage cap were also green. Private *Leichte Dragoner* had a *Cartouche-Riemen* bandolier with cartridge box wider than the cuirassiers'. The box contained 30 cartridges, the cover had no metal badge, and was carried upon a white leather shoulder belt. The

33 Karger, *Die Entwicklung der Adjustierung, Rüstung und Bewaffnung*, p.378.

Left: The reform of 1798 formed fifteen regiments of *Leichte Dragoner* dressed similarly to cuirassiers but with *meergrün* coats, and no armour. Horse furniture also differed from cuirassiers, since the light dragoons received the light cavalry harness. (Authors' archive)

Below: Another picture from the Mansfeld–Mollo series, depicting front and back of a private *Leichte Dragoner* with good details of equipment and weapons. (Authors' archive)

Left: *A Stabsoffizier* of a light dragoon regiment, 1798–1801. The *Adjustierungsvorschrift* of 1798 considerably simplified the uniform of the company officers as well as the field officers of all the German cavalry. Senior officers were identified by the laced cuffs of the coat, the lace edging of the saddle cover, the gilded accessories of the horse furniture. (Authors' archive)

Horse furniture for cuirassiers, established with the 1798 regulation, considerably differed to the previous model. This harness and saddle cover was later issued to dragoons also and, with minor changes, continued to be used until the 1850s. (Print from Teuber-Ottenfeld)

cartridge box belt was 6.5cm (2½ *Zoll*) wide, and all private horsemen were armed with carbines with brass fittings.

Further differences between *Cuirassieren* and *Leichte Dragoner* concerned the sword, with the latter provided with a new model of *Pallasch*. The hilt was in iron with folding knuckle bow, and the guard could be expanded with an additional bar mounted on a ring that doubled the defence. The *Pallasch* was completed by a black leather scabbard with iron lockets and chape. This weapon was later maintained by the chevauxlegers. Straps and belts were in white painted leather for troopers, NCOs and company officers, and in yellow-brown leather for field officers.

Jäger zu Pferd (Bussy Jäger Regiment)

The 1798 army reform created the light infantry from the volunteer units, and a mounted unit was also raised under the command of *Oberst* Frimont. The new regiment took the name Bussy Jäger Regiment (horse chasseurs). The regiment received the new 1798 helm, but with a green crest and no frontal brass plate. According to the regulation, the infantry and cavalry *Jäger* model had only the Imperial cypher in metal on the frontal side. The gilded plate was reserved for field officers only, but some contemporary illustrations show the metal plate for rank and file too. The coat was the typical Austrian *hechtgrau* (pike-grey) jacket with a single row of brass buttons, *grasgrün* collar, cuffs and turnback piping. The *Jäger zu Pferd* carried a bandolier made from black leather, which carried a single black *Patronen-Tasche* cartridge box with an Imperial eagle yellow metal badge on the cover. Breeches were in *hechtgrau* too. Belts and straps were also in black leather for all ranks.

The trumpeter wore the helm with the usual red wool crest. Field and company officers wore the regular yellow silk waist sash, the first had laced cuffs as usual. The side weapon was the new model 1798 sword, 96.5cm (102cm with scabbard), weighing 944g with double narrow guard bars like the one issued to the *Leichte Dragoner*.

Hussars

The 1798 regulation established the introduction of a new shako, or *Czako*, 21cm (9 *Zoll*) high, made of thick and sturdy felt. The pompom, under the plume, was joined to the yellow/black *Rosette* cockade, but a little smaller than the previous model, held by two vertical yellow laces as usual. Furthermore, the headdress now had a peak, fixed on the lower edge with three tiny hooks. The new shako had the usual combat chinstrap *Sturmbänder*, also known as *Bataillebänder*, with the top embroidered with a yellow/black lanyard, with two further lanyards on the left side ending with raquette-tassels manufactured in the traditional *Vitész Kötes* style. The plume was now 37cm high (14 *Zoll*), in black and yellow wool, with a flexible whalebone core, rather than the previous wire, which was more subject to cracking.

The troopers maintained the classical *Pelz* (pelisse) and the traditional jacket dolman – or *Attila* – with its 4cm (1½ *Zoll*) standing collar and cuffs of the regimental colour. The dolman was a single-breasted, tailless jacket like the *Leibel* worn under the *Gürtel* Hungarian sash; this was barrelled with mixed yellow and black cord. The *Dolman* had low-pointed cuffs piped with a *Vitész Kötes* knot (with three loops similar to a trefoil leaf), from 16 or 17 lanyard loops on the breast, each with five buttons, and cuffs with embroidering. All the pipings were in mixed black and yellow laces, trimming the collar, cuffs, skirts, front and back.

The tight breeches were the common hussar trousers, piped with black and yellow and with small knots on the thigh. On campaign, the 1798 regulations allowed also the use of grey overall trousers made of grey twill fabric, with black leather side buttons and leather reinforcements on the sabre side. The footwear remained the Hungarian *Czismen* boots with spurs, with black and yellow piping and with a black-yellow *Rosette* on the frontal 'V'.

Further items of the 1798 hussar uniform were the neckband as for the German cavalry, which replaced the old fashioned *halsflor*. The winter garment remained the traditional *Gepernek* mantel, but the new model completely lost the hood, replaced by a standing flap collar. However, German-style *Roquelor* were legally issued to the regiments. In field service, troopers were allowed to remove raquette and plume from the shako, or to protect the latter with a waterproof tube.

An *Oberoffizier* of the Jäger zu Pferd regiment, 1798–1801. Note the larger and square-shaped sheepskin of the saddle, identical for all the cavalry officers. (Authors' archive)

The waist belt was of dark red or red-brown 'Russiani' leather; the sabre belt became 6.5mm narrower than the pre-1798 belt, with small iron hooks for fixing the side weapon, instead of the straps. The *Säbelriemen* – sabre belt – pendant with tassel, for the sabretache, was 10.5cm (4 *Zoll*) longer than the previous model. Two red leather straps supported the sabre and three were needed for the sabretache. The red fabric *Säbeltasche* now had a yellow/black lace instead of the yellow/black pipings and replaced the disparate models employed until 1798. The crowned Imperial cypher was embroidered in yellow/black. The cover over the *Tasche* itself was made of calf leather and larger then the older model. The sabretache contained matches, tobacco and moustache dressing, but no personal papers.

The Hungarian sabre with curved blade 84cm long, and the metal scabbard, remained unmodified, except for a slot on the guard, to pass the strap through. The *Säbelhandriemen* – sabre knot – was made of red 'Russiani' leather and secured to the hilt so that it could never be removed, responding to its purpose. The carbine belt was the same as the German cavalry, with a separate belt for the cartridge box.

Above: Hussar *Oberoffizier*, 1798. The more evident change in the officer's uniform concerned the shako, identical to that issued to the private horsemen, but with the rank insignia on the top. Company officers bore a 2.3cm-width golden or silver lace, with yellow silk braids and *raquettes*. The chinstrap was fastened to a lion-face gilt boss on each side. Although personalised variations continued to be frequent, these distinctives remained unchanged in subsequent years. Note the larger model of sheepskin reserved for the officers' horse furniture. (Authors' archive)

Overleaf: *Gemeiner* hussar from the 1798 Regulation showing the common practice of wearing the *Pelz* as a coat, with the *Attila*-dolman carried with the horseman's baggage, and a waistcoat being worn under the *Pelz* instead. The barrel sash could be omitted unless the dolman was worn. Note the 'mixed grey' overall trousers, common to all Austrian cavalry for service dress. The 1798 hussars' uniform retained the cylindrical shako, but now with a peak. The top surface of the shako was not reinforced with leather and usually manufactured in the same colour as the body. (Authors' archive)

Unteroffizieren – NCOs – carried their rank insignia on the headdress as before 1798. They completed their distinctive marks with the cane and sword knot as usual. The trumpeter's uniform was like the corporal's but with a red plume on the shako. The *Wachtmeister*'s and *Estandartefürer*'s pelisse was tailored with the better *Primaplanisten* fabric,[34] but with a reduced fur trimmed as for the troopers, because it easily deteriorated. Sabres and scabbards were in iron for all ranks. As in the German cavalry, the *Stabs Trompeter* wore the uniform like the *Wachtmeister* but with the traditional red plume on the shako.

The 1798 regulation also dealt with the uniform of the *Professionisten*, who wore the same dress issued to the German cavalry, but with the hussar's

34 The *Primaplanisten* had the privilege to voluntarily dismiss themselves from military duty as and when they wanted. Since 1765 NCOs and *Primaplanisten*were armed with sabres (and probably also the *Pallasch*) with the lion-headed hilt.

shako for *Sattler* and *Schmied*.[35] Both these ranks wore the *Roquelor* without *Egalisierung* instead of the *Gepernek* cloak, white *Leibel* and Hungarian *Czismen* boots without piping. Weaponry consisted of a grenadier infantry sabre inside an iron scabbard for the saddler and infantry-pattern sword knot in white leather for the smith. The *Proviantknecht* continued to wear their informal uniforms as prescribed by their colonels.

According to the new regulation, the officers replaced their bearskin headgear with the new shako with distinctive marks on the headdress. A shako with gold or silver lace around the upper edge identified the company officers, whilst field officers had the same distinctive, but doubled. Loops and pipings were in golden lanyard where those for troopers and NCOs were in yellow/black. The shako for officers of all ranks was completed by golden/black lanyards and gilt lion bosses on the sides, from which a gilt chain was suspended by a ring on the right boss and a hook on the left, with decorative function.[36]

Dolman and pelisse sleeves were also embroidered with elaborate *Vitész Kötes* and embroidery, generally doubled for *Stabsoffizieren*. Officers retained the original weaponry but belts and slings were now black leather with gilded edgings. Further special distinctives issued to company and field officers included the cross belt for the cartridge box, manufactured in black leather with gilded buckle and fittings, measuring 5.2cm (2 *Zoll*) wide. On the cross belt there was a gilded brass shield with the Emperor's cypher, and a chain suspended from a lion-head boss.

New sabretaches were also introduced in two different and very elaborate patterns for company and field officers. These models remained unchanged, except for the Emperor's cypher, modified with 'F.I.' after 1805.

Hussar officers retained some freedom concerning their dress, and as with all Austrian cavalry officers, they could tailor the uniforms privately. The already elaborate hussar uniform became more and more diversified according to the personal taste and preference of the individual. Therefore, special instructions dealt with the hussar officers' uniform in order to identify them from rank and file in ordinary service as well as on campaign. These recommended officers of all ranks wear the complete uniform and weaponry with all their marks and accessories, avoiding replacement of the headdress and other garments with informal items.[37] The 1798 regulation prescribed that hussar officers follow the same regulation as their colleagues of the German cavalry in matter of rank insignias regarding cane, sword knot and saddle cover. The new regulation introduced further details regarding *Regiments Auditor* and *Rechnungsführer*, who had to wear the same uniform established for their colleagues of the German cavalry, but both retained

35 Karger, *Die Entwicklung der Adjustierung, Rüstung und Bewaffnung*, p.245.

36 The *Adjustierung* of 1811 states that: 'For the fastening of the Czako there is a gold-plated chain on the same headgear, fixed to gilded lion heads on both sides of the Czako, the right one with a ring, the left with one little hook (*Haggen*), and just below the *Rosette*, an even smaller hook in order to hang up appropriately.'

37 Karger, *Die Entwicklung der Adjustierung, Rüstung und Bewaffnung*, p.246.

Portrait of a *Rittmeister* from the Erdödy Husaren Regiment (Nr. 11), datable to 1799–1805, showing in detail the rank distinctives, such as the lion-head boss and shield on the cross-belt, the embroidered collar, the lace on the top of the shako, and the remarkable size of the plume. (Authors' archive)

some Hungarian clothing, such as the trousers with *Vitész Kötes* and the pointed cuffs for the coat.

Horse equipment comprised Hungarian saddle, saddle cover, large and heavy *Pferdekotzen* blanket, lambskin shabraque, complete horse tack and bridles, grooming brush, curry comb, stockpot and casserole pot made in Vienna by Josef Kuppelwieser in his *k.k. priv. Eisenfabrik*. The saddle cover had the same edging lace as for the German cavalry, but the saddle cover maintained the traditional Hungarian pointed pattern. According to the 1798 regulation, the lambskin shabraque was black for NCOs and troopers and white for officers as prescribed for the German cavalry, however this scheme seems to have been little respected among the hussars. As for firearms, the hussars had one gun holster, a hussar short Model 1798 carbine without ramrod and brass fittings,[38] a pair of light cavalry *Pistole* and a wooden canteen called *Csuttera*.

Uhlans

In 1798, the Austrian uhlans received a new model of *Czapka*. The main modification concerned the size and the introduction of the peak. The new headdress measured 21.8cm high and the top square diminished the size to 23cm each side, for 32.5cm of the diagonal. The new model had a black leather lower section replacing the fur headband, and a cloth upper section with a square top covered with cloth of the regimental colour: yellow for Nr.1, and green for Nr.2. The new headdress retained the plume, identical to that of the hussars, but usually with richer feathers. No chinstraps were necessary in order to fasten the headgear to the head, but there were two leather combat slings on both sides, and when they were not in use they were not outwardly visible.

The Polish-style *Kurtka* or *Ulanka* replaced the old double-breasted jacket, manufactured in *meergrün* cloth, as issued to all the cavalry regiments uniformed in green. The new model retained the yellow metal buttons, but introduced a standing collar, cuffs, lapels and turnbacks in ponceau red. On the right shoulder the *Kurtka* had green shoulder straps with red piping. As specified in a later explanation of the regulations, the *Kurtka* was essentially the same for all ranks and it was long enough to cover half the buttocks and had a standing collar 6cm high. Trousers were in *meergrün* with two red lateral strips called *Lampasse,* each 2.8cm (1 *Zoll,* 1 line) wide, worn over the boots. The lower sections were in black leather. Trousers and *Kurtka* were separated at

38 The hussars were armed with a short carbine, 90cm long, reduced to 85.2cm in 1798, and further reduced to 76.5cm in 1815.

Hussar *Stabsoffizier*, 1798. The field officer's shako bore the rank distinctive introduced with the new regulation. It consisted in a couple of golden or silver 'chain of rings' on the top of the headdress, with the upper chain usually larger than the one below, but also in this case variations were common. (Authors' archive)

the waistline by a yellow/black sash, identical in shape for NCO and troopers, made by a single band of 8cm (3 *Zoll*, 2 lines). The two outer as well as the central stripes were in yellow, while the two intermediate stripes were of black silk. This item was different from the hussar waist sash, not having any tassels, and it was fastened by a brass hook.

Fatigue dress comprised the *Leibel* with sleeves, piped in the regimental colour on the plain cuffs. Under the black–yellow lined sash the uhlans received overall trousers for riding, in grey *Zwilch* fabric. Footwear was the Polish short boot with a fixed spur. Underwear, shirts, neckband and waistcoat were identical to the hussars.

The original pattern of the sabretaches for company and field officers established in 1798, with the modification introduced in 1805 with the new Emperor's cipher. (Authors' archive)

The uhlans received the 'German' cavalry *Roquelor* as an overcoat. Troopers carried sabre and belts as the hussars, but without sabretache; waist belts had the loops to insert the scabbard and the pistol when dismounted, as for the German cavalry.

In addition to the lance, the Austrian uhlans were armed with two pistols, a curved sabre and a cavalry rifle. Each squadron of uhlans had eight men armed with a musket and eight with carbines. On the field, the two flank divisions of the regiment were equipped with belt and cartridge box for the carbine, the central divisions had the same equipment and the lance.

According to the Emperor's resolution related to the 1798 regulation on the uniform, the yellow/black pennant of the lance – *die Lanzenfähnchen* – was in taffeta (silk fabric on linen weaving) and measured 90 x 29cm (2 *Schuh*, 10¼ *Zoll* x 11 *Zoll*), split after 43cm in a dovetail.

As for the hussars, rank distinctives were placed on the headdress. The corporal's *Czapka* had a silver lace 2.6cm (1½ *Zoll*) wide; the *Estandarteführer* and *Wachtmeister* had the same lace with a further smaller lace 1.3cm (½ *Zoll*) wide above the previous. The *Trompeter*'s *Czapka* was as for the corporal but with a red plume. Cords and tassels for corporals and NCOs were in yellow/black lanyard as for the troopers.

According to the illustrations attached to the 1798 regulation, the *Kurtka* of the uhlan officers differed from the falling collar.[39] As usual, the officers could wear tailored uniforms and instead of the rough jacket issued to the rank and file, they adopted a finer dark green cloth for their dress. The colour of *Kurtka* and trousers had to be in accordance with the *meergrün* cloth as for the troopers, but the *Leibel* would have been lighter for the officers of both the uhlan regiments, and the uniform buttons would have been smooth. Officers' *Kurtkas* included yellow epaulettes on both shoulders. The strap had golden edges and the inner third was black, for the whole width of 5.2cm (2 *Zoll*, 1 line); the length of the golden bullion fringes was 3cm (1 *Zoll*, 2 lines).

The *Czapka* for the officers was the same issued to the troopers except for the golden lace separating the lower and the upper section. The company officers' *Czapkas* had a golden lace 3.2cm (1 *Zoll*, 3 lines)

39 *Abbildung der neuen Adjustirung der K.K. Armee, 1798*; plate n. 21.

wide, with a thin black piping inside. Lanyards and raquettes were in golden/black silk. The cockade had the Imperial cypher and the black–yellow plume was 26cm (10 *Zoll*).

Stabsoffiziere wore the *Czapka* as above but with a smaller golden lace large 1.3cm (½ *Zoll*) above the company officers' lace. Officers carried a small cartridge box called a *Ladownika*, displaying a black double-headed eagle on the cover, carried by a black leather belt 5.2cm (2 *Zoll*) wide as for the hussar officers but with silver fittings. The waist sash was of yellow/black silk for all officer ranks.

Instead of the overcoat for city dress, the uhlan officers wore a slightly longer dark green *Kurtka* with red lining, tailored as the ordinary *Kurtka*. Polish boots were shorter compared to those of the German cavalry, but were calf-length, and the spurs were as per the hussars. Overall trousers were like those of the German cavalry; neckband like infantry officers; gloves like the German cavalry. As for weaponry, uhlan officers carried a hussar-pattern sabre belt, 2.8cm wide, with a yellow metal hook; the difference from that of hussar officers was in the black leather with gilded edge piping. The sword knot for the *Stabsoffizieren* was in golden silk, whilst company officers had it in black leather with a fringed golden silk tassel.

The horse furniture and other items of equipment were the same of the hussars, only the saddle cover differed in the shape, having rounded edges *à la Polonaise* with edging lace like that introduced for the German cavalry. Saddle and equipment as that of the hussars.

Hair and moustaches were permissible as in the infantry, but not to be powdered; the moustaches had to be directed downwards, only reaching the upper lip.

The 1798 regulation introduced changes that fixed the pattern of the Austrian uniform for at least half a century. However, the regulations of any period describe how uniform was intended to look, not how it actually was. Although accurate and considerably enriched with details relating to the measures of all accessories, the 1798 regulation also partially resolved the question of uniformity in the Austrian army. The durability of some items made the replacement of these unnecessarily expensive. For instance, the leather equipment of the old regulation survived for some years in some regiments, and the same occurred for the hussar

Private hussar weapons and equipment of the 1798 Regulation after Teuber-Ottenfeld. Note the carbine ramrod hanging from the cross-belt.

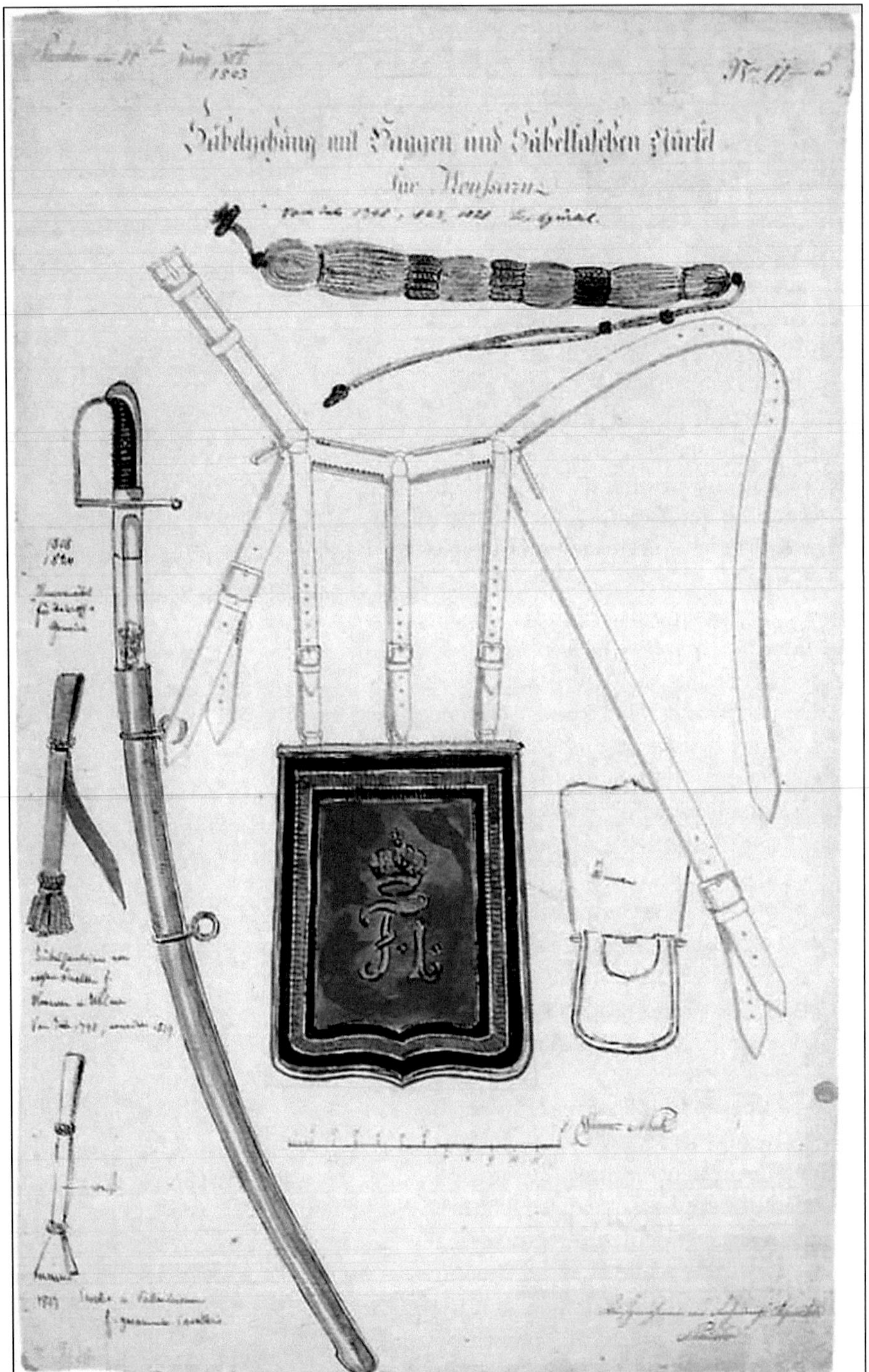

Details of hussar equipment according to the *Vorschrift* issued in 1805. Note the sabretache (red with black-yellow-black edging) and its internal section. Except for the new Imperial cipher, these items were the same introduced with the 1798 Regulation. (Authors' archive)

The new helm with higher comb and plate with the lion embossed, introduced for the senior cavalry officers after 1805, and the one issued to privates and NCOs. Note the cuirass in foreground with the short arrow head plate for *Oberoffizieren*. (Print after Teuber-Ottenfeld)

sabretaches. In this regard, the contemporary iconography shows such cases. The *Zürcher Bildserie* from 1800, compiled by an anonymous Swiss eyewitness, portrays some uniforms of the Austrian units that had fought the French with the Russians of Aleksandr Vasil'evič Suvorov the previous year. Among the cavalrymen there are two members of the light dragoons wearing a mixed version of the old and new regulation. The outdated felt headdress and the high boots are still worn alongside the new *Röckel* with the standing collar. Moreover, both horsemen's mounts retain the old saddle cover and pistol holster with the elaborate diamond pattern lace. An uhlan is also depicted wearing new items mixed with older ones, such as the pre-1798 *Czapka* without a peak and the uncommon hussar-pattern saddle cover. In this period hussars represent most cases of difformity in matter of uniform regulation. In 1799–1800 contemporary iconography shows hussar officers and NCOs still wearing bearskin busby with an *Egalisierung* bag of the older uniform. Obviously the replacing of the old items could not happen simultaneously for several seasons, but the poor compensation for the Hungarian officers implementing changes for their soldiers' dress may have produced these results. Furthermore, shortage of money influenced some choice. An oil painting by Seele dated 1800 portrays hussars wearing pre-1798 shakos with improvised front peaks. Difformities seem to be continued for several years in the hussar regiments. Another oil painting depicting a scene from the battle of Günzburg in 1805 shows the hussars of the Blankenstein regiment (Nr.6) still wearing the pre-1798 shako. One NCO has even retained his old-fashioned bearskin busby. In another painting dated 1805, the hussars of the Erzherzog Ferdinand Carl regiment (Nr.3) are depicted on horses with a regular post-1798 saddle cover but with old-fashioned pistol holsters.[40] Further uncommon and improvised items also appear in the uniforms of other cavalry branches. A sepia drawing by Seele dated 1799 depicts a *Leichte Dragoner* wearing a headdress obtained from the transformation of a chevauxlegers' black leather *Casquet*, to which a front peak has been applied. Moreover, his coat has a very unusual falling collar.

Changes in German Cavalry Uniforms, 1800–1803

After 1798 there were minor changes in the uniform. In 1800 the *Leibel* waistcoat became white throughout the German cavalry, while chevauxlegers adopted the hussars' low boots, but without yellow/black piping and *Rosette*. Further adjustments concerned equipment. After 1801 the cartridge box

40 Oil painting of Johann Adam von Bartsch. In his series entitled *Ceux Qui Bravaient l'Aigle*, Patrice Courcelle wrongly identifies the hussars as belonging to the 4th Regiment.

Private uhlan, 1798. The new *Czapka* and *Kurtka* mark the main changes in the Austrian uhlan uniform of this period. Note the profile of the lapels on the coat. (Authors' archive)

became somewhat broader and new *Pallasch* models were introduced in 1802. Dragoons and chevauxlegers received a new weapon with a folding knuckle bow iron hilt with perforated slots, the grip bound with black leather, a straight blade, and an iron scabbard with two lockets for suspension rings. In 1803 cuirassiers also received a new *Pallasch*, with an iron hilt, the grip bound with black leather, a straight blade, 84.5cm long and 3.5cm wide. The iron scabbard remained identical to the old 1775–98 pattern and was now distributed to all ranks, officers included. In 1802 the *Roquelor* greatcoat took an improved cut with a new standing collar without patches. Minor changes occurred for the officers' overall trousers, which were improved with leather layers on the internal sides and the lower edges.

In February 1802 the Aulic War Council transmitted to the 'German' cavalry regiments new orders regarding the trumpeters' dress. In order to preserve their coats, each regiment had to provide the trumpeters with a further *lichtgrau Röckel* with *Egalisierung* facing colours as for the ordinary uniforms. Cuirassier trumpeters retained the *Paroli* patches and buttons on the collar, and plain collar for dragoons and chevauxlegers. The Aulic War Council specified the quality of the cloth as that employed for NCOs.[41] In 1802 the coat was also modified for all branches of the German cavalry, with a new collar increased to 6.5cm high.

In 1803 black lambskin covers gradually replaced the previous model for troopers and NCOs, which remained white for cuirassiers, dragoons and chevauxlegers. In 1804 all the cavalry regiments replaced their muskets and other firearms with carbines.

Meanwhile, on 19 December 1801, Austrian cavalry uniforms changed again. The *Leichte Dragoner* were reformed into *Dragoner* and *Chevauxlegers*. The new chevauxlegers regiments, like those of the hussars and uhlans, now belonged to the actual 'light cavalry'.

Chevauxlegers and dragoon regiments wearing the same colour facings had to differentiate themselves by yellow or white metal buttons. Breeches remained in white cloth for all. As for the chevauxlegers serving on Hungarian horses, they also maintained the Hungarian saddle and bridles. Dragoons turned to the traditional white *Röckel*, and also the chevauxlegers had to replace their green uniforms with white ones, though some chevauxlegers regiments asked permission to maintain the green coats.

In subsequent years, some modifications concerned the German cavalry uniforms for the personnel of the *Regimentsstab*. The most important novelty was the introduction of the *Regiments Adjutant* for all the cavalry branches in 1802, and this required a specific uniform for the new rank. Following the Austrian rank classification, he held the title of *Unter-Lieutenant* and the only difference with this latter consisted in the *Feldbinde* carried on the left shoulder and the absence of the cane. However, this item continued to receive little favour in the cavalry, and after the *Vortrag* of 11 January 1803 the Aulic

41 Karger, *Die Entwicklung der Adjustierung, Rüstung und Bewaffnung*, p.203. Thera are no iconographic sources relating to this garment. Karger noticed that the Aulic War Council transmitted this order three times in 1802. There is no further evidence to suggest that the grey coat for trumpeters was still used in subsequent years, and also the regulations successively issued do not mention it.

Uhlan officer in 1799–1801. Note the *Kurtka* with lapels and falling collar. (Print after an engraving by anonymous artist. Authors' archive)

War Council retained the use of the officer's cane only for the colonels.[42]

Another important introduction was the uniform for the medical staff. An appropriate order was issued in June 1802 for avoiding the use of informal dress among the *Professionisten*, who usually tailored the uniform according to their personal taste. The uniform for the *Regiments Doctor* consisted of a felt hat with black *Rosette* cockade, *dunkelblau* coat with the regiment's facing colour, waistcoat and trousers, and black neckband. The clothing was manufactured to the same quality established for the *Primaplana*, but each physician could privately tailor the same uniform with finer cloth, Furthermore, as a distinctive they carried the usual silk *Portepee* as the officers.[43]

In February 1803 also, the *Fourier* replaced their regimental coat with a dark blue *Rock*, waistcoat and breeches, and a black felt *Corsican* hat and plume. The uniform retained the *Egalisierung* facing colour for collar, cuffs and turnbacks, and the rank insignias as for the *Primaplana*. The side weapon was the infantry *Grenadiersäbel*.[44] As winter coat, the *Fourier* wore the *Roquelor* without facings on the collar.

Changes in Hussar Uniforms, 1802–1804

Notwithstanding the resistance of the Hungarian officers' circle, hussar uniforms underwent further modifications, and after 1798 the most remarkable change was the introduction in 1802 of a new model of *Czako* with a dummy neck peak.[45] New overall trousers were also introduced, manufactured as for the German cavalry but with a black leather insert on the lower section of the legs.

42 Karger, *Die Entwicklung der Adjustierung, Rüstung und Bewaffnung*, p.49.

43 Karger, *Die Entwicklung der Adjustierung, Rüstung und Bewaffnung*, p.389.

44 Karger, *Die Entwicklung der Adjustierung, Rüstung und Bewaffnung*.

45 Karger, *Die Entwicklung der Adjustierung, Rüstung und Bewaffnung*, p.239.

According to the authoritative Joseph Karger,[46] in January 1802 it was proposed that all regiments should adopt *lichtblau* (light blue) uniforms with yellow lanyards and buttons, differing only by the *Czako*'s colour: pompadour red for Nr.1, ponceau red Nr.2, *hechtgrau* for Nr.3, *lichtblau* for Nr.4, *kaisergelb* for Nr.5, violet Nr.6, *dunkelgrün* Nr.7, orange Nr.8, white Nr.9, light green Nr.10, black Nr.11, and dark blue Nr.12. This measure was intended above all to rationalise the supply of clothing and consequently to bring significant savings, but the proposal met with a strong resistance and was therefore abandoned. The hussar' headdress was affected by further modification, and another order in 1802 prescribed a plume 26cm (10 *Zoll*) high.

In the same year, trumpeters of all ranks received the single-breasted *hechtgrau* undress coat like that of the German cavalry, with facing colour on the standing collar and buttons like the regiment's uniform. Between 1802 and 1803 the *Regiments Doctor* and *Fourier* received the same uniforms as for the German cavalry but with the usual Hungarian attributes.

In 1804 a new model of *Gepernek* cloak was introduced for all ranks. The new model lost the hood but it was improved with a removable cape on the upper section.

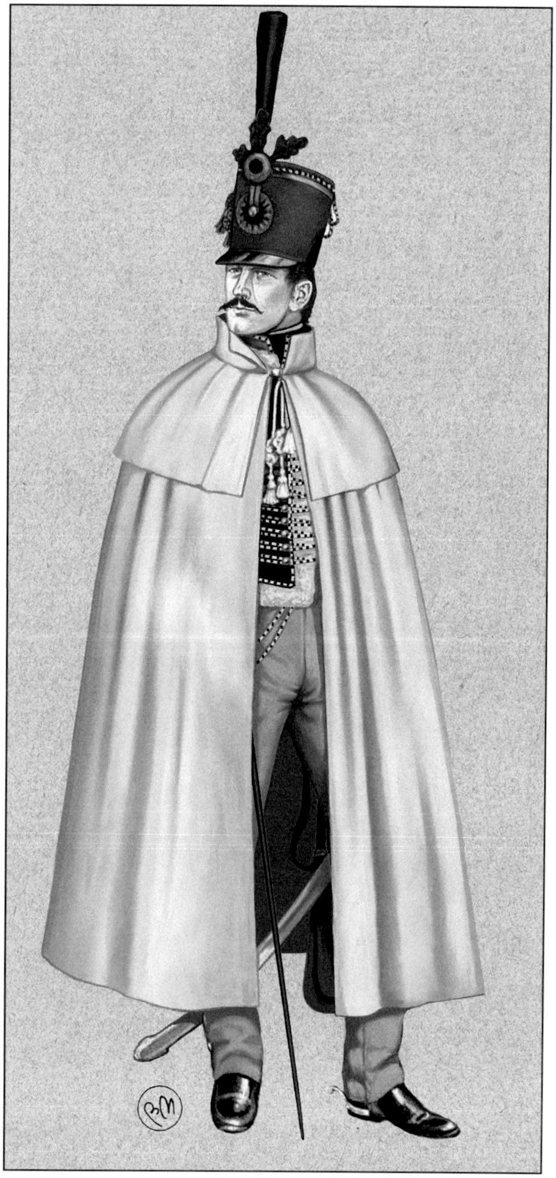

Hussar corporal, 1804, wearing the *Gepernek* with removable cape, according to a modern reconstruction by Alfred Umhey. Several models of cloak were issued to the hussar regiments but they were all manufactured from white-grey felted wool and lined with bay across the shoulders and to half of their length. (Illustration by Bruno Mugnai)

Changes in Uhlan Uniforms, 1801–1804

Between 1800 and 1801 the *dunkelgrün* cloth replaced *meergrün* for coat and trousers. As occurred in the hussar and German regiments, in 1802 the trumpeters received the single-breasted *hechtgrau* coat with the same facing colours as the *Czapka*. *Professionisten* took the uniforms with new rank insignias introduced in 1798 for the German cavalry.

In 1801, on the occasion of the creation of the 3rd Uhlan Regiment, whose *Inhaber* became Archduke Carl, a restyled *Czapka* was introduced. The new model was higher than the previous: 21.8cm (8 *Zoll* and ¼) provided with a top side measuring 23.4cm

46 Karger, *Die Entwicklung der Adjustierung, Rüstung und Bewaffnung*, p.245.

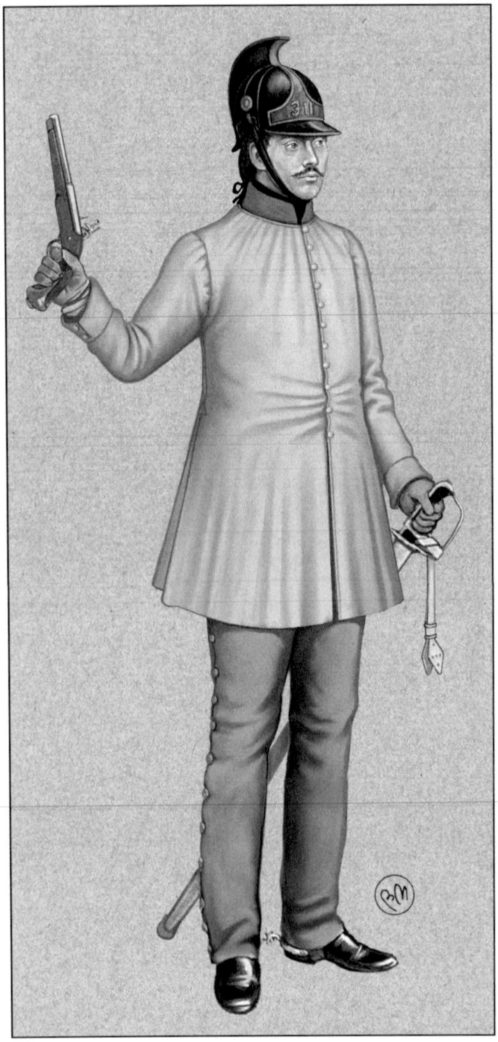

Austrian *Dragoner* in training session wearing the *Kittel*, 1802–1805. (Illustration by Bruno Mugnai)

wide, improved with a black leather neck flap turned up at the back and a new frontal peak. A narrow yellow lace separated the lower from the upper section. The upper section and the square top covered with the *Egalisierung* facing colours remained unchanged and was in black for the newly raised regiment.[47] Corporals had a golden silk lace 1.3cm high; senior NCOs added further yellow piping on the top square edge. The *Czapka* was the same shape for officers and troopers, with identical leather flaps, laced in gold for officers. In order to secure the *Czapka* on the head, there was a double lanyard with raquette tassels attached to the headdress in the same manner as prescribed for the hussar shako, and fixed on the right shoulder. On campaign the cords passed behind the head, but on parade they were fixed frontally on the right shoulder.[48] Among the company officers, the *Czapka* was surrounded above the leather skull part with a 4.6cm (1 *Zoll*, 3 *Strich*) wide golden lace. Field officers had double lace and the top square was edged with golden piping. Officers' *Czapkas* included a silver chain above the peak, fixed on the headdress with two lion-head bosses. In 1804, an ordinance replaced the trousers with a new model with only one red side band 4cm wide instead of two.[49]

As for the hussars, between 1802 and 1803 the *Regiments Doctor* and *Fourier* wore the same uniforms established for the German cavalry.

1805–1815 Uniforms

Cuirassiers, Dragoons and Chevauxlegers

Experience acquired from campaigns, and the strenuous work of reorganisation undertaken by Archduke Carl after 1805, also affected equipment and dress. In 1805 the German cavalry began to replace the helm with a new model characterised by a higher comb, measuring 12.4cm (5 *Zoll*) high and 2.3cm (1 *Zoll*) wide. Dragoons and chevauxlegers replaced their headdress first. The new helm improved the protection of the nape and increased its resistance with a stronger frame. In order to accommodate the suggestions submitted by the *Stabsoffizieren*, the Aulic War Council also authorised a new headdress with new gilded accessories and comb. This latter was designed with a gilded brass plate on each side with an embossed lion device, and a new larger crest in black/yellow

47 Karger, *Die Entwicklung der Adjustierung, Rüstung und Bewaffnung*, p.274.

48 *Militaria Austriaca*, Sonderdruck 3, 'Die Kopfbedeckungen der K.K. / K.u.K. Ulanen von 1784–1918', 1980, p.69.

49 Karger, *Die Entwicklung der Adjustierung, Rüstung und Bewaffnung*, p.206; order issued on 12 March 1804.

metallised chenille. This helm was confirmed in 1811 through the regulation introduced by Archduke Carl, and resulted in an imposing headdress, becoming very popular among senior commanders too. However, after 1805 another significant change occurred on the cavalry helm: the frontal plate now carried the cypher 'F.I.', since the old German–Roman Empire had been dissolved.[50]

In 1805 a new *Röckel* for the German cavalry was designed and issued during the next year to dragoons and chevauxlegers and then to cuirassiers within two years.[51] The most evident modification concerned the collar, which changed its size again, measuring 10cm (4 *Zoll*) high. Cuirassiers lost their traditional *Paroli*, replaced by new collar patches applied on both outer edges with a small button in white or yellow metal. Dragoon and chevauxlegers coats were tailored with the usual standing collar in the new size.

These modifications followed the attempt to rationalise the matter introduced in the previous years, which had caused several confusions, especially in the cavalry. This drawback concerned the chevauxlegers and dragoon uniforms in particular. Economic shortage put a focus on the green uniforms of the chevauxlegers, which had a higher cost compared to the white uniforms. According to the records produced after the muster, many units wore mixed uniforms, occasionally showing dragoons still in green, and chevauxlegers in white. Therefore on 27 January 1805 a new regulation was issued. The first two chevauxlegers regiments, plus Nr.4 – which was the heir of the former Latour Regiment, specially awarded for its loyalty during the Austrian Low Countries campaign – continued to wear the green jackets, while all the other chevauxlegers regiments definitively received the white ones. On campaign this resulted in problematic attempts to visually distinguish white dragoons from white chevauxlegers: except for the button colours, white metal for dragoons and yellow for chevauxlegers, the only difference was the bridles and reins used by the latter.

The economic shortage of the period 1814–1815 affected every aspect of the equipment of the Austrian army. Here is a *Husar Geimeiner* belonging to Kaiser Regiment (Nr. 1) who has replaced the regulation cloak with a blanket of buff and lamb fur of the type characteristic of rural Hungarian clothing. (Authors' archive).

50 Already before 1805, the German cavalry helm gradually had changed its shape, with a progressive heightening of the comb. Nevertheless, the practice of increasing the comb height seems to have spread among the cavalry officers since 1798, in order to differentiate their headdress from the infantry one.

51 Karger, *Die Entwicklung der Adjustierung, Rüstung und Bewaffnung*, p.202.

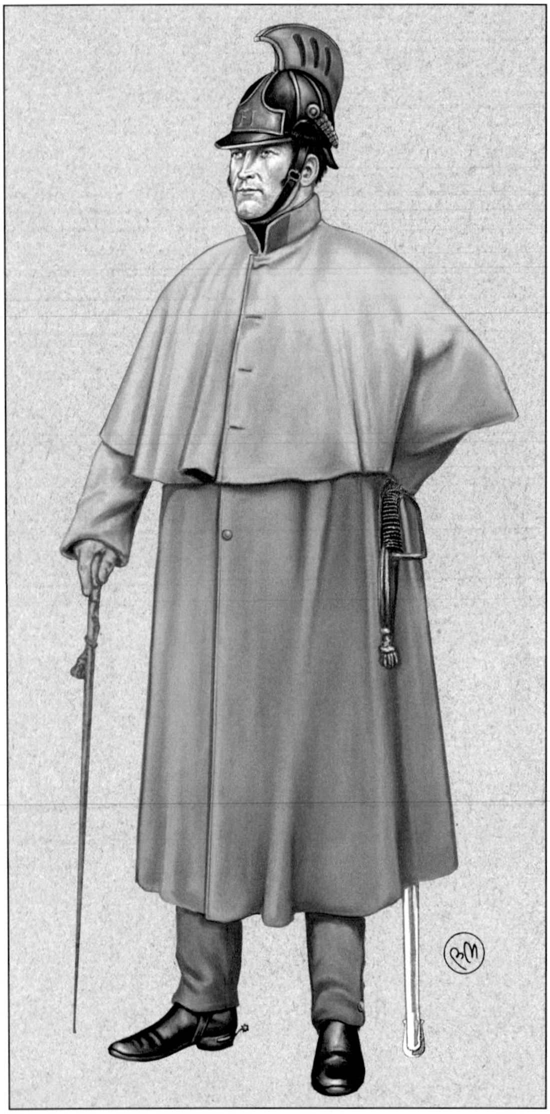

German cavalry *Rittmeister*, 1811–15, wearing the *Roquelor* with cape and the new collar with patch introduced in 1809. (Illustration by Bruno Mugnai)

In 1806 chevauxlegers regiments 1, 2 and 4 still wore the dark green *Röckel*, while 3, 5 and 6 were uniformed in white. It was during this period that chevauxlegers changed their old facings in order to have a new definitive *Egalisierung*. The case of the Walloon regiment Latour represented a significant exception, because it received a particular award upon the death of its colonel proprietor, Count Baillet de Latour. The Emperor himself, with a 'Supreme Resolution' dated 9 January 1806, dealt with the matter three days later, as stated in the regiment's history:

> The Chevaux-Legers Regiment Latour, which, from its former days, always had the green coat, must continue to maintain such and, to maintain also their dark red Egalisierung, received during the Seven Years War. Rank and file of the regiment, most of which were Walloons, having left behind their belongings in the lost homeland, were grateful and delighted for this, faithfully serving under the Imperial standards.[52]

However, the differences remained unresolved: in 1814 the newly established Chevauxlegers Regiment Nr.7 wore green coats with crimson facings and white metal buttons. Regiments Nr.1, 2 and 4 were allowed to wear green coats and white breeches as had been the case before 1798.

No significant changes occurred regarding the rank distinctives and uniforms, except for the *Fourier* in 1806, who received a new uniform identical for all the cavalry. This comprised a black felt bicorne hat with black silk *Rosette* cockade, *hechtgrau* coat with collar, cuffs and turnbacks in the regiment's *Egalisierung* facing colour; *hechtgrau* breeches and black gaiters. As a winter coat the *Fourier* wore the *Roquelor* in the German cavalry and uhlans, and the *Gepernek* in the hussars. The weapons included sword or sabre with *Portepee* like the *Primaplana* ranks.[53]

Also the *Fourierschützen* changed their uniforms, and in 1807 they were dressed with the regiment's uniform with reduced armament and equipment.[54] The same change affected the *Privatdiener*, except for the headdress, which remained the black felt *Corsican* hat.

52 Gustav Amon von Treuenfest, *Geschichte des k. k. Dragoner-Regimentes Feldmarschall Alfred Fürst zu. Windiscb-Graetz Nr.14* (Vienna: Verlag des Regimentes, 1886), p.383.

53 Karger, *Die Entwicklung der Adjustierung, Rüstung und Bewaffnung*, p.390.

54 Karger, *Die Entwicklung der Adjustierung, Rüstung und Bewaffnung*, p.392.

In the 1805 the hair queue was finally abolished, while moustaches remained obligatory only for rank and file.

The 1805 pattern was confirmed by Archduke Carl's regulations issued in 1811. Some changes concerned the helm, which was modified with new chinstraps covered with gilt scales alongside the black leather chinstraps for functional use. In the same year, some adjustments affected the *Roquelor* greatcoat, which regained the patches on the collar, in the facing colour. The waistcoat became white and tailless for all ranks and branches, with a short white standing collar and buttons in white or yellow metal.

Field officers retained the coat with laced cuffs. A unified version of overall trousers in grey cloth with metal buttons was also prescribed for all the cavalry branches. Every informal *Überrock* for officers was abolished and replaced by the one in *hechtgrau*, moreover they received a Spencer short coat tailored in the facing colours for undress uniform.[55] As the troopers in winter, officers wore the white *Roquelor* with metal buttons, but now with a removable cape extending to the elbow. Yellow leather gloves with cuffs continued to be issued to officers of all ranks. Belts and equipment with gilded fittings remained unchanged.

The 1811 regulation issued detailed rules for the rank insignia, specially for the *Professionisten*, who were often dressed with informal or arbitrary uniforms. Field and company officers maintained their traditional rank's marks and also NCOs and corporals held their distinctive sword knots and cane, while for *Cadett* and *Expropriis Cadett* was prescribed the same uniform as for the troopers, but with a company officer's helm with woollen crest, officer's sword with *Primaplana* knot and officer's leather gloves. The *Oberschmied* (senior smith) wore a felt bicorne with yellow and black tassels at the ends, a black silk piping edge 2.3cm (1 *Zoll*) high, a loop of silver or gold lace according to the buttons of the uniform on a 7.6cm diameter black cockade. The *Röckel* was as for the NCO but without shoulder strap for the cross belts; *dunkelgrau* waistcoat and trousers, facing colour and buttons as rank and file; sword, cane and sword knot like the *Wachtmeister*. The *Schmied* wore the same uniform but without cane and *Corporal*'s sword knot. After 1813, riding bags were used by *Schmied* and *Sattler* to transport their tools on horseback.

The *Profoss* continued to be uniformed like the NCO, but with a laced felt hat. Officer's servants – *Privatdiener* – wore

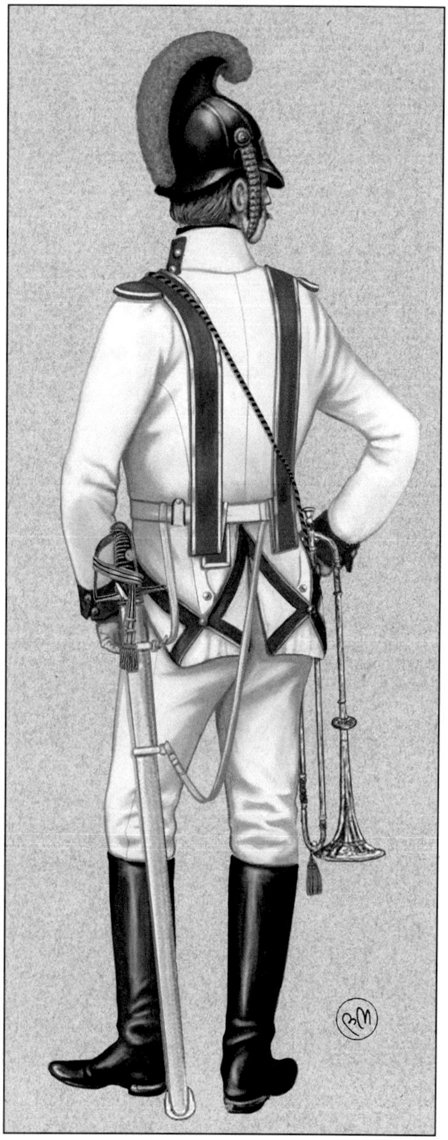

Cuirassier Trompete, 1813–15. According to some eyewitnesses, cuirassier musicians added accessories to their uniform for special events such as parades or festive days. Some cuirassier musicians are depicted in background in a painting of Wilhelm von Kobell wearing a coat with false sleeves and epaulettes in the regiment facing colour. Among the trumpeters, Kobell depicted also a group of horsemen with kettledrums, notwithstanding this instrument had been removed from the cavalry regiments in 1769. (Illustration by Bruno Mugnai)

55 A woollen outer tail-coat with the tails omitted. It was worn as a short, waist-length, single-breasted jacket. It was originally named after George Spencer, 2nd Earl Spencer (1758–1834), who was reported to have worn a coat adapted after the tails were burned by coals from a fire.

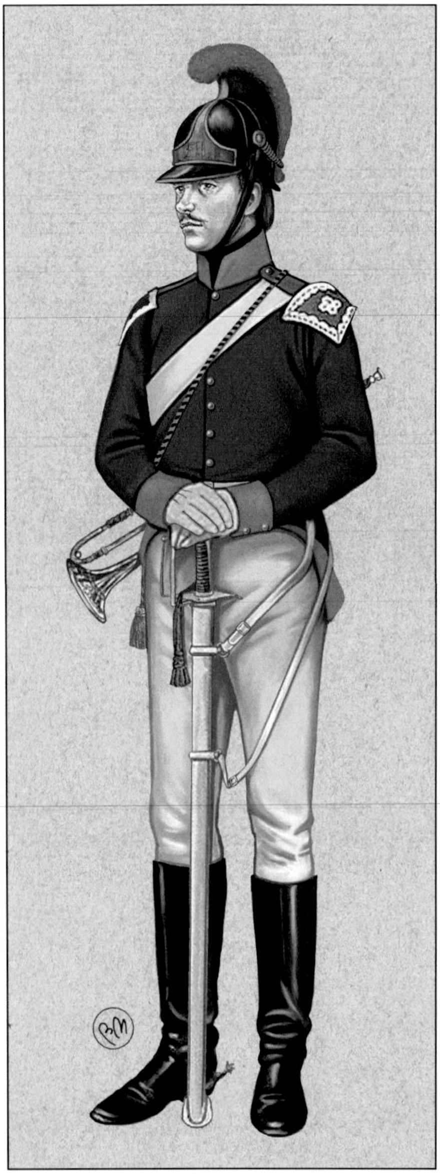

According to a French description of a trumpeter belonging to the Vincent Chevauxlegers Regiment (Nr. 4), captured in 1809 at Wagram, several arbitrary accessories persisted in the uniform of the musicians. The red crest on the helm seemed to be of 'regular' model, while the coat had a couple of violet(?) or probably *pompadourrot* shoulder straps with 'swallow nests', laced and embroidered in silver, like those issued to the infantry drummers. (Illustration by Bruno Mugnai)

the same uniform as the troopers but did not carry weapons. Despite the 1811 regulation addressing the matter in more detail, difformities and customised uniforms continued to be worn. According to the contemporary iconography, trumpeters carried accessories for modifying the ordinary dress in parade uniform. In 1814 some cuirassier trumpeters are depicted wearing the regular white *Röckel* with shoulder strap without fringes and false sleeve in the facing colour on the back.

Horse equipment was also regularised, introducing a new arrangement of the valise which now held spare legwear, shirt, handkerchief, socks, mittens, carbine cleaning-kit, pipeclay, razor, soap, small mirror, clothes brush and sewing kit with needles, thread, scissors and bodkin. The knapsack with the horseman's eating utensils was carried on the right side, while on the left another knapsack contained forage cap, haversack with bread, and the sickle and whetstone. Each horse was identified on the breastplate by a brass boss bearing the regimental number and the letter 'K', 'D' and 'C-L' for the respective branch.

Further changes affected the horse equipment, in order to preserve economic resources. In 1811 was a new saddle cover distributed to the troopers, modified with the elimination of the anterior section. This change halved the cost of the saddle cover not only concerning the cloth but particularly for the lesser quantity of laced edging required. The new model resulted in a saddle cover rectangular for German cavalry, pointed with a trapezoidal tail for hussars, and trapezoidal with rounded corners for uhlans. Now the pistol holsters were covered only by the lambskin cover, which increased its size in order to replace the cloth saddle cover for this function.[56] NCOs and officers retained the old model.

Hussars

In 1805, company officers adopted sword and sabretache with new model belts and slings of red-brown 'Russiani' leather with golden edgings.[57] Three years after, the cylindrical shako of all ranks was replaced by a new headdress quite similar to the French shako. Resistance was improved by a wide top and a dummy black leather turned up neck flap at the back. Further changes concerned the *Gepernek* cloak, which improved the protection for the neck with a wide turn-down collar. The typical hussar hair queues were dropped, but moustaches remained obligatory for all ranks.

56 Some contemporary illustrations the show lambskin cover with an enlarged cloth edge extending over the pistol holsters.

57 Karger, *Die Entwicklung der Adjustierung, Rüstung und Bewaffnung*, p.247.

With the 1811 regulations, further details affected the officers' shako. The front peak and rear flap neck were edged with golden lace. On the front of the headdress was a pleated *Rosette* cockade with a yellow edge, silver embroidery on the black, and golden lace loop. The regulation approved the field rank for *Stabsoffizeren*'s shako, formed by a double line of interlocking rings, the upper line usually of a large diameter than the lower. At the top was placed a hemispherical gold pompom with a black centre bearing the Emperor's cypher embroidered in gold silk, and black over yellow feather above. The functional chinstrap was of black leather like the trooper's model. The dimensions of the officers' shako were like those issued to the rank and file, however a higher headdress was allowed for field officers only.

In 1808 the *Profoss* adopted a long *dunkelblau* coat with *krapprot* facings and *lichtblau* trousers in the traditional Hungarian pattern.[58] The headgear was the black felt hat like that of the German cavalry's *Profoss*. The distinctives of rank were the same as the *Wachtmeister*.

After 1811, further modifications concerned the troopers' shako, replacing the deteriorable fabric cockade with a metal *Rosette* painted in yellow/black; the lace loop was also in metal. The *Professionisten* in the *Regimentsstab*, such as *Schneider*, *Ober Sattler* and *Ober Schmied* retained the distinctive ranks as for the *Wachtmeister*, while those in the squadrons ranked like the *Corporal*.

In 1814 were introduced some changes for the *Attile* Dolman, which took a new cut at the lower edge and its length was slightly diminished.

This shako belonged to *Oberst* Franz Adolph Prohaska, Baron of Guelfenberg, and commander of the Husaren Regiment Nr. 5 during the battle of Castel Guelfo, fought on 13 April 1814. Coeval writers referred that Prohaska suffered from a strong migraine for several days, but he survived the battle and became a *General der Cavallerie*. He died at the age of 94 in 1862. Note the double chain of rings on the upper section and the elaborated laces on the peak of the shako reserved to hussar field officers. (Collection of the Heeresgeschichtliches Museum, Vienna)

Uhlans

On 20 November 1806 the Aulic War Council abolished the golden laces for the top of NCO headgear. Their *Czapka* added as a distinctive a 1.3cm lace above the lower section. In 1809 the facing colour for Regiment Nr.3 was definitively established in *krebsrot*. In 1808, the top of the *Czapka* was covered with black leather for all ranks.

58 Karger, *Die Entwicklung der Adjustierung, Rüstung und Bewaffnung*, p.391.

Hussar shako bearing painted metal cockade and loops, 1813–15. (Private collection)

In 1809 a new *Kurtka* jacket was introduced. The major modification concerned the breastplate, which had an increased width and modified pattern. A new standing collar was added and increased to 10cm high (4 *Zoll*). Further changes concerned the introduction of a fringed woollen shoulder strap in yellow on the left shoulder for troopers, and in silk for NCOs. On the right shoulder was a simple shoulder strap in green cloth piped in red for troopers and in yellow for NCOs. The *Kurtka* for the officers of all ranks had two shoulder straps with silk fringes and black piping in the centre. However, poor observance of the regulations seemed to be a widespread practice, at least judging by the numerous appeals sent by commanders-in-chief to colonels concerning respect of the rules for uniforms. The Emperor also dealt with the matter, noting that almost in every regiment the officers had their uniforms modified according to their personal taste, forcing him to ask them to observe the regulations. The Imperial order was effective, therefore the uhlan officers donated their silver spurs to the national mint in 1810, and with them also the silver chains of the *Czapka*. Only use of silver on the cartridge box was tolerated, but only if already existing, and with the obligation to adopt the prescribed black leather item for the newly appointed officers. Irregular *Kurtka* and sashes were also abolished.

The regulation of 1811 replaced the *Czapka* of previous model with the new one introduced for the 3rd Regiment: now the square top diminished its diagonal to 30.5cm. The officers' headdress retained its particularities, but more detailed instructions concerned the gold laced peaks, gilt chains and lion-head bosses of the belt cartridge box. Furthermore, the leather skull of the *Czapka* was separated from the upper section by a wide 4.6cm (1 *Zoll*, 3 *Strich*) gold lace with two interwoven black stripes. The headdress had golden yellow/black cords and a 35cm feather plume in black over yellow. As their own rank insignia, field officers retained the golden piping on the square's edges. The golden button pattern cockade in yellow/black with the Emperor's cypher in its black centre was the same for company and field officers.

The *Kurtka* retained its traditional dark green, now with a *carmoisinrot* standing collar 10.5cm high (4 *Zoll*), pointed cuffs, lapels and turnbacks, with yellow metal buttons. The length of the *Kurtka* on the rear must be enough to cover the buttocks. The epaulettes on the shoulders were preserved. The *Roquelor* overcoat remained grey/white as for the German cavalry, now issued with the pike-grey *Überrock* for officers of all ranks, with the collar in *carmoisinrot* for all the regiments.

The *Vorschrift Adjustierung* issued in 1811 imposed more detailed regulations on the uhlan uniform. Double red lace on the trousers was allowed for field officers only. The *Leibel*, or *Zupanek*,[59] was manufactured in baize straw-cloth complete with sleeves and cuffs, with smooth yellow metal buttons. It was a very small garment always worn under the *Kurtka*. *Stabsoffizieren* had distinctive lace on the *Leibel* consisting of a golden border in the same shape and size of the *General Wachtmeister*'s laces. The uhlan saddle covers followed the hussar pattern, and lost the anterior section in the items issued to the troopers.

The *Adjustierung* issued in 1811 clarified the dress for *Professionisten* and other personnel within the regiments. The ranks of the *Regimentsstab* wore the *Czapka* with the distinctive on the headdress as for the NCOs. The *Fourier* retained the sabre knot as for the *Wachtmeister*, while the *Profoss* adopted the dark blue uniform and black felt hat as for the hussars, but with white trousers.

In 1813 a new Regiment Nr.4 was raised and the colonel proprietor became the Emperor Franz I in person. The facing colour on the *Czapka* was white.

In 1813, at the eve of the *Befreiungskrieg*, lack of resources reverberated in the shortage of uniforms and equipment. This forced the regiments to turn to every resource in order to dress the troops adequately. Radetzky left an impressive picture of the situation, saying that soldiers often appeared in linen smocks and underpants, while about one third of the infantry lacked ammunition pouches and then the cartridges were ruined by the rain.[60] The emergency lasted until November 1813, when finally a British transport docked in Fiume and delivered supplies and other war material to the exhausted Austrian intendancy.[61] The iconography of 1813–14 is mainly dedicated to immortalise victorious episodes and is little inclined to provide the real appearance of the soldiers. However some images seem to confirm the improvisation in matter of uniforms. German cavalry *Roquelor*s appear in the hussar dress instead of the traditional *Gepernek* and other unusual details indicate the disparate origin of certain items. Also in matter of colour some licenses were admitted. For instance, still in 1815, the Austrian commissars in France required cloth for uniforms in Lyon and Forez without asking too many details about regulation colours.[62]

Study of an Austrian dragoon, copy after Wilhelm von Kobell, 1814. This fine work shows in detail helm, equipment and the coat with the higher collar introduced after 1805. (Private collection)

59 The Polish name for this item.

60 Horstenau, *Die Tage von Dresden 1813*, p.31.

61 Rothenberg, *Napoleon's Great Adversary*, p.229.

62 In 1815, in occupied France, the Austrian Quatermaster Commissary, Chevalier Lehmann, of the Army of Upper Italy demanded the province deliver in 15 days 2,250 'aunes de Vienne' (0.779m) of black taffeta and the same of yellow for the pennants of the three (of four existing) uhlan regiments and a further 100,000 aunes of white cloth for infantry uniform, 8,000 aunes of light blue for the Hungarian infantry, 2,000 of brown for the Croatians, 1,000 of red for hussars, 1,000 of light grey for the *Jägers*, 54,000 skirts, 54,000 underpants, 10,000 pairs of gaiters or 8,000

Field Signs: *Eichenlaub*

The term *Feldzeichen* is commonly used in the military literature as a generic term for flags and standards, all Austrian regulations until 1918 referred also to a badge, which was equally worn in different forms, from the Supreme Commander to the common soldiers:

> The field emblem was to be taken by all detachments, disengaged troops and the generals who commanded them: on the birthday of His k. k. Apostolic Majesty, on the Day of Resurrection (Easter) and on the Corpus Christi day, and in all Parades adjustments afore His k. k. Apostolic Majesty, then on occasion of such ceremonies in which the generals, not in campaign, appear in high uniform.[63]

The *Feldzeichen* served as an identification mark for all members of a 'field side' which, due to the very undifferentiated military clothing, was absolutely necessary since the end of the seventeenth century for the identification between friend and enemy. Such signs, which were necessary in times in which no regular uniforms were introduced, continued to be worn in a great variety of patterns even when it was no longer essential.[64] Austrian soldiers carries three green oak-leaves – the *Laub* – on their headdress for distinguishing friends from enemies. This sign was already carried by the Austrian soldiers in the conflicts against Louis XIV, and became the typical field sign until the dissolution of the Habsburg Empire in 1918. According to Ottenfeld and Teuber, the custom began under Prince Eugene of Savoy: 'In summer, a soldier must be provided with a green foliage, in the winter with a straw stick [*Strohwisch*] or other marks decided by the commander-in-chief, in order to identify the side to which he belongs.' However, this was more than a military custom, and year upon year the oak leaves became the main symbol of the Imperial army. The importance of the field sign is confirmed on several occasions also in the Napoleonic wars: 'No oak leaves on their headgear' Baron Comeau said in his memoirs in 1793.[65] This means that oak leaves were a kind of field award and not a simple field sign.

---

aunes of black fabric, 10,000 breeches and 4,000 trousers *à la hongroise*, 12,000 aunes for smocks, 8,000 aunes for lining, 20,000 pairs of shoes for the German infantry, 10,000 Hungarian pairs of shoes and 20,000 complete infantry bags. Thanks to Löic Lilian for this information.

63 Herbert Breiteneder, 'Feldzeichen. Ein Begriff aus der Österreichischen Militärsprache bis 1918', in *Militaria Austriaca 1977*, Gesellschaft für Österreichisches Heereskunde, p.1.

64 At Warsaw in 1656 the Brandenburg and Swedish soldiers wore straw wisps on their hats. In the battle of Vienna on 12 September 1683 the Poles wore straw ropes around their headdresses in order to differentiate them from the Ottomans, who carried similar dress and equipment. The Prussians wore two red hearts on their headgear in front of Stralsund in 1715, probably indicating an alliance with the Saxons. In 1762 Frederick II issued to the Prussian cavalry white feathered headgear making it easier to distinguish them among similarly uniformed enemy cavalry. Among the great variety of allied uniforms in the War of 1813, the Prussians adopted a white band around the left forearm.

65 Sébastien Joseph Baron de Comeau de Charry, *Souvenirs des guerres d'Allemagne pendant la Révolution et l'Empire* (Paris: Plon, 1900), p.80: 'Ce qui touchait notre droite était deux bataillons du régiment hongrois de Giulay [*sic*] qui avaient été malheureux à la guerre et subissaient encore une punition à la guerre: point de drapeau, point de musique, point de canon, point de feuilles de chêne à leur coiffure!'

Plate A

General Stab

1. Hungarian *General der Cavallerie*, 1809–12; 2. *Feldmarschall* in field dress, 1805–11; 3. *Flügel Adjutant*, 1799–1810

(Illustration by Bruno Mugnai, © Helion & Company)

See Colour Plate Commentaries for further information.

Regimentsstab, Stabsdragoner and Botenmeister
1. Chevauxlegers Regiment Nr. 6, *Rechnungsführer*, 1801–1805; 2. Stabsdragoner Regiment, *Gemeiner*, 1812; 3. *Botenmeister*, 1813–1814
(Illustration by Bruno Mugnai, © Helion & Company)
See Colour Plate Commentaries for further information.

Heavy Cavalry, 1792–1805

1. Carabinier Regiment Nr. 1 (Nr. 5) Sachsen-Teschen, *Gemeiner* in high dress, 1792–1798; 2. Cuirassieren Regiment Nr. 8, Hohenzollern; *Rittmeister* in service dress, 1799–1805; 3. Cuirassieren Regiment Nr. 4, Kavanagh; *Trompete*, 1802–1805

(Illustration by Bruno Mugnai, © Helion & Company)

See Colour Plate Commentaries for further information.

Heavy Cavalry 1806–15

1. Cuirassieren Regiment Nr. 9, Nassau-Usingen; *Gemeiner* in service dress, 1807–1815;
2. Cuirassieren Regiment Nr. 1; Kaiser; *Gemeiner* in campaign dress, 1812–1815

(Illustration by Bruno Mugnai, © Helion & Company)

See Colour Plate Commentaries for further information.

Plate E

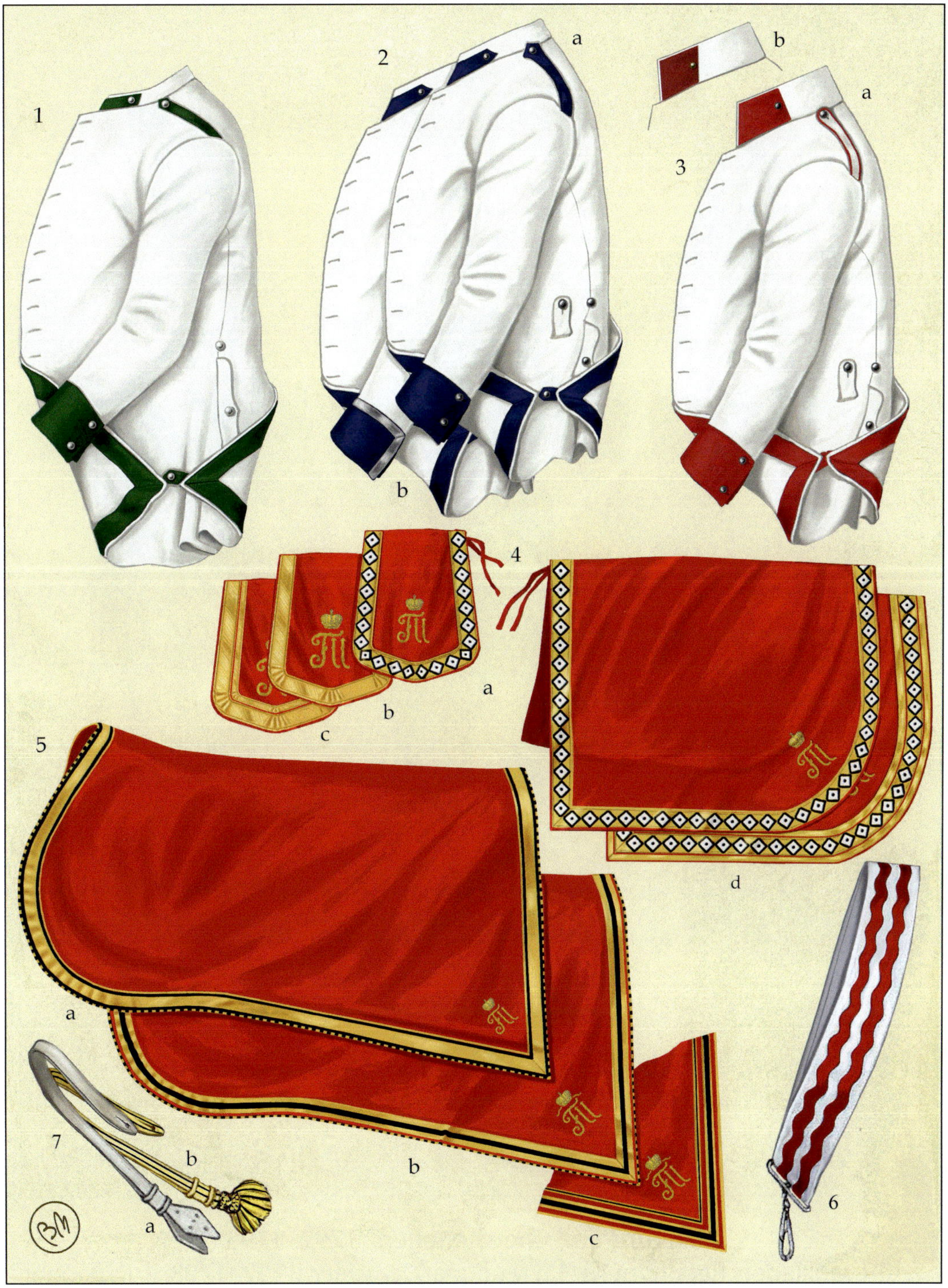

Cuirassier Uniform, Details
(Illustration by Bruno Mugnai, © Helion & Company)
See Colour Plate Commentaries for further information.

Plate F

Dragoons and Chevauxlegers, 1792–1798

1. Chevauxlegers Regiment Nr. 11, Modena; *Gemeiner*, 1792–1798; 2. Dragoner Regiment Royal Allemand; *Gemeiner*, 1792–1797; 3. Leichte Dragoner Regiment Nr. 11, Latour; *Wachtmeister*, 1799–1800.

(Illustration by Bruno Mugnai, © Helion & Company)

See Colour Plate Commentaries for further information.

Plate G

Dragoner, Chevauxlegers, and *Jäger zu Pferde*, 1798–1805

1. Regiment Jäger zu Pferd, Bussy; *Gemeiner*, 1798–1801; 2. Dragoner Regiment Nr. 1, Erzherzog Johann Baptist; *Gemeiner*, 1802–1805; 3. Chevauxlegers Regiment Nr. 1, Kaiser, *Rittmeister* with cloak, 1802–1803

(Illustration by Bruno Mugnai, © Helion & Company)

See Colour Plate Commentaries for further information.

Plate H

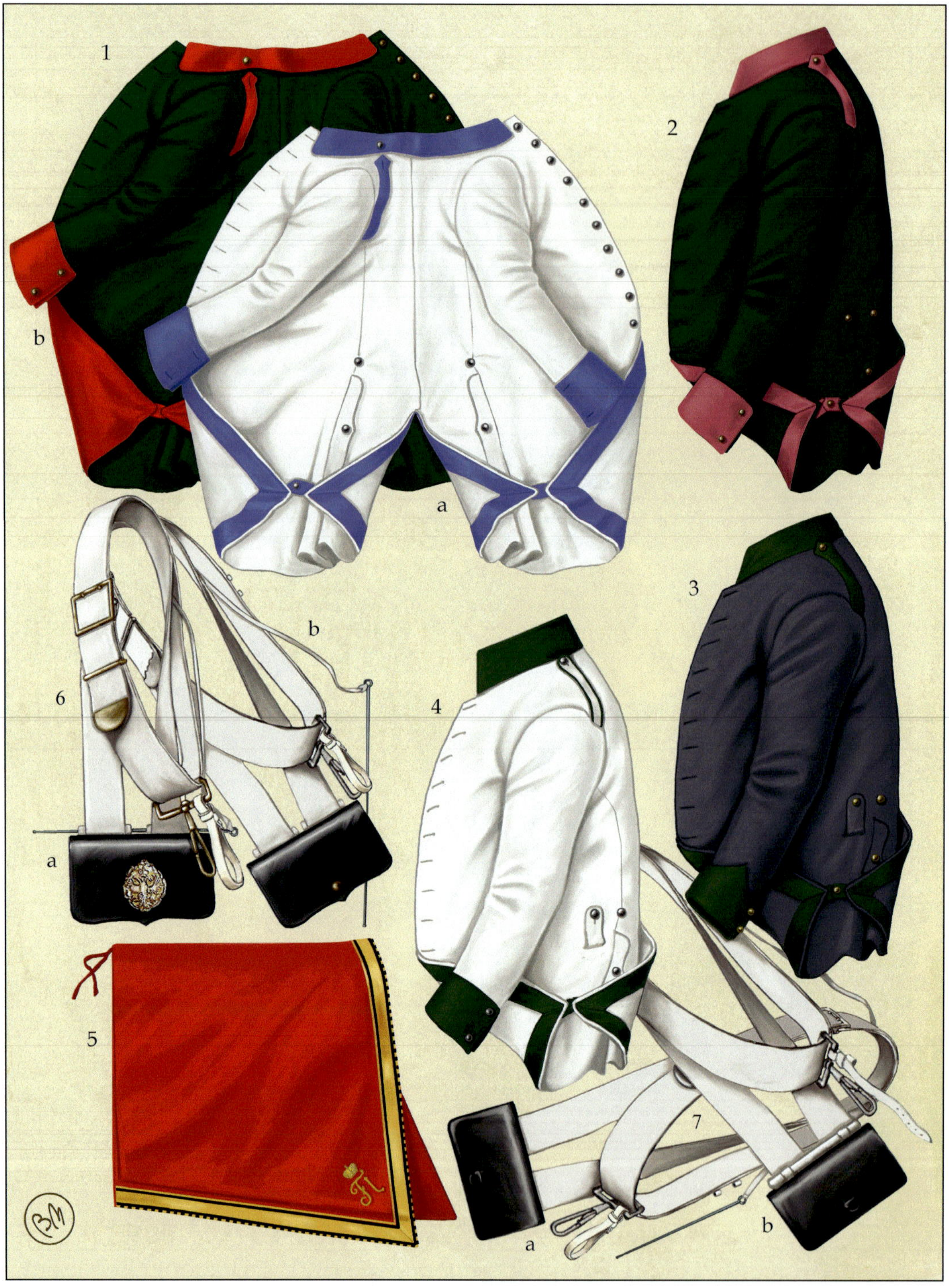

Dragoner, Chevauxlegers and *Jäger zu Pferd* Uniforms, Details

(Illustration by Bruno Mugnai, © Helion & Company)

See Colour Plate Commentaries for further information.

Hussars, 1792–1809

1. Frei Corps Rohan, *Gemeiner*, 1797–1798; 2. Husaren Regiment Nr. 1, Kaiser; *Wachtmeister* in high dress, 1799–1804; 3. Husaren Regiment Nr. 3, Erzherzog Ferdinand Carl; *Gemeiner* in service dress, 1805–1809

(Illustration by Bruno Mugnai, © Helion & Company)

See Colour Plate Commentaries for further information.

Plate J

Hussars, 1810–15

1. Husaren Regiment Nr. 5, Ott; *Unterlieutenant*, honorary standard bearer, 1814;
2. Husaren Regiment Nr. 10, Mészáros-Stipsicz; *Gemeiner* in *Gepernek* cloak, 1810–15

(Illustration by Bruno Mugnai, © Helion & Company)

See Colour Plate Commentaries for further information.

Hussar Uniform, Details

(Illustration by Bruno Mugnai, © Helion & Company)

See Colour Plate Commentaries for further information.

Plate L

Uhlans, 1792–1815

1. Uhlanen Regiment Nr. 2 (Uhlanen Freiwilligen Korps), *Gemeiner*, 1792–98;
2. Uhlanen Regiment Nr.3, Erzherzog Carl; *Gemeiner* in high dress, 1809–1810;
3. Uhlanen Regiment Nr. 4, Kaiser; *Oberst*, 1814–15

(Illustration by Bruno Mugnai, © Helion & Company)

See Colour Plate Commentaries for further information.

Uhlan Uniform, Details

(Illustration by Bruno Mugnai, © Helion & Company)

See Colour Plate Commentaries for further information.

Plate N

The Cavalry of the *Reichsarmee*

1. Schwäbischer Kreis, Dragoner Regiment Württemberg, 1792; 2. Fränkischer Kreis, Cuirassieren Regiment Tresskow, 1792–93; 3. Fränkischer Kreis, Dragoner Regiment Anspach, 1792–93

(Illustration by Bruno Mugnai © Helion & Company)

See Colour Plate Commentaries for further information.

Austrian Cavalry Ensigns

1. Ordinary standard pattern for all specialties, 1792–1804; 2. Ordinary standard pattern for all specialties, 1805–1815; 3. Ordinary standard, unknown hussar regiment, 1805–15; 4. Regimental standard, Husaren Regiment Nr. 5, 1809–15; 5. *Ehrestandarte*, 1814; 6. Standard finial, 1792–1805; 7. Ensign cover

(Illustration by Bruno Mugnai, © Helion & Company)

See Colour Plate Commentaries for further information.

Farbtabelle

The Uniform Colours Table of the Austrian Army

See Colour Plate Commentaries for further information.

In Germany the oak is the 'tree of the homeland'. Furthermore, in the ancient German language, it is said that: 'Who carries oak leaves, indicates his own determination and that thereby nobody will can stop him. So it was recommended, therefore, to be careful with those carrying oak leaves, and, above all, to avoid jokes with these fellows, who didn't allow jokes.' The warrior's weapons put 'at rest' during wars and campaigns were usually hung up on an oak. Therefore it is easy to understand why ancient Germans (and Austrians) went into battle with oak leaves. This tradition received a great tribute when on 3 February 1814 the order was given to carry green leaves on the soldiers' headgear, as a national mark among the troops of the allied army who were facing Napoleon in Germany, in order to follow the Austrians' custom.

Uniform Colour Schemes, German Cavalry 1798

Cuirassiers

	Nr. in 1798	Commander in 1798	Facings	Coat	Breeches	Buttons	1792–97
Kaiser	1	Conrad Weeber	*pompadourrot*	W	W	W	Karabinieren Regiment Nr.2
Este	2	Carl von Willenstein	black	W	W	W	Cuirassieren Regiment Nr.29
Sachsen-Teschen	3	Christian von Wolfskehl	*pompadourrot*	W	W	Y	Karabinieren Regiment Nr.1
Czartoryski*	4	Schmidlin	*dunkelblau*	W	W	Y	Cuirassieren Regiment Nr.27
Zeschwitz*	5	Dienersperg	*grasgrün*	W	W	Y	Cuirassieren Regiment Nr.10
Melas**	6	Ignaz Eggermann	*lichtblau*	W	W	Y	Royal Allemand
Lothringen	7	Johann Mercandin	*dunkelblau*	W	W	W	Cuirassieren Regiment Nr.21
Hohenzollern	8	Fabrizio Serbelloni	*ponceaurot*	W	W	Y	Cuirassieren Regiment Nr.4
Nassau-Usingen	9	Franz de Valvasor	*lichtblau*	W	W	W	Cuirassieren Regiment Nr.14
Leiberich	10	Joseph Walthür von Waldenau	black	W	W	Y	Cuirassieren Regiment Nr.20
Anspach*	11	Bolza	*ponceaurot*	W	W	W	Cuirassieren Regiment Nr.33
Kavanagh	12	Leopold Pálffy ab Erdödy	*grasgrün*	W	W	W	Cuirassieren Regiment Nr.12

*Disbanded in 1802
***Dragoner* in 1802

Light Dragoons

Denomination	Nr. in 1798	Commander in 1798	Coat	Facings	Breeches	Buttons
Kaiser (1. Chevauxlegers in 1802)	1	Pilati	*meergrün*	*ponceaurot*	W	Y
Erzherzog Ferdinand (Disbanded in 1802)	2	Philip von Grünne	*meergrün*	*kaisergelb*	W	W
Erzherzog Johann Baptist (1. Dragoner in 1802)	3	Carl De la Motte	*meergrün*	orange	W	Y
Karaiczay (2. Chevauxlegers in 1802)	4	Joseph Nimptsch	*meergrün*	*pompadourrot*	W	W
Modena (Disbanded in 1802)	5	Roschkovski	*meergrün*	*orange-gelb*	W	W
Coburg (Disbanded in 1802)	6	Hadik de Futak	*meergrün*	gris de lin	W	W
Vacant, ex Valdeck (2. Dragoner in 1802)	7	Weissmann von Weissenstein	*meergrün*	*schwefelgelb*	W	W
Württemberg (3. Dragoner in 1802)	8	Johann Festenberg	*meergrün*	gris de lin	W	Y
Liechtenstein (*Stabsdragoner* in 1798)	9	Görupp Von Besanez	*meergrün*	black	W	W
Lobkowitz (3. Chevauxlegers in 1802)	10	Max Joseph Thurn und Taxis	*meergrün*	*lichtblau*	W	W
Latour (4. Chevauxlegers in 1802)	11	Ferdinand de Mondet	*meergrün*	*ponceaurot*	W	Y
Kinsky (5. Chevauxlegers in 1802)	12	Albert Stahel	*meergrün*	*lichtblau*	W	Y
Vacant (1801: Rosemberg; (6. Chevauxlegers in 1802)	13	Joseph von Egger	*meergrün*	*ponceaurot*	W	W
Levenehr (4. Dragoner in 1802)	14	Joseph Zinn	*meergrün*	*kaisergelb*	W	Y
Prinz Eugen von Savoyen (5. Dragoner in 1802)	15	Malachias Hermann	*meergrün*	black	W	Y

German Cavalry Regiment Uniforms, 1802–1815

Cuirassiers

Regiments	Commander in 1802	Coat	Facings	Breeches	Buttons	Year	Proprietor or Denomination
1. Cuirassieren Regt.	Laurencin D'Armont	W	*pompadourrot*	W	W	1802	Kaiser

2. Cuirassieren Regt.	Stanislaw Auer	W	black	W	W	1802	Este
3. Cuirassieren Regt.	Josef Radetzky	W	*pompadourrot*	W	Y	1802	Sachsen-Teschen
4. (former Nr.12) Cuirassieren Regt.	Anton Picking	W	*apfelgrün*	W	W	1802	Kavanagh
5. (former Nr.9.) Cuirassieren Regt.	Anton Kirchner	W	*lichtblau*	W	W	1802	Nassau-Usingen
6. (former Nr.10.) Cuirassieren Regt.	Wöllwarth	W	black	W	Y	1802	Mack–Gottesheim–Liechtenstein
7. Cuirassieren Regt.	Clemens von Thünefeld	W	*dunkelblau*	W	W	1802	Lothringen
8. Cuirassieren Regt.	Josef Clary	W	*ponceaurot*	W	Y	1802	Hohenzollern

Dragoons and Chevauxlegers

Regiments	Commander in 1802	Coat	**Facings**	Breeches	Buttons	**Proprietor or Denomination**
Dragoner Regt. Nr.1	Speth	W	black	W	W	Erzherzog Johann Baptist
Dragoner Regt. Nr.2	Hager von Altensteig	W	*dunkelblau*	W	W	Hohenlohe-Ingelfingen
Dragoner Regt. Nr.3	Wodnjanski	W	*carmoisin*	W	W	Württemberg
Dragoner Regt. Nr.4	Franz von Tige	W	*krebsrot*	W	W	Levenehr
Dragoner Regt. Nr.5	Malachias Hermann	W	*grasgrün*	W	W	Prinz Eugen von Savoyen
Dragoner Regt. Nr.6	Strachwitz	W	*lichtblau*	W	W	Melas
Chevauxlegers Regt.. Nr.1	Johann De Best	G	*pompadourrot**	W	Y	Kaiser
Chevauxlegers Regt. Nr.2	Carl Provenchères	W	*grasgrün*	W	Y	Franz Hohenzollern
Chevauxlegers Regt. Nr.3	Bernhardt Grosser	W	*krebsrot*	W	Y	Joseph Fürst Lobkowitz
Chevauxlegers Regt. Nr.4	Armand Nordmann	G	*pompadourrot*	W	Y	Latour
Chevauxlegers Regt. Nr.5	Carl Kinsky	W	*lichtblau*	W	Y	Kinsky
Chevauxlegers Regt. Nr.6	Carl Civalart	W	black	W	Y	Rosenberg

*In 1807 the *Egalisierung* facing colour changed to *krebsrot*, then in 1810 to *ponceaurot*.
Note: after 1802, facing colours became definitive only for dragoons.

Chevauxlegers, 1814–1815

Proprietor	Number in 1802	Coat	Facings:	Breeches	Buttons
Kaiser	Chevauxlegers Regiment Nr.1	*dunkelgrün*	*ponceaurot*	white	Y
Hohenzollern	Chevauxlegers Regiment Nr.2	*dunkelgrün*	*carmoisin*	white	Y
Lobkowitz	Chevauxlegers Regiment Nr.3	white	*ponceaurot*	white	Y
Latour	Chevauxlegers Regiment Nr.4	*dunkelgrün*	*Pompadourrot*	white	Y
Kinsky	Chevauxlegers Regiment Nr.5	white	*lichtblau*	white	Y
Rosenberg	Chevauxlegers Regiment Nr.6	white	*carmoisin*	white	Y
Vacant, Notstitz in 1815	Chevauxlegers Regiment Nr.7	*dunkelgrün*	*carmoisin*	white	Y

Hussars (1798–1815)

Nr.	Denomination	Buttons	Shako	Pelisse and Attila	Breeches
1	Kaiser	Y	black	*dunkelblau*	
2	Erzherzog Joseph	Y	*graprot*	*lichtblau*	
3	Erzherzog Ferdinand Carl	Y	*hechtgrau*	*dunkelblau*	
4	Vecsey, later Hessen-Homburg	W	*lichtblau*	*papagei grün*	*ponceaurot*
5	Vacant, then Ott	W	*graprot*	*dunkelgrün*	*krebsrot*
6	Blankenstein	Y	black	*lichtblau*	
7	Vacant then Liechtenstein	W	*grasgrün*	*lichtblau*	
8	Würmser then Nauendorff and later Kienmayer	Y	black	*papagei grün*	*ponceaurot*
9	Erdődy then Frimont	Y	black	*dunkelgrün*	*pompadourrot*
10	Mészáros then Stipsicz	Y	*grasgrün*	*lichtblau*	
11	Székler Grenz-Husaren	W	black	*dunkelblau*	
12	Croatische-Slavonisches Grenz-Husaren*	W	black	*hechtgrau*	*hellblau*
	Palatinal-Husaren (1802)**	W	black	*kornblau*	*kornblau*

* Disbanded in 1801
** Raised in 1802

Uhlans (1798–1811)

Nr.	Denomination	Commander in 1798	Czapka	Kurtka	Facings	Breeches	Buttons	Note
1	Merveldt	Wilgenheim	Y	G	*ponceaurot*	G	Y	
2	Schwarzenberg	Kinsky	G	G	*krebsrot*	G	Y	
3	Erzherzog Carl	Mensdorf	B*	G	*krebsrot*	G	Y	Raised in 1801

*In 1806 this regiment replaced the black *Czapka* with one with a *roseel-hellrot* (light scarlet) cover. In 1809 it changed again, becoming *krebsrot*.[66]

Uhlans (1811–1815)

Nr.	Denomination	Commander in 1798	Czapka:	Kurtka	Facings	Breeches	Buttons	Note
1	Sachsen-Coburg	Alberti	Y	G	*carmoisin*	G	Y	
2	Schwarzenberg	Mengen	G	G	*carmoisin*	G	Y	
3	Erzherzog Carl	Grozkowski	R	G	*carmoisin*	G	Y	
4	Kaiser	Devay	W	G	*carmoisin*	G	Y	Raised in 1814

Freikorps 1809–1814

Nr.	Denomination	Strength	Shako	Pelisse and Dolman	Breeches	Buttons	Note
-	Husaren Abteilung des Schill'schen Freikorps*	2 sqn	black	dark blue	dark blue	Y	Raised in March 1809. Disbanded in May 1809
-	Erzherzog Carl Siebenbürgisches Husaren-Corps	4 sqn	*hechtgrau*	*dunkelblau*	*lichtblau*	Y	Raised in June 1809. Disbanded in January 1810
-	Carneville Frei-Husaren	½ sqn	Uniform unknown				Not completed 1809
-	Neutraer Husaren	2 sqn	Uniform unknown				Raised in June 1809. Disbanded in October 1809

66 Karger, *Die Entwicklung der Adjustierung, Rüstung und Bewaffnung*, p.274.

-	Österreichischer Kosaken	3 sqn	Cossack-style dark blue coat with red facings	Raised in May 1809 Disbanded in January 1810
-	Cavallerie Abteilung der Fränkischen Legion	3 sqn	Uhlan-style dark green uniform	Raised in July 1809 Disbanded in December 1809
-	Böhmisches Dragoner	8 sqn	Uniform unknown	Raised in May 1809 Disbanded in December 1810

Nr.	Denomination	Strength	Shako	Pelisse and Dolman	Breeches	Buttons	Note
-	Westphälischen Legion Husaren Regiment Nr.1	3 sqn	black	*dunkelgrün*	*graprot*	Y	Raised in April 1813 Disbanded in May 1814
-	Westphälischen Legion Husaren Regiment Nr.1	3 sqn	red	*kornblau*	*kornblau*	Y	Raised in April 1813 Disbanded in May 1814
-	Kosaken Regiment	4 sqn	Uniform unknown		Raised in September 1813 Disbanded in June 1814		

Cavalry Weaponry

Carbines

Taking advantage of its rapidity and its highly emotional nature, the well-trained military horse was especially fit for charging the enemy in open spaces, but the Austrian cavalry continued to place great importance on firepower and trained its units to the tactics considered more useful to this purpose.

Fire could be delivered by cavalry in two ways:

- Individually (for instance by trooper forming the skirmish sequence)
- or tactical units (squadrons, divisions, etc.) formed in two ranks

However, the horse easily got upset by the very close and loud discharges to his left, right and behind. Sometimes the gunpowder would burn over the horses throwing them into panic. The best solution was to load the carbines shortly before the action, then deliver just one volley, draw sabres and charge. Firing numerous times was not a problem for the skirmishers, who had more time to charge, to shoot, and to retreat in order to reload. It was completely different matter for cavalry in close formation, which had to maintain order and correct distance in manoeuvre.

All cavalry firearms must, in general, have the characteristics of the infantry weapons; hence the carbines were different only in calibre, and

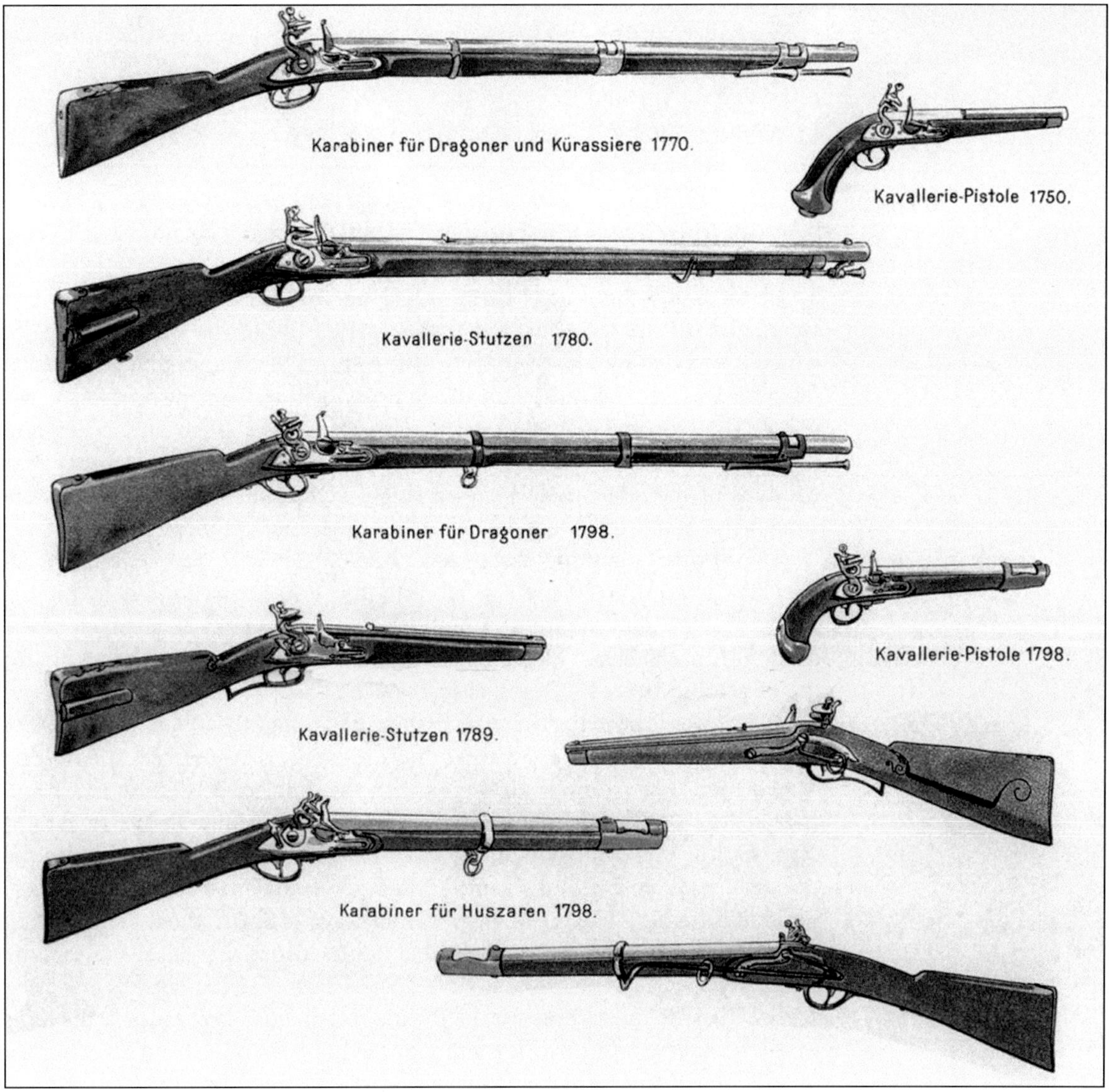

Cavalry carbines and pistols from Teuber-Ottenfeld's *Die Oesterreichische Armee von 1700 bis 1867.*

consequently also in charges and in ranges. In the Austrian cavalry two branches received 'karabiners': the dragoons and the hussars.

The dragoons' main firearm was the Model 1798 dragoon carbine, with a barrel length 91cm (2 feet 8 inches, 3 lines and 1 point),[67] with the stock it reached the overall length of 123.5cm, equal to 5 *Pfund* and 21 1/16 Löth (around 2.8kg). The hussar carbine was much shorter than that of the dragoons. The hussars' carbine was the 1798-pattern weapon with a barrel 45.7cm long

67 Ancient measurements, originally, were related to human body elements. Thus a *Klafter* corresponded to the widening extension of the arms sideways, an *Elle* (arm) corresponded to the length of an arm, a *Zoll* (thumb) corresponded to the width of a thumb. One *Fuss* or *Schuh* (foot) was = 12 *Zoll* (inches) = 31.6cm; 1 *Zoll* (inch) was = 12 *Linien* (lines) = 2.63cm; 1 *Linie* (line) = 12 *Punkte* (points) = 2.2mm; 1 *Punkt* (point) was = 0.18mm. These measurements are somewhat rounded; the correct measurements come from the ratio: 1 *Klafter* = 1.896484m.

(1 foot 6 inches). The overall length was 84.5cm. Moreover, the hussar carbine was much lighter compared to the dragoon model, only 4lb, 5 1/16 *Löth* (2.45kg),[68] so it could be held with one hand without difficulty, aiming and firing like a pistol. The lock was the same on both carbines, but smaller than that on the infantry weapons. However in the carbine's lock was attached a blocking device, on the lock plate behind the hammer, by means of which the hammer, when it was at rest, was locked, which could have not been so easy when riding.

Incidentally, the hussar carbine had no ramrod because this was not supplied with the weapons, but it was carried under the cartridge box, to which it was tied by a leather string. The ramrod for *Stutzen* and other short firearms was carried on the cartridge cross-belt and was also used for the pistol. This particular item was characteristic of the Austrian cavalry and known as *Carabiner-und-Pistolenladstock*. Both the dragoon and hussar carbines of the later models shot a single 17.5 calibre ball, and they were similar to the infantry weapons, namely 8 lines and 2 points.

The optimal shooting distance for the hussar carbine was 60 *Schritte* (steps)[69] or around 40 metres, while if the horseman wanted to hit the breast of the enemy, he must aim at the abdomen within 30 steps, or at the head within 100 steps. Nevertheless the horseman could have certainly hit the target still from 150 steps, at least from substantial elevation. However, because it was longer, the dragoon carbine had a slightly greater range of fire.

After 1807, in the Austrian army, only dragoons, chevauxlegers and hussars were armed with carbines, dragoons with the long models and hussars and chevauxlegers with the short ones. Before 1807 the cuirassiers also carried carbines, however limited to only 16 men for each squadron. This was also the case for the uhlans, with the same 16 men for each squadron. The difference was that cuirassiers had the dragoon carbines, while uhlans those of hussars. In general there was a common opinion that carbines would have been unusable by all cavalry specialties, and that their use could have been the cause of upsetting horses. Because the carbine was held with both hands like a musket, the reins were left hanging on an arm, but although having well-trained and quiet horses, they did not assure to stand still during an action, especially when skirmishing, and therefore the carbine shot was always uncertain. The carbine remained in use among the light cavalry, which was confirmed in every campaign. First of all, because the carbine needed in the skirmish, which usually lasted for hours, which skirmisher would have the best chance of success, the one who fought with the carbine or the one with the pistol?

68 Here the weight measures of the gun calibres (catalogued for the weight of the ball shot) are made simpler using the pdr (pounders, *Pfünder* for Austrians). However there were some important differences between French and Austrian measures. Austrian measured weights in *Löth*, 32 of which made a *Wiener Pfund* (Austrian pound). One *Löth* was equal to the current 17.5g (0.62oz) so a *Pfund* was 560g and equal to 1,235lb (Imperial pounds). At least 100 *Pfünder* made 1 *Zentner* (56kg).

69 The Austrian Army measured distances in footsteps (*Schritte*) or 0.63 metres. One *Schritt* = 2 *Füsse* (1 *Füss* = 316cm). The true Austrian length measure was the *Zoll* (inch). Twelve *Wiener Zoll* made one *Füss* (and two *Füsse* made a *Schritt*).

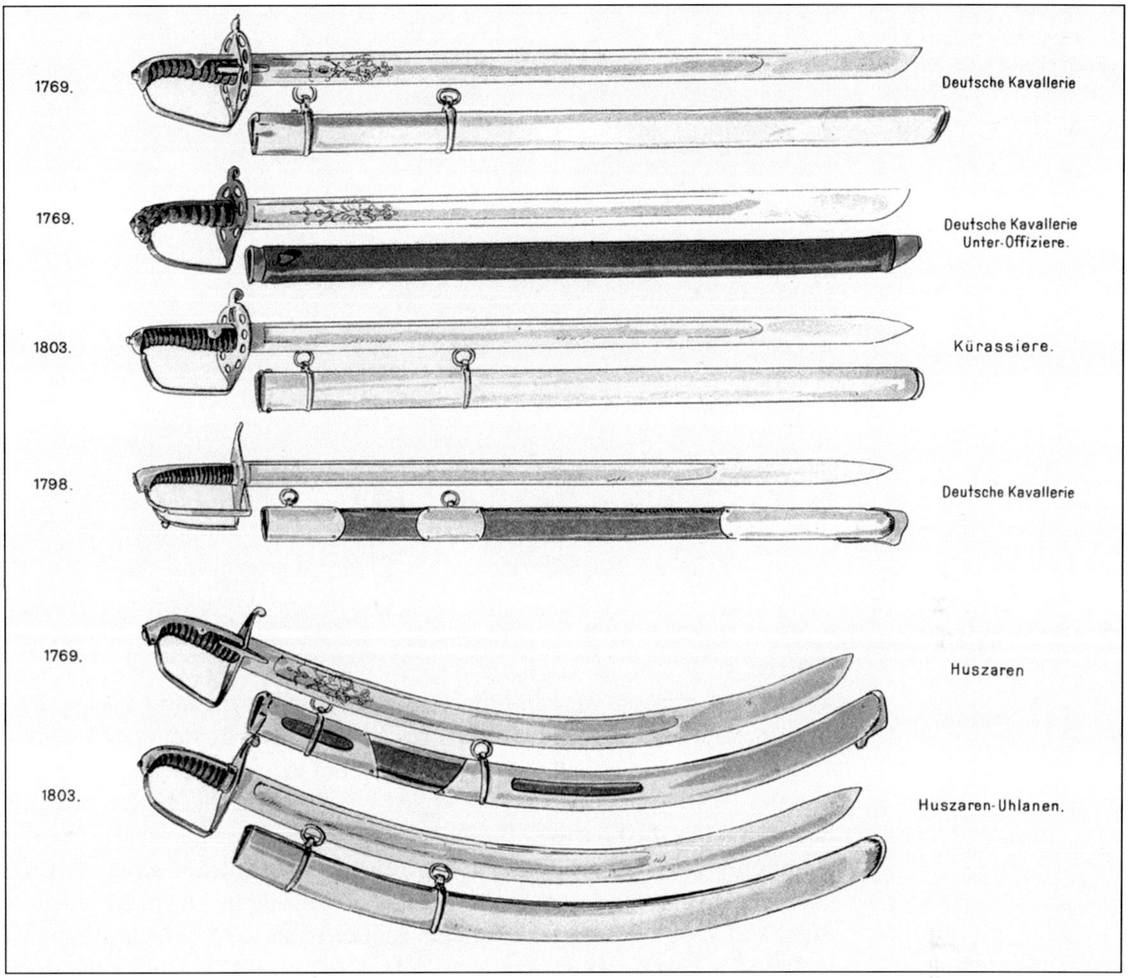

Swords and sabres from Teuber-Ottenfeld's *Die Oesterreichische Armee von 1700 bis 1867*. The Austrian cuirassier *Pallasch* was a very effective side weapon, copied by the British heavy cavalry in 1800. The Austrian light cavalry sabres were equally well reputed.

Muskets

Cavalry muskets were similar to the *Infanteriegewehr* Model 1798 musket, 150.6cm long for 4.2kg. This firearm had been produced in large quantities, but was later replaced with the *Infanteriegewehr* Model 1807, 150cm long, for 4.6kg. Both muskets had a rifled barrel and were commonly shorter than the infantry smoothbore muskets. The 1798-model cavalry rifle was 71cm long, and weighed 2.65kg.

Originally each squadron of cuirassiers trained eight men armed with muskets and eight with carbines. Six marksmen in each hussar squadron were designated to be issued with muskets as well. The old model of hussar musket was considered too heavy at 4.4kg, therefore it was replaced by the aforementioned shorter 1798-pattern, based on a Prussian design. The dragoons were also armed with carbines (similar to the cuirassiers), but each dragoon squadron had 16 men armed with cavalry muskets. The chevauxlegers carried the carbine, and from 1804 all troopers received the longer 1798-model dragoon carbine. Each squadron of chevauxlegers also had 16 men armed with cavalry muskets.

Detail of the *Pallasch*'s gilded hilt for NCO with the lion head embossed on the pommel. (Private collection)

Stutzen

Stutzen and *Büchsen* were hunting weapons issued to the *Jäger* troops. This firearm, in its external appearance, was characterised by the wooden stock that did not end after half the barrel length, but extended itself to the barrel mouth. This is the reason it was called a 'full stock rifle'. These firearms had generally rifled barrels. The Austrian army also used a cavalry *Stutzen* commonly referred as *Husar Stutzen*, issued to eight horsemen in each squadron in the light cavalry. It was shorter and lighter than the infantry ones, and shot a 7 lines and 5 points calibre (1.63cm) *5/4 Löth* (22 gram) bullets. The barrel was 32.5cm long (1 foot, 4 lines and 2 points); the stock was long 70.6cm (2 feet, 2 inches, 9 lines and 9 points). The cavalry *Stutzen* weighed 2.5kg (4 *Pfund* and 13 *Löth*). It had an iron ramrod of 23.6cm (9 inches), but with no place in the stock.

It was habitual to provide firearms to the light cavalrymen, who were destined to skirmish and attack the enemy from short distance. Therefore, if the horseman could have only a sure shot at a distance with the *Stutzen* or the musket, in such circumstances both weapons were better than carbines. Light cavalry, usually involved in skirmish, may have had special advantages from them. Officers opposed the use of *Stutzen* in the cavalry, saying that the weapon required more careful charging than ordinary carbines. However, loading on horseback was less complicated for soldiers equipped with the shorter and lighter *Stutzen*, which could easily be held with the left hand, while being charged by the right.

Pistols

Pistols were, after the sabre, the main cavalry weapon for they could be better managed on horseback than carbines and other firearms. It was true that, with a longer pistol, the shot was more accurate and carried further than with a shorter weapon, with which one could have aimed too uncertainly; but as

Personnel of the Remount Service in 1820. In 1769. Only officers wore the uniform, consisting of a tobacco-brown coat with yellow collar and cuffs, straw-yellow waistcoat and breeches, brass buttons, high boots and black felt tricorne laced in white. In 1798 a new uniform was issued to the officers only, replacing the tobacco-brown coat with a dark blue ***Röckel*** with black facings, and white breeches. In 1809, the Remount Service was split in two, and the Austrian section received the new uniform in ***hechtgrau*** with pompadour red facings, yellow metal buttons, white breeches and black felt headdress as shown in this later illustration. The Hungarian section received the same ***hechtgrau*** coat but in hussar style with yellow braids. (Authors' archive)

a somewhat longer pistol became too heavy to be comfortably handled with one hand, the Austrian cavalry pistols came out with only a 10-inch barrel (26cm), while the whole weight of this new type of pistol was around 1.2kg (2 *Pfund* and 6½ *Löth*).

Of course, the Model 1798 pistol of 17.8 calibre (1.76g) would have been even lighter, and would also have had a lesser recoil; but in this case a horseman had to carry bullets of two different calibres, namely 1.75cm for the carbines and 1.78cm for the pistol. Therefore it was easier, having discharged his pistol cartridges, to avoid the use of the carbine, utilising half of the powder charge from the carbine cartridges for the pistols.[70] The actual visual or point-blank distance of this new type of pistol, mounted with brass, was indeed only 10 to 15 *Schritte* (6–9m), but, with some elevation, they could easily hit a target within 25–30 *Schritte* (15–18m).

The pistol was used for defence, skirmishing and signalling duties. Nevertheless, because of the uncertain shot and the short distance at which the gun could be used, it was not a significant weapon. The greatest benefit was afforded when pursuing fugitives, when encircling groups of men, and other

70 The paper cartridges which took the whole load did not come into use until 1670; before small tin cans containing the charges were used. The balls were stone cast or made with iron moulds. *Anleitung zum Selbst-Studium der militärischen Dienstwissenschaft für Officiere der k.k. österreichischen Armee*, p.55.

similar occasions; but for flank attacking or skirmishing it was completely useless. As we have seen above, the gun shot properly only at a short distance so when the flanking squads came within gun distance the gun was certainly soon to be replaced by the sabre. But using the pistol at greater distances, such as 18m or more, was no use, because it was impossible to hit with them.

The Side Weapon – *Seitschwert*

Dealing with Austria (and Hungary) means hussars, and hussars evoke sabres. The sabre gained widespread use in the eighteenth century. The English word sabre derives from the French *sabre*, which is akin to the Hungarian *szablya*, Polish *szabla*, and Russian *sablya*. The word is believed to originate from the Turkic Kipchaks' *selebe*, with contamination from the Hungarian verb *szab*, which means 'to cut'. Regarding Austrian sidearms, the main difference was in the blades. The sabres with curved blades were called *Säbel*; those with straight, two-edged blades commonly referred as *Schwert*, and swords with a single straight blade were called *Pallasch*,[71] which were similar to the backswords.[72]

Almost all experienced cavalrymen preferred blades with sharp points, the thrust instead of the cut, for the reasons that firstly a thrust was deadlier, and could put an enemy permanently out of combat; and secondly because it was easier and safer to use, by not offering as many weak points as cuts did, and consequently it was far more capable of rendering ineffective the adversary's attack with parries. However, cavalrymen sought to have blades which could be used both thrusting and cutting. In general cuts were most applicable in individual battles, but in the shock or melée a thrust was most effective. In addition, a cutting blow was not as poor at a distance as a thrusting point, for the man's head was protected by the helm or by an iron cross under the hat, and elsewhere it rarely penetrated, having a whole different effect compared to the tip.

Austrian regulation was inspired by the concept that the length of the sabre was determined by the possibility of the cavalryman hitting the ground with the point of his weapon. This happened comfortably with a side weapon with a blade of 95–110cm (3 to 3½ *Schuh*). If the cavalryman fought against a mounted enemy, and therefore their horses stood head to head, the cavalryman would have been about 190cm from his opponent as opposed to the infantry, and an even longer side weapon would have given him more advantage in close combat. However, the swords were not long

71 The word comes from the Hungarian *Pallos* (Palló, long and broad), which in turn is similar to the Turkish *palas* and means a single-edged, long, heavy broadsword (perhaps in the time after the end of the independence war in 1711, when the first hussar regiments had been formed with Hungarian officiers in France, Prussia and Russia).

72 A backsword is a type of European sword characterised by having a straight single-edged blade and a hilt with a single-handed grip. Later examples often have a 'false edge' on the back near the tip, which was in many cases sharpened to make an actual edge and facilitate thrusting attacks. Backswords were used all over the world, it seems, first by the cavalry but later also by the infantry. Backswords were simple and easy to make and thus cheap. They were also easy to use. Soldiers who had a sword not as primary weapon but as last resort could not make very good use of a long double-edged blade since that needed considerable skill if it was to be used to full advantage. For further details see *Sword Types*, at <https://www.tf.uni-kiel.de/matwis/amat/iss/kap_1/basics/b1_1_3.html>.

enough to strike the infantryman and break the line. The designated length of 95–110cm was sufficient, to reach an infantryman not lying on the ground.

As far as the hardness of a blade was concerned, the power of a cutting blow depended mainly on the weapon's weight. Since, however, no cavalry sword could be heavier than what the weakest man was still able to manage, it would have been impossible to have a blade weighing over 840g (1½ *Pfund*), otherwise it would have caused hard discomfort.

In the Austrian cavalry there were two main side weapons in use: the strong *Pallasch* and the lighter hussar sabre. The *Pallasch*, issued to cuirassiers, dragoons and chevauxlegers, had a long and straight blade and a back, which gave it a sturdy impact. The blade was 84cm (32 *Zoll*) long, and used both for cuts and thrusts. The hilt was made of steel and weighed 507g (29 *Löth*) and the blade 568g (1 *Pfund* ½ *Löth*). The scabbard was all iron, and weighed around 1kg, while the whole sword, together with the scabbard, weighed 2kg 150g (3 *Pfund* and 27 *Löth*). It was a longer weapon so it was difficult to manoeuvre in tight or/and chaotic settings. The centre of gravity of this weapon was close to the hilt, so it was easier to keep the arm outstretched to reach out towards the opponent. The horseman would lean forward with the sword extended, this made him a smaller target and at the same time gave him the greatest reach, in addition he took advantage of the weight of the horse to better perform. However, with the centre of gravity so close to the hilt, it was a poor weapon for slashing and cutting. Therefore dragoons were armed with a straight (and heavy) *Pallasch*, 84–92cm long and unusually cutting on both sides. Chevauxlegers carried the sabre, however until 1802 they had the same heavy *Pallasch* like the dragoons. Like the hussars, the uhlans carried the curved sabre. The hussars received the 1803-model (84cm blade), with iron scabbard; it differed from the *Pallasch* only in the curved blade, which was more adapt at cutting than thrusting. The sabre was the more effective weapon in situations where squadrons broke into small groups and where individual cavalrymen were passing each other from left or right, or coming from behind, and a slash or cut was required. This weapon had its centre of gravity at the end of the blade, which added extra strength to the blow, but for exactly this reason it was not too handy a weapon when it came to using the point.

The Uhlan Lance

In the Austrian army, the uhlans from Galicia and Poland had as their main weapon the lance. It was carried under the right arm, with only two thirds of the pike-rod standing in front, and one third behind the body. A little metal sphere was attached under the tip to avoid the lance becoming stuck during the impact and consequently the horseman was not prevented from being able to pull it back after the shock. The pole was also provided with a 1 Schuh and 8½ *Zoll* iron bar on both sides, down from the sphere, in order to secure the lance from cutting and breaking. All the metal parts weighed no more than 3 *Pfund* and 12 *Löth* (1.9kg). The lance carried by Austrian uhlans measured 260cm in all (8 *Schuh*, 3 *Zoll*), and comprised the 21cm (8 *Zoll*) tip. The wooden pole was 218cm (6 *Schuh*, 11 *Zoll*) made from ash wood.

The lance was an effective offensive weapon, having great advantages over the sword, both in the charge and in pursuit of fleeing enemies. However, the lance had also several disadvantages. When engaged in a close combat it was almost unusable because of its length. To perform effectively the uhlans had to maintain a compact and regular formation, which could be difficult in rough terrain, and under enemy fire horsemen and falling horses caused disorder and overexcitement. A poorly trained lancer unit could turn into disorder and remain exposed to dangerous enemy counterattacks. In close combat, where a horseman had to parry blows from the left, right and rear, and do it quickly, the lance was too long and heavy. In such situations the uhlans usually discarded their lances and fought with sabres, as happened in 1809 at Wagram, when some of the uhlans of Regiment Schwarzenberg threw away their lances after being engaged by Polish Guard light horse, who were not yet armed with this weapon.[73]

Austrian Cavalry Horses

The Austrian and Hungarian domains were renowned for their horse-breeding programmes, based on a number of Imperial stud farms. The role of these farms was to produce farm horses for citizens, riding and carriage horses for the nobility, cavalry mounts and artillery horses for the military.

Military horses were acquired from three sources: the Imperial breeding farms in Hungary; Galicia and Bukovina Galicia and Poland (for light cavalry); Prussia and northern Germany (for heavy cavalry). Notable stud farms were located at Mezőhegyes and Bábolna; the first founded in 1785, the latter purchased by the government in 1789, both located in modern Hungary. Mezőhegyes bred the *Nonius* (in Hungarian *Nóniusz*) horse, originally bred to serve as a light draft and utility animal, which became a useful agricultural horse used for light work and for pulling artillery wagons. The Nonius was also the typical Hungarian military horse breed, named after an Anglo-Norman forefather. Generally of dark colour, the Nonius was muscular and heavy-boned. The Nonius, Shagya, Gidran, and several other strains were often referred to as the *Altösterreichische Pferderassen* (Old-Austrian horse breeds). Bábolna was originally an extension of Mezőhegyes, but in 1816 the administration decided to use only Arabian and Arab-bred stallions to achieve their military cavalry goals.

According to David Hollins:

> The Hussars preferred Hungarian and Transylvanian horses, or Polish ponies, between 4 and 7 years old, standing 14–15 hands … usually coloured wholly dark bay, brown or black, although each squadron tried to maintain as little variation in colour as possible … Horses had to be at least 14 Faust (hands) and two Zoll

73 The regulations of Saxon cavalry recommended an unusual kind of attack against the lancers. It was called a *ladebandade* and was executed in the widest intervals and only by the hussars or cuirassiers with body armour. The wide intervals allowed them to get behind the uhlans. It was assumed that the effectiveness of the lance was reduced, since the target was not in close order and the lancer would have to constantly aim his lance against a moving target rather than just point it forward. See also Haythornthwaite, *Napoleonic Cavalry*.

(inches) high, although a suitable good-quality horse a Zoll shorter was acceptable.[74]

Above: *Gemeiner Leichte Dragoner* in 1799 wearing a singular headdress obtained from a chevauxlegers black leather casquet with a front peak. Moreover, the coat has a very unusual falling collar. (Particular from a sepia of Johann Baptist Seele. Authors' archive)

Horses preferred by Hungarian cavalry were akin to a lighter version of the usual Nonius war horse. Each cavalryman was instructed to ride horses with 'a lively temperament, combining speed and stamina'. The horse's age was easily found by observing the teeth, as specifically remarked in the Austrian cavalry regulations of 1807. In order respect horse size, since the 1780s the regulations specified that no light horse lower than14 *Faust*, 1 *Zoll*, and no heavy horse under 15 *Faust*, 2 *Zoll* was accepted in the army, unless endowed with particularly good qualities, in which case a *Zoll* less was tolerated. The *Dienst-Reglement* of 1807 also specified that: 'Each officer had a Pferdemesser or Hippometer, more than 18 shoes long, finger-thickness in width, made of linen, impregnated with wax or turpentine, with a device at the bottom, on which shoes were divided and marked in inches and lines.'[75] In wartime, to officers with a rank of First Captain was assigned also a *Dienstpferd* service horse. In addition, the extent of a horse's service in the military was important for the Imperial treasury. In 1807 a 10-year usage of the horse was rewarded with three dukats; one more dukat for each year thereafter.

The Székler (Hungarian-speaking ethnic Turks, settled in Transylvania) held a special status being part of the *Militärgrenze* system, which required each family with a farm of 50 *Jach* (acres), or smaller combined family units, to provide one horse for each 50 acres.

For the cavalry regiment horses' procurement by horse dealers and suppliers, it was determined that the horses must be aged between five and seven years old, 14–15 *Faust* tall for the dragoons, and 15–16 *Faust* for the cuirassiers, strong enough and without major defects; also they must not have a pelt white, dappled, spotted or light coloured, but where possible only brown and dark. For a cuirassier horse 60 Imperial thalers were paid, and for one issued to dragoons, 50.

Although the Austrian army was famous for its light cavalry, the regiments also needed heavy, resilient horses to be used for strenuous work, such as artillery tasks and those requiring draft animals. Horse conscription in the hereditary territories was carried out in 1781, enumerating at the same time, the total number of horses present in the territories, and also fixing how they would be classified in the census, in order to raise the draft of pack

74 Hollins and Pavlovic, *Hungarian Hussar 1756–1815*, p.16. The *Zoll* (inch) was 26.34mm, the *Faust* (fist or hand) was 4 inches or *1/3* foot or 105.36mm. Another obsolete measure, utilised with horse, was the *Schuh* (shoe), 1 *Schuh* = 0.28812 metre or about 29cm.

75 *Dienst-Reglement für die Kaiserlich-Königliche Kavallerie*, vol. I (Vienna: K.k. Hof- und Staats-Druckerei, 1807), p.52.

Above, and facing page: Austrian *Leichte Dragoner* NCO and a private uhlan from the Zurich collection dated 1799–1800. Both figures are wearing a mix of items of the new and old regulation. Note the NCO with the hazel cane on the left wrist and the quartered pennant on the uhlan's lance. (Authors' archive)

horses in the event of a war, in proportion to the progress of mobilisation. This measure was omitted only in Galicia, since the horses there considered inadequate to serve in the army. The owner of a classified horse was obliged to provide the same in case of need, in return for payment. The release was the responsibility of the political authorities.[76] The prices for these horses were fixed at 50–80 florins, and for horses of special strength, if they were 15 percent or more *Faust* higher and above, the prices could be increased to 120 florins. With the Mobilisation Act of 1782 recruitment districts had been also assigned to single regiments and corps, which in case of war had to offer horses and riding materials. These districts also had to provide personnel to act as cavalrymens' servants in wartime.

The Austrians utilised Neapolitan, Spanish and Arabian breeds, developing local lines such as the Bohemian Kladrubers. The Kladruber (in Czech *Kladrubskýkůň*) is currently the oldest Czech horse breed and one of the world's oldest too. Today it is considered very rare. The main breeding centre was (is) at the National Stud Farm Kladrubynad Labem (Czech Republic), where the Kladrubers have been bred for more than 400 years. Kladrubers have always been bred to be *galakarossier*–a type of carriage heavy horse for the Habsburg court, usually used in a four- or six-in-hand, at ceremonies and funerals. The breed was based on imported Spanish (e.g. Andalusian) and Italian horses, crossed with Neapolitan, Danish, Holstein, Irish, and Oldenburg blood, in addition to the heavy Czech breeds. The Kladruber came in a variety of colours, including palomino and appaloosa, although in the nineteenth century the breed turned strictly to be grey or black, due to a breeding programme requiring 18white and 18 black stallions for various ceremonies of the court.

Other horse breeds included the 'mountain' horses, very solid and tenacious, and accustomed to hard and difficult routes, which served the army until the Great War. The Haflinger, also known as Avellinese, was a breed of horse developed in Austria and northern Italy (namely Hafling in South Tyrol) during the late nineteenth century, but was present during the Tyrol uprising of 1809. Haflinger horses are relatively small, are always chestnut with blonde mane and tail, have characteristic gaits described as energetic but charming. Haflingers have close connections to the Noriker,

76 The Horse Conscription Act was mandatory also in Hungary and Transylvania, but was not applied because of the hostility of the Regional Councils.

because of the mountain areas where the two breeds were developed.

Up to the end of the nineteenth century Noriker horses (from the Noric Alps, a Latin word) were important to allow trade between central Europe and the Adriatic Sea. The earliest breeding history of the Noriker horse began with the establishment of the stud farm Rif, near Salzburg in 1565. There began the phase of refinement by Neapolitan and Iberian stallions, which exerted their influence on the Noriker horse until 1806. Down to the present day this mixture is visible in their conformation: Roman heads with a powerful and compact topline, long manes and tails. Elaborate influences were also visible in coat colours, with a large number of black horses as well as blue roans, called *Mohrenkopf* (from the Italian phrase *testa di moro or capo moro*, meaning 'dark brown head' or 'Moor [dark] head'). Besides *Mohrenköpfen*, there was also a leopard-spotted coat colour, named *Tiger*.

Finally, it is important to remember, in two words, the famous horses of the Vienna Riding School. The Hungarian Lipizzaner horse was widely used by the Austrian cavalry. Lipica is the original town of the Lipizzan horse, today it is in Slovenia, very close to Trieste (Italy). Those horses were also known as being from a Spanish breed, but in fact the Lipica stud farm was established in 1580 and the first horses were bought from Spain in 1581. The Lipizzan breed was fully developed in the time of Maria Theresa of Austria, whose husband was greatly interested in horse breeding. During the Napoleonic wars the stud farm was relocated to Székesfehérvár (Hungary) at the time of the First Italian Campaign. In 1802 an earthquake struck Lipica, killing large numbers of horses. The stud farm was relocated to Đakovo in 1805, to Pecica (near Mezőhegyes) in 1809, and finally to Laxenburg during the First World War, and then to Kladrubynad Labem. This horse was the same size as the Arabian horse and enjoyed great reputation in Europe. Even Napoleon owned a Lipizzaner as a warhorse.

Left: Blankenstein Husaren Regiment (Nr. 6) charging at Günzburg on 9 October 1805. They are wearing the *Pelz* over the dolman as usual in action, but although more than six years have passed since the introduction of the regulation that replaced the old headgear, the officer still wears the busby with bag and his men retain the 1769-pattern shakos. Only the officer's sabretache is in compliance with the regulation, while the saddle cover and pistol holsters are probably a personal choice. (Authors' archive)

Below: Preparatory drawing by Johann Adam von Bartsch depicting hussars from the Erzherzog Ferdinand Carl Regiment on a march in 1805. Note the unusual zig-zag pattern of the pelisses and the pistol holsters of the horse furniture. (Authors' archive)

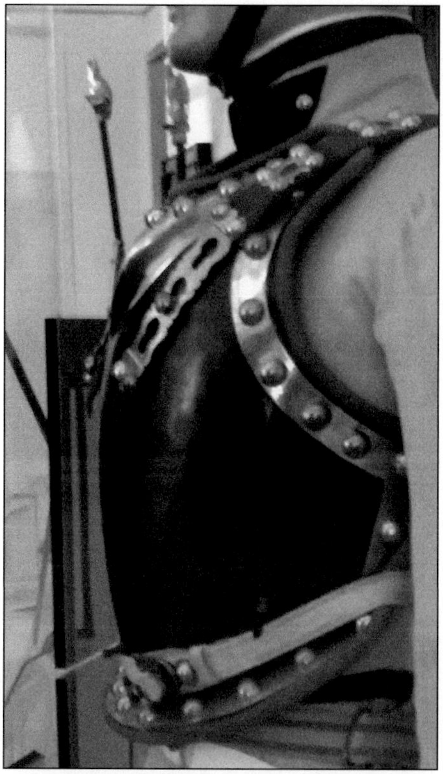

Left: Details of the officer cuirass with gilded edge and fittings. Preserved in the Heeresgeschichtliches Museum, Vienna. (Authors' photograph)

Below: Detail from the Battle of Hanau in 1813, painted by Wilhelm von Kobell, now preserved in Munich. Note the private cuirassiers and officers wearing the helm without crest. This is retained only by the trumpeters, who have it in red wool. The cuirassiers in the background are wearing *Roquelor* overcoats. As occurred after 1812, the Austrian cuirassiers served on campaign without carbines when on horseback. Note also the saddle covers of the private cuirassiers, which had lost the anterior section after 1811. (Bavarian State Painting Collections)

Right: NCO of the Erzherzog Johann Baptist Dragoner Regiment (Nr. 1), 1814–15, by an anonymous artist. The helm's comb with the crest removed is approximately depicted, however the other details appear accurate, like the sword knot in yellow-black and the *Pallasch's* hilt with the lion-head pommel. The decoration is the Army Cross medal awarded for the campaigns of 1813–14. After 30 years of distinguished service, individual soldiers were granted nobility as a *Freiherr*. Furthermore, in 1789, the Emperor introduced the Gold and Silver bravery medals for army-wide recognition. (Authors' archive)

Left: Austrian cuirassiers, 1815, wearing the helm without the wool crest. Note the overall trousers with the internal leather insert, probably one of the items sent from Great Britain in 1814. (Print of Genty. Authors' archive).

Left: Erzherzog Leopold Dragoner Regiment (Nr. 4) enters Naples on 23 May 1815, in a contemporary print published in Nurnberg. Note in foreground the trumpeters wearing a double-breasted *Röckel*, and behind them an NCO wears the same type of coat. Once again it is difficult to establish whether or not it is an artistic error, or if this is another macroscopic derogation from the official regulation. (Authors' archive)

Left: Hussars in 1804 by Wilhelm von Kobell. These horsemen wear the 1798-pattern shako with a plume, two bear the plume inside the cloth cover. Note the *Gepernek* cloak of the figure to left and its remarkable size. (Authors' archive)

Gemeiner uhlan and *Oberoffizier* published by Mollo and Mansfeld in the series relating the *Adjustierunvorschrift* issued in 1809. The main change concerned the new profile of the *Czapka*, here depicted with the leather reinforcements on the corner, definitely introduced after 1811 for rank and file. Note the officer with falling plume and trousers with double lace. (Private Collection)

Above, and overleaf: Contemporary iconographic sources suggest that the officers of the Hungarian and Galician-Polish light cavalry were particularly inclined to customize their uniforms with non-regulation accessories. Previously this habit had been the subject of warnings by the Aulic War Council and even the Emperor had intervened to enforce the regulations. However, especially when away from Vienna, the hussar officers, and especially uhlans, continued to modify their uniforms at times in a decidedly eccentric way. These caricatures by Jean Baptiste Baillot show two groups of Austrian cavalry officers and NCOs in 1814–15. While the chevauxlegers are wearing more or less regular items, the uhlans appear in very unusual uniforms. Some of them are wearing green Spencer jackets with red facings (or fur?), which were usually worn by officers as city dress, while two figures wear the Spencer like a hussars' pelisse. The officer below to right is wearing a very singular headdress with peak, red top, golden lace and brown fur skull; his Spencer also has he epaulettes. As their *Czapkas* have the top of green cloth, they belong to Uhlanen Regiment Nr. 2. (Private collection)

Ulanen

Two uhlan officers dated 1814–15 by Finart and Freyberg with non-regulation clothing. The first officer (above) wears a *Kurtka* with a broad lace on the breast and turnbacks; only collar and cuffs are of red crimson, while the turnbacks are green. Also the trousers are in green with the same broad golden lace on both sides. The white *Czapka* identifies him as an officer of Uhlanen Regiment Nr. 4. Note the chinstrap with gilded edgings. The second officer (left) belongs to the same regiment and he is wearing the city dress Spencer like a hussar pelisse. (Private collection)

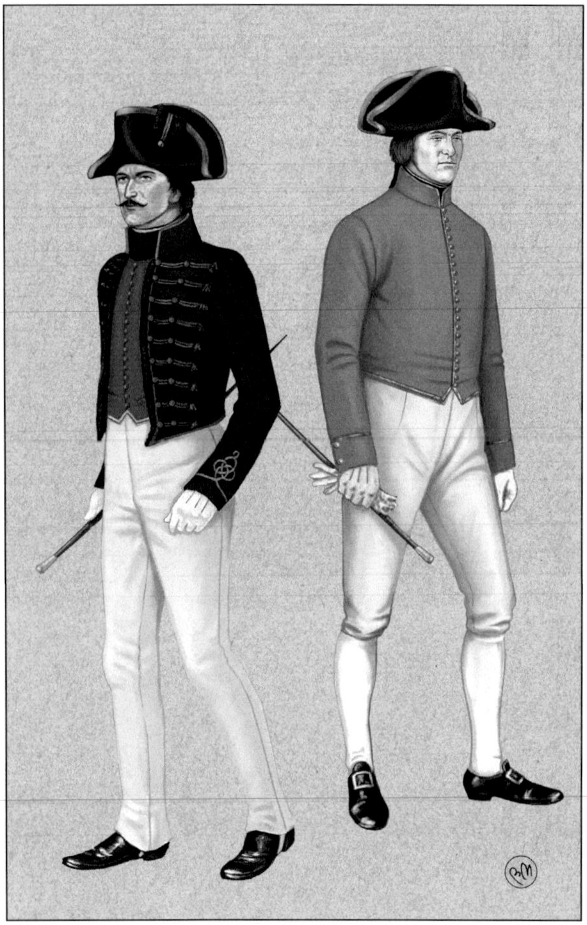

Hungarian and German cavalry officers wearing the Spencer, 1805–1810. Originally named after George Spencer, 2nd Earl Spencer (1758–1834) this coat was a short waist-length, single-breasted jacket without tail and turnbacks, tailored for the officers' undress or city dress after 1805. German cavalry officers had the Spencer in the regiment's facing colours, while hussars and uhlans had it like the *Pelz* and *Attila*. According to the iconographic sources, the hussar officer's Spencer followed the Hungarian pattern with fur lining and lanyards on the breast, and it could be worn over a short waistcoat of different colour. (Illustration by Bruno Mugnai)

Right: Uhlan *Oberoffizier* in *Überrock*, 1811–15. This is the most common version of the double-breasted greatcoat usually worn by all Austrian officers in winter as city dress, but also in active service where it was more practical (and more elegant) than the *Roquelor*, especially when dismounted. Coeval sources show uhlan officers wearing a single-breasted *Überrock* with lapels. (Illustration by Bruno Mugnai)

Left: The English artist Robert Dighton produced a lot of images of the allied occupation troops in France. Presumably, he could take notes on the uniform details, and nothing suggests that his artworks were arbitrarily reconstructed. In this fine watercolour dated 1818, Dighton portrays three uhlan officers from Regiment Nr. 1 and Nr. 3, wearing non-regulation uniforms. The officer to right wears gold laced crimson trousers which seems to be inspired by the French *charoual* style. The officer to left wears green trousers with side yellow-black hussar style piping. Other details appear very singular, like the cartridge box with the silver-flapped cover, and the sabretache carried by two of them. Also the epaulettes appear smaller than usual, while the lanyards seem manufactured from a very strong textile. All three figures have *Czapkas* without plume and reinforced corners, and a wide band of lace with interwoven zig-zag pattern at the base of the leather skull. (British Museum)

Below: A fine watercolour by Klein depicting two uhlans of the third regiment in 1814, identified by the red upper section of the *Czapka*. Every detail appears consistent with the changes introduced after 1809 for the uniform of the uhlans, except for the profile of the *Kurtka* lapels, which seem to be the ones of the old regulations. Note the shortened saddle cover issued to the troopers after 1811 and the reinforced corners of the *Czapka*. (Private collection)

Below: Hussars marching through a late-eighteenth-century German town, in a print after a drawing of Alois Greil. Economic shortage and lack of supplies had affected the Austrian army since the beginning of the wars against France. This resulted in inconveniences and improper armaments, as indicated by the size of the firearms carried by these hussars, which could be cavalry muskets instead of carbines. Note the officers bearing the bearskin headdress, with a bag and carrying pistol holsters. (Authors' archive)

4

Cavalry Tactics and Training

In addition to the unit-level organisation, the performance of the armies on the battlefield is always an extremely important field of investigation. While the structure of regiments, battalions, and squadrons interacts closely with the army's structure, the tactical organisation is the actual coefficient of the art of warfare. The military power of the Habsburg monarchy underwent the most spectacular and thorough change in this regard. However, this was not due to the internal development and evolution of the army but to external coercive forces. The army, and the cavalry, adapted to the changes in military art in Europe, not facilitating them, but following them. In this respect the close connection between the social system of a state and the efficiency of the army is clearly visible.

Historians have synthesised the French military success of the 1790s, focusing on numbers and best offensive attitude.[1] Taking advantage for the first time in modern history of an actual national conscription, French commanders could introduce a new style of war relying on the numerical superiority and availability of recruits to fill the voids. Moreover, lacking a regular supply train, the French armies lived off the land, quartered in improvised structures, and became capable of more rapid movement compared to their old regime enemies, who were instead slowed by complicated and often contradictory regulations. As often happens, simplistic explanations tend to circumvent other aspects and they are therefore only partially acceptable. The striking power of mass and mobility were not the only keys to success, as France forged effective battle tactics too. The manual of 1791 prescribed a refined use of line and column formations, combining fire and bayonet charges. Jourdan, Hoche, Pichegru and, naturally, Bonaparte temporarily abandoned most formal approaches in battle, but they knew perfectly the sophisticated field tactics developed after the Seven Years War. They implemented the theories of their predecessors, making them applicable in an army composed mainly of illiterate peasants. The new style of warfare was essentially based on a transformation in the role of infantry

1 Peball, 'Zum Kriegsbild der österreichischen Armee', pp.144–145.

and depended not only on political and social changes, but took advantage also of tactical innovations and effective training, which gave decisive results on the battlefield.

On the other hand, the Austrian army remained tied to the *Generalsreglement* of 1769 with its rigid and harsh discipline, attributing the primary role to line deployment. Infantry, with the exception of the recently established *Jäger Corps*, continued also to be drilled along formal lines. Austrian generals would not abandon their reliance on defence and on formally besieging any fortress which might threaten their communication lines. The phlegmatic attitude of the Austrian commanders had replaced the resolute and aggressive style of warfare of great captains of the past, such as Prince Eugene of Savoy, Claude de Mercy and András Hadik. The obsession with geometry and the symmetrical deployment of forces on the field were considered the best prerequisites for each commander. This doctrine was aggravated by the faulty organisation of artillery. Except for the regimental cannon, ordnance was massed into an artillery reserve and generally keep too far back to be effective.

Austrian cavalry tactics also remained formalised in the eighteenth-century mould of outflanking infantry or acting as a reserve for pursuit or defence. Though Austria tried to create large masses of cavalry as the French had just done, the Austrian armies included a relatively small number of cavalry brigades and divisions. Moreover, after 1763 the large formations of horse lost their tactical role on the field. As a result, there was a lack of instructions for multi-regiment units and large-scale exercises related to the *Divisionweise* employment. The Austrian commanders preferred to split regiments into a number of detachments, mainly for reconnaissance tasks: the *Abteilungsweise* employment. Naturally the consequences of this practice of scattering their cavalry in small corps, typical for dragoons, proved to be less useful and greatly reduced their combat effectiveness. During the Napoleonic Wars, dragoons generally assumed a cavalry role, though remaining a lighter class of mounted troops compared to the armoured cuirassiers, and usually did part of their service dismounted. However, at the end of the eighteenth century Austria tried to increase the mobility of the army and focus on the tasks of intelligence, reconnaissance and raids. For this reason the *Leichte Infanterie* battalions were raised in 1798, in order to improve speed on campaign. For some unimaginative military leaders, this light infantry could replace the dragoons in the foot tasks and then it was decided to transform the horsemen in light cavalrymen, creating the *Leichte Dragoner* regiments. The experiment lasted just three years, but it reduced significantly cavalry performance on campaign.

Although numerous military writers, such as Archduke Carl and Anton von Zach,[2] had pointed out that the new and more flexible tactics required to

---

2 Anton von Zach (1747–1826) was born at Pest, Hungary, and entered Austrian military service becoming a *Major* in 1788, an *Oberstlieutenant* in 1793, and an *Oberst* in 1795. He served as chief of the quartermaster general staff under *Feldmarschall* Johann Peter Beaulieu from 8 April to June 1796 during the Montenotte campaign, the battle of Lodi, and the battle of Borghetto. In June he was succeeded by Franz von Lauer when Würmser replaced Beaulieu. Subsequently

deal with the French also required a more human approach to the common soldier, in practice little was done. Corporal punishment remained the norm and except for some degrading practices abolished in 1792, the Aulic War Council did not change tack, and in May 1798 issued a circular denouncing officers who had become attracted to such 'subversive ideas' to the detriment of good order and discipline.[3]

On a tactical level, despite occasional efforts to modify the predominantly close-order deployment with an effective combination of light and mixed formations, the original methods remained practically unmodified.[4] Only on one occasion, at Novi in November 1799, did the Austrian army deploy in an actual open order, but it was driven off the field in disorder.[5] The wars of the coalition saw the usual confusion and contradiction among the allies, which did not favour a regular development of new tactics, because each army had primarily to balance the weakness of its allies in the open field. Therefore in 1798–99 the Russian weakness in cavalry had to be filled by the Austrian one in the Swiss and Italian campaigns. Moreover, strategic considerations kept the cavalry in a secondary role. Because a major portion of the likely theatres of operation in Switzerland, Italy and Tyrol offered little scope for major cavalry actions,[6] horse regiments – especially heavy regiments – were reduced,

---

he served on Paul Davidovich's staff during the battle of Rovereto on 4 September. In 1797, Zach served on a commission to analyse the causes of Austria's defeat. Among several reasons, he outlined that lower-ranking commanders displayed little initiative because there were too many regulations. He found that regimental officers showed more interest in pay and privilege and drill than in learning how to make fighting units more efficient. He saw that officers were indifferent towards the rank and file, and that the lower ranks had little trust or enthusiasm for their superiors. From January 1798 to March 1799, Zach was chief of staff of the army in Italy. He assumed the chief of staff role again from July 1799 to June 1800. On 9 June 1799 he received promotion to general *Wachtmeister*. Suvorov described him as 'sound, discreet and professional'. Zach performed capably at the Battle of Novi on 15 August 1799, and for his actions, the Emperor awarded him the Knight's Cross of the Military Order of Maria Theresa. A skilled mathematician, Zach was more at home in the field of military engineering than he was at combat leadership or in an operational role. At the battle of Marengo on 14 June 1800, he was chief of staff to Michael von Melas. Zach was promoted to *Feldmarschall-Lieutenant* in 1805, while he served as chief of staff in Archduke Carl's Army of Italy. After the war, Carl dismissed Zach as too old to serve as chief of staff. On 23 September 1807, Zach became *Inhaber* (colonel proprietor) of Infantry Regiment Nr.15 and held the post during his lifetime. At the beginning of the War of the Fifth Coalition, he was assigned again to the Army of Italy under Archduke Johann, participating at the battle of Sacile on 16 April 1809. Subsequently the French general retreated, Johann left a brigade under Zach to blockade the fortress of Palmanova. After the Austrian retreat from Italy in May, Zach served under Kalnássy in Slovenia and Croatia. After 1809 he was no longer employed in the field. He was deputy commandant of the Olomouc fortress from 1810 to 1812. In November 1812 he became commandant of the fortress and in 1815 he became governor of the city. Zach officially retired from military service in early 1825 and was appointed to the rank of *Feldzeugmeister*.

3 Rothenberg, *Napoleon's Great Adversary*, p.70.

4 By 1798 the Austrian army had learned how to fight in open order supported by closed formation, but this statement is not substantiated by the evidence. See Josef Rauch, *Erinnerungen eines Offiziers aus Altösterreich* (Munich: G. Müller, 1918), p.346.

5 Rothenberg, *Napoleon's Great Adversary*, p.70. Caning punishment was suppressed in 1807, but reintroduced in 1809.

6 However, also in the French *Armée d'Italie* the cavalry were reduced to a few units. In 1794 the cavalry deployed only the 5e and 9e Dragons, 6e and 8e Chasseurs á Cheval, and the 1er and 5e Hussars. In the following years further regiments arrived in Italy as reinforcements, but the total

Austrian Hussars engaging French horse chasseurs at Papa, on 12 June 1809, by Albrecht Adam. French and Austrian light cavalrymen faced each other several times from 1792, often with indecisive results. The long duel resumed during the Sixth Coalition War and finished with a substantial Austrian success. While the Austrians had assimilated past lessons, the French and their allies were unable to recover after the Russian campaign of 1812. In 1813 the gap appeared unbridgeable. On 14–15 September 1813, at Lippa, the Austrian infantry began a gradual withdrawal to a second position. During the withdrawal, the cavalry of the Kingdom of Italy took advantage of this situation and launched a charge. However, a half squadron of *Radetzky Husaren* pushed through the intervals in the withdrawing Austrian infantry and drove back six squadrons of the Italian *chasseurs-a-cheval* under General Perreimond, notwithstanding the incredible 0.5 versus 6 squadrons ratio. (Print from Riccardo Papi, *Eugène and Adam. The prince and his painter. The Leuchtenberg cycle and the Napoleonic campaigns 1809 and 1812*, Berlin 2012)

leaving the horsemen with few opportunities for exploiting their effectiveness. Furthermore, after centuries of history and battles, cuirassiers were not the most appreciated cavalry among Austrian officers. In this regard Charles Joseph de Ligne, the renowned and prolific writer, intellectual, and member of one of the most-signalled Austrian-Walloon princely family, wrote:

> What we have to say? All that is heavy for a man on horseback is a poor useful thing. Let us decorate our arsenals with all the cavalry cuirasses and let us enrol men up to five Shuh, 3 Zoll (165cm) at most. Let the cavalry have some more hussars, and be sure that a Dragoon captain at full speed can win a battle. How can so many unfortunates still charge with so much iron that only annoys them? The one behind (armour plate) is worth only to preserve miserable people, who turn their backs and whose existence is not worth the trouble to be. The frontal one would not be so useful, unless a General, who leads them, has enough intelligence to not expose them to blows, till when they are ready to react; besides all this, the hat crosses and these huge boots, too well waxed, have them take and finish as soon as they are dismounted. Without arguing, here, about fire or about

number of horsemen remained low. The 3e Dragons was headquartered in Milan in the spring of 1798, increasing the number to eight dragoon regiments, two line cavalry, six chasseurs à cheval and two hussars.

> the Exercise articles for hussars, nor for the one where I treat Dragoons, because it does not seem to me conceivable that, for some uncertain shots, that one shoots and which have so little effect, one loses the immense advantage of penetrating among the enemy with the greatest Impetus.[7]

Notwithstanding this authoritative comment, the Austrian cuirassiers retained their role of heavy cavalry, namely the 'battle cavalry', which charged knee to knee close order to overwhelm the enemy on its way. Though there were relatively small encounters that involved large formations of cavalry in this period, when well directed the Austrian horsemen performed well. On 24 September 1795 the Austrians cavalry routed the French at the battle of Handschuhsheim. The Austrian cavalrymen were placed in the hands of Johann von Klenau, recently promoted *Oberst*, and deployed a force of six squadrons each of the Hohenzollern Cuirassier Regiment (Nr.4) and Székler Husaren Regiment (Nr.44, later Nr.11), four squadrons of the Royal Allemand dragoon regiment (disbanded in 1798), and three squadrons of the Kaiser Dragoner Regiment (Nr.3). As French troops moved through open country, they were charged by Klenau. The Austrians first routed six squadrons of French *chasseurs à cheval* then turned against the footsoldiers who fled immediately after. As result of the encounter the Austrians overran the French camp outside Mannheim and placed the city under siege. The same outcome was obtained on 3 September 1796 at Würzburg by the Prince of Liechtenstein.

In the 1790s, the cavalry was the most powerful component of the Austrian army. Since the beginning of the century, like the whole army they suffered from lack of training. In earlier days, especially against the Ottomans, Austrian cavalry had made considerable use of mounted fire, but for some time this practice had been discouraged and shock action with cold steel was considered the primary task for all cavalry branches. Standards of training varied considerably; because of the financial contingency, regiments still remained widely scattered, and though this was undesirable for mobilisation, many units were stationed in the eastern domains, where their upkeep was cheaper. This practice also received a boost due to the reforms advocated by Archduke Carl, but was bitterly criticised by his opponents, who accused him of exposing the state to the threat of enemies.[8] Moreover, training was impeded by the unwise practice of sending a substantial proportion of enlisted men on unpaid furlough to save resources.

The reforms introduced after 1801 modified the regiment's organisation, but tactical dispositions remained antiquated. In the campaign of 1805 the Austrian cavalry was distributed into different corps. Though Mack understood that one of the main elements of French warfare was moving fast, he issued an army order sharply curtailing regimental and individual transport, in order to follow the enemy who lived off the land. Unfortunately the lack of baggage deprived half the troops of tents and the field army did not improve mobility as hoped. As it turned out, the Austrians were unable to operate like the French.

---

7 Charles Joseph de Ligne, *Préjugés et fantaisies militaires par un officier autrichien* (A Kralovelhota, 1783), p.16.

8 Rothenberg, *Napoleon's Great Adversary*, p.97.

The battle of Handschuhsheim, by Friedrich Rottman. The battle was fought on 24 September 1795 and resulted in a Austrian victory decided by the cavalry. *General Wachtmeister* Klenau commanded a mounted brigade that included the six squadrons of the cuirassier regiment Hohenzollern, two squadrons of the dragoon regiment Kaiser, six squadrons of the hussar regiment Szekler, and four squadrons of the French *émigré* regiment Royal Allemand. On 24 September 1795, seeing the French overwhelming the infantry under General Adam Bajalics von Bajahaza, Klenau quickly organised his own brigade into three columns and ordered the assault. In a battle-winning charge, Klenau's brigade with approximately 4,000 men dispersed the Dufour divisions of the French army of the Upper Rhine, under the command of General Charles Pichegru. The Austrian cavalry caught their enemy in the open, dispersed six squadrons of horse chasseurs, and cut down Dufour's infantry. With a loss of 193 men and 54 horses, the Austrians inflicted over 1,500 French casualties, including 1,000 killed; they also captured eight field guns, nine ammunition caissons with their teams, and General Dufour himself. (Kurpfälzisches Museum, Heidelberg)

Records written during the 1805 campaign outline the good behaviour of the Austrian cavalry, focusing on its endurance and ability to absorb casualties even in unfavourable conditions. At Austerlitz, in the initial phase of the battle, the hussars of the Hessen-Homburg Regiment suffered many losses in men and horses by the French skirmishers, but the enemy did not succeed in making them yield.[9] In the events that followed, *General-Major* Nostitz took advantage of the fog and smoke that had allowed the French infantry to take the village of Tellnitze by surprise, and now wheeled into action with two squadrons of hussars:

> The hussars, having been reduced to the role of spectators and targets for French marksmanship all morning, finally had their opportunity. The 1st Battalion of the 108th Line stood in line. Nostitz directed Mohr's men (Hessen-Homburg Husaren) into the exposed flank of the French infantry and they swept through

9 Gustav Amon von Treuenfest, *Geschichte des k.k. 11. Huszaren-regimentes Herzog Alexander v. Württemberg 1762 bis 1850 Székler Grenz-huszaren* (Vienna: Verlag des Regimentes, 1878), p.233.

> the French ranks, causing them to flee for the security of the village. One through the 1st Battalion, Mohr wheeled his hussars around and charged the 2nd Battalion, hitting it in the flank as well. Heudelet credited the grenadiers of the 2nd Battalion with blunting the Austrian charge sufficiently to allow most of the French troops of 15th Light and 108th Line in front of Tellnitz to escape into the village, but nonetheless many were cut off and captured.[10]

Actions like this seem to confirm that the quality of the individual regiments depended more on the individual initiative of the officers in command than on a homogeneous training standard. This situation continued until 1806, when Archduke Carl embarked on his army reform policy with renewed energy, which also affected cavalry training and tactics. The economic scenario did not permit an increase in cavalry strength, but the regiments were organised in a permanent structure in order to gather their regular strength in reasonable time. Cavalry regulations had been frequently updated until 1804,[11] and a new larger regulation issued in 1806 confirmed the original arrangements.

Compared to that of 1769, the 1806 regulation increased the speed of manoeuvres, and special emphasis was placed on the rapid and compact effects of the 'evolutions'. In 1769, the horseback training focused on the discipline and compactness of each units. In this regard, the regulation specifically mentions the whole-front attack and the retreats *enechiquier* (chessboard), in order not to disrupt the units. After any attack, the cavalrymen made a halt, from both wings each squadron rode to the last rank, since the cavalry was still ranked in three ranks. Four men, with a corporal, moved 150 steps before the front and formed themselves into two lines, in order to target the enemy with the firearms. Remarkably it appeared that the strict rules of the 1769 tactical regulations were intended only for peacetime training. In an emergency the formation should be left to the discretion of the commander, depending on the terrain and the situation. Against the Ottomans the retreat was ordered by a full front, however the cavalry could perform with significant autonomy compared to the infantry, and the personal responsibility of the officers was much clearer than in the infantry. Furthermore, the regulations already discussed mass formations, even manoeuvring with wide fronts and behaviour in enfilading fire. In the sense of adapting to the respective circumstances, further regulations had appeared in 1772 and 1784, the latter of which already contained provisions for avant-gardes and rearguards, flanks and side patrols, as well as the formation of an oblique front, to conceal the manoeuvring of the other regiments engaged in the action.

The 1806 regulation focused on the officers' training, considering them as the most important element in combat. Incidentally, in 1804 Archduke Carl had asked the officers to acquire knowledge in peacetime, to teach themselves

10 Robert E. Goetz, *1805: Austerlitz* (London: Greenhill Books, 2005), pp.131–133.

11 George Nafziger and Marco Gioannini, *The Defense of the Napoleonic Kingdom of Northern Italy 1813–1814* (Westport: Praeger Pub, 2001), p.50. Nafziger's comment that 'the Austrian 1805 Regulation is a miserable document' has already been noted.

Austrian uhlans of the Erzherzog Carl Regiment (Nr. 3), 1813–15, in a print published by Artaria. At the battle of Mincio River on 8 February 1814, Austrian *Feldmarschall-Lieutenant* Franz Mauroy de Merville urged his cavalry to remain ready for a charge from behind the earthen embankment when a squadron of uhlans from the Archduke Carl regiment returned, pursued by the French cavalry. As soon as the French came within sight, General Wrede's dragoon brigade and four squadrons of the Archduke Carl uhlan regiment were sent forward. At the head of the French force advanced two squadrons of the *1er Hussars*. The French, instead of countercharging, received the Austrians at a standstill and were routed. The Austrian Savoyen Dragooner then attacked the remaining French cavalry frontally, while the Hohenlohe dragoon regiment attacked their flank. The French, and the supporting Italian Regina dragoon regiment, were overthrown. The Austrians also captured a horse battery. The disorder of the cavalry spread to the adjacent troops. The French–Italian cavalry brigade was out of action for the rest of the battle, and unable to deploy again on the field. (Private collection)

by reading military writings and reflecting on their implementation. Experience taught that even a poorly trained cavalry could prevail better under skilled commanders than better-trained troopers led by poor officers. The 1806 regulation did not modify the basic tactical units – the *Division* – formed by two squadrons, but the two-deep line was now prescribed as the standard field formation. In addition, a regiment's *Abteilung* was made up to three squadrons for cuirassiers, dragoons and the Székler hussar regiment, and up to four divisions in chevauxlegers, hussars, and uhlans. Each *Division* was divided in two wings of two *Zuge* (sections or platoons). The tactical unit was considered an independent force, led by an officer under the command of the division's commander. However, the smaller corps should develop sufficient independence and flexibility in every situation. The best-trained horsemen were deployed at the wings, and the most spirited and determined troopers were in the first line. Since all ranks had to be occupied, in each section at least two troopers were to be reserved and trained as possible substitutes for those on the wings, a position which was also considered a sort of antechamber for the appointment to NCO.

The 1806 *Vorschrift* differentiated between heavy and light cavalry more precisely than the previous regulations, and indeed it appeared already in the numerical composition of the squadron, with 112 mounted and six dismounted men in the former, and 128 and eight in the latter. In the event of war, the dismounted horsemen formed the core of the reserve squadron for training of men and horses.[12] In the regulation chapter dealing with the charge, heavy cavalry was described as 'swift, firm, tearing', and the light cavalry as 'enduring and agile'. Cavalry had to act offensively whenever possible and the frontal charge, normally delivered at 12 pace intervals between divisions, was expressively recommended. The troopers were forbidden to receive any attack at the halt, but they were obliged to counter-attack in every circumstance.

Johann Josef Wenzel Anton Franz Carl Radetzky von Radetz (1766–1858), was a key figure in the Austrian army, particularly in the cavalry. After serving as attaché in Archduke Carl's headquarters, from 1809 to 1812 he was active in reorganising the army and its tactics. He served as chief of the general staff during the later period of the Napoleonic Wars under Schwarzenberg and had considerable influence in planning the offensive campaigns in Germany and France. A disciplined but fair man, he was so beloved by his troops that he was known as Vater Radetzky. (Print after an engraving of unknown artist. Authors' archive)

In addition to the frontal attack in a straight direction which, however, required favourable terrain, the oblique line was often recommended as formation because it was considered more effective and allowed threats on the flanks, forcing the enemy to give up a position or stop his advance. In rough terrain, as well as in the frontal attack with several divisions, it would have to hold back the wings or a part of them, deployed in *Staffeln* (echelons),[13] for the flanks' protection and in order to facilitate the offensive manoeuvre. The regulation recommended retaining a squadron as reserve in every circumstance. Speed was to be gradually increased from a walk to a trot, then to a canter and finally to a restrained gallop with only the last 80 or so paces before impact at full career.

Attacks against guns were specifically discussed, in order to force the gun to perform constant turns and to offer it a narrow front and small ranges of depth. Infantry squares were best attacked at the angles, and precisely

12 The squadron was no longer the basic tactical unit, as was thought, considering detachments which could operate independently on the battlefield. The reason that squadron establishments were similar in most armies was the fact that any number of men greater than 200 was difficult to control and unwieldy to manoeuvre.

13 The counterpart was the column which involved units deployed directly behind one another. This employed something of the principle of the echelon attack, with the leading squadron in charge of absorbing the fire of the enemy and then dispersing, while the succeeding squadrons sheltered from fire as they approached, then pressed the charge before the enemy could reload.

in line formation, as the effect of the fire of a square against columns was destructive. Adaptation to the situations, to the terrain, agility and offensive spirit were, therefore, always the main postulates that the new regulations recommended to cavalry officers.

Having declared the march in total frontline as the main rule in the regulations section, neither in peacetime nor in wartime, no small cavalry detachment was to march without avant-garde or rearguard and side patrols, unless all detachments were sent ahead for skirmishing or flanking. Two chapters of the 1806 regulation – I-23 and I-24 – were dedicated to the detached corps. The vanguard had to secure the main force, seeking to discover the enemy's intentions and ambushes, in order to give the main force time to start the battle formation, to mask their own movements, and to turn away enemy light troops.

The rules for skirmishing were similar to those issued to the infantry, except that there was no third rank in the cavalry and therefore one or more sections could have been moved and detached for skirmishing. One regiment sent out one platoon each as avant-garde and rearguard, two more as side patrols.

Movements on foot were now rather shortly dealt, and would have been performed by single *Divisions*. Deployment on foot was also in two ranks, and concerned not only dragoons, but also hussars, chevauxlegers and even cuirassiers. The third main section of the regulations was devoted to movements in larger formations,[14] and upon the use of the horse artillery. An artillery officer had his place in the avant-garde, the guns marched at intervals in front or on the flanks, each flank covered by a squadron. The regulations of 1806, likewise, focused on the necessity of speed and precision of movements. The officers had to have the necessary knowledge, especially because the new *Vorschrift* had simplified or omitted everything that was no longer compatible with the new kind of war. In the section dealing with the avant-garde, the officer was required to develop his first guidelines, drawn from the regulations, through his own reflection, reading and experience, and 'Above all, the Commander, who had to manoeuvre on horseback with larger formations and needed a practiced eye, correct mathematical notions, an active mind, and an awareness controlling the range of his activity sphere.'[15]

Columns were to be used for movement and deployment, but the regulation did not utilise compact columns for the charge, a practice increasingly common in the French cavalry. On occasion, the thin two-deep lines were a considerable disadvantage in a clash with the French heavy horse. An even greater disadvantage was the persistence of any precise instructions for multi-regiment charges. Alongside the absence of large-scale exercises which might have retained this shortcoming, this led to the use of single regiments, and even *Divisionen* and *Abteilungen*, for futile attacks.

The tendency to splinter cavalry strength was strongly opposed by Archduke Carl, but it was further reinforced by the new, and not always well understood,

14 Austria initially assembled brigades and divisions on a somewhat ad hoc basis, and showed an increasing tendency to dilute the cavalry's power by attaching units to protect the flanks of infantry formations, rather than assembling large corps to execute offensive manoeuvres on the battlefield.

15 *Vorschriften für die kaiserlich und königliches Kavallerie*, 1806.

battle movements, which called for large formations manoeuvring in columns during deployment. Though the new regiment organisation introduced by the Archduke tried to correct the lack of multi-regiment corps, the use of large tactical units remained little practiced. Despite this failure, the light cavalry always provided good reconnaissance and protection to the army, but an actual reserve corps made to collect the heavy cavalry was never organised. Fearing cavalry assault against their flanks, the Austrian commanders often insisted on cavalry support and received it in the form of small detachments. Instead of developing the capability of acting as an independent force on the battlefield, a role cavalry had repeatedly performed in the wars of the second half of the eighteenth century, the Austrian mounted arm was becoming a mere support for the infantry. The combat capabilities of the cavalry were further lessened by the fact that although the 1806 *Vorschrift* contained a section on the use of horse artillery, the mounted batteries were only partially mounted and in any case untrained to support cavalry charges.

Despite the reform remaining incomplete, in the war of 1809 the results of the new tactical approach proved their effectiveness in several encounters. On 22 April, during the retreat to Regensburg in the final phase of the battle of Eckmühl, the Austrian cuirassiers faced their French counterparts in a fierce encounter exploiting all the improvements achieved. The Austrian heavy horsemen were deployed before the village of Alt-Eglofsheim, in order to cover the retreat of their infantry and artillery. The French columns were obliged to halt until their cavalry came up to support engagement of the enemy. However, the Austrians charged first. The French cuirassiers, under Nansouty and Saint Sulpice, received the Austrian heavy cavalrymen with a volley of their firearms, followed by a countercharge at the gallop, which repulsed the Austrians upon their reserves. But these charged again, and the whole force mingled together, swayed backwards and forwards, in a desperate hand-to-hand struggle. Contemporary accounts related that the noise of steel clashing against steel, and of sword blades ringing upon helms and cuirass, raised above the other sounds of battle. The sun set and the moon rose before the loud clangs arising from the melee had ceased. After fearful losses the Austrian were obliged to give way. The Austrian cuirassiers, equipped only with frontal breastplates, had fought disadvantageously against the French horsemen, who were protected at the back also. One month later, at Aspern–Essling, 46 squadrons under *General der Cavallerie* Liechtenstein charged against the French light cavalry division of *Général de Division* Lasalle. This action was one of the rare multi-cavalry regiment actions performed by the Austrians, and succeeded in routing the enemy with a well-coordinated assault from the front and flank sides; Lasalle was killed in this action. At the same battle, regiments of French light cavalry under *Général de Brigade* Sahuc discharged their carbines and pistols at 10 paces against the Blankenstein Husaren (Nr.6) and O'Reilly Chevauxlegers (Nr.3). Despite the volley, the Austrian light cavalrymen closed and fought hand to hand. It did not take long before two French colonels and numerous troopers went down with wounds. In the following events, approximately 2,500 French heavy cavalry comprising four cuirassier regiments led by *Général de Division* Espagne attacked the Austrian centre defended by strong artillery and light cavalry. The French received canister fire and then encountered

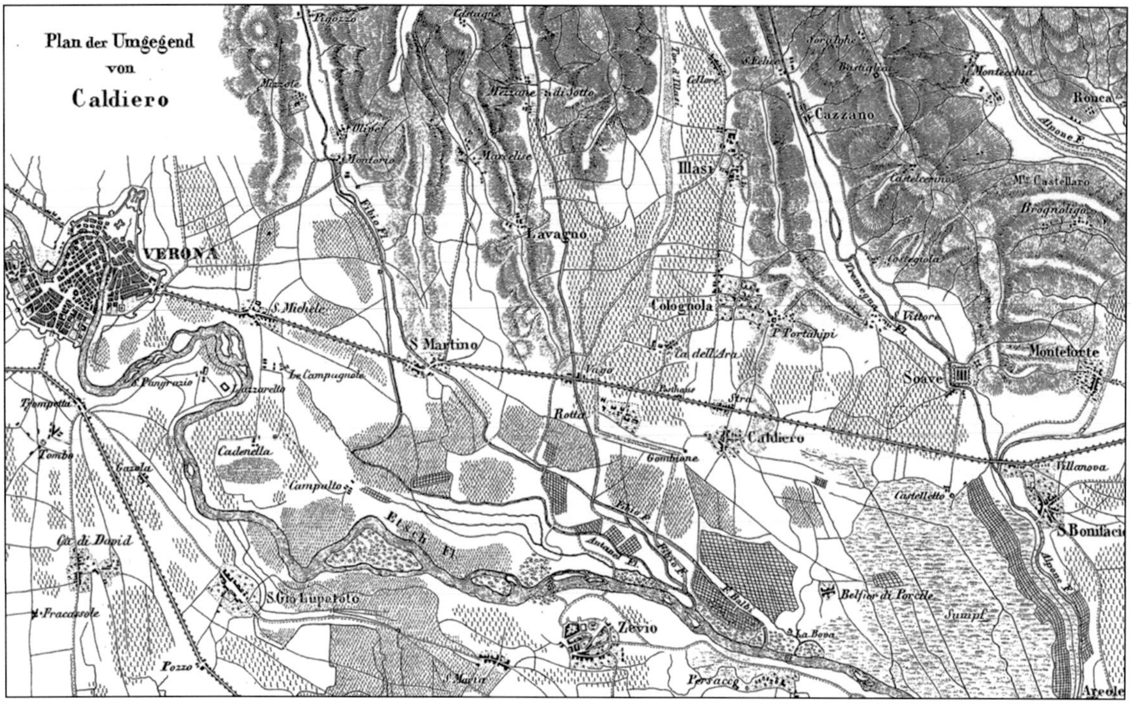

The battlefield of Caldiero, after the *Atlas der Schlachten, Treffen und Belagerungen aus der Kriege von 1792 bis 1815*, published at Freiburg in 1860. The battle was fought on 12 November 1796 and was the first defeat suffered by Bonaparte. The campaigns of Italy with the successes achieved at Bassano, Arcole and Rivoli made the reputation of Napoleon as a military commander, even if Caldiero underscored the fact that it was far from over. At the battle participated only 10 squadrons of Austrian cavalry: two squadrons of Husaren Regiment Würmser (Nr.8), four squadrons of Husaren Regiment Erdödy (Nr.11), and four squadrons of Uhlanen Regiment Mészáros (Nr.1). (Authors' archive)

four Austrian cavalry regiments deployed in a very long line. However, in contravention of the recommendations of the new regulation, the Austrians instead of countercharging remained stationary, but their impressive stance communicated great resolve, and the French wavered. Then two Austrian cuirassier regiments crashed into the French flank and sent them reeling backwards.

The second attack made by Espagne's cuirassiers took place a couple of hours later. This time the French took three Austrian cavalry regiments in the flank. The Prince Albert Cuirassiers, Archduke Ferdinand Cuirassiers and Knesevich Dragoons were routed. The Hungarian *Insurrectio* cavalry stood in second line. They were irregulars and fled before the enemies reached them. Fresh Austrian cavalry advanced against the cuirassiers and meanwhile the artillery and infantry opened fire. Espagne was struck in the face with canister shot and fell dead. Three of his four brave colonels died in this battle. The Hungarian mounted militia performed poorly in the second day of fighting, when *Maréchal* Bessieres charged the Austrian centre with two massive corps of 4,000 and 5,000 horsemen. When the mass of enemy cavalry emerged from the smoke of battle, two hussar regiments of

A nineteenth-century print showing the Austrian cuirassiers charging the French and Saxon cavalry in the opening phase of the battle of Leipzig, on 16 October 1813. (Authors' archive)

the *Insurrectio* broke in panic and the nearby infantry began to waver; only the personal intervention of Archduke Carl resolved the critical moment.[16]

Other failures occurred due to the poor discipline of the militia territorial cavalry and the unwise decision to employ them together with the line regiments. On 14 June 1809, at the end of the battle of Raab, Archduke Johann attributed the defeat to the Hungarian *Insurrectio* cavalry, stating in his report that 'the Hungarians neither could ride or manoeuvre'.[17] However, the line cavalry also suffered major drawbacks. On 22 April 1809 the Austrian dragoons were caught off guard by the Württemberg cavalry in reconnaissance near Geisling, who learned from local peasants that the Austrians were stationed in nearby towns and villages. At midnight the Württemberg horsemen crept to the lighted houses and saw Austrian dragoons drinking and smoking their pipes. The dragoons had neglected to place sentinels and were taken by surprise. The enemies emerged from the darkness and in few minutes the fight was over. Heavily outnumbered, the dragoons were routed and one whole squadron was taken prisoner.

However, it was clear that something had changed in Austrian tactics. Napoleon himself changed his mind. Before Aspern–Essling he had dismissed his opponents by saying that 'the Austrians fight poorly; they are a mere mob', but in 1809 declared that 'Austrians not only are strong, they also fight very well.'[18] This result was not just the effect of Archduke Carl's leadership on the battlefield, because even on other fronts the Austrian cavalry performed

16 According to legend, memorialised in many pictures and in the famous statue outside the Imperial palace in Vienna, the Archduke seized the regimental colours as he led his troops forward. However, he told an inquirer: 'you know how heavy the colours are. Do you really believe that a little man like me could have gone off with them?'

17 Rothenberg, *Napoleon's Great Adversary*, p.202.

18 Rothenberg, *Napoleon's Great Adversary*, pp.189–199.

Johann Frimont von Palota (1759–1831), lithography of Josef Kriehuber. (Authors' archive)

positively. The capture of the French 35ème Ligne near Pordenone, on 15 April 1809, was due to the good training of the new light cavalry divisions and to its excellent commander, *Feldmarschall-Lieutenant* Johann Frimont.[19]

In subsequent years the Austrian cavalry was confirmed to have acquired better training and tactical skill. After the positive performance in Russia in 1812, the following campaigns in Germany, France and Italy registered significant achievements and negligible failures. At the battle of Leipzig the enterprise of the hussars against the French heavy cavalry echoed in the allied chronicles of the battle. A French cuirassier witnessed the encounter between the elite French horse carabiniers and the Hungarian hussars:

> We were in column of regiments. The 1er Carabiniers were in front and general Sebastiani was to the right of the regiment: all at once a mass of enemy cavalry, mainly Hungarian hussars, rode furiously down on the carabiniers. 'Bravo!' cried the general, laughing and waving the riding crop which was the only weapon that he designed to use. 'This will be charming; hussars charging the horse carabiniers.' But when the Hungarians were 100 paces away, the 1st Carabiniers turned about and fled leaving behind their brave general! They hastily rode back on to the 2nd Carabiniers and both regiments fled away. It was such a disgrace that when after battle a group of carabiniers entered a farm seeking quarters, the cuirassiers from the 5th Regiment teased them: 'If you want hospitality, try the Hungarian hussars!'[20]

19 Johann Maria Philipp Frimont (or Fremont) (1759–1831) was born at Fénétrange, in modern French Lorraine. He entered the Austrian cavalry as a trooper in 1776, participating in the War of the Bavarian Succession, and successively in the Ottoman War of 1788–91. As colonel he took part in the early campaigns against the French, in which he frequently earned distinction. In the campaign of 1800, despite the final failure at Marengo, he distinguished himself as a light cavalry leader, and in the next year became *General Wachtmeister*. In the war of 1805 he was again in Italy and won further renown by his gallantry as light cavalry commander. In 1809, he again saw active service in Italy under Archduke Johann in the rank of *Feldmarschall-Lieutenant* , serving in Chasteler's Corps at the first battle of Sacile on 15–16 April, and Caldiero. He commanded the rearguard at the Piave, but was defeated at the second battle of Sacile and at San Daniele on 11 May. He commanded the cavalry reserve at the battle of Raab on 14 June 1809. In 1812, Frimont led the cavalry of Schwarzenberg's corps in the Russian campaign, participating at the action at Gorodetschna on 12 August. In January 1813 he replaced Schwarzenberg as commander in Poland. In the same year he led the V. Armeekorps under Hiller in Italy. After the Treaty of Paris (1814) he became military governor in Mainz. In 1815 he was commander-in-chief of the Austrian campaign in Italy, and his army penetrated France as far as Lyon, which was occupied on 11 July. With the army of occupation he remained in France for some years, and in 1819 he was appointed as a military governor of Venice. In 1831 he became president of the Aulic War Council.

20 Constant Rilliet, 'Tagebuch eines Kürassierenleutnants während des Feldzuges 1813', in G. Kircheisen (ed.), *Napoleons Untergang 1813* (Stuttgart: R. Lutz, 1919), vol. II, pp.298–299.

Austrian light cavalry performed valiantly at Leipzig. During the third day of the battle, the Poles and French strongly defended Dolitz with artillery and infantry:

> Although the French strongly held Dolitz, Oberst Simonyi with three squadrons of Hessen-Homburg Hussars and two horse guns resolved to march as quickly as possible to the other side of the village, so as not to lose the least time in striking the French. This movement was barely begun when the French first line struck at the Austrian hussars. Simonyi sounded the charge, and drove back not only the French infantry assault, but completely broke through the second French line and threw that back. Twice more the hussars charged forward in order to give the Austrian infantry time to arrive.[21]

József Simonyi de Vitézvár (1771–1832), master of the *Streifkorps*, was a prominent light cavalry commander and celebrated as the best hussar in the history of the Austrian cavalry. He entered the cavalry in 1787 as *Gemeiner* in the Husaren Regiment Würmser, and three years later became a corporal. Appointed as *Wachtmeister* from 1795 and a lieutenant in the Mészáros Uhlanen from 1797. His first major success happened at Ulm in 1805, when he saved two infantry regiments and artillery from being surrounded by the French. Soon, he earned the nickname of 'the bravest hussar'. In 1809 he took part in the battle of Wagram as a *Major*. Decorated at Leipzig. in 1814 he was appointed as *Oberst-Commandant* of the Hessen Homburg Regiment. He achieved great notoriety when led his regiment into Fontainbleu Palace in Paris, and imitating the famous Andras Hádik at Berlin in 1757, he emptied his pipe on Napoleon's throne. In 1816, he was transferred to Vienna, then to Oradea, before he received a command as military governor in 1819, which was withdrawn in 1828 because of the shooting of a cadet. In the course of this fact, he was also stripped of all titles and sentenced to 10 years in prison in Oradea, where he died. (Print after an engraving of unknown artist. Authors' archive)

Attachment to tradition did not always have a negative impact on the effectiveness of Austrian cavalry on campaigns. Since the beginning of the eighteenth century a characteristic feature of the Austrian cavalry had been the *Streifkorps* (intruder parties). Composed by volunteers or the most spirited horsemen, these units of variable size usually comprised light cavalrymen but also dragoons and sometimes artillery, ranging in size from 100–150 men to several thousand. They operated as part of a division or corps, scouting the area and disrupting the enemy's movements. Following the exploits achieved by cavalry commanders of the past such as Ebergeny and Hádik, after 1800 the Austrian commanders turned with increasing frequency to these formations. An example of such a *Streifkorps* was those led by *Major* (and later *Oberst Commandant*) József Simonyi de Vitézvár. He mastered this kind of warfare, forming squadrons of light horsemen assigned to one officer and four NCOs from his Hessen-Homburg Husaren (Nr.4), of which at least 10 troopers volunteered. The *Streifkorps* carried only personal arms and a small amount of equipment in their backpack, while reserves of ammunition, foodstuff and equipment were strategically placed in guarded secret places in the wilderness or in remote buildings. These tactics

21 Treuenfest, *Geschichte des k.k. 11 Huszaren-Regimentes*, p.303.

Feldmarschall Archduke Carl of Habsburg in 1796, by Rudolph von Ottenfeld. In the 1790s the Austrian army remained tied to the *Generalsreglement* of 1769 with its rigid and harsh discipline, attributing the primary role to the infantry and line deployment. As a consequence, Austrian cavalry tactics too remained formalised in the eighteenth-century mould of outflanking infantry or acting as a reserve for pursuit or defence. Archduke Carl and some other officers pointed out that the new and more flexible tactics required a drastic reform of the army organisation.

Cuirassier on campaign, 1814, by Wilhelm von Kobell. The horse to the left is carrying bags and other facilities. In the attempt to increase its mobility, in 1805 the Austrian cavalry had diminished the baggage train and part of the equipment and food for three days was transported by the horsemen. In background there is the regiment's music band with trumpeters and even a kettledrummer. (Staatliche Museum, Berlin)

returned in 1814 when *Feldmarschall* Carl Philipp von Schwarzenberg, after the decisive war council met at Frankfurt on 28 December 1813, agreed that numerous *Streifkorps* would precede the Bohemian Army into France. The general staff issued instructions for the organisation of six large cavalry parties to cover the army's flanks. The Austrian commander, haunted by his own demons in that difficult campaign, believed that upon entering France he must employ only bold and intrepid partisan commanders. The operation aimed to divert the enemy from the main strategic goal of the allies, and naturally the parties had to collect information about the enemy forces and their positions. In this regard a Russian officer remarked that, 'above all, [it is] the officers who, through their ability to speak the language of the land, can provide detailed information of the enemy movements'.[22] Schwarzenberg's plan proved to be one of the largest *Streifkorps* of the nineteenth century. The first *Streifkorps* would follow the Rhine through Colmar towards Strasbourg. The instructions issued to the commander of the second party initially directed him through the Moselle Valley to Nancy, but Schwarzenberg modified this operation to place the second *Streifkorps* on the army's left wing. In accordance with this change, the third party would proceed down the Moselle to Nancy. The Austrian commander planned the fourth *Streifkorps* to operate between the rivers Saône and Loire, while the fifth *Streifkorps* received orders to advance towards Besançon and Bourges. Finally, Schwarzenberg planned to send the last *Streifkorps* across France to Wellington's headquarters to deliver the allied operation plan. The operation involved 5,200 horsemen, including a part of the Russian cavalry. Although not all the *Streifkorps* managed to accomplish their assigned objectives, the allies advanced

22 Cited by Michel V. Leggiere, *The Fall of Napoleon*, vol. I, *The allied Invasion of France, 1813–1814* (Cambridge: Cambridge University Press, 2007), p.146.

deeply into French territory, where even the great Prince Eugene of Savoy had been reluctant to go at the beginning of the previous century.

The fact that the last Austrian victories in Napoleon's war against France have never received the attention of military historians, is perhaps due to the fact that the army of the House of Austria had only a few good leaders and capable cavalry generals were rare. Only Klenau, Liechtenstein and Frimont could compete against enemy cavalry generals such as Murat, Montbrun, Nansouty, Kellermann, Lasalle and many others. Moreover, the lack of good officers also affected the lower ranks. Some talented colonels and junior officers had the potential to became good commanders, but they never reached the rank of general, because the great number of aristocrats in the cavalry precluded them rising to higher ranks. Archduke Carl supported the promotion of talented officers, but he was never able to earn control over the army and many incompetent and mediocre generals remained in service.

5

Cavalry Regiments and Corps, 1792–1815

A - Cuirassiers and Carabiniers

Karabinieren Regiment Nr.6; Cuirassieren Regiment Nr.1					
Nr.	**Year**	**Proprietor/ 2nd Proprietor**	**Commander**	**Denomination**	Depot
6	1792	Kaiser Franz II / Moritz von Lacy	Rudolf von Kölbel	2. Karabinieren	Vienna
6	1793	" "	" "	2. Karabinieren	
6	1794	" "	" "	2. Karabinieren	
6	1795	" "	Eugen von Monroe	2. Karabinieren	
6	1796	" "	" "	2. Karabinieren	
6	1797	" "	Conrad Weeber	2. Karabinieren	Gaja
1	1798	" "	" "	1. Cuirassieren	
1	1799	" "	" "	1. Cuirassieren	
1	1800	" "	Carl Favier du Noyer	1. Cuirassieren	Steinamanger
1	1801	Kaiser Franz II / Wolfgang von Zezschwitz	" "	1. Cuirassieren	Vienna
1	1802	" "	" "	1. Cuirassieren	
1	1803	Kaiser Franz II / Joseph Prinz zu Lothringen	" "	1. Cuirassieren	Pécs
1	1804	" "	" "	1. Cuirassieren	
1	1805	" "	Wilhelm von Motzen	1. Cuirassieren	
1	1806	Kaiser Franz I / Joseph Prinz zu Lothringen	" "	1. Cuirassieren	Sárospatak -Gyöngyös

1	1807	" "	" "	1. Cuirassieren	Miskolc
1	1808	" "	" "	1. Cuirassieren	
1	1809	" "	Franz von Desfours	1. Cuirassieren	Sárospatak
1	1810	" "	" "	1. Cuirassieren	Nagy-Tapolcsán
1	1811	" "	" "	1. Cuirassieren	
1	1812	Kaiser Franz I / Henrich Bersina von Siegenthal	" "	1. Cuirassieren	
1	1813	" "	Carl von Wibbeking	1. Cuirassieren	
1	1814	" "	" "	1. Cuirassieren	Ungarisch Brod
1	1815	" "	" "	1. Cuirassieren	

A carabinier regiment recruited in all German hereditary lands (except Krain, Görz and Gradisca), after 1799 became cuirassiers, in Bohemia.
1793 – Assigned to the Upper Rhine, some divisions are engaged at Landau and in the capture of the Weissenburg lines. The chevauxlegers division is based in the Austrian Low Countries and performs with distinction at Huy, Tirlemont, Neerwinden, Saultain, Menin and Orchies.
1794 – Only a detachment takes part at the battle of Kaiserslautern; the chevauxlegers division fights at Landrecies and Tournai.
1795 – Transferred to the Rhine, the regiment distinguishes itself in the capture of the enemy entrenchments at Mainz; one division is engaged near Trippstadt.
1796 – The regiment fights at Würzburg, the chevauxlegers division is engaged near Kuppenheim and Neuburg.
1797 – Only the chevauxlegers division is involved in the encounter near Frankfurt am Main.
1799 – The regiment is quartered at Mannheim, then participates at the battles of Knittlingen and Wiesloch.
1800 – Near Eichen, covering the Austrian retreat after the battle of Biberach, the regiment rejects the enemy assaults with success, then fights at Gutenzell. Assigned to the rearguard, after the battle of Hohenlinden it is involved in the encounter near Salzburg.
1805 – The regiment moves from Vienna to Moravia. Three divisions take part at the battle of Austerlitz, where it performs positively covering the allied retreat. The third division forms the guard to the Emperor's encampment.
1809 – The regiment is divided within the 2. Reservekorps; a good performance at the battle of Eckmühl; successively it is engaged at Aspern–Essling. After the battle of Wagram the regiment claims the loss of 79 men. Some *Abteilungen* are engaged at Znaim.
1813 – Two divisions are involved in the battle of Dresden; the whole regiment participates at the battles of Liebertwolkwitz and Leipzig.
1814 – The regiment fights at Troyes, La Ferté and with success at Fère-Champenoise.
1815 – In France, with the corps of occupation.

Cuirassieren Regiment Nr.29; Cuirassieren Regiment Nr.2					
Nr.	**Year**	**Proprietor/ 2nd Proprietor**	**Commander**	**Denomination**	**Depot**
29	1792	Erzherzog Franz Joseph von Habsburg-Este / Joseph von Harnoncourt	Anton von Barco	Franz Joseph	St. Georgen
29	1793	" "	" "	Franz Joseph	
29	1794	" "	Giovanni Nobili	Franz Joseph	
29	1795	" "	" "	Franz Joseph	
29	1796	" "	Giuseppe Vigili von Kreuzberg	Franz Joseph	
29	1797	" "	Wilhelm von Willenstein	Franz Joseph	
2	1798	" "	" "	2. Cuirassieren	Vienna
2	1799	" "	" "	2. Cuirassieren	
2	1800	" "	Bernhard von Degelmann, then Stanislaus Auer	2. Cuirassieren	
2	1801	" "	Joseph von Theumern	2. Cuirassieren	Gyöngyös
2	1802	" "	" "	2. Cuirassieren	
2	1803	" "	" "	2. Cuirassieren	
2	1804	" "	" "	2. Cuirassieren	Miskolcz
2	1805	" "	" "	2. Cuirassieren	
2	1806	" "	" "	2. Cuirassieren	Moór – Vienna
2	1807	" "	" "	2. Cuirassieren	Güns
2	1808	" "	" "	2. Cuirassieren	Margarethen (Ödenburg)
2	1809	" "	Joseph de Hemmy	2. Cuirassieren	
2	1810	" "	" "	2. Cuirassieren	
2	1811	Vacant	" "	2. Cuirassieren	
2	1812	" "	" "	2. Cuirassieren	
2	1813	" "	Carl von Schaeffer	2. Cuirassieren	
2	1814	Erzherzog Franz Joseph / Ludwig Carl von Folliot de Creneville	" "	2. Cuirassieren	Saaz
2	1815	" "	" "	2. Cuirassieren	

Recruited in Oberösterreich and Niederösterreich, and from 1800 partially also in Bohemia.
1790 – Assigned to the Observation Corps against Prussia.
1793 – In the Austrian Low Countries and in Luxembourg. The regiment is involved in minor encounters. The *Oberstwachtmeister* division is assigned to the Corps Beaulieu, and performs with success at Courtrai.
1794 – The regiment distinguishes itself at Arlon, as well as at the two battles of Fleurus; one squadron fights at Quatre Bras.

1795 – On the Upper Rhine without actions.
1796 – In the corps Latour, fights at Kuppenheim, Malsch, Neresheim; a single division is engaged at Geisenfeld and Donauwörth; one detachment distinguishes itself at the battles of Ingolstadt. The regiment is later reunited but remains unengaged at Emmendingen; then employed to cover the siege of Kehl.
1797 – In quarters at Ulm and then moves to Carinthia.
1799 – The regiment is transferred to Germany; one platoon is engaged at Ostrach for the defence of the artillery train; later the regiment fights at Stockach, and is then assigned as reserve in the Rhine army. Detachments are involved in the encounters of Gross-Gartach (Weingarten), Bietigheim, Löchgau, Hoffenheim and Sintzheim during the relief of Philippsburg.
1800 – The regiment is engaged at Engenm, Möskirch, Memmingen, on the Iller, Wettenhausen, Gundelfingen and later at Hohenlinden, Anthering and Lambach.
1805 – Four *Divisionen* are on the Rhine. Some detachments fight at Werneck and Trochtelfingen while the rest of the regiment is captured after the capitulation of Ulm. Only 50 troopers join the Archduke Ferdinand corps, where they form a squadron with the Hohenzollern Cuirassieren Nr.8, which fight at Stecken.
1809 – The regiment joins the 1. Reservekorps in Germany; engaged at Eckmühl. Before Aspern, the regiment began the campaign with 851 men and 771 horses (three field divisions) in the Division Hessen-Homburg, Brigade Heinrich Bersina von Siegenthal. Engaged at Wagram and Znaim.
1813 – Two *Divisionen* are assigned to the cavalry corps of the main army and fights at Dresden, and later successfully at Leipzig.
1814 – The regiment is deployed with the Süd-Armee outside Besançon, where is reunited with the *Oberstlieutenant-Division* coming from the blockade of Dresden and later marches to Lyon with the main army without to sustain engagements.

Karabinieren Regiment Nr.5; Cuirassieren Regiment Nr.3					
Nr.	**Year**	**Proprietor / 2nd Proprietor**	**Commander**	**Denomination**	**Depot**
5	1792	Albert zu Sachsen-Teschen	Friedrich von Seckendorff	1. Karabinieren	Ödenburg
5	1793	" "		1. Karabinieren	Ödenburg
5	1794	" "	Mathias Karst	1. Karabinieren	
5	1795	" "	Hieronymus von Vimereatti	1. Karabinieren	
5	1796	" "		1. Karabinieren	
5	1797	" "		1. Karabinieren	
3	1798	" "	Christian von Wolfskehl	3. Cuirassieren	Ungarisch Brod
3	1799	" "		3. Cuirassieren	
3	1800	" "		3. Cuirassieren	
3	1801	" "	Joseph Radetzky de Radetz	3. Cuirassieren	Ödenburg
3	1802	" "		3. Cuirassieren	

3	1803	" "		3. Cuirassieren	
3	1804	" "		3. Cuirassieren	
3	1805	" "	Carl von Kroyher	3. Cuirassieren	
3	1806	" "		3. Cuirassieren	
3	1807	" "		3. Cuirassieren	
3	1808	" "		3. Cuirassieren	
3	1809	" "	Ferdinand Kuttalek von Ehrengreif	3. Cuirassieren	
3	1810	" "		3. Cuirassieren	Ödenburg and Vienna
3	1811	" "		3. Cuirassieren	Ödenburg
3	1812	" "		3. Cuirassieren	
3	1813	" "	Heinrich von Bayerwerk	3.Cuirassieren	
3	1814	" "		3.Cuirassieren	
3	1815	" "		3. Cuirassieren	

As a carabinier regiment, recruited in all German hereditary lands (except Krain, Görz and Gradisca); from 1798 recruited in Moravia.

1793 – With the *Chevauxlegers Division* the regiment is assigned to the army of the Austrian Low Countries. The chevauxlegers are engaged at Aldenhoven and Neerwinden; the whole regiment fights at Maubeuge and Wattignies.

1794 – Engaged at the battles of Landrecies and Fleurus, the *Chevauxlegers Division* distinguishes itself at Jülich.

1795 – The regiment is deployed in front of Mainz and takes part at the battles of Pfrimm and Lampertsheim. The *Oberstlieutenants Division* distinguishes itself at Bacharach.

1796 – The chevauxlegers division fights at Malsch and Bopfingen and later performs positively in the assault on Kitzingen. The *Majors Division* fights at Camberg, the others are engaged at Würzburg, where they especially distinguish themselves.

1797 – Only the chevauxlegers division is involved in action in some small encounters.

1799 – A cuirassier regiment is in the reserve corps on the Rhine. The *Oberstlieutenant Division* fights at Stetten; two divisions perform successful charges at Wiesloch.

1800 – Assigned to the reserve corps without actions at Engen and Möskirch. At Dellmensingen the colonel's division repulses the enemy cavalry after wading the Danube; the *Majors Division* distinguishes itself at Gutenzell. The regiment performs with special distinction under Colonel Count Radetzky at Hohenlinden and at Laufem.

1805 – In Germany with the corps of Werneck, the regiment distinguishes itself at Wertingen, Jungingen and Langenau. The regiment escapes the catastrophe of Ulm, which affects the Werneck Corps at Trochtelfingen, and joins the cavalry that has broken the French encirclement. The regiment is involved many times in pursuit attacks and in sturdy fighting during the Bohemian breakthrough. It takes part at the encounter of Stecken.

1809 – The regiment is assigned to the main army in Germany. At Eckmühl,

Rittmeister Andreas von Phannhauser seizes with a successful attack several guns already captured by the enemy. At Aspern–Essling the regiment is deployed on left flank of the IV Corps. At Regensburg, two squadrons cover successfully the retreat of the infantry rearguard brigade.
1813 – Only the *Oberst* and *Majordivisions* are with the main army in Saxony, but they are not involved in action at Dresden; later both divisions are engaged at the rearguard battle of Mulda and, positively, at Leipzig.
1814 – Two divisions are assigned to the Süd Armee, but they are not involved in action.
1815 – In Alsace without actions.

Cuirassieren Regt. Nr.27; Cuirassieren Regt. Nr.4 – disbanded in 1801					
Nr.	**Year**	**Proprietor / 2nd Proprietor**	**Commander**	**Denomination**	**Depot**
27	1792	Adam von Czartoryski-Sangusco	Christian von Schmidlin	Czartoryski	Pécs
27	1793	" "	" "	Czartoryski	
27	1794	" "	" "	Czartoryski	
27	1795	" "	" "	Czartoryski	Semlin
27	1796	" "	" "	Czartoryski	
27	1797	" "	" "	Czartoryski	
4	1798	" "	" "	4. Cuirassieren	Krain–Lugos
4	1799	" "	" "	4. Cuirassieren	Krain–Lugos
4	1800	" "	" "	4. Cuirassieren	
4	1801	" "	" "	4. Cuirassieren	Maria-Theresiopel

Recruited in Bohemia.
1796 – The regiment is assigned to the Army of Italy and involved in the blockade of Mantua.
1799–1800 – In Banat with no actions.
1802 – Disbanded; the *Oberst-Division* is merged into the regiment Melas (Dragoner Nr.12), the *Oberstlieutenants-Division* in the regiment Hohenzollern (Dragoner Nr.8), the *Majors Division* in the regiment Kavanagh (Dragoner Nr.4).

Cuirassieren Regiment Nr.12; Cuirassieren Regiment Nr.4					
Nr.	**Year**	**Proprietor / 2nd Proprietor**	**Commander**	**Denomination**	**Depot**
12	1792	Moriz von Kavanagh	Friedrich Xaver zu Hohenzollern –Hechingen	Kavanagh	Brandeis
12	1793	" "		Kavanagh	Brandeis
12	1794	" "		Kavanagh	

12	1795	" "		Kavanagh	
12	1796	" "	Leopold Pálffy ab Erdöd	Kavanagh	
12	1797	" "		Kavanagh	
12	1798	" "		12. Cuirassieren	Güns
12	1799	" "	Heinrich Bersina von Siegenthal	12. Cuirassieren	Güns
12	1800	" "		12. Cuirassieren	
12	1801	Erzherzog Ferdinand / Andreas von Karaczay	Anton von Ricking	12. Cuirassieren	Pécsvár
4	1802	" "		4. Cuirassieren	
4	1803	" "		4. Cuirassieren	Vienna
4	1804	" "		4. Cuirassieren	Maria Theresiopel
4	1805	" "		4. Cuirassieren	
4	1806	" "		4. Cuirassieren	
4	1807	" "	Philipp Christoph von Bechtold	4. Cuirassieren	Gyöngyös
4	1808	" "		4. Cuirassieren	Grosswardein
4	1809	Erzherzog Ferdinand, Kronprinz / Joseph Radetzky von Radetz / Ferdinand Peter Graf Hennequin von Fresnel und Carel		4. Cuirassieren	
4	1810	Erzherzog Ferdinand, Kronprinz / Ferdinand Peter Graf Hennequin von Fresnel und Carel		4. Cuirassieren	Moór
4	1811	" "	Paul von Taxis	4. Cuirassieren	Totis – Lovas/ Berényi
4	1812	" "		4. Cuirassieren	Veszprém
4	1813	" "		4. Cuirassieren	
4	1814	" "	Georg von Mann	4. Cuirassieren	Brandeis
4	1815	" "		4. Cuirassieren	

Recruited in Upper and Lower Austria.
1793 – In the Austrian Low Countries. The regiment distinguishes itself at Neerwinden, where the *Rittmeister* Wenzel von Hermann and Johann Menz capture a French artillery battery. At Leeuwen and Bierbeck the avant-garde engages the French cavalry in continued skirmishes. Later, at Tournai, one and a half squadrons perform a successful action. The other divisions are detached at Templeuve. The regiment is engaged at la Capelle and Cysoing and later at Maubeuge and distinguishes itself at Wattignies.

1794 – The regiment is involved at the battle of Landrecies, then fights at Charleroi with distinctions.
1795 – Transferred to Germany, the regiment is initially at Mainz; later it is assigned to the army on the Upper Rhine without engaging action.
1796 – In the Upper Rhine in the corps Latour; some detachments fight at Orloffen and Renchen. Successively the regiment is assigned to the army of Archduke Carl; engaged at Neumarkt, Amberg and Schliengen.
1797 – The regiment is quartered at Hüningen, then marches to Inner Austria without actions.
1799 – In the Italian theatre of war: siege of Mantua, later the regiment is assigned to the Frelich Corps and marches to Romagna.
1800 – The regiment is garrisoned in different places in Tuscany, then joins Brigade Sommariva and the main army during the retreat from Vicenza.
1801 – Assigned to the rearguard.
1805 – With the army of Germany; the regiment is separated from the main army at Landsberg, during the march against Ulm, but re-establishes the situation with a successful campaign in Tyrol. The regiment joins the Brigade Rohan and then capitulates at Castelfranco with the other Austrian troops.
1809 – The regiment is assigned to the 1. Reservekorps in Germany; engaged at Eckmühl, then covers the retreat from Regensburg on 23 April, suffering the loss of 162 men and 169 horses. Archduke Carl gives the regiment a mention of honour. The regiment fights at Aspern and Wagram, where on the second day it is employed against the French elite cavalry, but is targeted by canister shot from the enemy artillery, suffering the loss of 134 men and 143 horses. Battle of Znaim.
1813 – The regiment is assigned to the cavalry corps Nostitz: engaged at Dresden with heavy losses, then at Flöhe and Leipzig under Colonel Baron Taxis receiving a special mention for acts of bravery; *Major* Franz von Bolza rescues an endangered Austrian battery.
1814 – The regiment is initially assigned to the Southern Army at Macon in Bourgogne, but at the end of March is transferred to the main army without actions.
1815 – On the Upper Rhine.

Cuirassieren Regt. Nr.10; Cuirassieren Regt. Nr.5 – disbanded in 1801					
Nr.	**Year**	**Proprietor / 2nd Proprietor**	**Commander**	**Name**	**Depot**
10	1792	FML Caspar Wolfgang, Freiherr von Zezschwitz	Friedrich von Linken	Zezschwitz	Olmütz
10	1793	" "		Zezschwitz	
10	1794	" "	Carl Philipp von Schwarzenberg	Zezschwitz	
10	1795	" "		Zezschwitz	
10	1796	" "	Johann von Magnani	Zezschwitz	
10	1797	" "	Peter von Dienersperg	Zezschwitz	
5	1798	" "	" "	5. Cuirassieren	Prossnitz

5	1799	" "	" "	5. Cuirassieren	
5	1800	" "	Franz Heinrich	5. Cuirassieren	
5	1801	" "	" "	5. Cuirassieren	Ruszt
5	1802	" "	" "	5. Cuirassieren	Bar–Hont

Recruited in Moravia.
1793 – In the Austrian Low Countries: battle of Neerwinden and siege of Valenciennes. *Major* Simon Hartelm is awarded with the *Militär-Maria Theresien-Orden* (Order of Maria Theresa) for his actions at Neerwinden.
1794 – The regiment performs positively under Carl von Schwarzenberg at le Cateau, le Villers, Tourcoing, Charleroi and Maastricht; the colonel receives the Order of Maria Theresa.
1795 – Quarters at Rastatt in Baden.
1796 – The regiment distinguishes itself at Würzburg.
1799 – With the main army in Germany; the regiment is later transferred to the Upper Rhine.
1800 – In Germany: fights at Engen and on the Iller, then at the battle of Hohenlinden, and in the retreat at the battle of Lambach.
1801 – The regiment is disbanded; the *Obersts-Division* is merged with Dragoner Regiment Nr.6; the *Oberstlieutenants-Division* with Lothringen Dragoner Nr.7; the *Majors Division* with Erzherzog Franz Dragoner Nr.2.

Cuirassieren Regiment Nr.14; Cuirassieren Regiment Nr.9; Cuirassieren Regiment Nr.5					
Nr.	**Year**	**Proprietor / 2nd Proprietor**	**Commander**	**Denomination**	**Depot**
14	1792	Friedrich August von Nassau –Usingen	Johann von Risch	Nassau-Usingen	Vienna
14	1793	" "	Ferdinand Bouget	Nassau-Usingen	
14	1794	" "	Franz de Valvasor	Nassau-Usingen	
14	1795	" "		Nassau-Usingen	
14	1796	" "		Nassau-Usingen	
14	1797	" "		Nassau-Usingen	
9	1798	" "		9. Cuirassieren	Nyitra
9	1799	" "	Peter von Brady	9. Cuirassieren	
9	1800	" "		9. Cuirassieren	
9	1801	" "		9. Cuirassieren	Vienna – Herzogenburg
5	1802	" "	Anton Kirchner	5. Cuirassieren	Steinamanger
5	1803	" "		5. Cuirassieren	St. Georgen
5	1804	" "		5. Cuirassieren	
5	1805	" "	Friedrich von Minutillo	5. Cuirassieren	Vienna
5	1806	Hannibal Sommariva		5. Cuirassieren	Rzeszów
5	1807	" "		5. Cuirassieren	Niedwiecz

5	1808	" "		5. Cuirassieren	Rzeszów
5	1809	" "	Maximilian Graf Auersperg	5. Cuirassieren	Krakow
5	1810	" "		5. Cuirassieren	Vienna
5	1811	" "		5. Cuirassieren	Ödenburg – Báth
5	1812	" "		5. Cuirassieren	St. Georgen
5	1813	" "	Franz von Seymann	5. Cuirassieren	
5	1814	" "		5. Cuirassieren	Vienna
5	1815	" "		5. Cuirassieren	Vienna – St. Georgen

Recruited in Styria and Carinthia.
1793 – In the Austrian Low Countries: engaged at Neerwinden and at the siege of Valenciennes, later fights at Le Quesnoy and distinguished in the encounters of Avesnes-le-Sec.
1794 – Engaged in limited actions, then at Sólre-le-Chateau, Rouvroy, Erquelinnes and at the battle of Charleroi.
1795 – The regiment distinguishes itself in the assault on the Mainz entrenchments: the *Oberstlieutenant-Division* is engaged at the battle of Trippstadt.
1796 – With the army of the Lower Rhine: encounters of Wetzlar and Friedberg, where the *Oberstlieutenant-Division* supports the infantry retreat; the *Oberst* 2nd squadron participates with Brigade Alcaini at the battle of Lahn. The regiment fights at Amberg and Würzburg, where it performs positively.
1797 – The *Oberstlieutenant-Division* distinguishes itself at the battle of Hochheim-Frankfurt.
1799 – In Germany. The regiment performs with success at Stockach; campaign in Switzerland and battle of Zürich.
1800 – The regiment fights at Möskirch, Memmingen, Launingen and Nördlingen and Hohenlinden. In the following retreat the *Oberst-Division* distinguishes itself at the Salza bridges near Salzburg; the *Oberst* 2nd squadron is engaged at Neumarkt.
1805 – Assigned to the Korps Kienmayer: the regiment is heavily engaged at Austerlitz. One squadron under *Rittmeister* Baron von Gumpenberg forces out with success a pontoon train at Ulm and avoids capture moving to Tyrol.
1809 – Assigned to the VII Corps under Erzherzog Ferdinand: heavy losses at Raszyn.
1813 – With the Bohemian main army, distinguishes itself at Leipzig with a brilliant charge near Gröbern.
1814 – With the main army: detachments are engaged at Troyes, la Ferté, and la Fère-Champenoise.
1815 – In Germany without actions.

Cuirassieren Regiment Nr.6 – disbanded in 1801					
Nr.	Year	Proprietor / 2nd Proprietor	Commander	Denomination	Depot
6	1798	-	Ignaz Eggermann	6. Cuirassieren	Aschbach
6	1799	Michael von Melas	" "	6. Cuirassieren	Vienna
6	1800	" "	Leopold von Strachwitz	6. Cuirassieren	
6	1801	" "	" "	6. Cuirassieren	Szeged
6	1802	" "	" "	6. Cuirassieren	Grosswardein

Recruited in Bohemia.
1798 – Formed on 1 June at Aschbach in Lower Austria with both chevauxlegers divisions of the carabinier regiments Kaiser and Sachsen-Teschen and with the regiments Royal Allemand and Anhalt–Zerbst. The first denomination was a generic, Neu-formierte Cürassier Regiment, but before the end of the year, the regiment receives the number '6'.[1]
1799 – Quartered at Vienna.
1800 – Assigned to the Army of Italy in the Verona reserve corps without actions.
1802 – Merged with the *Oberst-Division* of the disbanded Czartoryski Cuirassieren (Nr.4), the regiment forms Dragoner Regiment Nr.6.

Cuirassieren Regiment Nr.20; Cuirassieren Regiment Nr.10; Cuirassieren Regiment Nr.6					
Nr.	Year	Proprietor / 2nd Proprietor	Commander	Denomination	Depot
20	1792	Heinrich von Jacquemin	Johann Karwinsky von Karwin	Jacquemin	Vienna
20	1793	Carl Mack von Leiberich		Mack.	
20	1794	" "	Franz Orsini-Rosenberg	Mack	
20	1795	" "		Mack	
20	1796	" "	Joseph Walthür von Waldenau	Mack	
20	1797	" "		Mack	Saaz
10	1798	" "		10. Cuirassieren	Pilsen
10	1799	" "		10. Cuirassieren	
10	1800	" "	Friedrich von Wöllwarth	10. Cuirassieren	
10	1801			10. Cuirassieren	Vienna
6	1802	" "		6. Cuirassieren	Gross-Kanizsa

1 The regiment occupied place number 12 in the cuirassiers' order of seniority, since 11 regiments had existed before 1798. However, the previous 11 regiments retained their rank numbers within the whole cavalry, and the number 12 had been already assigned in the old numeration, while number 6 was vacant.

6	1803	" "		6. Cuirassieren	Kesthély
6	1804	" "		6. Cuirassieren	
6	1805	" "		6. Cuirassieren	Moór
6	1806	Vacant	Franz Roussel d'Hurbal	6. Cuirassieren	Grosswardein Moór
6	1807	Vacant		6. Cuirassieren	Gyöngyös
6	1808	Friedrich von Gottesheim		6. Cuirassieren	
6	1809	Moriz von Liechtenstein	Carl von Flachenfeld	6. Cuirassieren	
6	1810	" "		6. Cuirassieren	St. Georgen (Pressburg)
6	1811	" "		6. Cuirassieren	
	1812	" "		6. Cuirassieren	Vienna
6	1813	" "	Andreas von Laitner	6. Cuirassieren	
6	1814	" "		6. Cuirassieren	Gaja
6	1815	" "		6. Cuirassieren	

From 1781 until 1807 the regiment recruited in Bohemia, later also in Moravia and Silesia.

1793 – In the Rhine theatre of war: detachments fight at the battles of Rheinzabern and Landau, at the siege of the Weissenburg lines, and at Brumpter Wald. The *Obersts-Division* distinguishes itself at Reichshofen (Uttenhofen) with a successful charge; at the battle of Neuweiler, *Major* Wallthör and his *Division* clean the enemy out of Schweighauser Wood.

1794 – In Germany without actions.

1795 – On the Upper Rhine: successful action at Mannheim and at Frankenthal, where one squadrons distinguishes itself in the fight.

1796 – Assigned to the Erzherzog Carl army: the regiment breaks a French three-battalion square during the battle of Amberg, and later distinguishes itself at Würzburg.

1797 – On the Rhine, without actions.

1799 – In Germany; encounters at Stockach and Löchgau.

1800 – The regiment is gathered at Donauwörth and later fights at Hohenlinden, and with the Austrian rearguard is engaged at Salzburg, Lambach and Kremsmünster.

1802 – The regiment joins the *Oberst-Division* of the disbanded Zezschwitz Cuirassieren (Nr.5).

1805 – With four *Divisions* in Germany: the *Major Division* distinguishes itself at the battle of Michaelsberg. Campaign in Bohemia under Erzherzog Ferdinand's successful action at Eschenau. Diminished to a single *Division* after suffering heavy losses, engaged at Stecken.

1809 – in the reserve corps of the army of Germany; at the battle of Eckmühl; five squadrons try to stop the French heavy cavalry at Alt Eglofsheim but they are routed with the loss of 50 men. In the two days of the battle of Aspern–Essling the regiment claims the loss of 42 men and 44 horses dead, 83 men and 41 horses wounded, 19 men and 22 horses missing. On the second day

at Wagram, the regiment is deployed with the Austrian right wing; after the collapse of the front, it covers the retreat engaging the enemy in rearguard encounters. For this action *Oberst* Flachenfeld earns the Order of Maria Theresa. At Znaim the regiment is deployed with the reserve cavalry under Schwarzenberg in Brigade Kroyher, without participating in the battle.
1813 – With the army of the Danube, later in the mixed Austrian–Bavarian Corps under Wrede: heavy losses at Hanau.
1814 – With the main army: engaged at Troyes, then in the battles at Areis-sur-Aube and the Fère-Champenoise, where the *Oberst Division* distinguishes itself in the action. Occupation of Paris but without engagements.
1815 – With the Upper Rhine Army without actions.

Cuirassieren Regiment Nr.21; Cuirassieren Regiment Nr.7					
Nr.	**Year**	**Proprietor / 2nd Proprietor**	**Commander**	**Denomination**	**Depot**
21	1792	Christoph Frh. von Wallisch	Joseph von Roth	Wallisch	Békéscsaba
21	1793	" "		Wallisch	
21	1794	Carl Eugen von Lothringen-Lambesc	Nicolaus Pálffy ab Erdöd	Lothringen	Vienna
21	1795	" "		Lothringen	
21	1796	" "	Johann Mercandin	Lothringen	
21	1797	" "		Lothringen	
7	1798	" "		7. Cuirassieren	Bechin
7	1799	" "		7. Cuirassieren	
7	1800	" "	Maximilian Kollonits von Kollograd	7. Cuirassieren	
7	1801	" "	Clemens von Thünefeld	7. Cuirassieren	Nagy-Patak
7	1802	" "		7. Cuirassieren	Steinamanger
7	1803	" "		7. Cuirassieren	Ungvár
7	1804	" "		7. Cuirassieren	Sáros-Patak
7	1805	" "		7. Cuirassieren	
7	1806	" "	Johann Piccard von Grünthal	7. Cuirassieren	Gródek
7	1807	" "		7. Cuirassieren	Krakow
7	1808	" "		7. Cuirassieren	Zółkiew
7	1809	" "	Ferdinand von Hessen-Homburg	7. Cuirassieren	
7	1810	" "		7. Cuirassieren	Zombor
7	1811	" "		7. Cuirassieren	Grosswardein
7	1812	" "		7. Cuirassieren	
7	1813	" "		7. Cuirassieren	
7	1814	" "	Ernst von Penz	7. Cuirassieren	Klattau
7	1815	" "		7. Cuirassieren	Grosswardein

Recruited in Moravia and Silesia.
1792–95 – Garrison duties in Hungary and Austria.
1796 – In Germany with the corps Latour. One *Division* distinguishes itself at Herbolzheim. The regiment performs positively at Isny, Memmingen and Schliengen.
1797 – Quartered at Kehl.
1799 – In Germany: encounters at Ostrach and Stockach; siege of Mannheim.
1800 – The regiment is engaged at Möskirch, Biberach, Ulm, Neuburg, Hohenlinden and Schwanenstadt.
1802 – As new Cuirassieren Nr.7, it receives the *Oberstlieutenant Division* of the *Zezschwitz* Cuirassieren (Nr.5).
1805 – With the corps Kienmayer in Germany: engagements of Amstetten and Stein. Heavy losses at Austerlitz, while the regiment protects the Russian Guard during the retreat from the battlefield.
1809 – With the VII Corps under Archduke Ferdinand: fight at Raszyn. During the following campaign four squadrons are engaged in the battle of Tachów (Wlostów).
1813 – With the main army: battle of Dresden; the regiment distinguishes itself at Leipzig, near Gröbern, on 16 October, where it defeats several infantry units. On 18 October, at Dölitz, *Oberstlieutenant* Wernhardt rescues some guns from the enemy.
1814 – With the Süd Armee: encounter of St. Léger, Belleville and Limonest; conquest of Lyon.
1815 – In France without actions.

Cuirassier Regiment Nr.4; Cuirassieren Regiment Nr.8					
Nr.	**Year**	**Proprietor / 2nd Proprietor**	**Commander**	**Denomination**	**Depot**
4	1792	Friedrich Anton zu Hohenzollern -Hechingen	Friedrich de Hotze	Hohenzollern	Saaz
4	1793	" "	Caspar von Oppeln	Hohenzollern	
4	1794	" "		Hohenzollern	
4	1795	" "		Hohenzollern	
4	1796	" "		Hohenzollern	
4	1797	" "	Fabrizio Serbelloni	Hohenzollern	
8	1798	" "		8. Cuirassieren	Wittingau
8	1799	" "		8. Cuirassieren	
8	1800	" "	Joseph von Clary	8. Cuirassieren	
8	1801	" "		8. Cuirassieren	Grosswardein
8	1802	" "		8. Cuirassieren	Alternately Nagy- Károly and Szatmár
8	1803	" "		8. Cuirassieren	
8	1804	" "		8. Cuirassieren	
8	1805	" "		8. Cuirassieren	
8	1806	" "		8. Cuirassieren	Nagy Károly
8	1807	" "	Jakob O'Ferral	8. Cuirassieren	Szikszó

8	1808	" "		8. Cuirassieren	Kittsee
8	1809	" "	Clemens Grosselsberg von Hohenforst	8. Cuirassieren	
8	1810	" "		8. Cuirassieren	Báth (Frauenmarkt)
8	1811	" "		8. Cuirassieren	Vienna
8	1812	" "		8. Cuirassieren	Gaja
8	1813	Constantin Cesarewitsch Grand-Prince of Russia / Ignaz von Hardegg	Valentin Veigl	8. Cuirassieren	
8	1814	" "	Alfred zu Windischgrätz	8. Cuirassieren	Vienna
8	1815	" "		8. Cuirassieren	Brandeis

Recruited in Bohemia.
The oldest cavalry regiment of the Austrian army. For its loyalty and valour, in 1648 the regiment earned special privileges from Emperor Ferdinand II, confirmed by Emperor Franz I on the occasion of the *Säkularfeier* which took place in 1810:

> On duty, this regiment may march, under the trumpet's sound and with raising banners, through the Court, k-k. Hofburg and in the Reichshaup und Residenzstadt in Vienna, also deploying in the imperial Hofburgplatz (Franzensplatz) itself and open a recruitment post after three days of free advertising. The regiment will then advance the commanders to the Hofburg in a pro-forma accommodation, where the Regiments banners were deployed near those of the Palace Guards, and where the respective regiment commanders were, on such occasion, admitted to appear, unannounced, in full armament before His Majesty the Emperor. The Regiment also has the assurance that it will never be reduced or dissolved as long as it continues to claim its previous merits and finally had the award that no man would be executed by the regiment, because of crime, punished with death; in such cases the culprit had to be sent to another regiment for the accomplishment of such a Sentence.

1792 – In Breisgau without actions.
1793 – With the Rhine army: detachments fight at Reichshofen, Dauendorf, Neuburg, Gamshaim, Pfaffenhofen, where many officers distinguish themselves.
1794 – In Upper Rhine, fights at Mannheim.
1795 – One detachment fights at Schriesheim, while the regiment is engaged at Handschuhsheim.
1796 – With the Upper Rhine army: some detachments are engaged at Ettlingen, Cannstadt, later at Geisenfeld, Emmendingen and Schliengen. Two *Divisions* are engaged in the siege of Kehl.
1797 – The regiment is engaged at Diersheim–Honau.
1799 – In Germany: encounters of Ostrach and Stockach and siege of Mannheim.

1800 – The regiment fights at Möskirch, Dillingen, Ingolstadt and Neuburg.
1805 – With the corps under Werneck in Germany: fight at Elchingen. After the capitulation of Trochtelfingen and Ulm, a great part of the regiment is made prisoner and only single detachments remain with the Archduke Ferdinand Corps.
1809 – With the 1. Reservekorps of the army of Germany; fight of Eckmühl (Alt-Egloffsheim) and Regensburg; battle of Aspern, where the regiment engages in a hard battle on the second day, attached to Brigade Lederer, with the loss of seven men and 15 horses. At the battle of Wagram, the regiment is assigned to the second column and sent to help the IV Corps under attack, a hopeless mission because of the infernal artillery fire: losses are reported as very high. Encounter of Tesswitz (Znaim).
1813 – With the main army at Dresden and Leipzig, where the regiment performs positively.
1814 – Under its commander, Prince Windisch-Graetz, fights with success at Troyes, Arcis-sur-Aube and la Fère-Champenoise. *Oberst* Windisch-Graetz and some officers are awarded the Russian Order.
1815 – In France without actions.

Cuirassieren Regt. Nr.33; Cuirassieren Regt. Nr.11 – disbanded in 1801					
Nr.	**Year**	**Proprietor / 2nd Proprietor**	**Colonel Commander**	**Name**	**Depot**
33	1792	Christian Friedrich von Brandenburg-Ansbach und Bayreuth	Franz Saint Amour	Ansbach	Grosswardein
33	1793	" "		Ansbach	Grosswardein
33	1794	" "		Ansbach	
33	1795	" "		Ansbach	
33	1796	" "	Werner von Bolza	Ansbach	
33	1797	" "		Ansbach	
11	1798	" "		11. Cuirassieren	Bayern
11	1799	" "		11. Cuirassieren	Salzburg
11	1800	" "	Anton Kirchner	11. Cuirassieren	
11	1801	" "		11. Cuirassieren	Gross-Tapolcsan

Recruited in Bohemia.
1793 – In the Austrian Low Countries; the regiment distinguishes itself at Valenciennes.
1794 – On the Upper Rhine.
1795 – In Germany, the whole regiment performs positively at the encounter of Eppstein.
1796 – The regiment fights at Willstedt (Kock) in the Upper Rhine, where Oberstlieutenant Kirchner distinguishes himself in the action, then at Biberach and Stockach.
1799 – With the army of Germany: encounter of Löchgau.
1800 – Battle of Engen and minor encounters. Rearguard battle at Salzburg.

1801 – The regiment is disbanded, the *Oberst-Division* is transferred to Nassau Cuirassieren (Nr.5), the *Oberstlieutenants-Division* to Kaiser Dragoner (Nr.1), the *Majors Division* to Sachsen-Teschen Dragoner (Nr.3).

B – Dragoons

Dragoner Regiment Nr.26; Leichte Dragoner Regiment Nr.3; Dragoner Regiment Nr.1					
Nr.	**Year**	**Proprietor / 2nd Proprietor**	**Colonel Commander**	**Denomination**	**Depot**
26	1792	Joseph Anton Grossherzog von Toskana Carl von Lilien	Heinrich Bellegarde	Toskana	Keszthely
26	1793	" "	Franz von Bueren	Toskana	
26	1794	" "		Toskana	
26	1795	Erzherzog Johann Baptist / Carl von Lilien		Herzherzog Johann	
26	1796	" "	Carl de La Motte	Herzherzog Johann	
26	1797	" "		Herzherzog Johann	
3	1798	" "		3. Leichte Dragoner	Kuttenberg
3	1799	" "	Joseph Gavre	3. Leichte Dragoner	Vorarlberg
3	1800	" "		3. Leichte Dragoner	
3	1801	" "		3. Leichte Dragoner	
1	1802	" "	Sebastian Speth von Zwiefalten	1. Dragoner	Rzeszow
1	1803	" "		1. Dragoner	
1	1804	" "		1. Dragoner	
1	1805	" "	Johann Belloute de Watters / Ludwig von Hentzy	1. Dragoner	
1	1806	" "	Johann Belloute de Watters	1. Dragoner	
1	1807	" "		1. Dragoner	Pápa
1	1808	" "		1. Dragoner	Keszthely and Vienna
1	1809	" "	Johann von Szombathely	1. Dragoner	Vienna

<table>
<tr><td>1</td><td>1810</td><td>Erzherzog Johann Baptist / Emanuel Schustekh von Hervé</td><td></td><td>1. Dragoner</td><td>Debrecen</td></tr>
<tr><td>1</td><td>1811</td><td>" "</td><td></td><td>1. Dragoner</td><td>Deés</td></tr>
<tr><td>1</td><td>1812</td><td>" "</td><td>Johann von Stück</td><td>1. Dragoner</td><td>Jaworów</td></tr>
<tr><td>1</td><td>1813</td><td></td><td></td><td>1. Dragoner</td><td></td></tr>
<tr><td>1</td><td>1814</td><td>" "</td><td></td><td>1. Dragoner</td><td rowspan="2">Török-Szent Miklós Szász-Régen, Zaskoutz (Bukowina)</td></tr>
<tr><td>1</td><td>1815</td><td>" "</td><td>Johann von Schuster</td><td>1. Dragoner</td></tr>
</table>

Since 1781 recruited in Inner Austria (Styria and Carinthia).
1792 – With the corps under Hohenlohe in Germany: one detachment suffers heavy losses during the defence of Speyer. Some detachments guard the outposts at Saarburg (Wavern) and engage the French in minor encounters; one *Abteilung* performs a successful raid against Schoden.
1793 – The *Oberst* and *Majorsdivisions* are engaged at the siege of Mainz: encounters of Marienborn and Weissenau, later the *Oberstlieutenant Division* is transferred to Trier. Detachments fight at Rippach, Eisweiler and Merzkirchen.
1794 –Two *Divisionen* are engaged at Saarlouis; the *Oberstlieutenant Division* fights in small encounters in Luxembourg, while other *Abteilungen* fight at Remich, Mondorf and Sandweiler. *Oberstlieutenant* Schwander distinguishes himself during the assault on Bastogne.
1795 – The *Oberstlieutenant Division* is involved in the defence of Luxembourg. The other divisions are with the army of Upper Rhine without actions.
1796/97 – Two divisions are assigned to the corps under Latour: the *Major Division* fights at Sandweyer and Rastatt (Kuppenheim). The whole regiment is engaged at Malsch and Esslingen. During the retreat the regiment is finally involved in the siege of Kehl.
1798 – The reorganised *Oberstlieutenant Division* is in Vorarlberg and distinguishes itself during the French attack on Bregenz; later it is engaged in the battle of Lauterbach. The divisions at the siege of Kehl fight at Diersheim–Honau. The *Oberstlieutenant Division* sends a squadron to the Army of Italy, and during the retreat from Tarvis is engaged in several encounters; the other squadron remains with the corps in Tyrol and fights at Kollomann-Klausen and Kiens.
1799 – In Tyrol, the *Oberstlieutenants* 2nd squadron is assigned to the Loudon Brigade, which fights at Taufers and Martinsbruck, then follows the brigade's retreat to Landeck. The regiment is transferred to Italy: encounter of Tortona, fight of San Giuliano, and Novi where it performs positively. The *Oberstlieutenant Division* fights at Lesegno; the whole regiment is engaged at Genola, where the *Ober-Lieutenant* Gordon distinguishes himself.
1800 – The regiment fights at Romano and then at Marengo.
1805 – With the corps Kienmayer on the River Inn, some single detachments came into action near Lambach. Two squadrons are at Austerlitz, the rest of the regiment is assigned to the protection of the ammunition columns.

1809 – With the II Corps under Kolowrat; only the *Major Division* is engaged in action at Regensburg. The regiment distinguishes itself at Aspern, deployed with the Division Kienmayer in the Brigade Rottermund and then in the Hiller column. Detachments are also with the Division Kottulinsky, VI Corps; after the battle it claims the loss of 36 men and 76 horses. At Wagram is assigned to Brigade Rothkirch, Nostitz Division, reserve corps and sent to Pischdorf and Glinzendorf; later as reinforcement for the left wing at Markcount-Neusiedl. Encounters of Korneuburg and Znajm, being part of the rearguard division under Schwarzenberg, Brigade Neckersfeld.
1812 – Two divisions are assigned to the Observation Corps in Galicia without actions.
1813 – With the Bohemian main army; under *Oberst* Stück the regiment decides the allied victory at Kulm. The regiment is not involved at Leipzig, but is engaged at Hochheim.
1814 – Quartered at Besançon, then with the Süd-Armee: the regiment is engaged at Lyon, and successively is divided into detachments and sent through the Jura for the expedition in the Loire and Auvergne.
1815 – In France without actions.

Dragoner Regiment Nr.39; Leichte Dragoner Regiment Nr.7; Dragoner Regiment Nr.2					
Nr.	**Year**	**Proprietor / 2nd Proprietor**	**Colonel Commander**	**Denomination**	**Depot**
39	1792	Christian Prinz zu Waldeck	Friedrich Carl Prinz zu Hohenlohe-Ingelfingen	Waldeck	Báth
39	1793	" "		Waldeck	
39	1794	" "		Waldeck	
39	1795	" "	Alexander Prinz von Württemberg	Waldeck	
39	1796	" "		Waldeck	
39	1797	" "	Johann von Motzen	Waldeck	
7	1798	Vacant	Franz Weissmann von Weissenstein	7. Leichte Dragoner	Vorder-Österreich
7	1799	" "		7. Leichte Dragoner	
7	1800	" "	Ferdinand von Wintzingerode	7. Leichte Dragoner	
7	1801	Maximilian Joseph, König von Bayern		7. Leichte Dragoner	Horodenka
7	1802	" "	Johann Nepomuk von Hager zu Altensteig	7. Leichte Dragoner	
2	1803	" "		2. Dragoner	Horodenka
2	1804	" "		2. Dragoner	
2	1805	" "		2. Dragoner	
2	1806	" "		2. Dragoner	Groß-Kanizsa
2	1807	" "		2. Dragoner	Vienna
2	1808	" "	Emerich von Bésán	2. Dragoner	Keszthely

2	1809	" "		2. Dragoner	
2	1810	" "		2. Dragoner	Pécs
2	1811	" "		2. Dragoner	
2	1812	" "	Friedrich Wilhelm von Schlotheim	2. Dragoner	Maria-Theresiopel
2	1813	" "		2. Dragoner	
2	1814	Maximilian Joseph, König von Bayern / Friedrich von Hohenlohe-Ingelfingen		2. Dragoner	Verona
2	1815	Maximilian Joseph, König von Bayern / Ignaz von Lederer		2. Dragoner	Ehrstein (Alsace)

Recruited in Bohemia; from 1807 in Upper and Lower Austria.
1793 – On the Upper Rhine: detachments fight at Rheinzabern, Landau, Killstett, Hördt, Bettenhofen and in the assault on the Weissenburg lines.
1794 – Encounters of Schifferstadt, Schwengenheim, Kaiserslautern, Frankenthal. One squadron distinguishes itself in the reconquest of the entrenchments at Zahlbach near Mainz.
1795 – Two divisions are involved in the battle of Bacharach.
1796 – The regiment fights at Malsch, Cannstatt, then with the corps under Latour at Friedberg, on the River Isar and at Schliengen.
1797 – On the Upper Rhine but without actions.
1799 – With the main army: encounter of Neuhaus, later with the corps under Hotze the regiment participates at the siege of Luciensteig. With the Austrian corps in Switzerland: battle of Winterthur and Zürich. The regiment remains in Switzerland on outpost duty, then is engaged at Lichtensteg.
1800 – Detachments are sent to the Voralberg and Tyrol borders and fight at Nesselwang, Reutte, Schongau. With the main army: encounter of Nieder-Heidenstein, and during the retreat after the battle of Hohenlinden, at Salzburg and Schwanenstadt.
1805 – In Germany: one division fights at Ulm, then with the corps under Archduke Ferdinand is engaged at Eschenau and Stecken. Two *Divisions* remain at Ulm and become prisoners after the surrender.
1809 – In Italy with Archduke Johann, assigned to the IX Corps, under Gyulai, Division Wolfskehl, Brigade Hager; battle of Sacile, encounter of Vicenza and then involved in the retreat behind the River Piave, where the regiment is engaged against the French; General Wolfskehl is killed in action and the regiment commander Bésán taken prisoner, but is able to escape and join the regiment at Marburg. In Hungary, assigned to Division Freemont, VIII Corps; battle of Raab. One squadron moves to Pressburg under siege in order to link the Army of Inner Austria with the main army.
1813 – In Inner Austria without actions.
1814 – In Italy: battle of the River Mincio, where its commander, Graf Schlotheim, is seriously wounded.
1815 – In southern France without combat, later as occupation force in Alsace.

Dragoner Regiment Nr.3 Leichte Dragoner Regiment Nr.2 – Disbanded in 1801					
Nr.	**Year**	**Proprietor / 2nd Proprietor**	**Commander**	**Denomination**	**Depot**
3	1792	Kaiser Franz II / Friedrich Moriz von Nostitz-Rieneck	Matthias Bauer	Kaiser	St. Georgen (Svätý Jur)
3	1793	" "		Kaiser	Pécs
3	1794	" "		Kaiser	
3	1795	" "		Kaiser	
3	1796	" "	Johann von Nostitz-Rieneck	Kaiser	
3	1797	" "		Kaiser	
2	1798	Kronprinz Erzherzog Ferdinand / Franz Xaver Friedrich von Hohenzollern-Hechingen	Philipp von Grünne	2. Leichte Dragoner	Olmütz
2	1799	" "		2. Leichte Dragoner	
2	1800	" "	Sebastian von Speth	2. Leichte Dragoner	
2	1801	Kronprinz Erzherzog Ferdinand / Andreas von Karaiczay		2. Leichte Dragoner	Siedlec
2	1802	" "		2. Leichte Dragoner	

Recruited in Upper and Lower Austria.
1792 – Garrison duty in Austria.
1793 – With the army on the Upper Rhine: encounters of Rheinzabern and Offenbach, conquest of the Weissenburg lines, and engagements at Schaidt, Reichshofen and other minor encounters in Alsace. In these actions, *Oberst* Bauer, *Oberstlieutenant* Klenau, *Major* Nostitz-Rieneck and other officers distinguish themselves.
1794 – On the Upper Rhine without actions.
1795 – The regiment distinguishes itself at Handschuhsheim, then at the siege of Mannheim.
1796 – Encounters at Mausbach and Rheingönnheim, and battle of Emmendingen.
1797/98 – On the Upper Rhine without actions.
1799 – The regiment performs positively at Stockach, then marches to Switzerland and later to the Upper Rhine: small encounters at Philippsburg. *Oberlieutenant* Franz Fichtl receives the Order of Maria Theresa and is promoted to *Rittmeister* (1801).
1800 – With the corps under Lothringen: encounter of Engen and minor skirmish on the River Iller; detachments fight at Steindorf and Kremsmünster.
1801 – Disbanded.

Dragoner Regiment Nr.38; Leichte Dragoner Regiment Nr.8; Dragoner Regiment Nr.3					
Nr.	**Year**	**Proprietor / 2nd Proprietor**	**Commander**	**Denomination**	**Depot**
38	1792	Carl Eugen Landprinz Württemberg – Stuttgart	Ferdinand von Ritschan (Rziezan)	Württemberg	Ujpécs
38	1793	Ludwig Eugen Herzog von Württemberg		Württemberg	Nagy Enyed
38	1794	" "		Württemberg	
38	1795	Friedrich Wilhelm Carl Erbprinz von Württemberg		Württemberg	
38	1796	" "	Marcus von Frossard	Württemberg	
38	1797	Friedrich Wilhelm Carl Herzog von Württemberg	Johann von Festenberg von Hassenwein	Württemberg	Vienna
8	1798	" "		8. Leichte Dragoner	Vienna, Fünfkirchen
8	1799	" "		8. Leichte Dragoner	Fünfkirchen
8	1800	" "	Johann von Wodniansky	8. Leichte Dragoner	Pécsvárad
8	1801	" "		8. Leichte Dragoner	Nyiregyháza
8	1802	" "		8. Leichte Dragoner	Maria Theresiopel
3	1803	Friedrich Wilhelm Carl Kurfürst von Württemberg		3. Dragoner	Vienna
3	1804	" "		3. Dragoner	
3	1805	" "	Wenzel von Ollenhausen	3. Dragoner	
3	1806	Friedrich Wilhelm Carl König von Württemberg		3. Dragoner	Ujpécs
3	1807	" "		3. Dragoner	
3	1808	" "		3. Dragoner	Sárvár
3	1809	Vincenz Knesevich von St. Helena		3. Dragoner	
3	1810	" "	Carlo Guicciardi	3. Dragoner	Grosswardein
3	1811	" "		3. Dragoner	Szász Régen
3	1812	" "		3. Dragoner	Fratautz (Bukowina)
3	1813	" "	Jakob Oláh de Nánás	3. Dragoner	Suczawa
3	1814	" "		3. Dragoner	Simmern (Pfalz)
3	1815	" "		3. Dragoner	Landau

Recruited in Silesia and Moravia, and until 1804 also in Württemberg.
1792 – Garrison in Banat.
1793 – In Banat and then to Budapest, to escort French prisoners to Banat's detention camps.
1794–1795 – In Banat and Siebenbürgen.
1796 – In Hungary.
1797 – In Italy with the left wing of the 2nd Army at Gorizia (Görz) in the Liechtenstein Brigade. Peace interrupted operations.
1798 – In Hungary.
1799 – In Italy, one division at the Trebbia. All three divisions are employed in the occupation of Piacenza, then to Tortona. At the beginning of September, the regiment fights positively at Carrosio and Novi; later is engaged at Fossano and Pinerolo, in the occupation of Cuneo, and detachments are engaged at Beinette, Genola and Mondovì.
1800 – In the reserve corps under Vukassovich on the River Sesia; encounter of Turbigo. One squadron attached to the main army participates at the battle of Marengo.
1805 – The regiment now has eight squadrons and is assigned to Italy, but later marches to join the army of Germany, in the corps of Archduke Johann in Tyrol.
1809 – With the 2. Reservekorps of the army of Germany; encounters at Landshut and Neumarkt; two squadrons are engaged at Ebelsberg. The regiment participates at the defence of Vienna, where part of the troops are captured. The regiment fights at Aspern assigned to Brigade Clary, *Division* Kienmayer – reserve corps, with the loss of 14 men and 95 horses dead, 24 prisoners and 119 wounded; after the battle deploys only two field divisions. At Wagram the regiment is with Brigade Neckersfeld, Division Schwarzenberg of the reserve corps. Deployed at Pischdorf and then at Rasdorf, the regiment suffers under heavy artillery fire, and claims the loss of 26 men and 105 horses dead, 25 men and horses are taken prisoners. With Brigade Rothkirch, Nostitz Division, the regiment is deployed at Tesswitz near Znaim without actions.
1813 – Two divisions are in the reserve corps in Galicia and later are assigned to the army of the Danube, or Österreichisch–Bayerische Korps Wrede. Three divisions fight positively at Hanau.
1814 – With the corps under Wrede: successful fight at Brienne and Bar-sur-Aube. Detachments are engaged at St. Martin (Troyes), la Guillotiére and at Arcis-sur-Aube.
1815 – In Germany, two squadrons fight at Selz, the regiment is involved in the blockade of Strasbourg.

Chevauxlegers Regiment Nr.19; Leichte Dragoner Regiment Nr.14; Dragoner Regiment Nr.4					
Nr.	**Year**	**Proprietor / 2nd Proprietor**	**Commander**	**Denomination**	**Depot**
19	1792	Franz von Levenehr	Michael Kienmayer	Levenehr	Rohatyn
19	1793	" "	Johann von Hildebrand	Levenehr	

19	1794	" "		Levenehr	
19	1795	" "		Levenehr	
19	1796	" "	Joseph Zinn	Levenehr	
19	1797	" "		Levenehr	
14	1798	" "		14. Leichte Dragoner	Friuli (Italy)
14	1799	" "		14. Leichte Dragoner	
14	1800	" "	Franz Tige	14. Leichte Dragoner	
14	1801	" "		14. Leichte Dragoner	Bursztyn
14	1802	" "		4. Dragoner	
4	1803	" "		4. Dragoner	
4	1804	" "		4. Dragoner	
4	1805	" "		4. Dragoner	
4	1806	" "	Anton Hardegg	4. Dragoner	Pécs
4	1807	" "		4. Dragoner	
4	1808	" "		4. Dragoner	Neusatz
4	1809	" "	Georg von Hirsch	4. Dragoner	
4	1810	" "		4. Dragoner	Maria-Theresiopel
4	1811	" "		4. Dragoner	
4	1812	" "		4. Dragoner	
4	1813	Erzherzog Leopold Erbgrossherzog von Würzburg / Ferdinand Bubna von Littitz		4. Dragoner	
4	1814	Erzherzog Leopold, Erbgrossherzog von Toscana / Ferdinand Bubna von Littitz	Franz von Zarczynski	4. Dragoner	Pécs
4	1815	" "		4. Dragoner	

Recruited in Upper and Lower Austria and from 1802 also in Moravia.
1794/1795 – In West Galicia.
1796 – In Germany; the *Majors Division* fights at Eglingen, while the *Oberst* 2nd squadron is engaged at Altmühl and Gerolshofen; encounters at Amberg, Neumarkt; the regiment distinguishes itself at Würzburg; later is engaged at the siege of Kehl. *Major* Joseph von Prochaska receives the Order of Maria Theresa for his actions at Eglingen.
1798 – In Piedmont-Savoy, encounter at Fenestrelle.
1799 – In Italy: battles of Verona, Magnano, Trebbia and Novi; three squadrons are engaged at Beinette and Genola. *Oberstlieutenant* Joseph von Prochaska, *Major* Franz Latour and other officers receive awards.
1800 – The regiment participates at the blockade of Genoa, then transfers to the main army.
1805 – In Italy without actions.
1809 – With V Corps in Germany, 2. Reservekorps under Kienmayer,

Brigade Clary. After the first battle of Landshut the regiment leaves the brigade to form a vanguard unit under *General-Major* Thierry with 4½ squadrons, while 1¼ squadron forms the *Abteilungen* under *Oberst* Hammer. The detachments are assigned to Division Lusignan in the III Corps, and are overrun during the battle of Abensberg, involved in the chaotic retreat and, for a large part, taken prisoner at Kloster-Rohr. During the two days battle of Aspern–Essling, the regiment lost 98 men, included the *Oberstlieutenant* Bachmann, and further 280 men wounded or missing; 293 horses are lost. The regiment is transferred to the camp of Rohrendorf for reorganising and employed in small detachments for watching the outposts along the left Danube bank from Grafenwörth and beyond assigned to Brigade Hardegg.
1812 – In Russia with the Auxiliary Corps under Schwarzenberg: encounters of Podubnie and other limited engagements.
1813 – With the main army in Germany: one division under *Major* Menninger distinguishes itself at Dippoldiswalde; one squadron is engaged at Altenburg. The regiment performs positively at Pretsch but with heavy losses, and Leipzig, where *Rittmeister* Ast captures a French battalion on 17 October.
1814 – With Light Division Bubna in southern France and Savoy; detachments fight at Givry and Charnay. Later the regiment is involved at St. Georges and takes part in the siege of Lyon.
1815 – The regiment is with the Corps Bianchi in the campaign against Murat. One squadron distinguishes itself at the occupation of Cesenatico and later at Tolentino and Macerata.

Dragoner Regiment Nr.9; Leichte Dragoner Regiment Nr.15; Dragoner Regiment Nr.5					
Nr.	**Year**	**Proprietor / 2nd Proprietor**	**Commander**	**Denomination**	**Depot**
9	1792	Ferdinand von Tige	Franz Janota von Janthal	Savoyen	
9	1793	" "	Carl von Bey	Savoyen	
9	1794	" "		Savoyen	Chelm (Galicia)
9	1795	" "		Savoyen	Rajowice
9	1796	" "		Savoyen	
9	1797	" "	Marcus von Frossard	Savoyen	
15	1798	" "	Malachias Hermann	15. Leichte Dragoner	Reps
15	1799	" "		15. Leichte Dragoner	
15	1800	" "		15. Leichte Dragoner	
15	1801	" "		15. Leichte Dragoner	
15	1802	" "		5. Dragoner	
5	1803	" "		5. Dragoner	
5	1804	" "		5. Dragoner	Vienna
5	1805	" "	Carl von Aichelburg	5. Dragoner	
5	1806	" "		5. Dragoner	Moór -Jenikau

5	1807	" "		5. Dragoner	
5	1808	" "		5. Dragoner	
5	1809	" "	Franz von Gabelkoven	5. Dragoner	Iharos-Berény
5	1810	" "		5. Dragoner	Reps
5	1811	Vacant		5. Dragoner	
5	1812	" "		5. Dragoner	
5	1813			5. Dragoner	
5	1814	" "		5. Dragoner	Vicenza
5	1815	Johann Friedrich von Mohr	Franz von Chorinsky	5. Dragoner	

Recruited in Upper and Lower Austria.
During the First Coalition Wars, 1792–97 and 1799–1801, the regiment is quartered in Transylvania.
1794–1797 – In the Second Polish Partition, the *Oberst* and *Majors Divisions* are in Galicia in the Corps gathered on the Vistula River and remain there until 1797 in the newly constituted West Galicia province.
1798 – The *Oberst Division* marches to Vienna and joins the reserve corps, then in Inner Austria. The *Majors Division* is transferred to Bukowina to protect the border from Ottoman raids; detachments are engaged in minor encounters.
1800 – The *Oberstlieutenants Division* is transferred to Hungary in the reserve army.
1805 – In Italy without actions.
1809 – In Italy with the army of Archduke Johann; encounter of Pordenone and Fontanafredda. After the first advance to Vicenza, the regiment withdraws behind the River Piave. Assigned to cover Piavesella, right of Campana, with three artillery batteries, the regiment is then deployed in second line with 2. Dragoner. The Austrian cavalry is targeted by the French artillery and suffers heavy losses. After two hours of heavy gunfire between the opposing artilleries the regiment moves ahead but is countercharged by the French. General Wolfskehl and the *Oberst Commandant* Aichelburg are killed. The regiment loses 81 men dead and many wounded. Retreat to Styria; detachments take part in minor encounters at Windisch and Feistritz, at the siege of Graz and Leoben; the reserve squadron fights at the battle of Raab.
1813 – With the Army of Inner Austria without actions.
1814 – The regiment fights with distinction and heavy losses at Mincio.
1815 – In southern France without actions.

Dragoner Regiment Nr.6					
Nr.	**Year**	**Proprietor / 2nd Proprietor**	**Commander**	**Denomination**	**Depot**
6	1802	Michael von Melas	Leopold von Strachwitz	6. Dragoner	Grosswardein
6	1803	" "		6. Dragoner	
6	1804	" "		6. Dragoner	
6	1805	" "		6. Dragoner	

6	1806	Johann von Riesch		6. Dragoner	Nagy Enyed
6	1807	" "	Franz von Fröhlich	6. Dragoner	Leipnik
6	1808	" "	Heinrich von Scheither	6. Dragoner	Krakow Nikolsburg
6	1809	" "		6. Dragoner	Caslau
6	1810	" "		6. Dragoner	Rohatyn
6	1811	" "		6. Dragoner	
6	1812	" "		6. Dragoner	
6	1813	" "	Wilhelm von Kronenberg, then Heinrich von Hardegg	6. Dragoner	
6	1814	" "	Friedrich von Wangen	6. Dragoner	Moór
6	1815	" "		6. Dragoner	

Recruited in Bohemia.
1802 – Formed from the disbanded Cuirassieren Regiment Nr.6 and the *Oberst-Division* of the disbanded Cuirassieren Regiment Nr.4: the only dragoon regiment which avoided the light dragoon stage.
1805 – In North Tyrol: detachments are involved in outposts skirmishes defending the pass of Strub.
1809 – With the 1. Reservekorps of the army of Germany. The *Major* 1st squadron is captured after an unsuccessful raid against Straubing. The regiment fights positively at Aspern, assigned to the Brigade Rottermund, Division Kienmayer, reserve corps with 623 men in all. During the battle the regiment is engaged by the French cavalry together with other Austrian regiments of the right flank. Part of the regiment shifted back to support the third line, which includes the Hungarian *Insurrectio* militia cavalry, and several men are taken prisoners. After the battle the regiment claims the loss of 19 men and 74 horses dead, 52 men and 13 horses wounded, 5 men and five horses missing. At Wagram, the regiment is assigned to the Brigade Rothkirch, Nostitz Division, in the reserve corps under Liechtenstein. The *Oberstlieutenants Division* remains under enemy artillery fire, while the *Majors Division* is the only dragoon unit to attack the French. The regiment loses 89 men and 103 horse dead, 39 men and 37 horse wounded, 34 men and 26 horse missing, for a total of 162 men and 165 horses. At Znaim, without action, in the Brigade Neckersfeld, Schwarzenberg Reserve Division.
1812 – Russian campaign with the auxiliary corps under Schwarzenberg with two divisions; encounter of Liubomil. The commander of the regiment, *Oberst* Scheither, distinguishes himself in some actions with his autonomous *Streifkorps* at Gradniki and Pinsk. *Ober-Lieutenant* Joseph Pfister, seizes with just 50 dragoons and 30 infantrymen the village of Lohiczin.
1813 – With the army of Germany: battle of Dresden, Arbesau and Leipzig, where it is distinguished for its action.
1814 – With the Süd Armee without actions.
1815 – In France; some *Abteilungen* are engaged in minor skirmishes near Strasbourg.

Chevauxlegers Regiment Nr.13; Leichte Dragoner regiment Nr.5; Disbanded in 1802					
Nr.	Year	Proprietor / 2nd Proprietor	Commander	Denomination	Depot
13	1792	Hercules Herzog von Modena / Carl von Sauer	Andreas O'Reilly	Modena	Rohatyn-Grodek
13	1793			Modena	Rohatyn-Grodek
13	1794		Friedrich Ludwig von Hessen-Homburg	Modena	Rohatyn-Grodek
13	1795			Modena	Rohatyn-Grodek
13	1796			Modena	
13	1797		Carl von Roskowszky	Modena	
5	1798			5. Leichte Dragoner	Bavaria
5	1799			5. Leichte Dragoner	Bavaria
5	1800	Hercules Herzog von Modena / Antoine Bussy de Mignot		5. Leichte Dragoner	
5	1801		Johann Nepomuk Hager von Altensteig	5. Leichte Dragoner	Troppau
5	1802			5. Leichte Dragoner	East Galicia

Recruited in Bohemia.
1796 – In Germany; encounters of Neuburg and Schliengen.
1799 – The regiment is transferred to the Vorarlberg with Corps Hotze and participates in the siege of Luciensteige and Chur; battle of Zürich and encounter of Brunnen. *Major* Petz and *Rittmeister* Managetta distinguish themselves in these actions.
1800 – In North Tyrol.
1802 – The regiment is disbanded: the *Oberst-Division* is merged with Dragoner Regiment Nr.4; the *Oberstlieutenants* division with Dragoner Regiment Nr.5, and the *Majors Division* with Dragoner Regiment Nr.2.

Dragoner Regiment Nr.37; Leichte Dragoner Nr.6; Disbanded in 1802					
Nr.	Year	Proprietor / 2nd Proprietor	Commander	Denomination	Depot
37	1792	Friedrich Josias zu Sachsen-Coburg-Saalfeld	Joseph Maria von Lothringen-Vaudemont	Coburg	Cheb
37	1793		Anton Canisius	Coburg	
37	1794			Coburg	
37	1795			Coburg	

37	1796		András Hadik de Futak	Coburg	
37	1797			Coburg	
6	1798			6. Leichte Dragoner	Hohenmauth
6	1799			6. Leichte Dragoner	
6	1800			6. Leichte Dragoner	
6	1801		Franz Ambschel	6. Leichte Dragoner	
6	1802			6. Leichte Dragoner	Pilsen-Klattau

Recruited in Bohemia.
1792 – In the Austrian Low Countries; three squadrons fight at Bossut, one division at Florennes, the regiment distinguishes itself at Jemappes.
1793 – Battles of Aldenhoven, Berlaimont and Maubeuge, later at Bassuyan. The commander *Oberst* Canisius, the *Majors* Hadik and Schauroth, and several officers receive praise for their service.
1794 – The regiment is deployed in front of Landrecies; encounters of Le Cateau, St Croix, and other minor actions on the River Sambre; later involved at Maastricht and Kreuznach.
1795 – On the Rhine without actions.
1796 – With army of the Lower Rhine; encounter of Wetzlar, battles of Würzburg and Schliengen.
1798 – The regiment gives up its 4th *division* for the formation of the Leichte Dragoner Nr.13.
1799 – With the army of Germany: encounter of Stockach; in Switzerland: battle of Zürich.
1800 – The regiment forms the vanguard on the Upper Rhine; fights at Engenand and in the following battles on the River Iller and at Hohenlinden.
1802 – The regiment is disbanded; the *Oberst Division* is merged with Chevauxlegers Regiment Nr.6, the *Oberstlieutenants Division* with Chevauxlegers Nr.1, the *Majors Division* with Chevauxlegers Nr.5.

***Stabsdragoner* Regt.; Leichte Dragoner Regiment Nr.9 – Disbanded in 1801**					
Nr.	**Year**	**Proprietor / 2nd Proprietor**	**Commander**	**Denomination**	**Depot**
-	1792	-	Christoph Wieser	*Stabsdragoner*	-
-	1793	-		*Stabsdragoner*	
-	1794	-	Joseph Döller	*Stabsdragoner*	
-	1795	-		*Stabsdragoner*	
-	1796	-		*Stabsdragoner*	
-	1797	-	Carl von Wolfskehl	*Stabsdragoner*	
9	1798	-	Franz Gorüpp von Besanez	9. Leichte Dragoner	Aspern an der Zaya
9	1799	Johannes von Liechtenstein		9. Leichte Dragoner	

9	1800		Carlo Belcredi	9. Leichte Dragoner	
9	1801		Franz von Kinsky	9. Leichte Dragoner	Laibach
9	1802			9. Leichte Dragoner	

1792 – In March the *Major Division* is transferred to Germany.
1793 – In Italy; one *Division* fights at Sospello.
1794 – A *Stabsdragoner* division is formed in the Austrian Low Countries under *Major* Belcredi; the *Stabsdragoner* in Italy fight at Carrosio.
1796 – Detachments fight at Mondovì, Codogno (Fombio) and other minor encounters; two divisions are involved in the siege of Mantua. The *Oberst Division* joins the army corps in South Tyrol; detachments are engaged at La Rocchetta, Deutschmetz, San Michele and Cadine, then also at Rovereto and finally at Arcole.
1797 – The same division is engaged in the battle of Rivoli, then in the encounters at Lavis and Salurn. The other two divisions return to Austria after the surrender of Mantua.
1798 – After the order of 25 April, the regiment in Italy becomes the Leichte Dragoner Regiment Nr.9. The *Stabsdragoner Division* in Germany is disbanded.
1799 – In Italy; the regiment fights at La Trebbia and distinguishes itself during the siege of Cuneo.
1800 – Heavy losses at Marengo.

C – Chevauxlegers

Chevauxlegers Regiment Nr.1; Leichte Dragoner Regiment Nr.1; Chevauxlegers Regiment Nr.1					
Nr.	**Year**	**Proprietor / 2nd Proprietor**	**Commander**	**Denomination**	**Depot**
1	1792	Kaiser Franz II / Ferdinand von Harrach	Johann Fitzgerald	Kaiser	Gaja
1	1793	" "	Peter von Bolza	Kaiser	
1	1794	" "		Kaiser	
1	1795	" "		Kaiser	
1	1796	" "	Franz von Pilati	Kaiser	
1	1797	Kaiser Franz II / Heinrich Bellegarde		Kaiser	
1	1798			1. Leichte Dragoner	Radkersburg
1	1799			1. Leichte Dragoner	
1	1800		Carl von Kölbel	1. Leichte Dragoner	
1	1801	" "	Albert De Best	1. Leichte Dragoner	Gaja
1	1802	" "		1. Chevauxlegers	Nikolsburg
1	1803	" "		1. Chevauxlegers	Troppau
1	1804	" "	Joseph Baillet de Latour	1. Chevauxlegers	

1	1805	" "		1. Chevauxlegers	Leipnik
1	1806	Kaiser Franz I / Heinrich Bellegarde		1. Chevauxlegers	Ried
1	1807	" "		1. Chevauxlegers	Eperjes
1	1808	" "	Carl von Raigecourt	1. Chevauxlegers	Gródek
1	1809	" "		1. Chevauxlegers	
1	1810	" "		1. Chevauxlegers	Gyöngyös
1	1811	" "		1. Chevauxlegers	
1	1812	" "	Simon Fitzgerald	1. Chevauxlegers	
1	1813	" "		1. Chevauxlegers	
1	1814	" "		1. Chevauxlegers	Ungarisch-Brod
1	1815	" "		1. Chevauxlegers	

Recruited from Moravia.
1793 – In the Austrian Low Countries; *Oberstlieutenant* Bolza distinguishes himself in a raid against Stablo and Malmedy. Detachments fight at Tirlemont and Arlon.
1794 – In Luxembourg, *Major* Lackenau leads a successful combat near Rochefort. Other detachments on the Sambre are involved in minor actions.
1795 – With the army of the Rhine at Mannheim.
1796 – With the army of Archduke Carl; *Oberst* Bolza distinguishes himself at Maubach. *Rittmeister* Vécsey, as avant-garde commander, forces the fortress of Rottenberg to surrender. The same officer distinguishes later at Riegel and during the siege of Kehl. For these actions he obtains the Order of Maria Theresa. The regiment is engaged at Würzburg.
1798 – As *Leichte Dragoner*, the regiment receives a division (*Oberst-Division*) from the Coburg Dragoner (Leichte Dragoner Nr.6)
1799 – In Italy: encounter of at San Giuliano and, positively, at Novi, where *Major* Kees leads his division in a successful action. Detachments of the regiment fight at Beinette, Genola, Carra and Mondovi.
1800 – The regiment fights at Romano, Marengo and later on the River Mincio. *Rittmeister* Gasser receives the Order of Maria Theresa for his conduct at Romano, and in the previous campaigns.
1805 – Again in Italy where, at Caldiero, *Oberstlieutenant* Hardegg prevents multiple enemy attempts to seize key Austrian positions, and gains the Order of Maria Theresa.
1809 – With the VII Corps of Erzherzog Ferdinand in Poland; two squadrons take part in the attack at Jedlinsko.
1813 – With the Light Division under Liechtenstein in Germany; encounter of Marienberg, battles of Dresden, Freiberg, Altenburg and Naumburg, then Leipzig, and, finally, at Hochheim.
1814 – The regiment is involved in limited actions at Troyes and Rouvigny.
1815 – With the Rhine Army: one division is involved in the siege of Strassburg; encounters at Schlettstadt, Hüningen and Basel.

Chevauxlegers Regiment Nr.18; Leichte Dragoner Nr.4; Chevauxlegers Regiment Nr.2					
Nr.	Year	Proprietor / 2nd Proprietor	Commander	Denomination	Depot
18	1792	Andreas von Karaiczay de Vale-Sakam	Anton von Elsnitz	Karaczaj	Sedziszów
18	1793	" "		Karaczaj	
18	1794	" "		Karaczaj	
18	1795	" "	Maximilian von Merveldt	Karaczaj	
18	1796	" "	Joseph von Nimptsch	Karaczaj	
18	1797	" "		Karaczaj	Treviso
4	1798	" "		4. Leichte Dragoner	Inner-Österreich
4	1799	" "		4. Leichte Dragoner	
4	1800	" "	Carl von Provenchères	4. Leichte Dragoner	
4	1801	Friedrich Xaverzu Hohenzollern-Hechingen		4. Leichte Dragoner	Bassano
2	1802	" "		2. Chevauxlegers	Agram
2	1803	" "		2. Chevauxlegers	
2	1804	" "		2. Chevauxlegers	
2	1805	" "		2. Chevauxlegers	
2	1806		Leopold von Ludwigsdorff	2. Chevauxlegers	Warazdin
2	1807	" "		2. Chevauxlegers	Agram
2	1808	" "		2. Chevauxlegers	Pécs
2	1809	" "	Theophil von Zechmeister	2. Chevauxlegers	
2	1810	" "	Matthias Löderer	2. Chevauxlegers	Wels and Vienna
2	1811	" "		2. Chevauxlegers	Debrecen
2	1812	" "		2. Chevauxlegers	
2	1813	" "		2. Chevauxlegers	
2	1814	" "	Carl von Scheibler	2. Chevauxlegers	Nagy-Enyed
2	1815		Franz von Fichtel	2. Chevauxlegers	Zółkiew

Recruited in Moravia and Silesia, from 1809 also in Bohemia.
1793 – In the Austrian Low Countries; the *Major Division* distinguishes itself at Herve, capturing 17 guns. Detachments fight at Neerwinden, at the siege of Camp-César, at Dünkirchen and Cysoing.
1794 – The regiment fights at Landrecies, Tourcoing, Tournay and the second Fleurus. Major Schustekh, destined for a brilliant career, distinguishes himself several times and receives the Order of Maria Theresa.
1795 – Two squadrons are engaged at Millingen-Vreden; the regiment is

engaged at Urdingen, on the Pfrimm and Lauterecken, while one division fights at Meissenheim and one squadron takes part at the siege of Thalheim.
1796 – With the army of the Archduke Carl; one *division* distinguishes itself at Wetzlar-Ukerath, as well as the whole regiment at Amberg and Würzburg. Detachments fight at Hirschaid, Emmendingen and Schliengen, the regiment standing later – and in 1797 – at Kehl.
1799 – In Italy; encounter of Novi, detachments fight at Pastrengo, Verona, Magnano and then on the Trebbia. Detachments are involved in the encounters of Fossano, Centallo, Borgo San Dalmazzo and Genola. The commander, *Oberst* Nimptsch, earns the Order of Maria Theresa for his action at the battler of the River Trebbia.
1800 – In northern Piedmont, one squadron fights at Susa; heavy losses at Marengo. The regiment is engaged at Valeggio-Pozzolo.
1801 – The regiment fights at Caldiero and Mantachie-Maggiore.
1802 – Change to Chevauxlegers Regiment Nr.2 and receives the *Major Division* of the disbanded Leichte Dragoner Regiment Nr.5.
1805 – In South Tyrol, later in Pustertahl. The only action performed is the assault of the *Rittmeister* Esch's squadron on Bozen with the Brigade Rohan. Later, the regiment is taken prisoner and interned in Castelfranco with the rest of the brigade.
1809 – With the VIII Corps in Italy; two divisions are transferred to Tyrol, while the *Erste Major* second squadron marches to Dalmatia. The squadron in Italy performs positively: the *Oberst-Division*, under the regiment's commander Baron von Ludwigsdorff, who is seriously wounded, achieves a success at Pordenone, and later with the vanguard at Rorai Grande. The 2nd *Majors Division* under Major Lachowski fights at Sacile and is later sent to Tyrol as reinforcement: detachments protect the retreats of the Chasteler Corps to Carinthia, performing positively at St. Veit and Klagenfurt. In mid June the division joins the rest of the regiment with the army of Archduke Johann at Pápa. *Abteilungen* from the squadrons in Tyrol are involved in the battle of Laditscher Brucke and Volano, then they move to North Tyrol fighting at Wörgl and Berg Isel. After the retreat of the Corps Chasteler in Tyrol, one squadron is engaged at Trento. Among the detachments in North Tyrol, *Oberlieutenant* Altmann distinguishes himself with one *Zug*, at Murnau, saving the local *Landesschützen* from the destruction. *Oberlieutenant* Altmann and *Rittmeister* Martyn are awarded the Order of Maria Theresa as well as the regiment's *Oberst Inhaber* Prinz Hohenzollern.
1812 – The regiment is in Russia with the auxiliary corps under Schwarzenberg; good performances in the encounters of Podubnie, Divin, Rudnja, in the assault on Nieswicz and at Glinki.
1813 – Three divisions fight at Dresden; one division under *Oberstlieutenant* Gasser joins the Russian Corps Thielemann in the encounters of Merseburg, Altenburg and in the siege of Zeitz. Two divisions take part at the battles of Chemnitz, Penning and on the River Flöha. The same divisions fight at Liebertwolkwitz and Leipzig. The regiment is involved in the blockade of Dresden and then marches to Italy.
1814 – Battle on the River Mincio.
1815 – In Bohemia in the reserve corps, without actions.

Chevauxlegers Regiment Nr.28; Leichte Dragoner Regiment Nr.10; Chevauxlegers Regiment Nr.3					
Nr.	Year	Proprietor / 2nd Proprietor	Commander	Denomination	Depot
28	1792	Joseph von Lobkowitz	Carl Mack von Leiberich	Lobkowitz	Zółkiew
28	1793	" "	Paul von Winkler	Lobkowitz	
28	1794	" "		Lobkowitz	
28	1795	" "		Lobkowitz	
28	1796	" "	Annibale Sommariva	Lobkowitz	
28	1797	" "		Lobkowitz	
10	1798	" "		10. Leichte Dragoner	Padua
10	1799	" "	Max Joseph von Thurn und Taxis	10. Leichte Dragoner	
10	1800	" "	Bernhard Grosser	10. Leichte Dragoner	
10	1801	" "		10. Leichte Dragoner	Tarnów
3	1802	" "		3. Chevauxlegers	Siedlec
3	1803	Andreas O'Reilly		3. Chevauxlegers	
3	1804	" "		3. Chevauxlegers	
3	1805	" "	Friedrich von Degenfeld-Schonburg	3. Chevauxlegers	Siedlec
3	1806			3. Chevauxlegers	Lauffen
3	1807	" "	Leopold von Rothkirch	3. Chevauxlegers	Ried
3	1808	" "		3. Chevauxlegers	Wels
3	1809	" "	Simon von Sardagna	3. Chevauxlegers	
3	1810	" "		3. Chevauxlegers	Bochnia
3	1811	" "		3. Chevauxlegers	Gródek
3	1812	" "	Johann Heinrich von Auersperg	3. Chevauxlegers	Zółkiew
3	1813	" "		3. Chevauxlegers	
3	1814	" "		3. Chevauxlegers	Rzeszów
3	1815			3. Chevauxlegers	

Recruited in Upper and Lower Austria, in 1807 in Bohemia and from 1813 also in Galicia.
1793 – The *Oberstlieutenants Division* under Sommariva is in the Austrian Low Countries: battle of Marchiennes, half squadron fights at Orchies.
1794 – The same *Division* is engaged at Landrecies and then joins the other two *Divisions* which have fought at Le Cateau. The regiment is involved in the encounters on the Sambre, at Charleroi and Fleurus, one squadron takes part in the defence of Liège.
1795 – In Germany; the regiment performs positively in the assault on the fortified camp near Mannheim, where *Rittmeister* Friedrich von Schwarzenber distinguishes himself, as does *Oberlieutenant* Zerboni in the defence of Edigheim.

1796 – On the Upper Rhine; detachments fight at Schwetzingen, Frankenthal and Rastatt, then also at Teining-Amberg, Emmendingen and at the siege of Kehl. *Rittmeister* Sardagna, at the command of commanding a mobile column, distinguishes himself in these actions.
1797 – The regiment moves to Tyrol, then to Carinthia without actions.
1799 – In Italy; encounters of Verona and Magnano, siege of Tortona; the regiment distinguishes itself at Marengo and also at the battle of the Trebbia. Detachments are involved at Novi, Fossano, Pinerolo, Castelletto, Madonna dell'Olmo, Centallo, Beinette and Genola; the regiment commander Annibale Sommariva, from Lodi, earns the Order of Maria Theresa.
1800 – Detachment fights at Ivrea, Casteggio, then at Marengo and later at Valeggio. *Rittmeister* Sardagna receives the Order of Maria Theresa for the action at Casteggio.
1802 – As *Chevauxlegers RegimentNr.3*receives the *Majors Division* from the disbanded Leichte Dragoner Regiment Nr.2 (Kronprinz).
1805 – With the corps under Kienmayer on the River Inn, the whole regiment is involved in the encounters after Austerlitz. The proprietor of the regiment, *Feldmarschall-Lieutenant* O'Reilly, earns the Order of Maria Theresa award for his action at Caldiero.
1809 – In Germany with the Division Jellacich near Salzburg, where detachments fight at Waging and Anthering. One squadron remains with Jellacich while the other seven squadrons are assigned to the main army in the Marchfeld; they fight positively at Aspern. After the battle the losses are 19 men and 78 horses dead, 125 men and 79 horses wounded, 13 men and 16 horses missing. Battle of Wagram, the regiment claims the loss of 50 men and 89 horses dead, 50 men and 19 horses wounded, 17 men, included the commander and 15 horse prisoners, 49 men and 34 horses missing. After the battle the 1. Majors Division is attached to the IV Corps under Rosenberg. The *2. Majors Division* is detached for the defence of the bridgehead at Pressburg. After the campaign, the regiment's commander *Oberst* Rotkirch is promoted to *General Wachtmeister*.
1812 – With the auxiliary corps under Schwarzenberg in Russia; encounters of Podubie, Ploska, Krimini and Guidawa. After a surprise Russian attack against the regiment's camp at Nieswiez, three squadrons lose many soldiers captured by Russians.
1813 – In Germany; battle of Dresden, detachments fight at Freiburg, on the Flöha, Chemnitz and Penig. The regiment performs positively at Liebertwolkwitz and Leipzig. *Oberstlieutenant* Windisch-Graetz earns the Order of Maria Theresa.
1814 – With the Light Division under Liechtenstein; detachments fight at Salins, Maisons-Blanches, Moret, Villemaure and Troyes.
1815 – In Alsace with the 1. Reservekorps without actions.

Chevauxlegers Regiment Nr.31; Leichte Dragoner Regiment Nr.11; Chevauxlegers Regiment Nr.4					
Nr.	Year	Proprietor / 2nd Proprietor	Commander	Denomination	Depot
31	1792	Maximilian Baillet de Latour	Carl von Pforzheim	La Tour	Tournay
31	1793	" "	Franz von Roe	La Tour	
31	1794	" "		La Tour	
31	1795	" "		La Tour	
31	1796	" "		La Tour	
31	1797	" "	Ferdinand de Mondet	La Tour	
11	1798	" "		11. Leichte Dragoner	Dittmaning
11	1799	" "		11. Leichte Dragoner	
11	1800	" "	Armand von Nordmann	11. Leichte Dragoner	
11	1801	" "		11. Leichte Dragoner	Ungarisch-Brod
4	1802	" "		4. Chevauxlegers	Gaja
4	1803	" "		4. Chevauxlegers	
4	1804	" "	Ignaz von Lederer	4. Chevauxlegers	
4	1805	" "		4. Chevauxlegers	
4	1806	Carl von Vincent		4. Chevauxlegers	Neuhaus
4	1807	" "		4. Chevauxlegers	Gross-Tapolcsán
4	1808	" "		4. Chevauxlegers	Gaja
4	1809	" "	Goswin de Fierland	4. Chevauxlegers	St. Georgen (Pressburg)
4	1810	" "		4. Chevauxlegers	Rakonitz
4	1811	" "		4. Chevauxlegers	Esseg (Osijek)
4	1812	" "	Franz von Gallois	4. Chevauxlegers	Radkersburg
4	1813	" "		4. Chevauxlegers	Gross-Kanizsa
4	1814	" "		4. Chevauxlegers	Bochnia
4	1815			4. Chevauxlegers	

A Walloon regiment which recruited in the Austrian Low Countries until 1801, then in Lower Austria.

1792 – Detachments fight at Lamain, Glisuelle, Harlebeke, Orchies, Lille, Mons and Jemappes, where the *2. Majors Division* rescues lost guns. Later two divisions protect the retreat of the Corps Clerfayt behind the Roer.

1793 – The regiment distinguishes itself at Aldenhoven, Neerwinden and Famars; later is engaged at Maubeuge, Beaumont, Merbes-le-Chateau, Fauquemont and Condé.

1794 – Detachments fight at Landrecies, Belleghem, Courtray-Ingelmunster and Rousselaer. The *2. Majors Division* originally deployed at Douay is assigned to the defence of Valenciennes and after the evacuation returns in the Austrian Low Countries. Two divisions cover the retreat of the army and both fight at Tongeren.
1795 – On the Lower Rhine, then at Mannheim; encounters of Hachenburg and Frankenthal.
1796 – With the Corps Werneck; encounters of Sulzbach, Amberg and battle of Würzburg, then at Giessen and Freilingen with success.
1797 – the *Oberstlieutenant* Division suffers heavy losses at Kirburg.
1798 – The regiment becomes Leichte Dragoner Nr.11 and gives *2. Majors Division* to the newly raised Leichte Dragoner Nr.13.
1799 – In Germany; encounters of Ostrach and Stockach, then in Switzerland; battle of Zürich, later as garrison in Mannheim.
1800 – The regiment suffers heavy losses at Engen; encounter of Möskirch and Neuburg, where it distinguishes itself; later is involved at Ampfing and Salzburg (Viehhausen), at Schwanenstadt it rescues the artillery train.
1802 – As a *Chevauxlegers* regiment, it incorporates the *Oberstlieutenants Division* of the disbanded Leichte Dragoner Nr.2 (Kronprinz).
1805 – With the main army; the *Oberstlieutenants Division* distinguishes itself at Wertingen, and the whole regiment at Jungingen. Two divisions escort the artillery to Bohemia; the other two divisions are assigned to the corps of Archduke Ferdinand. Because of the low number of effectives, the regiment deploys a single *Division* which fights at Stecken.
1809 – With II Corps in Germany; encounters of Dinzling, Schierling, Eckmühl and Regensburg, then at Alt-Eglofsheim with heavy casualties, losing 23 men and 103 horses dead, 54 men and 33 horses wounded, 24 men prisoners, 16 men and 76 horses missing. At Aspern the regiment fields a strength of 746 men, deployed with army's vanguard in Brigade Stutterheim, Rohan Division, IV Corps. Some *Abteilungen* are also with Brigade Grätze in the same Rohan division. The regiment distinguishes itself in the assault against Baumersdorf. One division is with the *Streifen-Korps*, which carries out some successful actions. After the battle the losses amount to 10 men and 63 horses dead, 80 men and 61 horses wounded; *Oberstlieutenant* Ficquelmont dies of wounds on 23 May. At Wagram the regiment deploys the *Oberst Division* and the *1. Majors Division* under *Oberst* de Fierlant on the left flank. Both divisions engage the French advancing along the Russbach. The *2. Majors Division* under *Major* Laitner is on the right. While the French are attacking Baumersdorf, defended by the Brigade Hardegg, the regiment pursues the French units withdrawing to Raasdorf. On the second day, the French repeat the assault on Raasdorf; being under stiff artillery fire, Hardegg is forced to withdraw and the regiment covers the movement. After the battle the losses are 18 men and 122 horses dead, 47 men missing, 97 men and 62 horses wounded.
1813 – The regiment fights at Dresden; two squadrons assigned to the rearguard distinguish themselves during the retreat. The regiment is involved in the siege of Freiberg, then at Stössen-Wethau and Leipzig. One detachment performs a raid on Neuchatel and captures ammunition and other war material.

1814 – Blockade of Besançon and siege of Chalons-sur-Saone, later the regiment is involved at Maison-Blanches, Macon, Lyon and Romans.
1815 – The regiment is quartered at Schlettstadt; one squadron fights at Markolsheim.

Chevauxlegers Regiment Nr.7; Leichte Dragoner Regiment Nr.12; Chevauxlegers Regiment Nr.5					
Nr.	**Year**	**Proprietor / 2nd Proprietor**	**Commander**	**Denomination**	**Depot**
7	1792	Joseph Kinsky von Kninitz und Tettau	Johannes von Liechtenstein	Kinsky	Mährisch-Ostrau
7	1793	" "		Kinsky	
7	1794	" "	Joseph von Stipsicz	Kinsky	
7	1795	" "		Kinsky	
7	1796	" "		Kinsky	
7	1797	" "	Albert Stahel	Kinsky	Brüx
12	1798	" "		12. Leichte Dragoner	Aurolzmünster
12	1799	" "		12. Leichte Dragoner	
12	1800	" "		12. Leichte Dragoner	
12	1801	" "	Carl Kinsky	12. Leichte Dragoner	Saaz
5	1802	" "		5. Chevauxlegers	
5	1803	" "		5. Chevauxlegers	
5	1804	Johann Klenau von Janowitz		5. Chevauxlegers	
5	1805	" "		5. Chevauxlegers	
5	1806		Joseph von Mayer	5. Chevauxlegers	Pardubitz
5	1807	" "		5. Chevauxlegers	Gabel
5	1808	" "		5. Chevauxlegers	Pardubitz
5	1809	" "	Raban von Spiegel	5. Chevauxlegers	
5	1810	" "		5. Chevauxlegers	Saaz
5	1811	" "		5. Chevauxlegers	
5	1812	" "	Johann von Kopp	5. Chevauxlegers	
5	1813	" "		5. Chevauxlegers	
5	1814	" "		5. Chevauxlegers	Saaz Gabel
5	1815	" "		5. Chevauxlegers	Saaz

Recruited in Bohemia.
1792 – with the corps under Hohenlohe on the Rhine; operations in Champagne, later in Luxembourg.
1793 – The regiment fights at St. Croix (Arlon). In the second battle of Arlon, four squadrons repulse several enemy attacks. The regiment and its

commander Fürst Liechtenstein distinguish themselves at Avesnes-le-Sec, in a frontal assault against the French squares. Detachments participate in the seizure of the entrenchments at Merbes-le-Chateau and at the encounter of Berlaimont.
1794 – Siege of Landrecies and battle of le-Cateau; the regiment is engaged at Cense-du-Fagnel, Erquelinnes, Charleroi and, with success, at Fleurus.
1795 – The regiment distinguishes itself in the siege of Mannheim Camp; encounters of Schopp, Landstuhl and Trippstadt.
1796 – Four squadrons fight at Wetzlar, two squadrons at Kircheip. Detachments are engaged at Malsch and Rothensohl, then at Stüttgart, Cannstadt, Aalen, Heidenheim, Bopfingen and Kirchheim. The regiment fights at Teining, Neumarkt, Amberg, Forchheim and, positively, at Würzburg. Some *Abteilungen* are involved also at Aschaffenburg, Hanau, Kron-Weissenburg, and finally one squadron at the battle of Emmendingen.
1797 – On the Rhine without actions.
1799 – With the army of Germany; encounters of Ostrach, Stockach, Frauenfeld, with heavy losses; detachments fight at Winterthur and in the first battle of Zürich; later the regiment performs with success at Neckarau–Mannheim.
1800 – Battle of Engen, Möskirch, Biberach, on the Iller, then at Neresheim, Neuburg, and Hohenlinden, where the retreat is assured by the sacrifices of *Rittmeister* Tettenborn. During the retreat, the regiment is involved at Rosenhain. The *Oberst Division* performs an effective assault at Viehhausen (Wals) against superior enemy forces. The regiment fights also at Schwandorf and Kremsmünster.
1802 – Changed again to a *Chevauxlegers* regiment, numbered '5' and receives the *Major Division* of the disbanded Leichte Dragoner Nr.6 (Coburg).
1805 – With the main army in Germany; four squadrons are assigned to the Archduke Ferdinand Corps and are involved in a series of rearguard fights after the capitulation of Ulm; in these actions, *Rittmeister* Tettenborn with his squadron distinguishes himself at Waldmünchen. The remaining four squadrons are in the corps under Jellacich in Vorarlberg and avoid with a night march the effects of the capitulation of Bregenz, joining the army in Bohemia.
1809 – In Germany, with IV Corps under Rosenberg; detached in the Brig. Baron Peter Vécsey, and then assigned to III Corps Hohenzollern. At Eggmühl four squadrons are deployed to the right wing under Vécsey, while other four squadrons are with the reserve under Liechtenstein. The regiment is involved in the cavalry encounter at Regensburg, and claims the loss of 87 men and 107 horses dead, 35 men and 41 horses wounded, 23 men and 80 horses missing. After the retreat, Brigade Vécsey is assigned to the Treuenfels Division in the Corps under Hohenzollern. At Aspern the whole regiment participates in the attacks on Essling with the loss of 24 men and 44 horses dead, 89 men and 91 horses wounded, 13 men and 43 horses missing. In the battle of Wagram, the regiment is assigned to the Brigade Stutterheim, Fresnel Division, I Corps under Bellegarde, and is engaged in rearguard encounters; the losses are 14 men dead, 45 wounded, 17 missing. After Wagram the regiment retreats to Brenditz with the main army to Znaim, with five squadrons in charge of escorting the artillery with the Fresnel Division,

Brigade Stutterheim. The remaining three squadrons are in the vanguard. The encounters are hard and the losses results to 15 men and 35 horses dead.
1813 – In Germany; the regiment is engaged at Dresden, Naumburg, Leipzig and Hochheim. The *Oberstlieutenants*1st Squadron is attached to the Russian Corps Platov and distinguishes itself under Rittmeister Puchner in the actions at Altenburg, Zeitz and Chemnitz.
1814 – The regiment takes part in the battles at Bar-sur-Aube, Brienne, Troyes, with heavy losses, Bar-sur-Seine, Arcis-sur-Aube and Vitry.
1815 – With the main army in France, encounters near Belfort.

Leichte Dragoner Regiment Nr.13; Chevauxlegers Regiment Nr.6					
Nr.	**Year**	**Proprietor / 2nd Proprietor**	**Commander**	**Denomination**	**Depot**
13	1798	Vacant	Joseph von Egger	13. Leichte Dragoner	Engfurt (Bavaria)
13	1799	" "	Carl von Vincent	13. Leichte Dragoner	
13	1800	" "	Carl Civalart	13. Leichte Dragoner	
13	1801	Franz von Rosenberg-Orsini		13. Leichte Dragoner	Brandeis
6	1802	" "		6. Chevauxlegers	Klattau and Laufen
6	1803	" "		6. Chevauxlegers	Klattau
6	1804	" "		6. Chevauxlegers	
6	1805	" "		6. Chevauxlegers	
6	1806	" "		6. Chevauxlegers	Brandeis
6	1807	" "		6. Chevauxlegers	
6	1808	" "	Joseph Chotek	6. Chevauxlegers	
6	1809	" "	Carl Latuillerie	6. Chevauxlegers	
6	1810	" "		6. Chevauxlegers	Klattau and Himberg
6	1811	" "		6. Chevauxlegers	Inzersdorf
6	1812	" "		6. Chevauxlegers	Kecskemét
6	1813	" "		6. Chevauxlegers	
6	1814	" "		6. Chevauxlegers	Gyöngyös
6	1815	" "	Peter von Gasser	6. Chevauxlegers	Vienna

Recruited in Bohemia.
1798 – Raised on 26 April 1798 with officers and troopers from the Coburg Regiment (6. Leichte Dragoner), Latour (14. Leichte Dragoner), and Saxe and Bercsényi hussars (French emigrants). The regiment is gathered in Engfurt in Bavaria and enters the Austrian cavalry as Leichte Dragoner Regiment Nr.13.
1799 – On the Upper Rhine; detachments take part in the assaults against Leimen and Gamshorst; the whole regiment is engaged at Offenburg, Renchen, Neckarau, Löchgau, and Wiesloch.
1800 – Battle on the Iller, at Hohenlinden the regiment covers the Austrian retreat.

1802 – Changed to a chevauxlegers regiment with the number '6', receives the *Oberst Division* of the disbanded Leichte Dragoner Nr.6.
1805 – In Germany, the regiment fights at the first battle of Ulm and at Albeck, where it captures almost a whole French infantry brigade; then at Herbrechtingen, and after the capitulation joins the Archduke Ferdinand Corps; encounters of Eschenau and Stecken. One division is detached to Tyrol.
1809 – With the corps under Hiller in Germany; encounters at Pfaffenhofen, Landshut and Neumarkt; the regiment protects the infantry retreating to Traunviertel. At Aspern the regiment is deployed in the 1st Column under Hiller, Vincent Division, Brigade Provenchères; during the advance to Enzersdorf and Essling, the *2. Majors Division* forms the vanguard of the column. The regiment is then transferred to the IV Corps under Rosenberg. On the second day, all the divisions fight between Essling and Enzersdorf; the losses are eight men and 23 horses dead, 42 men and 40 horses wounded. After the battle half regiment is assigned to Brigade Neustädter, Dedovich Division, IV Corps, while the other half is with Brigade Stutterheim, Rohan Division in the same IV Corps. Battle of Wagram; in the reserve corps under Liechtenstein, Schwarzenberg Division, Brigade Neckersfeld; two divisions successfully relieve the menaced Austrian artillery. Rearguard encounters in Moravia.
1813 – The regiment fights at Dresden, detachments are involved in the encounters at Dippoldswalde, Naumburg, Eckartsberga and Hochheim. The regiment distinguishes itself at Hüningen, charging the French infantry.
1814 – Detachments are engaged at Vandeouvres, Troyes and St. Bar, where they suffer heavy losses. Later the regiment fights at Arcis-sur-Aube, Fère-Champenoise and Paris.
1815 – in Germany without actions.

Chevauxlegers Regiment Nr.7					
Nr.	**Year**	**Proprietor / 2nd Proprietor**	**Commander**	**Denomination**	**Depot**
7	1814	Vacant	Bartolomeo Alberti de Poja	7. Chevauxlegers	Cremona
7	1815	Johann von Nostitz-Rieneck		7. Chevauxlegers	Güns and Ödenburg

1814 – After the reacquisition of the Italian provinces in Lombardy the regiment is formed at Cremona with parts of the former Italic Kingdom Army (dragoon regiments Re and Regina, Guardia Reale and 1° 3° and 4° Cacciatori a Cavallo. Is assigned Lombardy as a recruitment place.
1815 – The regiment is mobilised for the Rhine but is not employed in action.

D – *Jäger zu Pferd*

Jäger Regiment zu Pferd – Disbanded in 1801					
Nr.	**Year**	**Proprietor / 2nd Proprietor**	**Commander**	**Denomination**	**Depot**
-	1797	Antoine Bussy de Mignot		Bussy	Heilbronn
-	1798	" "	Johann von Frimont	Bussy	
-	1799	" "		Bussy	Veszprem
-	1800	" "		Bussy	
-	1801	" "	Claude Bussy de Mignot	Bussy	Laibach-Ljubljana

Formed with troopers and officers from the *Jäger-Freikorps* raised in 1795 by the bishops of Paderborn and Hildesheim as *Reichskontingent* for the Westphalian circle; entered Austrian service in March 1797 and completed in 1798 with officers, rank and file of the disbanded Freikorps Rohan, Bourbon and Carneville. Recruited in Carinthia.
1798 – On the Upper Rhine.
1799 – In Italy, with the Corps under Ott; blockade of Mantua; six squadrons are engaged in the encounter of San Giovanni; siege of Ancona. In October the regiment marches to Piedmont; encounter of Serravalle and Novi; *Major* Degenfeld is awarded the Order of Maria Theresa.
1800 – Encounter of Croce di Fiaschi; later in the Corps under Vukassovich; encounter of Turbigo and battle of Marengo; rearguard engagements on the River Mincio.

E – Hussars

Husaren Regiment Nr.2; Husaren Regiment Nr.1					
Nr.	**Year**	**Proprietor / 2nd Proprietor**	**Commander**	**Denomination**	**Depot**
2	1792	Kaiser Franz II / Ignáz Almásy	Paul von Blascovich	Kaiser	Novosielica
2	1793	" "		Kaiser	
2	1794	" "	Ferenc Nagy de Felsö-Eör	Kaiser	
2	1795	" "		Kaiser	
2	1796	" "		Kaiser	
2	1797	" "		Kaiser	Mühldorf (Bavaria)
1	1798	" "	Keglevich	1st Hussars	Möhringen
1	1799	" "	Keszler	1st Hussars	
1	1800	" "		1st Hussars	
1	1801			1st Hussars	Zloczów
1	1802	" "		1st Hussars	
1	1803	" "		1st Hussars	

1	1804	Kaiser Franz II / Pal Esterházy		1st Hussars	
1	1805	" "	Graffen	1st Hussars	
1	1806	Kaiser Franz I / Pal Esterházy	Neipperg	1st Hussars	
1	1807	" "		1st Hussars	
1	1808	Kaiser Franz I / Sigmund Szent-Kereszty		1st Hussars	Siedlec
1	1809	" "	Andras de Szent-György	1st Hussars	
1	1810	" "		1st Hussars	Troppau
1	1811	" "		1st Hussars	
1	1812	" "	Jünger	1st Hussars	
1	1813	" "		1st Hussars	
1	1814	" "		1st Hussars	Gródek
1	1815		Legeditsch	1st Hussars	

From 1781 it recruited in the District of Alt-Ofen (old Buda –Óbuda, today part of Budapest).
1792 – In Germany: skirmishes near Windisch-Borna, Fürstenau, Peilau.
1793 – In Galicia; siege of Chotin; one division in the Austrian Low Countries; encounter of Avesnes-le-Sec.
1794 – Encounters of Valje-Szaka, Focsani and Martinestie. In the Austrian Low Countries; engagements at Catillon, Erquelinnes, Charleroi, Fleurus, and in the rearguard on the Roer.
1795 – Garrison on the border with Wallachia. In Germany at Ilbesheim and Kreuznach while the 2. Majors *Division* is engaged at Bacharach.
1796 – Detachments fight at Amberg, Würzburg, Aschaffenburg and on the Lahn.
1798 – One division is transferred to the newly formed Husaren Regiment Nr.5.
1799 – In Italy, later on the Upper Rhine; encounters of Ostrach, Liptingen and Stockach; outposts skirmish at Neumühl, Unter-Grombach and Wiesloch.
1800 – Encounter of Ulm, later in Upper Palatinate, heavy losses at Abbach.
1805 – Garrison in Hungary, then move to Moravia; battle of Austerlitz and encounter of Kostel.
1809 – With the VII Corps under Archduke Ferdinand in the Polish campaign; encounters of Grochow and Jedlinsko.
1812 – Three divisions are assigned to the auxiliary corps under Schwarzenberg in Russia.
1813 – With the main army in Bohemia, later in Saxony; encounters of Wüst-Olbersdorf, Reichenberg, Kratzau and battle of Leipzig (Hochheim).
1814 – With the Southern Army; outpost encounters at Meximieux, Macon and Saint Julien.
1815 – Blockades of Strasbourg and Hüningen, encounter of Hausbergen.

Husaren Regiment Nr.17; Husaren Regiment Nr.2					
Nr.	**Year**	**Proprietor / 2nd Proprietor**	**Commander**	**Denomination**	**Depot**
17	1792	Erzherzog Leopold Alexander, Palatin von Ungarn / Mihály Splényi de Miháldy	Carl Ott de Bátorkéz	Erzherzog Leopold	Schässburg
17	1793	" "		Erzherzog Leopold	
17	1794	" "	Andras Szent-Kereszty	Erzherzog Leopold	
17	1795	Erzherzog Joseph Anton Palatin von Ungarn / Mihály Splényi de Miháldy		Erzherzog Joseph	
17	1796	" "		Erzherzog Joseph	
17	1797	" "	Vincenz Knesevich de St. Helena	Erzherzog Joseph	
2	1798			2. Husaren	Inner Austria
2	1799	" "		2. Husaren	
2	1800	" "	Ferenc Szabó	2. Husaren	
2	1801			2. Husaren	Nagy-Enyed
2	1802	" "		2. Husaren	
2	1803	" "		2. Husaren	
2	1804		Ignaz Splényi de Miháldy	2. Husaren	
2	1805	" "		2. Husaren	
2	1806			2. Husaren	Pettau
2	1807	" "		2. Husaren	Radkersburg
2	1808			2. Husaren	
2	1809	Erzherzog Joseph Anton Palatin von Ungarn / Daniel von Mecséry	Leopold von Geramb	2. Husaren	
2	1810	" "		2. Husaren	Nagy-Enyed
2	1811	" "		2. Husaren	
2	1812	" "		2. Husaren	Suczawa
2	1813	" "		2. Husaren	
2	1814	" "	Emanuel Bretfeld zu Kronenburg	2. Husaren	Trier
2	1815			2. Husaren	

Recruited in Transylvania.
1792/93 – On the Upper Rhine; encounters of Landau, Bien-Walde, Lauterburg, St. Jean-de-Luz.
1794 – One detachment takes part at the defence of Luxembourg.
1796 – In Italy, detachments are engaged in several encounters and in the attempts to relieve Mantua.

1799 – The regiment fights at Cassano, Trebbia, Novi, Genola and during the blockade of Cuneo.
1800 – With the Army of Italy; encounters at Casteggio and Pozzolo-Valeggio.
1805- In Italy, the regiment is engaged in rearguard actions.
1809 – With the VIII Corps in Italy; assigned to the Frimont Division, Brigade Besán; the regiment fights at Pordenone and Sacile; then encounters at Treviso and Sala di Campagna. After the battle of the Piave on 8 May, two squadrons are with Brigade Kálnassy to cover the left army flank at Cimadolmo and both are engaged at Cisterna. In Hungary; encounter of Csanak and battle of Raab.
1813 – With the Army of Danube, and later in the Austro-Bavarian Corps under Wrede; encounter of Rothenberg and battle of Hanau.
1814 – Detachments fight at Brienne, Nangis, St Martin, Bar-sur-Aube and Arcis-sur-Aube.
1815 – In Alsace without actions.

Husaren Regiment Nr.32; Husaren Regiment Nr.3					
Nr.	Year	Proprietor / 2nd Proprietor	Commander	Denomination	Depot
32	1792	Vacant	Paul Dévay	Esterházy	Pardubitz
32	1793	-		Esterházy	
32	1794	Erzherzog Ferdinand Carl von Este / Rudolph von Otto	Ladislaus von Szent-Kereszty	Erzherzog Ferdinand	
32	1795	" "		Erzherzog Ferdinand	
32	1796	" "		Erzherzog Ferdinand	
32	1797	" "	Franz von Löpper	Erzherzog Ferdinand	
3	1798			3. Husaren	Sigmaringen
3	1799	" "		3. Husaren	Bohemia
3	1800	" "		3. Husaren	
3	1801		Janos Andrássy	3. Husaren	Moór
3	1802	" "		3. Husaren	
3	1803	" "		3. Husaren	
3	1804		Petar Vécsey de Hajnácskeö	3. Husaren	Radkersburg
3	1805	" "		3. Husaren	Radkersburg
3	1806			3. Husaren	Troppau
3	1807	" "		3. Husaren	Gabel Jitschin
3	1808			3. Husaren	Troppau
3	1809		Ferdinand von Sachsen-Coburg	3. Husaren	
3	1810	" "	István Wesselényi	3. Husaren	Sáros-Patak

3	1811	Erzherzog Ferdinand Carl von Este / vacant		3. Husaren	
3	1812	" "		3. Husaren	Christianopol
3	1813	" "	Joseph von Gosztonyi	3. Husaren	
3	1814	Erzherzog Ferdinand Carl von Este / Adam Albert von Neipperg		3. Husaren	Troppau
3	1815			3. Husaren	

Recruited in the *Werbebezirk* of Ofen (today Budapest).
1792 – Detachments fight at Tirlemont, Neerwinden, Maubeuge, Templeuve, Annapes (Lille), Etreux, Mons-eu-Pévelle, Cysoing and at the siege of Marchiennes.
1793 – With the corps under York in the battles of Abscon and Vaux; *Major* Löpper with his division captures several enemy guns; the regiment is engaged at Landrecies, Tournay, Tourcoing, Tongeren and Houtain-Saint Siméon.
1795 – The regiment is successfully engaged in several actions before Mannheim.
1796 – On the Upper Rhine, detachments fight at Mündelheim, Appenweier, Oberkirch, Dillingen, Neresheim, Friedberg and Biberach.
1797 – On the Rhine without actions.
1798 – The *3. Majors Division* is transferred to Husaren Regiment Nr.7.
1799 – In Germany, encounters of Ostrach, Stockach, Donaueschingen and Alt-Breisach.
1800 – On the Upper Rhine; the regiment fights at Breisach and Schliengen, Wettenhausen, Schwabmünchen and Hohenlinden.
1805 – In Italy, encounter of Castelvecchio and battle of Caldiero; detachments are engaged at Villanova and San Pietro in Gú.
1809 – With the III Corps in Germany; battles of Alt-Egglofsheim. On the eve of the battle of Aspern the regiment deploys 821 men; assigned to the IV Corps under Rossenberg. Rohan division: two divisions are in Brigade Stutterheim and two in Brigade Grätze. The regiment covers the left flank of the Austrian army during the attack on Essling. The loses are 7 men and 33 horses dead, 56 men and 48 horses wounded, and one man missing. At Wagram the regiment is transferred to the cavalry reserve in the Nostitz Division then with the Radetzky Division in the light brigade under Dollmayer on the left wing. After the battle the regiment claims the loss of 107 men and 192 horses dead or wounded, and may deploy only one tactical division with 377 horsemen in all.
1813 – With the army of Bohemia; battles of Dresden and encounters of Zeitz, Chemnitz, Penig, Liebertwolkwitz; good performance at Leipzig.
1814 – With IV Corps, six squadrons fight at Langres, Brienne, Montereau, Fontaine-Guerins, Arcis-sur-Aube and positively at Fère-Champenoise. The *2. Majors* and both the *Velite* divisions are assigned to the Süd-Armee.
1815 – In France, encounters of Dannemarie and Belfort.

Husaren Regiment Nr.34; Husaren regiment Nr.4					
Nr.	Year	Proprietor / 2nd Proprietor	Commander	Name	Depot
34	1792	Siegbert Vécsey de Hajnácskeö	Joseph von Spiegelberg	Vécsey	Zloczów
34	1793	" "		Vécsey	
34	1794	" "		Vécsey	
34	1795	" "		Vécsey	
34	1796	" "	Johann Skaritza	Vécsey	
34	1797	" "		Vécsey	
4	1798	" "	Pal Esterházy	4. Husaren	Wasserburg
4	1799	" "		4. Husaren	
4	1800	" "	Carl Johann von Tevalle, (interim)	4. Husaren	
4	1801	" "	Timotheus von Kerekes	4. Husaren	Janowice
4	1802	" "	Franz Kinsky	4. Husaren	
4	1803	Friedrich Erbprinz zu Hessen-Homburg		4. Husaren	Radom
4	1804	" "	Johann von Mohr	4. Husaren	
4	1805	" "		4. Husaren	Radom and Stassów
4	1806	" "		4. Husaren	Mährisch-Ostrau
4	1807	" "		4. Husaren	Konskie
4	1808	" "	Severin von Kisielewsky	4. Husaren	
4	1809	" "	Gustav zu Hessen-Homburg	4. Husaren	
4	1810	" "		4. Husaren	Zółkiew
4	1811	" "		4. Husaren	
4	1812	" "		4. Husaren	
4	1813	" "	Raban von Spiegel	4. Husaren	
4	1814	" "	Joseph Simony de Vitézvár	4. Husaren	Rohatyn
4	1815	" "		4. Husaren	

Recruited in the Fünfkirchen (Pécs) District.
1793 – Six squadrons are assigned to the Rhine Army, four squadrons are in West Galicia.
1794 – On the Rhine; three divisions fight at Schifferstadt, Schwengenheim and Eppstein and positively at Kaiserslautern.
1795 – Encounters at Hartberg near Mainz, Landstuhl and Kaiserslautern.
1796 – On the Lower Rhine; detachments fight at Wallhausen-Neukirchen, Wetzlar and Burgebrach. The regiment reunited at Sulzbach, Amberg and Würzburg, its detachments fight at Aschaffenburg and Gießen.
1797 – Six squadrons are engaged on the Lahn and in the battle of Cambach (Limburg).
1798 – The *3. Majors Division* is transferred to Husaren Regiment Nr.7.

1799 – In Germany; the regiment fights at Ostrach, Stockach, Schaffhausen; one squadron distinguishes itself in the defence of Wehr. Siege of Mannheim, encounters of Neckarshausen and Philippsburg.
1800 – Minor encounters in southern Germany. Four squadrons protect the infantry retreat at Landshut, and later at Neumarkt, where friendly units are encircled by the enemies and rescued by the charge of two squadrons.
1805 – With the corps under Merveldt on the Inn. In rearguard at Amstetten, Krems, Schöngraben; battle of Austerlitz, where two squadrons distinguish themselves during the retreat.
1809 – With the II Corps in Germany; with the III Corps under Hohenzollern, in reserve duties and then assigned to Brigade Pfanzelter, Vukassovich Division. The regiment has a small part in the combats of the first battle of Landshut, deployed to the flank of Radetzky's vanguard, and in the encounter of Regensburg. The regiment marches to Upper Austria and fights at Gallnenkirchen and Urfahr-Linz. After the retreat in Bohemia, the regiment is assigned to Vukassovich Division and fights at Urfahr). One squadron is with Brigade Pfanzelter, the other three under the command of *Oberst* Timotheus von Winzian. Two squadrons are assigned to Waldsee Division in Brigade Schneller in patrol duties along the Danube, and later to the outposts between Gallneukirchen and Neumarkt. With main army at Wagram; with the avant-garde of the left wing, in Brigade Vécsey, Nordmann Division. *Oberst Commandant* Kisielewsky receives an artillery shot to the foot, and bleeds to death. On 6 July half the regiment remains on the left wing while the other half is transferred in the centre, under *Major* Simonyi, in Brigade Hardegg alongside the Vincent Chevauxlegers Regiment (Nr.4) before Baumersdorf. After the battle the regiment claims the loss of 375 men dead and wounded. Attached again to the IV Corps under Rosenberg in the Radetzky Division during the retreat to Bohemia.
1812 – With the auxiliary corps in Russia; detachments fight at Kartuszkaja-Bereza, Kobrin and Sielo-Welykoje.
1813 – With the main army in Bohemia, small engagements at Dresden, later at the battle of Kulm; one squadrons fights at Tilisch, and Dolma. The regiment distinguishes itself at Leipzig, in the crossing of the Rhine and at Colmar.
1814 – Detachments fights at Troyes and Moret (Fontainbleau) and, with the Southern Army, at Bourg-en-Bresse. In the battle of Lyon the regiment distinguishes itself during the crossing of the River Rhône and outflanking the enemy.
1815 – In France, limited actions at Dannemarie, Belfort and others.

Husaren Regiment Nr.5					
Nr.	**Year**	**Proprietor / 2nd Proprietor**	**Commander**	**Name**	**Depot**
5	1798	Vacant	Anton von Révay	5. Husaren	Warazdin
5	1799	" "		5. Husaren	
5	1800	" "	Andreas Szörényi	5. Husaren	

5	1801	Carl Ott de Bártokéz		5. Husaren	Conegliano
5	1802	" "		5. Husaren	
5	1803			5. Husaren	
5	1804	" "		5. Husaren	
5	1805	" "		5. Husaren	
5	1806	" "		5. Husaren	Güns
5	1807	" "		5. Husaren	Ödenburg
5	1808	" "	Wilhelm von Fulda	5. Husaren	Esseg
5	1809	Joseph Radetzky de Radetz	Ludwig Boros de Rákos	5. Husaren	
5	1810	" "		5. Husaren	Warazdin Kanizsa
5	1811	" "		5. Husaren	Esseg
5	1812	" "	Anton Gundaker von Starhemberg	5. Husaren	
5	1813	" "	Adolph von Prohaska	5. Husaren	
5	1814	George, Prince Regent of England / Joseph Radetzky de Radetz		5. Husaren	Bologna
5	1815	" "	Matthias von Gavenda	5. Husaren	Bologna and Crema

Recruited in the Ödenburg District (Sopron).
1798 – With Imperial decree dated 28 April, the regiment is formed at Warazdin with the third divisions from the regiments 1. Husaren (Kaiser), 2. Husaren (Erzherzoh Joseph), 8. Husaren (Würmser) and 9. Husaren (Erdödy).
1799 – With the Army of Italy; encounters of Verona-Pastrengo, Parona, Magnano, siege of Pizzighettone, Milan, Alessandria and Tortona. One division takes part in the siege of Cremona, at the battles of San Giuliano and Novi, where it performs positively. One squadron is engaged at Fressonara, Acqui and Pasturana.
1800 – The regiment is quartered near Genoa; encounter of La Bocchetta, Cremona; distinguishes itself at Marengo and later at Pozzolo-Valeggio.
1805 – Encounters during the retreat at Gonars on the River Tagliamento; a good performance during the assault of superior enemy forces.
1809 – One squadron under *Major* Luszensky fights at Caporetto; the whole regiment is engaged at Sacile, where it suffers heavy losses, and at the Piave. Detachments fight at San Daniele, Tarvis and Raab.
1813 – Three divisions are in Inner Austria; encounters of Weixelburg, St. Marein, Groß-Laschitz and Zirknitz. One division distinguishes itself at Krainburg, Podpetsch-Brücke, capturing two enemy brigades. Another division is engaged at Castelnuovo, while one *Abteilung* takes part at the siege of the Istria. The regiment engages the enemy on the River Isonzo; many officers distinguish themselves at Boara and Forlì.

1814 – The regiment is quartered at Parma; detachments fight at Cadeo, Fiorenzuola, Pontremoli, Parma, Reggio and on the River Nura. One division is engaged in the blockade of Venice, two at the blockade of Mantua.
1815 – Detachments are engaged in the fighting against Murat at Cattolica, Panaro, Rubiera and in the Tolentino battle, where six squadron destroy a whole enemy regiment. Later the regiment marches to southern France without actions.

Husaren Regiment Nr.16; Husaren Regiment Nr.6					
Nr.	**Year**	**Proprietor / 2nd Proprietor**	**Commander**	**Denomination**	**Depot**
16	1792	Ernst von Blankenstein	Carl Hadik de Futak	Blankenstein	Bruxelles
16	1793	" "		Blankenstein	
16	1794	" "	Sigmund de Szent-Kereszty	Blankenstein	
16	1795	" "		Blankenstein	
16	1796	" "		Blankenstein	
16	1797	" "	Anton Vogl	Blankenstein	
6	1798	" "		6. Husaren	Troppau
6	1799	" "		6. Husaren	
6	1800	" "	Joseph von Prohaska	6. Husaren	
6	1801	" "		6. Husaren	Reichstadt
6	1802	" "		6. Husaren	Brandeis
6	1803			6. Husaren	
6	1804	" "		6. Husaren	
6	1805	" "	Ferdinand von Wartensleben	6. Husaren	
6	1806	" "		6. Husaren	Klattau
6	1807	" "		6. Husaren	Nagy-Tapolcsán
6	1808	" "		6. Husaren	Gabel
6	1809	" "	Vincenz von Gillert	6. Husaren	
6	1810	" "		6. Husaren	Rzeszów
6	1811	" "		6. Husaren	
6	1812	" "	Georg von Wieland	6. Husaren	
6	1813	" "		6. Husaren	
6	1814	Kronprinz Wilhelm / Ernst von Blankenstein		6. Husaren	Stanislaus
6	1815	" "		6. Husaren	Altkirchen (Alsace)

Recruited at Grosswardein (today Oradea in Romania).
1792 – In the Austrian Low Countries; Jemappes and other minor actions. In Luxembourg; encounter of Agneau and Corioule.
1793 – *Abteilungen* are engaged in minor actions; after these, the regiment

acquires its terrifying reputation for its achievements. Encounters at Aldenhoven, Neerwinden, Löwen, at the sieges of Condé and Valenciennes, at Poperinghe and Hondschooten; battle of Maubeuge and encounter of Bassuyan.
1794 – The regiment deploys its whole *Divisionsweise* at the battles of Landrecies, then at Tournay, Ypres and Moescroen. Rearguard actions during the retreat from the Low Countries.
1795 – On the Lower Rhine; engagements at Höchst, at the siege of the lines of Mainz, at the encounter of Kirchheim, Kreuznach and Meissenheim.
1796 – With the Corps Wartensleben; encounter of Herborn, Kircheip with detachments, then at Amberg, Würzburg, Giessen and Altenkirchen with the whole regiment; distinguishes itself at Kehl.
1797 – One division is engaged in the encounter at Grüningen.
1798 – The *3. Division* is transferred to Husaren Regiment Nr.7.
1799 – On the Rhine; engagements at Oberkirch, Ober-Kappeln, Bietigheim and Wiesloch.
1800 – The regiment protects the retreat after the battle of Biberach; rearguard actions in Upper Austria.
1805 – Two divisions are engaged at Günzburg. The regiment is assigned to the corps under Jellacich, and so avoids the capitulation of Bregenz, and then marches to Bohemia.
1809 – In Bavaria with I Corps under Bellegarde, Hennequin Division, Brigade Wintzingerode with two squadrons; Vogelsang Division, Brigade Wartensleben, former commander of the regiment, with six squadrons; engagement at Amberg-Ursensollen. Two squadrons are in the vanguard with the Brigade Wintzingerode, I Corps; the rest of the regiment is deployed in the centre with the Brigade Wartensleben, Fresnel Division. On the first day of the battle, the squadrons under Wartensleben successfully assault the flank of the French heavy cavalry. On the second day, *Oberst-Lieutenant* Vieland leads his division against the French cavalry. At Aspern the regiment loses 35 men and 72 horses dead, 78 men and 44 horses wounded, 1 man missing. In June the regiment receives two new squadrons as reinforcement and is deployed with the cavalry reserve under Liechtenstein in the Brigade Wartensleben, Nostitz Division. Two *Divisionen* are transferred to Inner Austria, and later fight at Raab. At Wagram, Nostitz's reserve cavalry forms the vanguard in the left wing of IV Corps; encounters at Markgraf-Neusiedl. On the second battle day, IV Corps forms two columns for the unsuccessful assaults on Grosshofen and Glinzendorf. Rearguard encounters at Hollabrunn, Schöngrabern and Znaim.
1812 – With the auxiliary corps in Russia; encounters of Signiewiczi, Pruszany, Kobrin, Liuboml, Stara-Wizwa and siege of Ogorodnicki.
1813 – With the Light Division Bubna in the main army; encounters of Gabel, Stolpen and Lohmen; detachments are engaged at Leipzig.
1814 – In southern France; siege of Genf, battles of Bourg-en-Bresse and Polign; one division is engaged at Macon and in the blockade of Auxonne.
1815 – In Alsace; encounter of Strasbourg.

Husaren Regiment Nr.7					
Nr.	Year	Proprietor / 2nd Proprietor	Colonel Commander	Denomination	Depot
7	1798	Vacant	Carl von Schauroth	7. Husaren	Verocze
7	1799	" "		7. Husaren	Wolfsberg in Krain
7	1800	" "		7. Husaren	
7	1801	Johannes Fürst zu Liechtenstein	Joseph von Mesko	7. Husaren	Görz and Troppau
7	1802	" "		7. Husaren	Bochnia
7	1803			7. Husaren	
7	1804	" "		7. Husaren	
7	1805	" "		7. Husaren	
7	1806	" "		7. Husaren	St. Georgen (Pressburg)
7	1807	" "	Franz von Vlasits	7. Husaren	Mölk and Vienna
7	1808	" "		7. Husaren	Ungarisch-Brod
7	1809	" "		7. Husaren	
7	1810	" "		7. Husaren	Grosswardein
7	1811	" "		7. Husaren	Békés-Csaba
7	1812	" "		7. Husaren	
7	1813	" "	Ferdinand von Zichy	7. Husaren	Zloczów
7	1814			7. Husaren	Turin
7	1815	" "		7. Husaren	Cremona, then Lambach

Raised at Veröcze, in Slavonia, on 28 April 1798 with the *3. Majors Divisions* from Husaren Regiment Nr.3 (Erzherzog Ferdinand), Nr.4 (Vécsey), Nr.6 (Blankenstein) and Nr.10 (Mészáros). Recruited in the Fünfkirchen (Pécs) District.

1799 – In Italy; engagements at Verona, Magnano and Trezzo; later in Piedmont; battle of Rivoli. One squadron is involved in the siege of Mantua, where on 8 May it repulses an enemy sortie.

1800 – In Piedmont; encounter of Pozzolo-Valeggio (battle of the River Mincio).

1801 – Rearguard actions; encounter of Colognola.

1805 – With the corps under Kienmayer on the Inn. Originally the regiment retreats to Vöcklabrück, then an autonomous column led by Colonel Mesko crosses the Pyhrn Pass in the Upper Enn valley sustaining engagements. At Marburg the regiment joins the Corps Chasteler.

1809 – With the Corps Hiller in Germany; one division distinguishes itself at Haag and Landshut. In May the regiment moves to Vienna and one division is in the defence garrison deployed between the Burgtor and Kärntnertor. The regiment is involved in the battles of Aspern, where its seven squadrons are deployed with the vanguard in the Nordmann Division of VI Corps under Hiller and later are involved in the defence of Kagran and Hirschstetten. At Wagram, the regiment deploys all eight squadrons in Brigade Wallmoden,

Vincent Division. After the battle the regiment claims the loss of 148 men and 172 horses. Rearguard actions at Korneuburg and Hollabrunn.
1812 – In October the regiment joins the corps under Schwarzenberg in Russia; encounters at Wysoko-Litowsk and Izabelin, while detachments distinguish at Mokrany, capturing many ammunition carriages.
1813 – On the Bohemia–Saxony border; encounters at Böhmisch-Leipa, Niemes, Rumburg and Stulpen; the regiment distinguishes itself during the defence of the bridgehead at Pirna. With the main army; battle of Leipzig; two squadrons perform positively in the encounter of Weimar.
1814 – In southern France; detachments are engaged at Genf.
1815 – In Italy; campaign against Murat, encounters of Ronco and Pesaro; three divisions take part to the occupation of Naples. The *Velite Division* is quartered in Milan.

Husaren Regiment Nr.30; Husaren Regiment Nr.8					
Nr.	**Year**	**Proprietor / 2nd Proprietor**	**Commander**	**Denomination**	**Depot**
30	1792	Dagobert Sigmund von Würmser	Friedrich von Nauendorf	Würmser	Troppau
30	1793	" "	Franz von Wachenheim	Würmser	
30	1794	" "		Würmser	
30	1795	" "	Johann von Klenau	Würmser	
30	1796	" "		Würmser	
30	1797	" "	Emanuel von Schustekh	Würmser	Graz
8	1798	" "		8. Husaren	Rovigo
8	1799	Friedrich August von Nauendorf		8. Husaren	
8	1800	" "	Timotheus Kerekes	8. Husaren	
8	1801	" "	Joseph Tevalle	8. Husaren	Tarnopol
8	1802	Michael von Kienmayer	Timotheus Kerekes	8. Husaren	
8	1803			8. Husaren	
8	1804	" "		8. Husaren	
8	1805	" "		8. Husaren	
8	1806	" "		8. Husaren	Bochnia Krakow
8	1807	" "		8. Husaren	Troppau
8	1808	" "	August von Vécsey	8. Husaren	Nagy-Topolcsán
8	1809	" "	Ferenc Bánffy	8. Husaren	Vienna
8	1810	" "	Franz Bubna von Warlich	8. Husaren	Horodenka
8	1811	" "		8. Husaren	
8	1812	" "	Philipp von Lilien	8. Husaren	
8	1813	" "		8. Husaren	
8	1814	" "		8. Husaren	Zolkiéw
8	1815	" "		8. Husaren	

Recruited in the District of Pressburg-Poszony (Bratislava).
1792 – One division is in the Austrian Low Countries; encounter of Florennes. The rest of the regiment is with the Rhine army; engagements at Landau, defence of Pellingen and encounters of Merzkirchen and Ober-Lenken.
1794 – In the Austrian Low Countries; detachments fight at Charleroi, Fleurus, Ernoux, Liège, Trier, Sprimont and other minor encounters. Two squadrons take part at the occupation of Mainz.
1795 – Detachments are involved in the siege of Hartberg, near Mainz, and later at Mannheim, Pfrimm, Frankenthal and Schwengenheim.
1796 – In Italy; detachments fight at Brescia, Saló, Desenzano and Peschiera. After the defeat at Bassano, three divisions fight with the corps under Mészáros at Cerea, Castellaro and La Favorita, then at Mantua in the attempt to relief the besieged city. One division is with the Friaul Corps; encounters at Fontaniva, Verona, Caldiero and battle of Arcole.
1797 – After the capitulation of Mantua the regiment is gathered in Styria; one division fights at Rivoli and on the River Tagliamento.
1798 – The *3. Division* is transferred to Husaren Regiment Nr.5.
1799 – In Italy; encounters of Legnago and Magnano and siege of Mantua. With the corps under Klenau in Italy; occupation of Modena, Sarzana and Lerici.
1800 – Blockade of Genoa and encounter of Casteggio (Montebello); battle of Marengo. At the end of the year the regiment is involved in the actions on the River Po; detachments fight at Finale and Bondeno.
1805 – The regiment distinguishes itself at Caldiero.
1809 – With the V Corps under Hiller in Germany; detachments are engaged at Landshut, Kloster Rohr and Riedau; the regiment fights at Ebelsberg, and at Aspern with only 434 men in Brigade Mesko, Vincent Division; successful assault against the French cavalry charging the Austrian infantry. The loss are two men and 19 horses dead, 16 men and seven horses wounded. At Wagram the regiment is transferred to Brigade Wallmoden in VI Corps under Klenau. Rearguard engagements at Korneuburg and Hollabrunn.
1812 – Three divisions are assigned to the corps under Schwarzenberg in Russia: encounters of Pruzany, Diwin, Rudnja and Wiczulki.
1813 – With the army of Bohemia; battle of Dresden, encounters of Kninitz-Arbesau (Leipzig), Hochheim and in the blockade of Kassel. One squadron is attached to the multinational mobile column under Thielemann; encounters of Naumburg and Altenburg.
1814 – In France; blockade of Besançon, and encounter of St. Ferjeux.
1815 – In Alsace; encounters of Strasbourg and Hausbergen.

Husaren Regiment Nr.11; Husaren Regiment Nr.9					
Nr.	**Year**	**Proprietor / 2nd Proprietor**	**Commander**	**Denomination**	**Depot**
11	1792	Johann Nepomuk Erdődy de Monyorókerek	Ladislaus Kosztolányi	Erdődy	Esseg
11	1793	" "	Carl Christoph von Piacsek	Erdődy	

11	1794	" "		Erdődy	
11	1795	" "		Erdődy	
11	1796	" "		Erdődy	
11	1797	" "	Franz von Stephaics	Erdődy	Pettau
9	1798	" "		9. Husaren	
9	1799			9. Husaren	
9	1800	" "		9. Husaren	
9	1801	" "	Constantin von Ettinghausen	9. Husaren	Esseg
9	1802	" "		9. Husaren	
9	1803	" "		9. Husaren	
9	1804	" "		9. Husaren	
9	1805	" "		9. Husaren	
9	1806	Johann Frimont		9. Husaren	
9	1807	" "		9. Husaren	
9	1808	" "	Georg von Wrede	9. Husaren	Pettau
9	1809	" "	Friedrich von Bretschneider	9. Husaren	
9	1810	" "		9. Husaren	Radkersburg
9	1811	" "		9. Husaren	Groß-Kanizsa
9	1812	" "		9. Husaren	Hód-Mezsö-Vásárhely
9	1813	" "		9. Husaren	Zółkiew
9	1814	" "		9. Husaren	Milan
9	1815	" "	Anton von Callot	9. Husaren	Lodzs

Recruited in the Hungarian District of Veszprém and later in Slavonian District of Esseg (Osijek).
1793 – With the Rhine army; minor engagements at Offenbach, Ottersheim and Knittelsheim.
1796 – In Italy; six squadrons are in the corps under Provera and four with Davidovich; detachments are engaged in the retreat after Castiglione; three divisions fight at Caldiero and Rivoli.
1797 – Encounter of Tarvis, where two officers earn the Order of Maria Theresa.
1798 – The *3. Division* is transferred to the Husaren Regiment Nr.5.
1800 – In Italy and Tyrol; battle of Marengo and encounter of Valeggio-Pozzolo.
1805 – In Italy, the regiment distinguishes itself at Caldiero.
1806–08 – Garrison duties in Slavonia.
1809 – With the army of Inner Austria, IX Corps under Gyulai, Wolfskehl Division, Brigade Splényi; on campaign with 1,305 men and 1,101 horses. Two squadrons are detached to the Croatian defence force under Knesevich in Brigade Tomachich, then Brigade Gyurkovich. At Sacile four squadrons serve with the Brigade Splényi. At the battle of the Piave, all six squadrons are assigned to the Frimont Division on the rearguard with Brigade Splényi. In June the regiment is with the vanguard on the right bank of the Mur River; four squadrons are engaged at Graz; while two squadrons are on the

left bank of the Mur in IX Corps under Gyulai with the Brigade Kengyel. Two squadrons are assigned to patrol duty and engaged the French at St. Leonhardt.
1813 – With the Army of Italy, then in Inner Austria; encounters at Hermagor, St. Georgen and Brunecken; one division is detached in Veneto; encounters at Castelfranco, Cittadella, a positive performance at Rezzonico, where it defeats superior enemy forces; two officers are awarded with the Order of Maria Theresa.
1815 – In Italy then in France, without actions.

Husaren Regiment Nr.35; Husaren Regiment Nr.10					
Nr.	**Year**	**Proprietor / 2nd Proprietor**	**Commander**	**Name**	
35	1792	Vincenz von Barcó	Tobias Quietowsky	Barcó	Tarnopol
35	1793		Michael von Kienmayer	Barcó	
35	1794		Joseph Levachich von Latischlowitz	Barcó	
35	1795			Barcó	
35	1796		Johann Keglevich	Barcó	
35	1797	Joanos Mészáros		Barcó	
10	1798		Johann von Schauroth	10. Husaren	Teschen
10	1799	" "	Danielde Mecséry	10. Husaren	Teschen
10	1800	" "	Andreas von Schneller	10. Husaren	Werschetz
10	1801			10. Husaren	
10	1802	Joseph Stipsicz von Ternova		10. Husaren	Ujpécs
10	1803	" "		10. Husaren	
10	1804			10. Husaren	
10	1805	" "		10. Husaren	
10	1806			10. Husaren	Saatz
10	1807	" "		10. Husaren	Ungarisch-Brod
10	1808		Franz von Frölich	10. Husaren	Vienna
10	1809	" "	Anton Gundaker von Starhemberg	10. Husaren	
10	1810	" "		10. Husaren	Ujpécs
10	1811	" "	Maxmilian von Paumgarten	10. Husaren	Veszprem
10	1812	" "	Franz von Genczy	10. Husaren	
10	1813	" "		10. Husaren	Ujpécs
10	1814	Friedrich Wilhelm III, König von Preussen / Joseph Stipsicz von Ternova		10. Husaren	Milan
10	1815			10. Husaren	Enisheim (Alsace)

Hungarian–Slovakian regiment; recruited in the District of Kaschau (Košice) and from 1809 also in Eperjes.
1793 – In the Austrian Low Countries; encounters of Valenciennes-Saultain, Neuville, Villers-en-Cauchies and Bouvignies; battle of Famars, where some *Abteilungen* assault the enemy entrenchments and capture an artillery battery.
1794 – Detachments are engaged at Landrecies, Rouvroy, Liège, Aachen, Henri-Capelle.
1795 – In Germany; detachments fight at Mainz, Meissenheim and Morbach.
1796 – The regiment fights at Uckerath, Amberg, Würzburg, detachments are engaged at Aschaffenburg, Bingen and other minor encounters.
1797 – Heavy losses at Hochheim.
1798 – One division is transferred to Husaren Regiment Nr.7.
1799 – In Germany and then in Switzerland; encounters at Ostrach-Stockach, Andelfingen and Brunnen; at Embach the regiment rescues two captured infantry companies.
1800 – The regiment fights at Engen, Möskirch, Biberach, Schwabmünchen, Hohenlinden and Asten.
1805 – In Italy; battle of Caldiero.
1809 – Seven squadrons are assigned to the corps under Rosenberg; encounters at Wenig (Landshut), Dinzling and battle of Eckmühl. The whole regiment is engaged in the siege of Passau; encounter at Aderklaa. Battle of Aspern, with the vanguard in the Klenau Division, Brigade Frehlich, with 861 men, engagements at Stadtl-Enzersdorf and Esslingen with the loss of six men and 21 horses dead, 41 men and 50 horses wounded. At Wagram the regiment is deployed to the left wing with the Nordmann Division with seven squadrons, which cover IV Corps under Radetzky during the retreat; the last squadron is detached to the Army of Inner Austria, Brigade Bach. After Wagram the regiment is engaged at Mistelbach.
1813 – In Inner Austria; encounter of Krainburg, then in Italy; engagements of Villanova, Monzambano and Caldiero.
1814 – Four squadrons are with the division under Sommariva; blockades of Mantua, Legnago and Venice.
1815 – In southern France; encounters of Macon, then in Alsace as occupation force.

Husaren Regiment Nr.44; Husaren Regiment Nr.11					
Nr.	**Year**	**Proprietor**	**Commander**	**Name**	**Depot**
44	1792	None	György Nemes	Székler	Sepsi-Szent-György
44	1793		József Borra	Székler	
44	1794			Székler	
44	1795			Székler	
44	1796			Székler	
44	1797		József Barbaczy	Székler	
11	1798			11. Husaren	
11	1799			11. Husaren	
11	1800			11. Husaren	

11	1801		Gabriel Geringer von Ödenburg	11. Husaren	
11	1802			11. Husaren	
11	1803			11. Husaren	
11	1804			11. Husaren	
11	1805			11. Husaren	
11	1806			11. Husaren	
11	1807			11. Husaren	
11	1808		Martin von Rakovsky	11. Husaren	
11	1809			11. Husaren	
11	1810			11. Husaren	
11	1811			11. Husaren	
11	1812		Ernst von Fickweiler	11. Husaren	
11	1813			11. Husaren	
11	1814			11. Husaren	
11	1815			11. Husaren	

Originally a *Grenz regiment*, recruited in the Székely Districts of Háromszék, Csik, Aranyos and in the Hunyadi County.

1793 – Six squadrons are on Upper Rhine; siege of the Lauterburg lines and encounters at Drusenheim, Wanzenau, Hördt, Weyersheim and Bischweiler.

1794 – Heavy losses at Schwegenheim; encounters of Westheim and Schifferstadt.

1795 – The regiment fights at Heidelberg, Handschuhsheim, Frankenthal and Gross-Fischlingen.

1796 – The regiment is engaged at Malsch, Bopfingen, Neresheim, Nurnberg, Würzburg, Kircheip and Mutterstadt.

1797 – Detachments fight at Wiesbaden.

1798 – The regiment maintains its original strength with only six squadrons in three divisions.

1799 – After the Peace of Campoformio, the regiment is quartered in Bohemia, then on the Rhine.

1800 – Two squadrons fight at Nidda; the regiment moves to the Palatinate; battle of Bamberg.

1805 – With the main army in Germany; rearguard actions at St. Pölten with the corps under Kienmayer; positive performance at Austerlitz.

1809 – With the Archduke Ferdinand Corps; encounter of Sandomierz.

1813 – With the Austro-Bavarian corps under Wrede; battle of Hanau and encounter of Saint Croix.

1814 – In France; engagements at La Rothiere, Troyes, Bar-sur-Aube, Vandeuvre and Arcis-sur-Aube.

1815 – On the Rhine without actions.

Freikorps Würmser; Croatisch-Slavonisches Grenz-Husaren Regiment; Husaren Regiment Nr.12 – Disbanded in 1801					
Nr.	**Year**	**Proprietor**	**Commander**	**Denomination**	**Depot**
-	1793	None	Bogovich	Freikorps Würmser	None
-	1794		Johann Morberth	Freikorps Würmser	
-	1795		Christian Uz	Croatisch-Slavonisches Husaren	
-	1796			Croatisch-Slavonisches Husaren	
-	1797			Croatisch-Slavonisches Husaren	
12	1798		Wiedersperg	12. Husaren	
12	1799		Johann Carl Fresnel	12. Husaren	
12	1800		Stanislaus Auer	12. Husaren	
12	1801		Ludwig Daniel	12. Husaren	

Formed as Freikorps Husaren in 1793 with volunteers enlisted in Croatia and Slavonia.

1793 – On the Rhine; engagements at Landau, Hagerbach, Offendorf and Killstedt; siege of the Lauterburg and Weissenburg lines.

1794 – Encounters at Eppstein, Frankental, Oggesheim; at Mainz in the reserve corps.

1795 – On the Upper Rhine; encounters at Mainz and Höchst.

1796 –The regiment deploys 10 squadrons in five divisions. With the corps under Fröhlich at Dachau and Giessen, and then at the siege of Kehl.

1797 – Encounters of Kehl, Neuwied and Hanau.

1798 – On the Rhine, without actions.

1799 – Encounter of Stockach, then in Switzerland; battle of Zürich and encounters of Albisried, Altstadt and Schännis.

1800 – In Germany; skirmishes at Buchloe, Schongau, Haag, and assault on Schwabmünchen.

Husaren Regiment Nr.12					
Nr.	**Year**	**Proprietor / 2nd Proprietor**	**Commander**	**Name**	**Depot**
12	1801	Erzherzog Joseph Anton, Palatin von Ungarn	Gabriel von Hertelendy	Palatin	St. Georgen (Pressburg)
12	1802	" "		12. Husaren	
12	1803	" "		12. Husaren	Nagy-Tapolcsán
12	1804	" "		12. Husaren	Neutra
12	1805	" "		12. Husaren	
12	1806	" "		12. Husaren	Nagy-Tapolcsán
12	1807	" "		12. Husaren	Rzeszów
12	1808	" "	József Csanády	12. Husaren	Zółkiew-Rohatyn
12	1809	" "	Alexander von Illésy	12. Husaren	Rzeszów
12	1810	" "		12. Husaren	Stanislau Nagy-Körös

12	1811	" "		12. Husaren	Vienna
12	1812	" "		12. Husaren	Rohatyn
12	1813	" "		12. Husaren	
12	1814	" "		12. Husaren	Kecskemét
12	1815	" "	Ignaz von Hoditz-Wolframitz	12. Husaren	Gyöngyös

1800/1801 – Formed with a strength of six squadrons with part of the Hungarian *Insurrectio* of central Hungary, and recruits from the Jazygier-Kumanier[2] districts of Nagy Kun and Szolnok, and from the Hajduk towns.[3] Before the end of the year two more squadrons are raised.
1802/1804 – Garrison in Hungary.
1805 – In Germany; two divisions are engaged in the battle of Günzburg; the regiment is involved in the Ulm capitulation even performing valiantly against Murat's cavalry. One division is captured at Memmingen. One *Flügel* (half squadron) joins the corps under Jellacich and then with the Corps Rohan in Tyrol.
1809 – With the VII Corps under Archduke Ferdinand in Poland; battles of Raszyn, encounters of Jedlinsko, Gorzyce and Zarnowice.
1813 – With the main army in Bohemia and then in Germany with the corps under Klenau; battle of Dresden; three squadrons are assigned to the Russian corps under Thielemann; encounters of Windisch-Laupa, Altenburg and Chemnitz. Later the regiment fights at Penig, Liebertwolkwitz and Leipzig.
1814 – In France; four squadrons are assigned to the Leichte Division under Liechtenstein.
1815 – On the Upper Rhine and then in France, without actions.

F – Uhlans

Uhlanen Regiment Nr.1					
Nr.	Year	Proprietor / 2nd Proprietor	Commander	Denomination	Depot
-	1792	Janos Mészáros	Anton von Schubirz	Mészáros	Rosenau
-	1793	" "		Mészáros	Lodi
-	1794	" "		Mészáros	

2 Jász is the Hungarian term for an ethnic minority settled in Hungary since the thirteenth century. The Jász originated as an Ossetian people in Sarmatia. The Jász live mostly in a region known as Jászság, which comprises the north-western part of Jász-Nagykun-Szolnok County. Although they live in the same area, the Jász should not be confused with the Iazyges, who lived in a similar area after the eighteenth century. Even though there is no direct connection between the Jász and the Iazyges, both were recruited into Husaren Regiment Nr.12.

3 Hajdú, formerly known as *Hajdúság* in Hungarian, was an administrative *comitatus* (county) of the Kingdom of Hungary in present-day eastern Hungary. The main city of the county was Debrecen. In the sixteenth century this area originated the *Haiduk* light infantry soldiers. The territory is now part of the Hungarian county of Hajdú-Bihar.

-	1795	" "		Mészáros	
-	1796	" "	Ezechiel von Mattyásovszky	Mészáros	
-	1797	Maximilian von Merveldt		Merveldt	
1	1798	" "	Achilles von Brea	1. Uhlanen	Straubing
1	1799	" "		1. Uhlanen	
1	1800	" "	Ludwig Wallmoden-Gimborn	1. Uhlanen	
1	1801	" "		1. Uhlanen	Pardubitz
1	1802	" "		1. Uhlanen	
1	1803	" "		1. Uhlanen	
1	1804	" "		1. Uhlanen	
1	1805	" "		1. Uhlanen	
1	1806	" "		1. Uhlanen	Gabel
1	1807	" "	Joseph von Bogdan	1. Uhlanen	Bischof-Teinitz
1	1808	" "		1. Uhlanen	Klattau
1	1809	" "	Ludwig von Wilgenheim	1. Uhlanen	
1	1810	" "		1. Uhlanen	Pardubitz
1	1811	" "		1. Uhlanen	Gaja
1	1812	" "		1. Uhlanen	Gyöngyös
1	1813	" "		1. Uhlanen	Nagy-Tapocsán
1	1814	" "	Bartolomeo Alberti de Poja	1. Uhlanen	Debrecén
1	1815	Ernst, Herzog von Sachsen-Coburg-Gotha / Carl von Civalart		1. Uhlanen	St. Florian

Recruited in Galicia.
1794 – With the Army of Italy without actions.
1795 – Detachments fight at Savona and San Giacomo, where *Rittmeister* Brochowsky earns the Order of Maria Theresa; then the whole regiment is engaged at Voltri and Loano.
1796 – Encounters of Millesimo, Codogno (Fombio) and Lodi. At Lodi, the *2. Oberstlieutenants* squadron under *Rittmeister* Domokos protects the retreat of Sebottendorf's Corps and earns the Order of Maria Theresa. Further engagements with the corps under Davidovich at Calliano, Bassano, Castellaro and La Favorita then, with the rest of Würmser's troops, three divisions march to Mantua to join the defence of the city. The *2. Majors Division* fights at Caldiero, Arcole and Rivoli.
1797 – After the capitulation of Mantua, six squadrons return to Austria. The *2. Major Division* continues the campaign in Carinthia. After the truce, one squadron marches to Dalmatia as occupation force.
1799 – In Germany; positive performance at Ostrach; then on the Middle

Rhine in the corps under Sztáray. The regiment takes part in the defence of the outposts around Kehl.

1800 – Encounters at Möskirch, Biberach, Schwabmünchen, Neresheim and Odelzhausen. In June, the *Oberstlieutenant* Wallmoden leads a raid through the valleys of the Murg and Kinzigtal. In late autumn the regiment is at Regensburg, where its detachments are engaged in several encounters; *Rittmeister* Scheibler distinguishes himself during an engagement with a French cuirassier regiment near Öttingen.

1805 – Six squadrons are in Germany with the corps under Kienmayer. The *Oberstlieutenants Division* is assigned to the reserve corps and, after the disaster of Ulm joins Erzherzog Ferdinand's corps at the battle of Stecken. During the retreat to Upper Styria, *Rittmeister* Mengen with one squadron relieves two encircled infantry battalions of the Austrian rearguard, for this action he earns the Order of Maria Theresa.

1809 – With the main army in Germany in II Corps under Kolowrat; *Major* Mensdorff distinguishes in the avant-garde battle at Ursensollen–Amberg. Detachments take part at the battles of Am Hof and Regensburg, where on 21 April they encircle a French cavalry squadron. Later, six squadrons are assigned to the division under Sommariva participating in several actions. In July, the *1. Majors Division* fights at Gefrees and Nurnberg against the Saxons. *Oberstlieutenant* Mensdorff is awarded the Order of Maria Theresa for these actions.

1813 – In Inner Austria with three divisions; the *2. Majors Division* fights at Loibl, while detachments of the *Oberstlieutenant Division* are engaged at Feistritz, Lippa and Krainberg. In the Italian campaign, detachments fight at Bassano and San Marco; two squadrons are quartered at Palmanova.

1814 – The regiment takes part in the blockade of Mantua; encounters on the River Po; one squadron is engaged at Monzambano.

1815 – With the army in France without actions.

Uhlanen Regiment Nr.2					
Nr.	**Year**	**Proprietor / 2nd Proprietor**	**Commander**	**Denomination**	**Depot**
-	1792	Vacant	Bernhard von Degelmann	Freikorps	
-	1793	" "	Carl Philipp zu Schwarzenberg	Freikorps	
-	1794	" "	Johann von Keglevich	Freikorps	
-	1795	" "		Freikorps	
-	1796	" "	Anton Vogl	Freikorps	
-	1797	" "	Joseph von Motschlitz	Freikorps	
2	1798	" "		2nd Uhlans	Jaroslawl
2	1799	" "	Emmanuel von Trach	2nd Uhlans	
2	1800	Carl Philipp zu Schwarzenberg	Moriz von Liechtenstein	2nd Uhlans	
2	1801	" "		2nd Uhlans	Holleschau
2	1802	" "		2nd Uhlans	

2	1803	" "		2nd Uhlans	Ungarisch-Brod
2	1804	" "		2nd Uhlans	
2	1805	" "	Ignaz von Hardegg	2nd Uhlans	
2	1806	" "		2nd Uhlans	Reichenau
2	1807	" "		2nd Uhlans	Nachod-Hohenmaut
2	1808	" "		2nd Uhlans	Saaz
2	1809	" "	Carl Schmuttermayer	2nd Uhlans	
2	1810	" "		2nd Uhlans	Brandeis
2	1811	" "		2nd Uhlans	
2	1812	" "	Ferdinand Kinsky	2nd Uhlans	
2	1813	" "	Carl von Mengen	2nd Uhlans	
2	1814	" "		2nd Uhlans	Vienna
2	1815	" "		2nd Uhlans	Gaja

Recruited in West Galicia.
Formed in September 1790 with the O'Donnell Freikorps, a uhlan division of volunteers, which became an independent Uhlanen Freikorps in 1792.
1792 – In the Austrian Low Countries; three squadrons distinguish themselves at Bossut.
1793 – Detachments fight at Neerwinden-Tirlemont; the newly appointed *Oberst Commandant* Carl Philipp von Schwarzenberg distinguishes himself at Famars and Valenciennes: The regiment is engaged in the battle of Bassuyan.
1794 – Battle of Landrecies, then encounter at Pont-á-Marque and Guise; *Rittmeister* Bogdan distinguishes himself in both actions.
1795 – *Oberstlieutenant* Keglevich distinguishes himself during the assault on the entrenchments of Mainz. The regiment is involved in the battle of Meissenheim.
1796 – Encounters of Amberg and Giessen.
1797 – With the Lower Rhine corps on the River Lahn.
1799 – The regiment fights positively at Ostrach and Stockach. One squadron under *Rittmeister* Bretschneider distinguishes himself in the siege of Luciensteig. In Switzerland; 1st battle of Zürich, then in Germany, where under the commander Fürst Liechtenstein, the regiment distinguishes itself in the assault against the entrenchments of Neckarau near Mannheim. In the battle of Neckarhausen the regiment engages a whole French division. *Rittmeister* Bogdan, with only 15 uhlans, defends the bridge on the Neckar.
1800 – The regiment distinguishes itself at Lohdorf-Möskirch, then at Biberach; rearguard actions at Lambach. *Oberst Commandant* Liechtenstein and *Major* Bogdan are awarded the Order of Maria Theresa.
1805 – The main part of the regiment is taken prisoner at Ulm. Some *Abteilungen* join the Archduke Ferdinand's corps in Bohemia. One squadron fights at Austerlitz.
1809 – Six squadrons are assigned to the 1st Corps under Bellegarde in Germany, while two squadrons are on the Bohemia–Saxony border. The squadrons in Germany fight at Ursensollen, then four squadrons are engaged at Bersching and Pruck-Nittenau. The day before the battle of Aspern, the

regiment under *Oberst* Hardegg engages the enemy at Esslingen. Battles of Wagram and Znaim. The squadrons in Bohemia are involved in the defence of Cheb, where *Lieutenant* Carl Steindl distinguishes himself in the sturdy defence, saving the town and obtaining the Order of Maria Theresa.
1813 – Assigned to the Austrian–Bavarian cavalry corps under Wrede; encounter of Gelnhausen, battle of Hanau and finally, on 31 December, engagement of Saint Croix. General Wrede expresses to the regiment his highest appreciation for its valour.
1814 – With V Corps of the Southern Army, the regiment distinguishes itself at Brienne; detachments fight at Nogent, Nangis and Troyes; battles of Bar and Arcis-sur-Aube. *Oberst Commandant* Mengen is awarded the Order of Maria Theresa after his actions at Hanau and Brienne, while several officers receive the High Russian Order award.
1815 – In France, without actions.

Uhlanen Regiment Nr.3					
Nr.	**Year**	**Proprietor / 2nd Proprietor**	**Colonel Commander**	**Denomination**	**Depot**
3	1801		Heinrich Bersina von Siegenthal	3. Uhlanen	Tarnów
3	1802	Erzherzog Carl		3. Uhlanen	
3	1803	" "		3. Uhlanen	Gródek
3	1804	" "		3. Uhlanen	
3	1805	" "	Johann von Klebelsberg	3. Uhlanen	
3	1806	Erzherzog Carl / Philipp von Grünne		3. Uhlanen	Vienna
3	1807	" "		3. Uhlanen	St. Georgen
3	1808	" "		3. Uhlanen	
3	1809	" "	Heinrich von Hardegg	3. Uhlanen	
3	1810	" "	Emanuel von Mensdorff-Pouilly	3. Uhlanen	Gaja
3	1811	" "		3. Uhlanen	
3	1812	" "	Carl von Grozkowski	3. Uhlanen	Pécsvár
3	1813	" "		3. Uhlanen	Güns
3	1814	" "		3. Uhlanen	Linz
3	1815			3. Uhlanen	

Recruited in Galicia.
1801 – Formed in Krakow with officers and troopers from the uhlan regiments Nr.1 and Nr.2, and Leichte Dragoner regiments Nr.11 (Kinsky) and Nr.15 (Savoyen).
1805 – In Italy; distinguishes itself at Caldiero. In the retreat through Styria, *Rittmeister* Truchsess commands the vanguard and achieves a successful combat at Ehrenhausen. *General Wachtmeister* Radetzky leads the regiment in battle at Marburg.
1809 – In Germany; encounters at Landshut and Neumarkt; battle at

Gayersdorf, where *Major* Wilgenheim distinguishes in the action, and successful encounters at Lambach and Ebelsberg. During the retreat the regiment is engaged at Blindenmarkt. The regiment is attached to the Vincent Division and forms the rearguard at Ebelsberg. In the following events, the *1. Majors Division* acts as support of the retreating infantry and sustains several rearguard encounters with the French light cavalry. The largest encounter happens at Ybbs, where four squadrons fight under *Oberst Commandant* Klebelsberg. The regiment loses 63 men dead, 31 wounded, 96 prisoners, 53 horses dead and 44 wounded. The regiment moves to Mautern, to control the Danube from Stockerau to Tulln.

During the battle of Aspern the regiment is at Stockerau, and at Wagram only the *Oberst Division* takes part in the battle; at Stammersdorf, *Rittmeister* Eugen von Wratislaw succours the 6th Vienna Volunteers battalion hardly engaged. Rearguard skirmish at Schöngraben and Hollabrunn; good performance at Znaim; where *Oberst Commandant* Heinrich von Hardegg receives the Order of Maria Theresa. In 1809 the regiment incorporates troopers from the disbanded *Kosakenpulk*.

1813 – With the Army of Inner Austria; in Friuli and Northern Italy; encounters of Tolmin and Villanova.

1814 – The regiment distinguishes itself at the battle of Mincio.

1815 – On the Upper Rhine without actions.

Uhlanen Regiment Nr.4					
Nr.	Year	Proprietor / 2nd Proprietor	Colonel Commander	Denomination	Depot
4	1813	Kaiser Franz I / Johann von Klebelsberg zu Thumburg	Stanislaus von Poradowski	4. Uhlanen	Gródek
4	1814	" "		4. Uhlanen	Pardubitz
4	1815	" "	Joseph von Devay	4. Uhlanen	Milan

Recruited in East Galicia.

1813 – Raised at Gródek by Galician Nobles with volunteers and troopers from the three previous uhlan regiments and also with officers from the Chevauxlegers Regiment Nr.3 (O'Reilly) and Husaren Regiment Nr.8 (Kienmayer).

1815 – With the main army on the Upper Rhine.

G - *Freikorps*

Freikorps Carneville				
Year	Proprietor / 2nd Proprietor	Commander	Denomination	Depot
1792	*Oberst* Franz Vicomte de Carneville	*Oberlieutenant* Bastieu (1st squadron)	Carneville	None
1793		*Rittmeister* Robert de la Marre	Carneville	

1794			Carneville	
1795		*Rittmeister* Vaudreville (1st Sq.)	Carneville	
1796			Carneville	
1797		*Rittmeister* Robert de la Marre (2nd Squadron)	Carneville	
1798			Carneville	

The detachments of the Carneville Freikorps were originally one squadron of uhlans, followed by another squadron of light cavalry.
1792/94 – In the Austrian Low Countries; battle of Landrecies and encounters on the Sambre and Liège, rearguard engagements at Courcelles.
1795/96 – In Germany; encounter of Lengenfeld and battle of Würzburg.
1798 – Disbanded and both the squadrons assigned to the newly formed Bussy Jäger zu Pferde Regiment.

Freikorps Rohan				
Year	**Proprietor / 2nd Proprietor**	**Commander**	**Name**	**Depot**
1793	Louis de Rohan		Rohan	None
1794			Rohan	
1795			Rohan	
1796			Rohan	
1797		*Oberst* Contades	Rohan	
1798			Rohan	

Raised in 1795 from the Legion de Rohan, with a strength of four, later six, squadrons, as *Reichs Contingent* for Brunswick. On 1 May 1797 it entered Austrian service, was disbanded in 1798 and merged into the newly formed Bussy Jäger zu Pferde Regiment.

Kosaken Pułk (Regiment)				
Year	**Proprietor / 2nd Proprietor**	**Commander**	**Name**	Depot
1809		*Major* Franz Freiherr von Fichtl	*Kosaken*	None
1810			*Kosaken*	

The hussar detachments of the Freikorps Schill or Schlesisches Freikorps, were raised on March 1809 in Silesia, in total 240 hussars divided into three squadrons, which on May 1809, joined the Austrian Kosaken-Pułk. The corps operated with the 7th Corps in Poland and later in Bohemia. In 1810 the unit were partially disbanded and partially assigned to the 3rd Uhlan Regiment.

Erherzog Carl Husaren Corps (Siebenbürgen Husaren Korps)				
Year	**Proprietor / 2nd Proprietor**	**Commander**	**Name**	**Depot**
1809		*Oberstlieutenant* Anton von Schmidt		Transylvania

The corps was raised in June 1809 in Siebenbürgen with four squadrons of 150 men each, and dismissed in 1810 without any fighting.

Fränkischen Cavallerie Legion (Uhlans)				
Year	**Proprietor / 2nd Proprietor**	**Commander**	**Name**	**Depot**
1809	*Oberstlieutenant* Emanuel Graf Mensdorff	*Oberstlieutenant* Graf Nostitz		Bohemia

Raised with volunteers on the Bohemian border with rank and file from the Braunschweig-Oels' Freikorps, the unit deployed three squadrons of Uhlans. Dismissed in December 1809.

Böhmische Dragoner Regiment				
Year	**Proprietor / 2nd Proprietor**	**Commander**	**Name**	**Depot**
1809		*Oberstlieutenant* Graf Kinsky		Bohemia

Intended to be raised in autumn 1809 with Bohemian noble volunteers under Count Kinsky, with four dragoon divisions, but was never completed.

Österrechischen Kosaken Pułk (Regiment)				
Year	**Proprietor / 2nd Proprietor**	**Commander**	**Name**	**Depot**
1813		*Major* Franz Graf Neuhaus de St. Mauro	*Kosaken*	None
1814			*Kosaken*	

Another *Kosaken-Regiment* was raised in 1813 under Major Neuhaus with a planned strength of three field divisions and one reserve division (1,436 men). In 1814, two *Pułk* of Cossacks with 460 horsemen marched to Italy, and were dismissed before the end of 1814.

1. Westphälisches Husaren Regiment				
Year	**Proprietor / 2nd Proprietor**	**Commander**	**Name**	**Depot**
1813	GM Wilhelm Graf Bentheim-Steinfurt	*Oberst* Wilhelm Freiherr von Hammerstein		Transylvania
1814				

2. Westphälisches Husaren Regiment				
Year	**Proprietor / 2nd Proprietor**	**Commander**	**Name**	**Depot**
1813	GM Wilhelm Graf Bentheim-Steinfurt	*Oberst* von Penz		Transylvania
1814				

The two Husaren-Regimenter der Österreichisch-Deutschen oder Westphälischen legions were raised in 1813 with recruits coming from Germany and completed with Austrian troops. The Legion was formed by two (later three) infantry battalions, 1 *Jäger* battalion, and two hussar regiments. 1813 they followed the army in Germany without fighting. In 1814 the legion was detached to the Southern Army in France, where both the hussar regiments took part in the seizure of Lyon; Colonel von Hammerstein was awarded with the LO (Leopold Orden). *Oberstlieutenant* Freiherr von Boyneburg of the 2nd Regiment also distinguished himself.

The legion was disbanded in 1814 after the Peace of Paris. The rank and file returned to their homes, while the officers entered the Austrian Army.

1813 – Followed the army in Germany without fighting.

1814 – Detached to the Southern Army in France, where both regiments took part in the siege of Lyon; *Oberst* von Hammerstein was awarded the Leopold Orden.[4] *Oberstlieutenant* Freiherr von Boyneburg of the 2nd Regiment also distinguished himself.

4 The Austrian-Imperial Order of Leopold was founded on 8 January 1808 by Emperor Franz I.

6

Allerhöchste Oberbefehl – the Austrian High Command

Since the introduction of a permanent army, the Emperor was the supreme warlord of his army, and thus exercised a strong influence in all military matters. His status was clearly expressed in every act, considering that all functions in the army were always provided in the name of the Emperor. However, he actually oversaw only a few matters, while transferring most of the work to his subordinate commanders and offices. Maria Theresa's husband, Francis Stephen of Lorraine – Franz I as Holy Roman Emperor – represented a significant exception when he independently issued orders to the army utilising the *Reichs-Hofkanzlei* (Reich Chancellery), while he signed all further resolutions in the name of his wife, the Empress. Even Emperor Joseph II, who personally took over command of the army against the Ottomans in 1788, as well as Emperor Franz II, who took command in 1805 before the battle of Austerlitz, sporadically held the senior commander's place on the battlefield, however their successors retained the supreme command of the army only for strategic affairs and the formal designation of commander-in-chief became limited with the introduction of the 1867 Constitution, which partially passed the matters to the parliament.

Since 1761, during the reign of Empress Maria Theresa, the *Staatsrat* (State Council) replaced the *Hof-Kanzlei* (court chancellery) as the main political instrument, in which converged the work of the various states' authorities. After its abolition in 1801 Archduke Carl assumed military affairs, as Minister of War. In 1809 all these matters returned to the State Council, which had its own military section until 1848. Indeed, the presence of a *Staatskanzler,* among the Emperor's advisers, was actually very important during the wars against Revolutionary France, but nothing changed in the chain of command because the strategic decisions continued to be reserved for the *Kaiser*. Likewise, it was obvious that Franz II (later Franz I) liked to assume decisions, but only after consultation with his allies and advisers, and he passed the direction of the army on campaign to his generals. But who were these advisers? A permanent council of war had already been created by Emperor Maximilian I of Habsburg

Archduke Ferdinand of Habsburg-Este (1754–1806) portrayed as Austrian *Feldmarschall*. High-ranking officers, including army commanders, were selected by seniority and birth rather than by merit and experience. In early 1800, the scenario was still unchanged. Archduke Ferdinand held a post in the army with two further archdukes: Johann and Ludwig. Other command posts were entrusted to three princes: Hohenzollern, Orsini-Rosenberg, and Liechtenstein. (Österreichisches Nationalbibliothek)

in the early sixteenth century. In 1556 Emperor Ferdinand I established the *Steter Kriegsrat*, a council of five generals and senior civil officials who controlled army activities and warfare finances, as well as the repartition of the forces in the garrisons and armies. It also handled civil and military administration of the Croatian border region. With the institution of a permanent army in the seventeenth century, the council became a court instrument and was named the *Hofkriegsrat* (Aulic War Council). This council managed all bureaucracy dealing with the standing military force. The importance of this office was considerable, because the distribution of the troops in campaign depended on the opinion of its president, who usually was selected from among a group of well-experienced commanders. Adjutants, copyists and other employees in unskilled jobs also worked in the council. Its major function concerned the coordination and centralisation of all the military affairs of the Habsburg territories. This matter included primary duties that centred on coordinating provisioning and equipment in wartime, appointment of commanders and generals and organising the maintenance of fortresses on the military frontier. Throughout the centuries, the Aulic War Council extended its influence also within the Empire, but the establishment of a standing army enormously increased the burden upon the hereditary domains. Concerned with matters of organisation and administration, the Aulic War Council was also the supreme legal authority for the army. In order to avoid any financial mishandling, expenditure could be authorised only with the Council's permission. All military funding became subject to continuous checks and inspections in order to avoid any mistakes or attempts at financial misappropriation. In order to manage these affairs, from 1650 all funds destined for the army were administered by an independent office, the *General Kriegscommissariats-Amt* (General War-Commissar's Office) under the direction of a *General Kriegscommisar* appointed by the Emperor. He supervised the work of the commissars, whose principal duty was to control the muster of the troops and the supplies for the army and fortresses, as well as the payment of the soldiers' salaries. The office of general war commissary was established in Vienna and the appointment increased in importance until at the end of seventeenth the century it became a court position. The general war commissar had under his command an *Oberst-Kriegscommisar* (colonel war commissar), or several, who, while the general remained in Vienna, went to the armies as directors of the *Feldzug Commissariats-Amts-Directeur* (field commissariat office). The main task of the war-commissars consisted of verifying the strength of the units and the general condition of the troops, and the commissar had to send to the Vienna office reports of the general reviews, to be carried out twice a year. Furthermore, each month the

Left: *General Wachtmeister*, print from the *Artaria's Schema aller Uniformen der Kaiserl. Königl. Kriegsvölkern* published in 1792. White–ponceau red coat, waistcoat, breeches, saddle cover and pistol holster with golden lace and buttons. (Authors' archive)

Right: *General-Stab Offizier* in 1792, wearing dark blue coat, ponceau red cuffs, waistcoat breeches, saddle cover and pistol holster with golden lace and buttons. (Authors' archive)

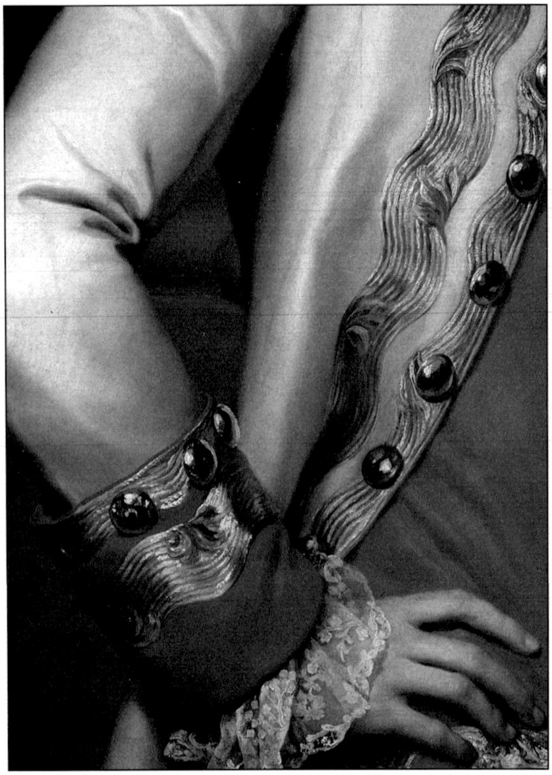

Detail of the golden woven lace for the uniform of *Feldmarschall*, after the portrait of Emperor Leopold II by Anton Raphael Mengs. Except for minor changes, this pattern remained unchanged until the 1840s. (Museo del Prado, Madrid)

war commissioners received reports on the strength of the individual companies from the regiments. The two general annual reviews, one carried out during winter quarters and the other – the most important, called *Haupt-Musterung* – performed before the war campaign, took place under the supervision of the war commissar. During the muster all the anomalous cases eventually found were recorded and then transmitted to Vienna to the general war commissar.

Under the supervision of the Aulic War Council and in conjunction with the War Commissariat, further major offices managed military matters. These were the *General Feld-Kriegauditoriats-Amt* (General Office of the War Court of Justice); the *Obrist Land und Haus Zeug-Amt* (Office for the Arsenals); the *Fortifications Bau-Zahl-Amt* (Administrative Office for the Construction and Maintenance of Fortresses); and the *Obrist Schiff und Brücken-Amt* (Office for the Pontoon and River Flotilla).

The Aulic War Council also raised the *Leibgarde* (Lifeguards) for the Emperor, as well as the field officers' staff, managing and coordinating military campaigns. Furthermore, it maintained diplomatic relations with the Ottoman Empire, while running the *Militärgrenze* (military border). All general commanders had to refer to the Aulic War Council in order to obtain authorisations for any strategic decisions, the exception being the extraordinary rank of *Generalissimus*, a rank that was heir to the ancient Roman *Dictator*, which ensured centralised conducting of the war; although the rank had some limitations when facing an aggressive opponent such as Frederick II of Prussia. In 1780, Emperor Joseph II further centralised the Council and gave it supreme authority over all branches of the military administration.

When, in 1801, the reforming Archduke Carl was directly appointed president of the Aulic War Council by Emperor Franz II (later Franz I of Austria), he divided the council into three departments, dealing with military, jurisdictional, and administrative matters. After the Napoleonic Wars the Aulic War Council was simply one of four components of the revivified State Council (*Staatsrat*), and continued to exert control over the military matters as delegate of the Emperor of Austria. This concurred to maintain the important role of the *Generalsstab* (General Staff) on a secondary step in respect of what would be the final decisions of the Aulic War Council. While the *Generalsstab* was growing in importance in other countries (notably Prussia), in Austria it remained a sort of academy divided into two branches, writing the topographical and military plans.

General-Quartiermeisterstabs Corps (General Quartermaster Staff Corps)

The office was formed as an independent corps in 1705. In subsequent years the Pioneers, the *Stabsinfanteristen* (Staff Infantry) and *Stabsdragoner* (Staff Dragoons) were subordinated to the General Quartermaster Staff Corps. Later, also the Pontoon Corps and *Jäger* Corps passed under its authority.

The positive behaviour of the corps during the Seven Years War influenced the decision to retain the General Staff with its stable organisation. However, some restrictions were imposed in matters of personnel. In peacetime colonels acted like chiefs of the general staff, and the office's strength would have been restricted to a minimal presence in order to be operative. Its full strength could be resumed only in the event of war, completing the personnel with conscription or individuals from the regiments. Before 1792 the Stabsdragoner Regiment had around 1,000 men, divided into five squadrons. Their main task was to escort trains and convoys of the General Staff on campaign. The *Stabsinfanterie* regiment had 4,112 men in three battalions, with 51 officers and 34 staff officers. It also handled the infantry had tasks of field organisation and surveillance on campaign.

One of the most important tasks of the staff officers was topography. According to the instructions issued in 1797–98, this service was carefully regulated. In order to pay expenses, each map designer received an account of 60 florins. Only the personnel or the officers employed in the triangulation of topographic maps received fixed allowances of 40 to 60 florins a month.

The rapid progress in this branch very soon led from simple mapping to the description of the military country, a useful element for writing plans of war. *General-Major* Mayer von Heldenfeld published in 1806 an *Instruction*, which was the upgraded to an Act by Archduke Carl. For the most part it contained the requirements to describe and to determine in advance the favourable military positions of a province. In the same year Transylvania was described in this manner by Colonel Quosdanovich, and 30 border locations against Moldavia and Wallachia, 12 on the Bukovina frontier; the same happened in Lower and Upper Austria, and after 1808, in Inner Austria.

Feldmarschall-Lieutenant Radetzky developed this project by giving useful benefits to the country description, preparing plans for future campaigns. In 1810–11 all matters were carried out down to the smallest details.

Marching tables were compiled including the more common eventualities:

A. In case of a war against France, the office had to specify:
   1– if the concentration of the army had to happen at the quickest rate;
   2 – if there were three months available;
   3 – if perfect training was possible.

B. Against Russia for cases 2 and 3.

C. Against the Ottoman Empire for all cases.

D. Concentration of the whole army at Budapest, Olmütz, Arad or Temesvár.

For the further training of the General Staff officers, on 29 May 1811 were established winter schools in which, without prejudice to other obligations and during the afternoon hours of the General Staff service, further matters were learned, with the exception of field fortifications. Matters with practical exercises were learned in spring, with the involvement of the Pioneer Corps.[1] Under such detailed care and with so much restless eagerness in learning, it was naturally a consequence that the Austrian General Staff, towards the end of the second period (1758–1816), was already trained in a way that could not be compared with the level which it occupied at its establishment. Over the years, the institute developed administrative and police services, which incidentally ran into tactical elements and military strategy. Now this had become the actual General Staff field of application.

Already from 1794, strategy was included in the tasks, by demanding of the General Quartermaster a written report or memoir about military operations after the expiration of each campaign. He had to explain the performed operations, eventual failures, causes, connections, and consequences. However, the need for an army reorganisation had proved to be unquestionable, especially after the experience in the French Revolutionary Wars. Archduke Carl took the initiative in setting up his general staff in Italy (that of the army under his command) in a well-timed manner. In September 1805 the *Dienstvorschrift für den General-Quartiermeisterstab* was issued, which soon after became authoritative for the whole Austrian army. The Archduke freed the General Staff from the restraining burden of administrative and police service, and indicated tactical matters as their exclusive competence. The *Jäger Corps*, which had been alienated from its original purpose of serving on reconnaissance tasks for the General Quartermaster, and as other light troops was used on vanguards, was definitively retired from the General Staff. The same happened also with the *Stabsinfanterie*, the *Stabsdragoner* and the Audiences Bureau. The first three corps came under the command of a *General Commandant*, the latter, with all its bureaus, was subordinated to the Army General Command. Under the General Quartermaster remained only the Pioneer Corps, the Pontoons Corps and the *Tschaikistens* Corps, the *Quartier-Generals-Wagenmeister*, and the *Wegmeister Amt*, which dealt with the roads bureau. The colonel became a brigadier of the troops assigned to the General Staff, directing the chancery, wrote the operations diary by his own hand, was the immediate assistant to the generals, assuming the tasks of general quartermaster, and for that reason he could never be detached, but always had to remain in the headquarters. With this reform, the service of the General Staff was greatly relieved and closer to its actual purpose. They were to be regarded as forerunners of the next, most important innovation, the 1809 division of the Army in Army Corps, each with its independent General Staff.

1 In 1811 the matters were: training regulations, the evolutions and comparative tactical diversity of the cavalry (*Major* Geppert), the service regulations, geometry and trigonometry (*Hauptmann* Augustin); finances and economy, style and learning disposition (*Oberst-Lieutenant* Rothkirch). In addition, the officers received a riding lesson every morning.

Uniforms

1792–1797

The simplifications of the general's uniform, which had already been introduced during the reign of Joseph II, continued with the *Adjustierungsvorschrift* (adjustment regulations) issued before 1798. Austrian generals wore the traditional tricorne manufactured with black *Seidenfilz*, a fabric made with mixed silk and felt, completed with a large *Goldborte*-golden lace, on the left side of which was a black butterfly-shaped cockade, held by a loop of gilt braid and a black and golden button. Already in the 1780s the front corner became flatter so as to more resemble a bicorne. The single-breasted coat was of white cloth, more or less laced depending by rank. The *Feldmarschall*'s coat was decorated with a composite broad-weave lace on the cuffs and breast 2 *Zoll* wide (5.2cm); the *General der Cavallerie* and *General Feldzeugmeister* had one broad lace 1 *Zoll* (2.6cm) wide, and one narrow lace half a *Zoll* wide (1.3cm); the *Feldmarschall-Lieutenant* a single broad lace and the *General Wachtmeister* a single narrow lace. Cuffs and lining were in ponceau red cloth. Pocket flaps were also decorated with lace as the cuffs. Gilded buttons with a star and spruce edge completed the regular uniform for generals, without further distinctions. The waistcoat was of ponceau red with yellow-gold lace. In 1796 ponceau red breeches for the *Feldmarschall* replaced the straw-coloured ones. Senior commanders also had chamois leather gloves with flaps, and as footwear, cavalry boots with buckled spurs. The sword had gilded fittings and golden leather straps. The prescribed *Feldbinde* (field sash) was not used after 1790. Before 1798, general officers did not carry a plume on their headgear. Generals also carried a wooden cane with a golden pommel on the top. Prior to 1798 most Hungarian generals wore either a red uniform or a white version with a *hechtgrau* pelisse trimmed with fur. They could wear their regimental uniforms, as did *Feldmarschall* Würmser in 1796 during the Italian campaign, wearing a parrot-green pelisse, lined with white fur and laced with gold. In winter and on campaign, the generals wore the double-breasted *Überrock* greatcoat in grey cloth with ponceau red collar and golden laces on the cuffs.

With regard to the general staff officers' uniform, no special regulation was issued during its permanent service period. Some evidence suggests that they followed the scheme established in 1771, but with several exceptions and flexibility. An order dated 7 April 1798, which refers to the earlier Aulic War Council regulations concerning the uniforms, required 'uniformity of dress', and it is likely to serve as proof of the previous assumption.[2] During daily service the *General Stab* officers wore long-tailed single-breasted coats of *dunkelblau* cloth with ponceau red collars, lapels and cuffs. Laced shoulder cords, as distinctives, identified the officers on parade. Therefore it may be considered that the blue coat with red cuffs and gold-embroidered buttonholes remained a characteristic feature of the Austrian General Staff officers until 1798.

2 Karger, *Die Entwicklung der Adjustierung, Rüstung und Bewaffnung*, p.348.

Even an authoritative source such as the monumental work of Rudolf von Ottenfeld and Oskar Teuber is not without errors or dubious interpretations. He are illustrated a *General Feldzeugmeister*, wearing the *Rock* with the less common falling collar, alongside with a *Flügel Adjutant* awaiting for orders. Behind them, a *Stabsoffizier* wears a laced headdress, which seems to be an error of the artist's.

The *General-Adjutant* wore the uniform of the Kaiser's Chevauxlegers Regiment (Nr.1), consisting of a dark green coat with ponceau red *Egalisierung* facings, and yellow metal buttons with yellow embroidered buttonholes. The *Stabsoffiziere* (staff officer) uniform comprised a dark blue coat with red cuffs, with buttonholes embroidered with gold. The breeches could be white, otherwise like the senior officers. The *Quartermaster Staff General* wore the same uniform with laced cuffs, red waistcoat and breeches, the latter were as the infantry officers' models.

1798–1805

Generals of all ranks wore a new single-breasted white coat, narrower and shorter compared to the previous models. The resulting pattern was less aulic and more similar to the uniform of the troops, but retained the typical features of the senior ranks. A white standing collar replaced the previous items, but exceptions continued to be common among the higher ranks. The silk waist sash in yellow, with fringed tassels, was reintroduced as the main rank insignia for all officer commanders. This item was manufactured in yellow and black silk, worn only on active duty. Waistcoat and breeches were always in ponceau red.

For special celebrations, festivities and parades, generals wore the gala uniform, which remained unchanged, with the three top buttons of the coat closed, the sword knot and the recently introduced *Feldbinde* over the waistcoat. At the same events, they wore straw-yellow breeches. On campaign or out of service, generals of all ranks wore as ordinary uniform the coat without lace with sword and *Feldbinde* over the buttoned coat, while out of service they carried both over the waistcoat. The laced hat was worn only with the gala uniform, otherwise worn without lace and with a 28.5cm green feather bush. The golden edge of the headdress could be richer compared to that of the regiment's officers. After 1798, the Austrian generals were also identified by a green *Federbusch*(feather bush), which in the nineteenth century transformed into green floppy plumage, as for duty and high uniforms as well. The *Federbusch* was only allowed to be carried on service duty. The generals had to adopt the same hairstyle as that prescribed for the staff and senior officers of the regiment. On gala days, when the only footwear generals were previously allowed to appear in at court were stockings and shoes, they could now appear as they pleased and even with boots.

After 1800, Hungarian generals usually wore the hussar-style parade uniform, comprising a white *Pelz* with 16 or 17 rows of golden yellow loops each with five *Oliven* buttons, and trimmed with white or brown fur. Above the barrelled waist sash, there was the sabretache waist belt with an 'S'-shaped clip buckle. Also tight breeches in ponceau red with golden embroidery and boots in Hungarian style with fixed spurs; the sabre was the Hungarian

Left: *General-Adjutant* in 1798 uniform in dark green coat, ponceau red cuffs and lining, yellow metal buttons, and straw yellow breeches. Note the black headdress with golden tassels but without edging lace and green feather bush, the *Feldbinde* sash worn on the left shoulder, and the yellow/black belt with silver buckle with the gold double-headed eagle embossed. (Authors' archive)

Right: *Feldmarschall Lieutenant* wearing the uniform introduced in 1798; print from the illustration of the *Adjustierungsvorschrift* published by Mollo and Mansfeld. (Authors' archive)

Right: *Flügeladjutant* in 1798, from Mollo and Mansfeld. He wears the same uniform of the *General-Adjutant* except for the white metal buttons and the 1.6cm lace on the cuffs, while the senior officer has it measuring 2.3cm. (Authors' archive)

Left: *Generalstabs-Offizier*, 1798; dark green coat with black facing and yellow metal buttons. (Authors' archive)

Officer of the *General-Quartiermeisterstab* wearing the uniform introduced in 1809. The colours remained the same of the previous uniform, green with black facings, and the change concerned essentially in details like the new headdress and horse furniture. (Authors' archive)

curved sword. The headgear carried the *Federbush* like the German generals. On campaign Hungarian generals also wore the shako, manufactured in black silk felt with the distinctives as for the hussar field officers.

A grey/white cloak or double-breasted frock coat *Überrock* completed the Hungarian general's uniform in winter. The *Überrock* also belonged to the German generals, but in *hechtgrau* (pike-grey),with an unlined red collar, red lapels, and cuff flaps closed by two small plain gilt buttons with the same gold edging as for the coat, embroidered in gold for field marshals. Generals also had a dark grey single-breasted *Roquelor* greatcoat with a detachable short cape, high standing collar and plain gilded buttons. The sword belt was the same as that carried by the infantry field officers.

All generals had the same ponceau red saddle cover edged with the same lace pattern of their rank, with the Emperor's cypher and crown embroidered in the four corners, of which those in the front corners were somewhat smaller. On campaign the saddle cover was replaced by another model, to preserve the previous item. This saddle cover had the same shape as that of the regiment field officers, with the same edged lace, and in addition to this, on the inside there was also a black and yellow border for edging. The size

General Bellegarde and his staff at the battle oft he Mincio River, 1814. Behind him there are a *General-Adjutant* and a *Flügeladjutant* both wearing the coat of dark green and red facing with the yellow-black sash fixed with a golden loop on the left shoulder. Their uniforms bore the same distinctives introduced in 1798. (Exhibited in 2001, Roslyn Harbor, Nassau County Museum of Art, Napoleon and his Age)

of the saddle cover was based on the size of the horse and the type of saddle, therefore the Hungarian generals could have the hussar-shape saddle cover.

In 1798 the *General Stab Quartermaster* completely changed the uniforms. While dress and equipment generally followed the regulations for infantry officers, after 1798 he adopted a black felt hat with golden laces, similar to the regiment's field officers, but with a green feather plume and black silk neckband with white edging. The new single-breasted coat was tailored in *dunkelgrün*, with black velvet standing collar and 'German' cuffs with golden lace, plain gilded buttons, red lining and turnbacks without piping. The coat was tailored with two vertical pockets at waist level with flaps fastened by a small single gilded button at the centre of each flap. Altogether the coat had 18 buttons. A *Paillefarben* – straw yellow – single-breasted waistcoat with small plain gilded buttons were common, worn under the coat.

Quartermaster staff generals wore the silk *Feldbinde* waist sash like the general commanders. As a winter coat, they wore a dark green double-breasted frock coat *Überrock* with black velvet collar and cuffs, and plain gilded buttons. The *Überrock* was lined of ponceau red with a standing collar higher than that of the coat. This was a common city and service dress to be worn on campaign and everyday service.

The *General Adjutant* and *Flügel Adjutant* had the same dark green uniform established for the General Staff, but the *Feldbinde* sash was worn diagonally on the left shoulder. The standing collar, cuffs and turnbacks were in ponceau red.

Wigs assumed a new style without side curls, but with a 5 *Zoll* (13cm) *Zopf* queue.

1805–1810

Generals of all ranks continued to wear the felt bicorne hat, which was actually more and more similar to a bicorne. The headdress readopted the lace as before 1798. In1806 the *Rock* coat added a white higher standing collar. The single-breasted coat became shorter, and cuffs were red with rank insignia as usual. The same laces appeared on the breast along the button panels of the gala uniform. Generals of all ranks wore the waist sash of golden silk as usual. Breeches remained ponceau red and were worn inside cavalry boots. Officers had to be clean shaven, except the Hungarians.

A significant novelty in the dress of the generals occurred with the introduction of the field coat. Since on campaign, especially on muddy ground, the white uniform tended to get dirty very easily, a single-breasted coat was introduced with the same pattern as the white *Rock*, in order to replace all the items introduced before, such as cloaks or other informal clothing. The first models of field coat were tailored in *dunkelhechtgrau* (dark pike-grey) cloth, later replaced by *hechtgrau*, and soon became very popular among generals of all ranks. The rank's laces followed the same pattern as the white coat.

The uniform for different occasions was regulated in the *Adjustierung* of 1807.[3] The text explained:

> 1 – At the first reception of the Supreme Order, when such generals arrive in a garrison, and when they are on leave of absence, during the revue, manoeuvres and when engaged in an extraordinary parade is ordered, or when a gala is announced at court, the gentleman generals have to wear with a fully laced uniform [coat], long trousers, boots and spurs, field armband, trimmed hats with green feather bushes.
>
> 2 – In all service affairs without exception, and when leading the troops, all generals have to appear in plain white uniforms, laced hats and green feather.
>
> 3 – When engaged in exercise and training, the generals who command their troops, who either exercise or training, carry the Feldbinde [waist sash], as do the generals in active service and generally as long as they are in a service to which they are commanded for replacing others.
>
> 4 – In the future, unlaced hats will only be allowed out of service, but the feather bush will be worn in and out of service.

3 Österreichisches Staatsarchiv – Kriegsarchiv, Vienna, *Hofkriegsrath 1807*, C7 – 121, signed 26 July 1807.

General der Cavallerie Adam Albert von Neipperg, portrayed by Josef Lanzedelli in 1810. He wears the regular uniform for Hungarian generals of white dolman and pelisse, golden buttons and braids, and ponceau red breeches. His pelisse has 24 pairs of braids, as usual for senior commanders. Note the shako with three laces of chained rings as distinctive for generals of all ranks. (Private Collection)

1811

The *Adjustierungs-Vorschrift* of 1811 confirmed for all members of the General Staff the dark green coat of 1798, but with a higher collar. The coat was in dark green baize cloth, with red lining and black collar and cuffs. The coat was so long that its turnbacks, always of red cloth, touched the ground when kneeling. It was closed with 10 smooth brass buttons. The collar was not allowed to exceed 10cm (4 *Zoll*) in height, the cuffs had wide laces but not over 8cm (3 *Zoll*) wide, and had two small side buttons. The new regulation also prescribed a higher bicorne felt hat, with a rear ridge 26cm high (10 *Zoll*), while the anterior one was 22.5cm (8½ *Zoll*) high. It had a 26cm (10 *Zoll*) standing green plume, a black velvet hat rosette, and gold laces. As a rank distinction the staff officer had a 5cm wide (2 *Zoll*) golden edging and a little golden lace of 1.5cm (½ *Zoll*). The *General Adjutant* and *Flügel Adjutant* followed the 1798 regulations but with updated headdress and pattern.

From 1811 the *Überrock* for senior commanders became definitively *hechtgrau*, while the one for the *Generalsstab* was of the same dark green cloth, with cuffs, collar, turnbacks and lining as the coat. The *Generalsstab* officers wore under the coat a straw-coloured single-breasted *Leibel* with yellow buttons. All *Generalsstab* personnel wore white German-style breeches, worn inside the boots, and were provided with 'German' steel spurs.

Stabsdragoner

The Staff Dragoons regiment was created for the first time by *Feldmarschall-Lieutenant* Count Lacy in 1758. Its main role was to guard the headquarters and to escort the baggage on campaign. The personnel came from the ordinary dragoon regiments and admission to this unit was very coveted, because serving close to the headquarters each horseman expected to receive better treatment, and usually did. Special distinctive and better equipment were usually issued to the *Stabsdragoner*, at least until the last year of the eighteenth century.

Generally the existence of the *Stabsdragoner* coincided with the military involvement of the Austrian army, and then the regiment was raised

This imperious Hungarian horseman has been portrayed in 1816 by English artist Robert Dighton. This officer seems to wear a personalised version of the Hungarian uniform for *General Wachtmeister*. The uniform has been tailored with the colours of the Erzherzog Joseph Husaren Regiment (Nr. 2), which replace the white–ponceau red pattern. The pelisse carries 22 pairs of braids each with the regular five buttons. The sabretache bears a simple design, but is enriched with a broad golden lace. Also the old-fashioned saddle cover is edged with a golden lace. The shako shows with good detail the chain of rings also forming the rank distinctive for the field officers' headdress, as introduced in 1798, but single, with golden piping on both sides. The top of the shako is edged by more golden piping. (British Museum)

every time until the war against the Porte in 1788–91. In the opening phase of the First Coalition War, one *Division* was raised in February 1790 and quartered in Breisgau. A further two *Stabsdragoner* squadrons were formed in November and assigned to the Army of Italy. In 1791 another division joined the one in Italy, composed of *Halb-Invaliden*, namely aged cavalry personnel who had been retired from active duty. In the spring of 1792 the division quartered in Breisgau headed to Italy and joined the divisions already serving in Lombardy. A fourth division was finally formed for the Austrian Low Countries.

The squadron staff was the same as for the ordinary dragoons, but the *Stabsdragoner* had a restricted regiment staff with their designated *Oberst* and other field officers, but no *Klein Regimentsstab*. After the campaign of 1797 the divisions in Italy were reformed and in 1798 joined the newly raised Leichte Dragoner Regiment Nr.9.[4] Meanwhile a new division had been formed in the Austrian Low Countries in 1794 and then a further division formed in November 1798 to serve with the Austrian headquarters in Germany. The first division was disbanded in 1799, while the second followed in 1801. The *Stabsdragoner* reappeared in 1805, in preparation for the Third Coalition War, this time with a strength of two divisions, one for the army of Germany and the other for that in Italy. As occurred every time, both these units were disbanded in April 1806 after the Peace of Pressburg signed in December. In April 1809 a single squadron of *Stabsdragoner* was formed for the army of Archduke Carl, disbanded in January 1810. This trend underwent a radical change at the end of 1812, when the new Stabsdragoner Regiment was raised in Vienna with a strength of six squadron for three *Divisionen*. The first division was assigned to the *Observations-Armee* in Galicia, the second headed to the Inner-Österreich Armee, which marched to Italy in October 1813, under the command of Major Philipp Freiherr von Zedlitz; and the third joined the headquarters of the Austrian main army under *Feldmarschall* Schwarzenberg in Bohemia, and later in Germany and France. In late summer of 1813, the first division was also assigned to the main army.

A further *Stabsdragonerdivision* was raised in January 1814 at Mistelbach under *Rittemeister* Franz Rauschenfeld, followed by *Major* Christoph Schäser. This division was in France in 1814 with the Southern Army, and in 1815 operated in Alsace. The *Stabsdragoner* served with the Austrian headquarters until 1816, when all the divisions were disbanded.[5]

Before 1791, the *Stabsdragoner* wore the same patter uniform of the ordinary dragoons, but with *dunkelblau* coat with ponceau red facings and white metal buttons. In 1792, a new uniform was issued to the two *Divisionen* in Italy, which differed from the previous one for the coat now in *grasgrün* with black *Egalisierung* facings.[6] Also weaponry was like the ordinary dragoons, except for the sword. As special weapon exclusively of this corps, in 1793, troopers received a special *Pallasch* with gilded brass hilt, inside a black leather scabbard with brass fittings. According to the Austrian *Kriegsarchiv*, the division raised

4 Wrede and Semek, *Geschichte der K. und K. Wehrmacht*, vol. III, part two, pp.940–941.

5 Wrede and Semek, *Geschichte der K. und K. Wehrmacht*, vol. III, part two, pp.943–945.

6 The same uniform was retained by the Chevauxlegers Regiment Nr.9.

The only known images depicting a *Botenmeister* are a watercolour by an anonymous artist (left) and the drawing from the Venturini series (right), representing a messenger during the campaign against Murat in 1815. He is receiving orders from a field officer of the Dragoner Regiment Nr. 4. (Authors' archive)

in 1798 for the war theatre in Germany received the old blue coat with red facings, replaced in 1800 by a new coat in *hechtgrau* with ponceau red facings and yellow metal buttons.[7] Weaponry, headgear and white breeches. In 1812, when the Stabsdragoner Regiment was raised again, the uniform consisted of a *dunkelgrün* coat with *carmoisinrot* facings, yellow metal buttons, white breeches and German cavalry helm like the ordinary dragoons.

Botenmeister

The need for intelligence, as well as the training of reliable individuals for espionage missions, which could not easily be carried out by officers but which could not easily be entrusted to just anyone, resulted in the 1813 establishment of a separate *Berittenes Botenmeister Corps* (Messenger Corps). It consisted of 30 individuals selected from the most qualified and most capable NCOs of the *Grenzer* or *Feldjäger* battalions. They were all mounted and served as couriers, accompanied by the General Quartermaster in marches, observing and reporting; however they often had, chiefly, the execution of secret assignments, for which purpose 20 of the most prepared among them, in addition to the uniform, were also provided with civilian clothes. The corps served in Italy under the command of *Rittmeister* Herbert.

The uniform of this corps consisted of a Corsican hat with a brass horn as emblem, instead of the common *Jäger* eagle, a green uhlan *Kurtka* with black cuffs, collars and lapels, green woollen epaulettes, a green *Leibel* with sleeves and yellow buttons; also green uhlan trousers with lateral black stripes and grey leather chaps or riding pants, a yellow/black uhlan-style waist belt, grey-white German cavalry *Roquelor*, uhlan-style boots with spurs and red saddle mantle bag. Armament included a hussar sabre, carbine, powder horns with green cords; the straps and cartridge box were of black leather.[8] The horse equipment was as the uhlans. The *Botenmeister* received double wages for his rank, together with an extraordinary contribution on campaign. Furthermore he managed 12 trained soldiers, assigned to him as adjutants and horse-keepers.

Mounted Palace Corps

Ungarische Adelige Leibgarde (Hungarian Noble Guards)

The first sovereign approval of the Empress and Queen Maria Theresa on the establishment of a bodyguard formed of Hungarian nobles for her personal lifeguard, was issued by the Hungarian Court Chancellor, Count Nikolaus Pálffy, on 25 October 1759. This order received a new confirmation on 4 December 1759 and a third followed on 12 February 1760 issued by the *Hofminister* Count Anton Corfiz Uhlfeld. The corps received the title Ungarische Adelige Leibgarde but later was also known as Ungarische

7 Wrede and Semek, *Geschichte der K. und K. Wehrmacht*, vol. III, part two, p.942.

8 This uniform is described in the *Oesterreichisch-ungarische Militär Zeitung*, March 1876.

Ungarische Adelige Leibgarde, 1792–1815, after a coeval print. The officers, NCOs and Guards had to belong to the Hungarian aristocracy with at least one year in the infantry or cavalry with an immaculate state of service. The guards were selected from soldiers, cadets, NCOs, and junior officers of the regiments, but, in addition to the otherwise necessary training, they had to be at least 173.78cm (five feet eight and a half inches) tall and with the finest appearance. In 1810 only 50 men were selected from the regiments; the remaining 100 guards were taken among candidates who had served into the Hungarian *Insurrectionis*. The final authorisation to enter the corps was reserved to the Emperor. (Authors' archive)

Nobelgarde or *Praetoriana Nobilis Turma*.

Alongside their main task, the Noble Guard had the purpose of serving as an academy for the nobility, where a young aristocrat had to be educated in civil matters as well as military ones. The lessons included the German, French and Italian languages, field service and arithmetic, state and politic sciences, and finally riding, fencing and dancing.

The Hungarian Noble Guard was regarded as a military corps and served under the command of a *Oberst-Hofmeister* (colonel court-master), otherwise, if the rank was vacant, they passed under direct control of the Aulic War Council. As quarter the guards were assigned to the Palais Trautson.

However, in 1764 the Hungarian State Parliament in Pressburg refused to advance the funds for maintaining the Noble Guards. Maria Theresa ordered the disbanding of the corps, but weeks later, after negotiations with the Hungarian parliament, she withdrew her decision, declaring the Hungarian Guard as 'an Imperial Guard detachment at her Service'.

Nevertheless, between the late eighteenth century and early nineteenth century, several reductions affected the corps. During the 1809 campaign the Emperor had as personal lifeguard in the field the *Unterkommandant* Henneberg, the lieutenants Medzihradsky, Illyes, Morway, Adam, Bodo, Baan, four lifeguards and three field orderlies. However, before the outbreak of the war of 1809 the Hungarian Noble Guard were almost dissolved, and it was only in subsequent years that the Emperor considered a reorganisation. With the Supreme Resolution dated 16 March 1810, Franz I rebuilt the Guards and prescribed for them a new organisation, which not only preserved their original purpose of forming a Guard for the King (of Hungary), but also maintained the military academy, from which would emerge many experienced officers for the army and the national *Insurrectio*. As a result the Noble Guard was raised with a strength of 183 men and consisted of one guard captain and first captain (who was a *Feldmarschall-Lieutenant*) one *Feldzeugmeister*; one *Zweites Rittmeister*, two Guard lieutenants (who were

Oberstlieutnants or colonels), two *Zweites Lieutenanten* (captains or majors), two *Gardewachtmeister* (first lieutenants); 12 corporals (second lieutenants), and 150 Guards (*Fähnrich*, junior officer). In addition they had also one chaplain, one auditor, one accountant, one adjutant, one Guard medical doctor, one *Schmied*; one *Profoss*; four trumpeters and 65 extra personnel, consisting for the most part of gratified invalids for the service of the 169 Lifeguards.

The officers, NCOs and Guards had to be Hungarian nobles with at least one year in the infantry or cavalry with an immaculate service record. The guards were selected from soldiers, cadets, NCOs, and junior officers of the regiments, but in addition to the other necessary training, they still had to be at least 173.78cm (5 feet 8 inches; 5 *Schuh*, 6 *Zoll*) tall with the finest appearance. In 1810 only 50 men were selected from the regiments; the remaining 100 Guards were taken among candidates who had served in the Hungarian *Insurrectionis*. Final authorisation was reserved for the Emperor. Service in the corps lasted five years, after which the men returned to their regiments as lieutenants. However, the Noble Guards could also ask to leave their service and obtain a better civil position in the state where they lived, whereby they were given special consideration. The Noble Guards could also retire completely after five years, receiving 'honoris causa' the rank of second lieutenant. They continued, as before, to serve under the command of the *Oberst-Hofmeister*. In order to avoid the disputes that occurred several times before 1809, the Hungarian Noble Guards had been equated as a military corps with the rank of *Erstes Arcièren*. The Noble Guard retained this organisation until 1848, but their number was progressively reduced to 70 effectives. The corps was disbanded after the 1848 Hungarian Revolution and rebuilt on 21 April 1867, coinciding with the *Ausgleich*.

Members of the *Ungarische Adelige Leibgarde*:

Period	Capitain	Capitain-Lieutenant	Garde-Oberlieutenant	Garde-Lieutenant
September 1791–January 1794	FML Anton Esterhazy de Galantha	1784–1809 GM.-FML Michael Splényi de Mihaldy	1790–1794 Ob. Abraham von Barcsay	1791–1794 ObLt. Nikolaus Esterhazy de Galantha
January 1794–December 1803	Vacant	Vacant	1794–1803 FML Nikolaus *Fürst* Esterhazy de Galantha	1794–1804ObLt. (later Ob.) Joseph Johann von Szarvassy
December 1803–November 1833	FML-FZM Nikolaus Esterhazy de Galantha	1813–1824 FML Maximilian Kollonitz	1795–1813 GM.-FML Maximilian Kollonitz	1812–1824 Ob (later GM) Andreas Freiherr von Martonitz 1812–1835 ObLt Franz Zichy-Ferraris

Galizische Adelige Leibgarde in 1792–1809. Recruited among Galician noble volunteers, this unit served under the command of a 'colonel' directly subordinated to the Aulic War Council. In 1790 Emperor Leopold II disbanded the Guard, and on 1 May 1791 incorporated the 30 best subjects with the Arcièren-Leibgarde as a Galician *Abteilung*. In 1809, due to the shortage of court funds, the unit was dissolved. (Authors' archive)

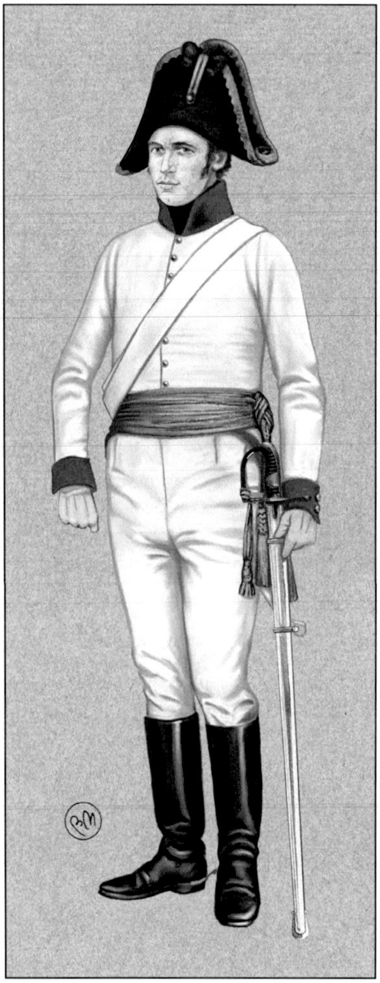

Böhmische Adelsgarde, 1813–14. The uniform consisted of a white *Röckel*, similar to the German cavalry, with ponceau red cuffs, collar and turnbacks, white breeches replaced on campaign with *schwarz-grau* overall trousers with yellow buttons, and a red stripe 5cm wide on both sides. Buttons and laces were golden yellow. Each private guard had the rank of corporal. (Illustration by Bruno Mugnai)

Hofdienstadjustierung – Uniform for the Court Service

Guard NCOs and private Guards wore a brown fur *Kalpak* with a black heron feather, white plume and *Apfelgrün* busby bag, a ponceau red *Attila* with silver olive and lanyards, a short mantle in leopard fur with silver accessories and buckle, ponceau red trousers with silver lace, an *apfelgrün* and silver waist sash, green velvet cartridge box and belts with silver fittings. Also a Hungarian sabre with a green velvet sabre belt and silver silk *Portepee*, straw-yellow gloves, *Czismen* boots in yellow or black leather, and a wooden cane for NCOs. The saddle cover comprised a leopard fur edged with white and black lace, and an *apfelgrün* cloth laced with silver.

Guard captain and Guard senior officers wore the same uniforms, but *Hofdienstattila* pelisse and trousers in ponceau red with silver embroidery, old Hungarian-style sabre, black velvet sabre belt with silver fittings – *Hofdienstsabelkuppel* – and golden silk *Portepee*, straw-yellow leather gloves, and a rank wooden cane. All lace on the uniform and saddle cover was double.

Galizische Adelige Leibgarde

Recruited among Galician nobles volunteers, this unit served under the command of a *Oberst-Hofmeister*, directly subordinated to the Aulic War Council.

After the first partition of Poland in 1773, Joseph II established a new territorial Palace Corps. This 'Galician Noble Guard' was intended as a higher educational institution for young Polish noblemen for training them in civil and military matters as occurred for their Hungarian counterparts. The corps entered service on 1 January 1782, and received the 'Credential' on 16 November. Each guardsman performed service in the so-called battalion room alongside the Hungarian Noble Guard and the Arcièren-Leibgarde. They were quartered in the former *Kaiserspital* in the Viennese Rennweg.

As a military obligation, the Guardsmen participated in the wars against the Porte. In 1790 Emperor Leopold II disbanded the Guard, and on 1 May 1791 incorporated the better subjects with the Arcièren-Leibgarde as Galician *Abteilung*, with a strength of 30 men. In 1809, due to the shortage of court funds, the unit was dissolved, and as a consequence some guardsmen who served with the army in Galicia deserted with their horse and weapons to the French side. In 1813 the guard was re-established and joined to the *Böhmische Adelsgarde*, but 120 men were recruited among Bohemian noble volunteers. Nonetheless, its formal dissolution took finally place in July 1816.

The uniform followed the uhlan style, with white cloth *Czapka* with black peak with gilded edge and cords; red *Kontusch* (overcoat)[9] with blue sleeves; blue *Zupan* (long coat to the knees) with gold-trimmed edgings, the sleeves of which were split to the top and lined with cherry-red velvet; standing collar of red cloth, epaulettes; *Pass* (long woven belt, embroidered in gold and silver); belt with cavalry cartridge box, red boots.

Sabre yellow-mounted (with gilded metal) with a leather scabbard; riding horse with precious bridles; two pistols in the holsters; an uhlan lance with black and yellow pennant.[10]

Böhmische Adelsgarde

At the beginning of the 1813 campaign it happened that the *Arcièrenleibgarde* was unable to set up a detachment for the Emperor's security. The Guards consisted exclusively of veterans, who also had to continue to serve the court and protect the Empress. For this, several high nobles came to Prague on 3 August, who had already served in the *Landwehr* during the 1809 campaign, and asked the commanding general in Bohemia, *Feldmarschall* Graf Kolowrat-Krakowsky to form 'at their own expense a Bohemian Nobles Guard'. This request was sent on August 4 to Franz I, and he issued a handwritten letter from Brandeis on August 4 1813 to Count Kolowrat, in which he accepted the offer and left him the organisation 'at the requests of these Chevaliers'.

The Bohemian noble, Colonel Count Georg Waldstein, Major Altgraf Johann Salm, Major Count Ernst Waldstein, Colonel Count Johann Pachter and Major Count Josef Nostitz wrote, consequently, a proposal for the establishment of this Guard, which also became executive in its essential parts.

The Böhmische Adelige Leibgarde zu Pferd was established for the whole duration of the 1813 campaign, with the task of escorting the Emperor in all his movements, and protecting him against every possible danger until the last man 'with the sacrifice of goods and blood'. At the same time, the Guards could be used for all sorts of services, such as the delivering of orders, courier riding, or escorting enemies to captivity.

Although it was originally intended to deploy one squadron with 4 *Züge* of 30 Guards each, this strength was later disregarded, as the corresponding number of noblemen was not always available. In fact, only a detachment of 38 Guards with two trumpeters was actually raised. It comprised one *Kapitän*, one *Kapitän Lieutenant*, two *Erstes Lieutenanten*, three *Zweites Lieutenanten*, 30 Guardsmen, one *Fourier* and three stablemen.

From August 1813 until June 1814, the Kapitän der Kaiserliche Böhmischen Adeligen Leibgarde, was the *Generalmajor* (later *Feldmarschall-*

9 The *Kontusz* (sometimes with the same meaning of *Kurtka*) was the uhlan overcoat. The name derives from the ancient Median *kantuš* which means the kaftan worn over the *Kurtka* with false sleeves. The fashion of the Polish military of the first half of the eighteenth century prescribed that Polish uhlans would wear a *Zupan* under their *Kontusz* or *Kurtka*. Peter Broucekr, Georg Zivkovic, Herbert Klima, 'Geschichteder k. u. k. Wehrmacht, VI. Band, DerAller hochste Oberbefehl, Die Garden', *Militaria Austriaca*, vol. VI (Vienna, 1988), p.77.

10 The reason for the lance was that noble horsemen (*Towarzysz*, in the traditional Polish military terminology) were always armed with lances, while the *Pocztowy* (retainers or troopers) carried firearms.

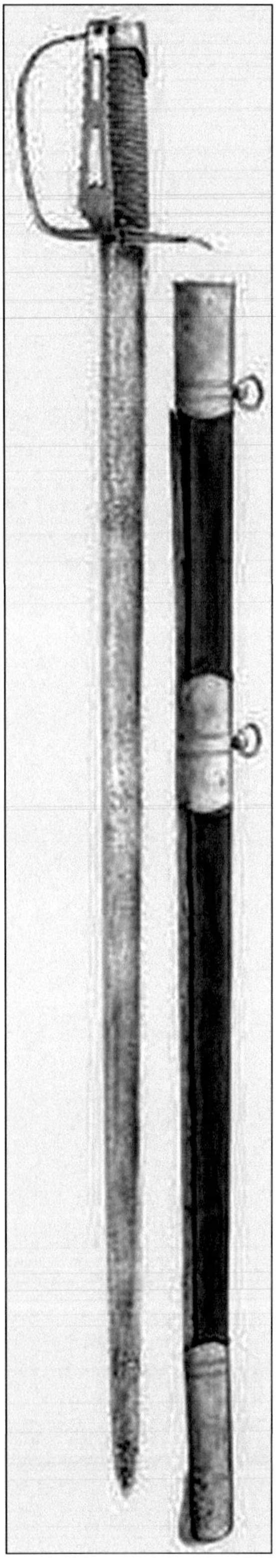

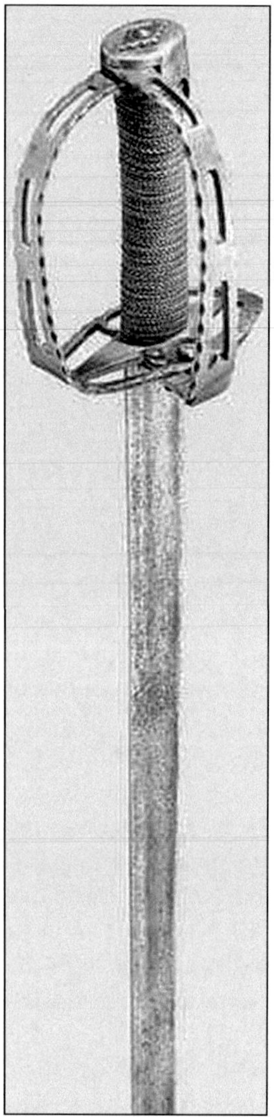

Pallasch issued in 1798 to the *Stabsdragoner*: gilded hilt and black leather scabbard with brass fittings. (Private Collection)

Lieutenant) Emanuel Wratislaw von Mitrowitz-Nettolitzky. During the 1813–14 campaign, three Guardsmen joined the army. As a result of a letter from the Emperor's of 27 June 1814, the Bohemian Noble Guard was disbanded.

The uniform consisted of a white coat, similar to that of the German cavalry, with ponceau red cuffs, collar and turnbacks, white trousers, replaced on campaign with *schwarz-grau* overall trousers with yellow buttons, and a red stripe 5cm wide on both sides. All ranks wore German-style high boots with fixed spurs. The bicorne hat, in the 1811 style, was provided with a jagged gold lace. With the exception of the officers, all the Guards had cartridge boxes like the hussar officers, sabres with an iron scabbard, an ordinary *Portepee*, and silk waist sash. As among the German Noble *Arcièren* Guards, the rank distinctive consisted of the black cane with round pommel and red band. The Guards' winter coat was the white *Roquelor* like the line cavalry. Furthermore, the Guards had also an iron-grey *Kaputröck* mantle with red cuffs and collars. The equipment for the horses was the same as that issued to the German cavalry.

Also, when licensed from the service, the former guardsmen were allowed to wear the uniform. To Count Wrbna, senior commander of corps, the Emperor paid a tribute to their service by offering a cross, bearing the inscription *Nobilibus Bohemis bello Gallicofidis corporis custodibus Franciscus Augustus MDCCCXIV*.

Left: Ladislaus Skulteti, *Estandarteführer* of the Kienmayer Husaren Regiment (Nr. 8), portrayed in 1814 or 1815. He was probably the only hussar to have served across the period from 1792 to 1815. Note the two-pointed standard still used as ensign, as usual in the hussar regiments. (Authors' archive)

Below: The reverse of the *Ehrestandarte* presented to the Hessen Homburg Husaren after the escort of Pope Pius VII in 1814, bearing the inscription *Hungariae Patrona Pium comitatur ad Urbem – O felix tanto Roma sub aupicio*. (Authors' archive)

Appendix

Austrian Major Staffs, 1792–1815

Emperor's *General-Adjutanten* 1792–1815	
Month – Year	**General-Adjutanten**
March 1792–September 1805	GM.-FML Kamillo von Lambertich
March 1792–August 1796	GM-FML Franz von Rollin
March–June 1794	Field General-Adjutant-ObLt. Josef von Stipsicz
March 1796–June 1797	GM-FML Friedrich von Linken
August 1796–October 1798	Ob Lt. then Oberst Carl von Vincent
October 1798–1808	FML Franz von Rollin
November 1805–July 1832	FZM Johann von Kutschera

Aulic War Council (*Hofkriegsrat*) 1792–1815	
Month–Year	**President**
December 1791–May 1796	FM Michael Johann von Wallis
May–November 1796	FM Friedrich Moritz von Nostitz-Rieneck
November 1796–January 1801	(ad interim) GdC Ferdinand von Tige
January–November 1801	FM Erzherzog Carl
War Minister (*Kriegsminister*)	
November 1801–February 1809	FM Erzherzog Carl
After February 1806, Supreme Chief Generalissimus of all Military Forces **Deputy Minister:** September–December 1805, FM Josef Maria von Colloredo-Waldsee	
February 1809–December 1814	FM Josef Maria von Colloredo-Waldsee
President	
April 1805–July 1806	FZM Maximilian Baillet de Latour
August 1806–April 1810	FZM-FM Wenzel Josef von Colloredo-Waldsee
April 1810–November 1813	FM Heinrich von Bellegarde

November 1813–June 1814	FM Wenzel Josef von Colloredo-Waldsee
June 1814–July 1820	FM Carl Philipp zu Schwarzenberg

Armies and Commanders 1792–1815			
From	**Until**	**Army**	**Commanders 1792–1801**
April 1792	November 1792	Niederlanden Armee	FM Albert von Sachsen-Teschen *adlatus*: FM Franz Moritz von Lacy
November 1792	February 1793		(ad interim) FZM Charles Clerfayt de Croix
February 1793	August 1794		FM Friedrich Josias von Sachsen-Coburg-Saalfeld
August 1794	April 1795	In 1796 united with the Rhein-Armee	FZM Charles Clerfayt de Croix
February 1793	January 1794	Rhein-Armee	GdC Dagobert Siegmund von Würmser
January 1794	March 1794		FZM Johann Georg von Browne
March 1794	April 1795	Divided into Oberrhein-Armee and Niederrhein-Armee	FM Albert von Sachsen-Teschen
April 1795	August 1795		FZM-FM Charles Clerfayt de Croix
August 1795	February 1796	Niederrhein-Armee	FM Charles Clerfayt de Croix
February 1796	August 1796	Again reunited in a single Rhein-Armee	FZM Erzherzog Carl von Este
August 1795	June 1796	Oberrhein-Armee	GdC-FM Dagobert Siegmund von Würmser
June 1796	August 1796	Again re-united in a single *Rhein-Armee*	FZM Maximilian Baillet de Latour
August 1796	February 1797	Neue Rhein-Armee	FZM Erzherzog Carl d'Este
February 1797	April 1797		FZM Maximilian Baillet de Latour
April 1797	November 1797		FZM Erzherzog Carl von Este
November 1797	January 1798	*Transformed into* Reichs-Kontingent *Transformed into* Deutsches Armee	FZM Maximilian Baillet de Latour
February 1798	November 1798		FML Josef Staader von Adelsheim
November 1798	March 1800		FZM Erzherzog Carl von Este
March 1800	August 1800		FZM Paul Kray von Krajova und Topolya
August 1800	December 1800		Obst. Erzherzog Johann Adlatus: FZM Franz von Lauer
December 1800	March 1801		FZM-FM Erzherzog Carl von Este
December 1792	August 1794	Italienisches Armee	FZM Josef Nikolaus de Vins
August 1794	March 1795		FZM Olivier Remigius von Wallis
March 1795	November 1795		FZM Josef Nikolaus de Vins
November 1795	March 1796		FZM Olivier Remigius von Wallis
March 1796	June 1796	Lombardisches Armee	FZM Johann Peter von Beaulieu
June 1796	November 1796		FM Dagobert Siegmund von Würmser

November 1796	March 1797	Friaul Armee Transformed into Inner-Österreich Armee	FZM Josef Alvinczi de Borberek
March 1797	April 1797		FZM Erzherzog Carl von Este
April 1797	January 1798		FZM Ludwig von Terzi
January 1798	July 1798	(Disbanded)	FML Friedrich von Hotze
April 1797	November 1797	Hungarian Insurrektions-Armee	FM Erzherzog Josef Anton, Palatin von Ungarn
January 1798	November 1798	Italienisches Armee	FZM Olivier Remigius von Wallis
November 1798	January 1799		FZM Friedrich von Oranien-Nassau
January 1799	April 1799		FML Paul Kray von Krajova und Topolya
April 1799	November 1800		GdC Michael von Melas
November 1800	March 1801		GdC Heinrich von Bellegarde
January 1799	May 1799	Armee in Tirol (Later joined with the Army of Italy)	GdC Heinrich von Bellegarde
November 1800	March 1801	Neue Hungarian Insurrektions-Armee	GdC Erzherzog Josef Anton, Palatin von Ungarn

1805

From	Until	Army	Commanders
November 1805	January 1806	Imperial Army	Emperor Franz I
November1805	October 1805	Armee in Deutschland Disbanded for Capitulation	GdC Erzherzog Ferdinand Carl von Este, adlatus: FML Carl Mack von Leiberich
November 1805	December 1805	Armee in Italien	FM Erzherzog Carl
December 1805	January 1806		GdC Erzherzog Johann (interim)
November 1805		Armee von Tirol Reunited with Army of Italy	GdC Erzherzog Johann
October 1805	January 1806	Insurrektions-Armee von Ungarn	GdC Erzherzog Josef Anton, Palatin von Ungarn

1806

Period:	Army	Commanders
September 1806	Neutrality Army	-

1809

From	Until	Army	Commanders
February 1809	July 1809	Hauptarmee	*Generalissimus* (GS) Erzherzog Carl von Habsburg
February 1809	February 1810		Emperor Franz I
February 1809	July 1809	Hauptarmee	*Generalissimus* (GS) Erzherzog Carl
July 1809	December 1809		GdC-FM Johann Josef von Liechtenstein

February 1809	December 1809	Armee von Innerösterreich	GdC Erzherzog Johann
		Armee von Böhmen	GdC Erzherzog Ferdinand Carl von Este
April 1809	November 1809	Insurrektions-Armee in Ungarn	GdC Erzherzog Josef Anton, Palatin von Ungarn

1813–1814

From	Until	Army	Commanders
May 1813	June 1813	Observations-Armee in Böhmen (became Hauptarmee)	FM Carl Philipp zu Schwarzenberg
May 1813	June 1813	Observations-Armee in Galizien (became 1st and 2nd Reserve Korps)	FZM Heinrich von Reuss-Plauen
June 1813	June 1814	Hauptarmee (Böhmische Armee)	FM Carl Philipp zu Schwarzenberg
July 1813	November 1813	Inner-Österreich Armee Later: Armee in Italien	FZM Johann von Hiller
November 1813	December 1813		FZM Johann von Hiller
December 1813	March 1815		FM Heinrich von Bellegarde
July 1813	October 1813	Donau-Armee (subordinated under the Bavarian army as Austrian army *Abteilung*)	FZM Heinrich von Reuss-Plauen
February 1814	March 1814	Reserve-Armee	GdC Friedrich von Hessen-Homburg
March 1814	May 1814	(became Süd-Armee)	GdC Friedrich von Hessen-Homburg

1815

From	Until	Army	Commanders
April 1815	October 1815	Armee in Oberrhein	FM Carl Philipp zu Schwarzenberg
March 1815	October 1815	Armee in Italien	GdK Johann von Frimont
	October 1815		FML Paul von Radivojevich
April 1815	June 1815	Naples Army	FML Federico Bianchi di Casalanza

***General-quartiermeisterstabs* Chiefs (from November 1865) or of the *Generalstab* 1792–1815**		
From	Until	Commanders
November1790	May1793	GM Andreas von Neu
May 1793	February 1794	FZM Friedrich Wilhelm zu Hohenlohe-Kirchberg
May 1794	August 1794	GdK Christian August zu Waldeck
August 1794	December 1795	FML Johann Peter von Beaulieu
March 1797	March 1798	FML Carl Mack von Leiberich*

* Until April 1797 also Chief of Staff in the Army of the Low Countries, then in the Rhine army and Niederrhein		
March 1798	March 1799	GM Heinrich von Schmitt
1799–1801 *General-quartiermeister* of the army of Germany and Italy		
March 1801	April 1805	FML Peter von Duka
April 1805	October 1805	FML Carl Mack von Leiberich
January 1806	February 1809	GM Anton Mayer von Heldensfeld
February 1809	May 1809	GM Johann von Prochaska
May 1809	August 1809	GM Maximilian von Wimpffen
August 1809	February 1813	FML Josef Radetzky de Radetz
February 1813	March 1815	GM.-FML Franz Xaver Richter von Binnenthal Temporary chief of the Quartermaster General Staff, and, from July 1813, at the same time Chief of Staff of the Army of Inner Austria and of Italy
May 1813	June 1814	FML Josef Radetzky de Radetz Chief of the General Staff of the Main Army and Quartermaster General: GM Friedrich Carl von Langenau
March 1815	October 1815	FML Josef Radetzky de Radetz
October 1815	March 1816	*Oberst* Josef von Koudelka

Colour Plate Commentaries

Plate A : *General Stab*

1. Hungarian *General der Cavallerie*, 1809–12

Although the General der Cavallerie was the counterpart of the infantry and artillery *Feldzeugmeister*, the senior ranks of the Austrian army did not reflect a division between the different components of the army, and both generals could command mixed corps of horse and foot. In practice, this rank identified the commanders who came from the cavalry, and only after 1809 were generals appointed to the command of actual cavalry corps. This figure is depicted in *The Military Costume of Europe*, published in England in 1812. The Hungarian commander wears a personalised uniform of the *General der Cavallerie*. As very often happens with coeval documents, it is difficult to establish whether the representation is true to reality, however it is known that the Hungarian officers enjoyed wide autonomy in the matter of clothing. The great helm for cuirassiers field officers was introduced after 1805 to better differentiate this item from the one worn by the company officers, and soon became very popular. The coat has the regular lace prescribed for the *General der Cavallerie* and the Hungarian trousers conform to the regulation of 1798. The decorations are, at the collar, the Maria Theresia Ritter Order, and the cross of the Saint Stephen Order on the breast.

2. *Feldmarschall* in field dress, 1805–1811

This general wears the field coat in *hechtgrau* introduced in 1805, certainly more practical on campaign compared to the white one. The pattern followed the white coat version, with ponceau red cuffs, lining and turnbacks. The rank distinctive appears on the cuffs only. The laced headdress conforms to the order issued in 1807, which prescribed its use in active service with the green *Federbush*. This pattern was modified after 1812, when the plain grey collar was replaced with one in ponceau red laced with the rank distinctive. The saddle cover is the model introduced in 1798 for senior commanders and remained unmodified until the 1850s. Gilded buckles and accessories for the horse furniture were reserved for field officers also.

3. *Flügel Adjutant*, 1799–1810

The *Vorschrift* of 1798 introduced a new uniform for the officers of the general staff, and essentially consisted of the dark green *Rock*, which replaced the blue one introduced in the 1770s. As a distinctive feature, the *Flügel Adjutant* and *General Adjutant* carried the sash on the left shoulder. They also wore a waist belt in yellow/black closed by a white metal buckle with gilded double-headed eagle embossed. In subsequent years this uniform changed very little, except for the felt headgear, replaced by the new higher model after 1811.

Plate B: *Regimentsstab, Stabsdragoner* and *Botenmeister*

1. Chevauxlegers Regiment Nr. 6, *Rechnungsführer*, 1801–1805

According to the authoritative work of Johann Karger, the *Rechnungsführer* (Regiment's Accountant) wore the same uniform of the *Ober-Offizierien*, being ranked as an *Ober-Lieutenant*. After 1798, further details regarding the uniforms for this officer prescribed the use of the felt edged, laced headdress without plume in all the cavalry branches. As for all the professionals and specialists, the cuirassier *Rechnungsführer* did not wear armour.

2. Stabsdragoner Regiment, *Gemeiner*, 1812

The existence of the *Stabsdragoner* coincided with the involvement of the Austrian army in the war, and then the regiment was raised every time until the war against the Porte in 1788–91 and successively in 1792–1801 when Austria faced Revolutionary France. Further *Stabsdragoner* divisions were raised in 1805 and a single unit in 1809. Finally, in 1812, a new *Stabsdragoner* regiment was raised in Vienna with a strength of six squadrons for three tactical divisions. The uniform followed the same pattern established for the line dragoons.

3. *Botenmeister*, 1813–14

Except for the description published in the *Oesterreichisch-ungarische Militär Zeitung* of March 1876, there is very little information about the uniform worn by this corps of messengers raised in 1813. A *Botenmeister* is depicted in the Venturini series dated 1814. The illustration shows the messenger wearing a pair of Hungarian *Czizme* boots instead of the uhlan short boots described in the text of 1876.

Plate C: Heavy Cavalry, 1792–1805

1. Karabinier Regiment Nr. 1 (Nr. 5), Sachsen-Teschen, *Gemeiner* in High Dress, 1792–98

The uniform of the *Karabinieren* was the same issued to the cuirassiers, though the hat lace on the headdress was indicative only for the two carabinier regiments: in yellow for Regiment Nummer 5 (first regiment) and white for Nummer 13 (second regiment). Cuirassier uniform was simplified after 1767. The jacket was now single-breasted with regimental facing colours on the cuffs, turnbacks edge and the typical *Paroli* patches on the collar. The cuirasses continued to be blackened. The headdress was fitted with a black over yellow plume and gradually had assumed the bicorne form in the 1780s. Note the high boots with removable spurs, also issued to cuirassiers, dragoons and chevauxlegers, replaced after 1798 with the shorter model.

2. Cuirassieren Regiment Nr. 8, Hohenzollern; *Rittmeister* in Service Dress, 1799–1805

Cuirassier officers carried breast armour like the private cuirassier, but showed the main distinctive rank insignia, consisting in the gilded brass arrowhead plate on the breast. Field officers' plate extended to the bottom of the cuirass, while *Ober-Offizieren* (company officers) had a shorter arrow, like the one here represented. The armour was edged in gold for officers and brass for the rank and file. The red cloth lining is plainly visible on the breastplate of officers only. The *Pallasch* scabbard is the model with the black leather cover for the cavalry officers, replaced in 1805 by the one in full metal. Also the helm with gilded comb and fittings was reserved for officers, but without difference among the officers' ranks until 1805. Note the *Feldbinde* waist sash partially concealed by the lower edge of the cuirass.

3. Cuirassieren Regiment Nr. 4, Kavanagh; *Trompete*, 1802–05

Cuirassier trumpeters followed the pattern established for the German cavalry, and the only difference consisted in the collar with coloured *Paroli*. A cuirassier trumpeter did not have cuirass and firearms, except for pistols in the saddle holsters. The main distinctive of rank for musicians was the red crest on the helm. In 1802, in order to preserve the white *Röckel*, trumpeters of all cavalry branches received a field coat in *lichtgrau* cloth, with the facing colour only on the collar. This item is rarely represented and less mentioned, but the use is documented in several coeval accounts as being worn in training and quarter duties. Cuirassiers replaced the helm with the new higher model in 1807, but in 1805 the frontal plate changed the cipher to 'F-I'.

Plate D: Heavy Cavalry 1806–15

1. Cuirassieren Regiment Nr. 9, Nassau-Usingen; *Gemeiner* in Service Dress, 1807–1815

This private cuirassier wears the uniform introduced after 1805, the new helm with higher comb distributed between 1806 and 1807, and grey service overall trousers. This is the uniform of the Austrian cuirassiers as it would appear through the end of the Napoleonic wars. The helmet is now more classical in style as with other European armies. It bears the black over yellow crest and a sprig of oak leaves when on campaign.

2. Cuirassieren Regiment Nr. 1; *Kaiser*; *Gemeiner* in Campaign Dress, 1812–15

Cuirassier trooper wearing the *Roquelor* greatcoat. The very large skirts protected equipment and horse as well from bad weather. The *Roquelor* changed little from the original pattern, except for minor details, as for the patches on the collar, reintroduced after 1811. Note the helm with removed woollen crest, as waas usual on campaign. Crests were retained only by NCOs, trumpeters and officers.

On campaigns and transfers, the iron-shod picket stake was usually carried on the horse by all Austrian cavalry troopers. The picket was secured with a coiled rope between the valise and the left knee, and transported at the right side strapped with the carbine, in this case a cavalry *Stutzen*. Though several cavalry officers opposed the use of *Stutzen*, saying that every weapons required more careful charging than ordinary carbines, loading on horseback was less complicated for troopers equipped with the shorter and lighter *Stutzen*, which could be easily held with the left hand, while the right charged it. However, after 1812, when cuirassiers served on horseback, saddle pistols were the only firearms. Only the canteen and the cartridge box were worn over the *Roquelor*, other equipment being concealed beneath it.

Plate E: Cuirassier Uniform, Details

1. Cuirassier's Coat for Private and NCO, 1792–98

At the eve of the wars against France, the 'German cavalry' coat was essentially the same introduced in 1767, consisting in a single-breasted *Rock* manufactured with white cloth and lined of white coarse fabric. The plain cuffs measured 8cm, and were closed with two buttons on the lower edge. On the breast, 10 smooth buttons remained hidden under the cuirass. The cavalry coat was 10.5cm shorter than the coeval infantry one, and tailored following a different pattern. The standing collar of the cuirassier coat was a narrow 2.6cm high (1 *Zoll*) strap with small button and *Paroli*, collar patch. *Paroli*, cuffs and edging of the folded turnbacks were in the regimental facing colour, known as *Egalisierung*.

2. Cuirassier's coat, a: private and NCO, b: field officers, 1799–1805

For all the German cavalry, a new coat replaced the older model after 1798. The new jacket – *der Röckel* – was manufactured in white cloth for cuirassiers only. The collar maintained the traditional *Paroli* patches but increased its size, now measuring 3.2cm height. Compared to the previous model, the new coat reduced the size of the skirts, but held the same 10 large buttons on the breast and two at the back, with further two small buttons on each cuff, one to each pocket, and one to each turnbacks. A single strap of the facing colour was at the left shoulder, with another small button in order to maintain the cross-belts. In the later model, a further strap was added to the left side at the waist level, fastened by a button, to accommodate the sword belt. The officer's coat followed the same pattern, but without the shoulder strap. Field officers' coats bore a lace on the cuffs in silver or gold as a distinctive insignia.

3. Cuirassier's Coat for Private and NCO, 1806–1815

In 1805, a new *Röckel* for the German cavalry was designed and issued in the next year to dragoons and chevauxlegers, and then to cuirassiers within the next two years. The most evident modification concerned the collar, which again changed its size, now measuring 10cm high. Cuirassiers lost their traditional *Paroli*, replaced by new collar patches applied on both outer edges, with a small button in white or yellow metal. According to the period iconography, the patches appear to be of various patterns (a–b).

4. Saddle cover 1792–1798, a: private, b: company officers, c: field officers, d: NCOs

5. Saddle cover 1799–1805, a: private and NCO, b: company officers, c: field officers

6. Standard Belt for German Cavalry 1792–1815

The standard belts were made from leather or a double layer of canvas, lined with cloth of the regiment's facing colour and decorated with a broad woven white or yellow lace echoing the metal of the buttons. Hussar regiments carried a similar belt with the background colour as for *Pelz* and *Attila* with silver or golden lace. Uhlan standard belts were red with golden lace.

7. *Porte-epée* for Cuirassiers, Dragoons, Chevauxlegers and *Jäger zu Pferd*, a: private, b: corporal

The *Porte-epée* sword knot carried the important task of identifying the rank of the Austrian cavalry, as well as infantry and artillery. The *Primaplana* sword knot was manufactured of yellow/black camel hair with a fringed tassel, while the corporal had the same but in *Harras* fabric with the tassel in camel hair. This rule concerned all the German cavalry, and did not change in subsequent years.

Plate F: Dragoons and *Chevauxlegers*, 1792–1798

1. Chevauxlegers Regiment Nr. 11, Modena; *Gemeiner*, 1792–98

Dragoons and chevauxlegers followed the same uniform scheme prescribed for the German cavalry, except for the headdress: the felt headgear for the former and the leather *Kasket* for the latter. In 1792 four of six chevauxleger regiments were dressed with white coats, while the other two wore a *grassgrün* version reminiscent of their seniority in the specialty. Breeches and other items were the same for all the regiments.

2. Dragoner Regiment Royal Allemand; *Gemeiner*, 1792–97

This figure is a reconstruction from a coeval print depicting the uniform of the regiment in the 1790s. This version differed strongly to the official uniform described in the documents of the Austrian *Kriegsarchiv*, which refers to a dark blue coat with red *Egalisierung*. Also the authoritative Teuber-Ottenfeld work depicts this latter version, adding seven white lanyards with tassels on the breast. Probably this uniform was only prescribed, but never worn, as the regiment was dissolved in 1798.

3. Leichte Dragoner Regt. Nr. 11, Latour; *Wachtmeister*, 1799–1800
Physical logistic difficulties, the need to save resources, resulted in several cases in regiment dressed with mixed items from the new and old regulations. This light dragoon, depicted in the *Züricher Bilderserie* dated between 1799 and 1800, is wearing the regular coat and equipment introduced with the 1798 regulation, while headdress, boots and probably also the breeches belong to the older uniform. This and other examples are common whenever there was a transition between old and new regulations, however in Austria some items of the old uniforms continued to be used long after the new models came into force. Note the wooden cane with brass top as a rank distinctive for NCOs, and the waist belt with the loops provided to insert the scabbard and pistol when the horsemen was in action dismounted.

Plate G: *Dragoner*, *Chevauxlegers*, and *Jäger zu Pferde*, 1798–1805

1. Regiment Jäger zu Pferd, Bussy; *Gemeiner*, 1798–1801
The newly raised regiment of horse chasseurs adopted the same uniform of the 'German' cavalry with the colour of the dismounted *Jäger* Corps. Further differences were for the helm's crest, in dark green wool, and the belt equipment in black leather. According to coeval iconography, the helm had no plate on the front, only a separate gilded brass cipher 'F.II.' Company and field officers wore the helm with the gilded comb, and the latter with the yellow/black silk crest. Horse furniture followed the German pattern.

2. Dragoner Regiment Nr. 1, Erzherzog Johann Baptist; *Gemeiner*, 1802–1805
After the dissolution of the *Leichte Dragoner* the Austrian dragoons readopted the white uniform, though this had been never dismissed in some regiments, according to eyewitness and iconographic evidence for the period 1799–1801. In 1802 there were also chevauxlegers regiments dressed in white, and therefore the facing colours were allocated in pairs: the dragoons had white metal buttons and the chevauxlegers yellow. This trooper is armed with a German *Pallasch* sword and cavalry musket Model 1798. All horsemen, except officers, have a moustache.

3. Chevauxlegers Regiment Nr. 1, Kaiser, *Rittmeister* with cloak, 1802–1803
Austrian officers could tailor their uniform privately; moreover, there was large discretion regarding the overcoat. In addition to the *Roquelor* used on campaign, the officers could wear the *Überrock*, or, as in this case, the cloak, which had been the traditional winter garment of the Austrian cavalry. This cloak, manufactured in white cloth with the high collar lined with the regiment's facing colour, was used only for special events, preferably out of service. However, many of these licenses were limited after 1805, and *Roquelor* and *Überrock* became the only winter clothing for officers, the latter worn especially for city dress. This officer carries the sword issued to

the *Leichte Dragoner* with leather and metal scabbard prescribed for officers until 1803. Officers' hairstyles throughout the cavalry were like those of the infantry: hair powder and a 'queue', bound with black ribbon, were still being used, replacing the rolls of hair over the ears prescribed before 1798.

Plate H: *Dragoner*, *Chevauxlegers* and *Jäger-zu-Pferd* Uniforms, Details

1. Dragoon and Chevauxleger Coat for Private and NCO, 1792–98

Dragoons and chevauxlegers wore the same uniform except for minor difference, and in turn it was similar to the one issued to the cuirassiers and carabiniers, but their *Rock* had a turn-down collar with the regimental facing colour, instead of the standing collar with *Paroli*. The same facing colour appeared on the strap fastened on the left shoulder of the private and NCO's coat.

2. *Leichte Dragoner* Coat for Private and NCO, 1799–1805

3. *Jäger zu Pferd* Coat, for Private and NCO, 1798–1801

The new 1798 *Röckel* coat in *meergrün* cloth was issued to the newly formed regiments of light dragoons, while *Jäger zu Pferd* had it in *hechtgrau*. Both followed the same changes introduced for the heavy cavalry uniforms, included the new standing collar. As for the previous uniform, the facing colour appeared on the broad edging on the turnbacks.

4. Dragoon Coat for Private and NCO, 1806–15

The major change occurred for the coat after 1805 concerning the collar, which increased its height to 11cm. The chevauxlegers coat followed the same pattern, but with yellow metal buttons.

5. Private's Saddle Cover for all German Cavalry Specialties, 1810–15

Shortage of funds and 'good economy measures' forced the Austrian military administration to spare whenever possible on material and other goods destined for the army. In this regard, saddle covers for privates distributed after 1810 were deprived of the anterior section. This change halved the cost of the saddle cover, not only concerning the cloth but also for the lesser quantity of laced edging required.

6. Cross-belts and cartridge boxes, a: for carabiniers, 1792–1798, b: for cuirassiers, 1799–1804

7. Cross-belts and cartridge boxes, 1805–1815, a and b variants for all cavalry branches

The ramrod was a distinctive feature of Austrian cavalry equipment. Since the Austrian cavalry carbines and pistols were deprived of their own ramrod, and in order to preserve the item from being dropped when in action, it was carried upon a leather strap and secured to the underside of the shoulder belt. The variety of firearms required different equipment when the horseman carried musket, carbine or the short *stutzen*, which required the same ramrod as the pistol.

Plate I: Hussars, 1792–1809

1. Frei Corps Rohan, *Gemeiner*, 1797–1798

The hussars corps Rohan was originally recruited between 1794 and 1795 by the Prince Louis de Rohan-Montbazon. With his ambitious plan, the French noble intended to form a personal army attracting French loyalist horsemen to join the Rohan-Étrangères infantry regiment, in order to form the Legion du Prince de Rohan in British service. However, at the end of 1796 the legion was disbanded and the cavalry entered the service of Austria on 1st May 1797 under the name Frei-Corps Rohan, and later also the Rohan Husaren Regiment. The cavalry retained the uniform established in 1795, but with the Austrian headdress with black/yellow plume, lanyards, pompom and *Rosette* on the headdress. The uniform of the Rohan regiment exemplifies the variety of clothing existing among the Austrian hussars before 1798.

2. Husaren Regiment Nr. 1, Kaiser; *Wachtmeister* in High Dress, 1799–1804

Hussar uniform was a restyling of the traditional dress of the Hungarian light cavalry. While maintaining the traditional features, such as the bearskin cap and the fur trimmed *Pelz*, after 1798 the hussar uniform gradually lost some of its Hungarian attributes and was regulated as carefully as that of the German cavalry. However, for several years a lot of informal clothing coexisted together with that prescribed in the regulations. Notwithstanding the difference of pattern and accessories, the main features are here represented and this senior NCO shows a substantial regularity concerning the uniform issued to the hussars after 1798. The main change concerned the new peaked shako, which replaced the cylindrical headdress of the previous regulation. The pompom, under the plume, was joined to the yellow/black *Rosette* cockade, but was a little smaller than the previous model, and held by two vertical yellow laces as usual. The neckband as for the German cavalry replaced the old fashioned *halsflor*. The *Pelz* illustrated here has button and lanyard braid tailored in the usual pattern, but contemporary iconography show them arranged in a zig-zag design, a variation which appears in some pictures as late as 1805. Rank markings for *Wachtmeister* are displayed in the form of a double golden lace around the top of the shako, and the hazel cane with brass top. The scabbard is the old model in black leather with gilded brass fittings, replaced from 1805 by the full iron model.

3. Husaren Regiment Nr. 3, Erzherzog Ferdinand Carl; *Gemeiner* in Service Dress, 1805–1809

A standard feature of the Austrian-Hungarian hussars was the fact that the Pelz and dolman, including collar and cuffs, were invariably of the same colour and coincided with the *Egalisierung*. However, shako and breeches could be of different colours in order to identify the regiments, as occurred for this hussar belonging to a regiment dressed in blue, like the previous figure, but with the *hechtgrau* shako identifying the 3rd Regiment. The shako of this horseman now has a wider top and a dummy rear peak, replacing the cylindrical headdress of the previous uniform. Plume, raquette and oak leaves are carried on the shako, but usually on campaign only the latter was retained as field sign by the troopers, while NCOs and officers also continued to bear a plume in action. The 'mixed-grey' overall trousers were common to all the Austrian cavalry for service dress, but those worn by hussars had a leather insert at the lower edges. This trooper is armed with the hussar carbine model 1798, which differed in length from that issued to the German cavalry.

Plate J: Hussars, 1810–15

1. Husaren Regiment Nr. 5, Ott; *Unterlieutenant* – Honorary Standard Bearer, 1814

After 1769, the rank of standard bearer did not belong to the officer corps, but he was associated to the NCO. However, a consolidated tradition in the army of the House of Austria, provided that in the event of promotion or for the reception of awards, the regiment's standard was assigned to the officer receiving the prize. For these ceremonies special ensigns and a standard belt were used, of which some items have survived to our day, also because they were less subject to deterioration through continuous use. The unusual standard belt is preserved in the Hungarian Army Museum and evidently destined to ceremonies and parades, as suggested by the elaborate decorations and rich accessories. This *Ober-Offizier* wears the uniform prescribed for company officers in 1798, but with the new shako introduced in 1805. His sheepskin is plainly black while other sources describe them as white.

2. Husaren Regiment Nr. 10, Mészáros-Stipsicz; *Gemeiner* in *Gepernek* Cloak, 1810–15

The *Gepernek* cloak was the Hungarian counterpart of the German *Roquelor* overcoat worn by the cavalry in winter. This garment was very simple and existed in different versions, completed by an additional cape and even hood in the older model. Manufactured in coarse white/grey wool, the *Gepernek* was usually deprived of *Egalisierung* facing colours. Under the cloak, in the cold, snowy weather, this hussar is wearing his fur-lined pelisse instead of carrying it over his shoulder. Note the removal of the plume and other accessories of the shako for field service.

Plate K: Hussar Uniform, Details

1. *Pelz* 1792–1815, a: *Gemeiner*, b: detail of the cuffs for NCO

2. *Pelz* 1792–1815; *Ober-Offizieren* (company officers)

3. *Pelz* 1792–1815; *Stabs-Offizieren* (field officers)

4. *Attila* 1792–1813; a: *Gemeiner*, b: NCO, c: company officers

5. *Attila* 1792–1813; field officers

6. *Attila* 1814–15, a: *Gemeiner*, b: NCO
There are several pictures illustrating *Pelz* (pelisse) and *Attila* (dolman), all depicting a wide variety of patterns even after the introduction of the 1798 *Vorschrift*, which considerably diminished the particularities of the hussar uniform. Brown or white fur edging was originally prescribed only for officers, but after 1798 a wide variety of examples are represented and successively black or brown furs became the more common for all ranks. These features lasted until 1813, when shorter dolmans without pointed edges begin to appear more and more frequently. After 1811 further modifications concerned the trooper's shako, which replaced the perishable cockade in fabric with a metal *Rosette* painted in yellow/black; the lace loop was also in metal.

7. Breeches, a: *Gemeiner* and NCO common variants, b: detail of the back for *Gemeiner* and NCO, c: field officers

8 – *Säbeltasche* 1805–15, a: field officers, b: company officers
These elaborate patterns for the officer's sabretache were introduced with the regulation of 1798 and remained unmodified until the 1830s, except for the Imperial cipher 'F.I.', which replaced the previous 'F.II.' in 1805. The cover was manufactured in cloth and embroidered with silk and metal accessories, and surely both were the most expensive items of the hussar's uniform.

9. *Rosette* Cockade and Pompom for Officers of all Ranks

10. Equipment for *Ober-Offizieren* (company officers), 1799–1815, a: belt, b: detail of the badge, c: ammunition pouch
Field Officers and company officers shared some rank insignia, such ase the cockade and pompom of the shako, but further distinctives qualified the senior ranks, such as the cartridge box, which carried the gilded double-headed eagle on the cover.

Plate L: Uhlans, 1792–1815

1. Uhlanen Regiment Nr. 2 (Uhlanen Freiwilligen Korps), *Gemeiner*, 1792–98

This horseman wears one of the various uniforms attributed to the early uhlans in the 1790s. As often occurred in the Austrian cavalry, the presence of differences in the uniform of the early units was the result of the use of heterogeneous equipment and dress. Before 1791 Austrian uhlans formed irregular corps or were distributed into the chevauxlegers regiments, and this resulted in a wide variety of dress, which could probably be recycled when the regular regiments were raised. The pre-1798 uhlan uniform comprised the yellow, peakless, topped *konfederatka* cap with fur headband and black/ yellow plume, and this item is confirmed in all the coeval iconographic sources. Coats in dark green with red lapels are also confirmed with little differences in the details, while the waistcoats appear represented in white, green or red, as for the figure here reproduced. Further differences consists in the presence of a black and yellow epaulette on the right shoulder, while contemporary pictures show a green shoulder strap, piped red. Breeches in red or in white with yellow/black braid are also usually depicted.

2. Uhlanen Regiment Nr. 3, Erzherzog Carl; *Gemeiner* in High Dress, 1809–10

This figure shows the change occurred in the uhlan uniform, after the distribution of the new large *Czapka* in 1802, which replaced the previous smaller model, and the new *Kurtka*, which in 1809 modified the lapels with the new profile of the *plastron* enlarging to the shoulders. The horse furniture is conformed to regulation, but in a few years the saddle cover would be replaced with the 'economic' model deprived of the anterior section.

3. Uhlanen Regiment Nr. 4, Kaiser; *Oberst*, 1814–15

The last uhlan regiment raised in 1814 adopted white as facing colour limited to the *Czapka*, as occurred for the other uhlan units. This colonel wears a customised single-breasted *Kurtka* with wide golden lace as rank distinctive. The *Czapka* follows the pattern established for field officers, identified by the golden edge on the top. After 1812, panache-style feathers became usual, and some coeval illustrations show black leather reinforcements on the corner of the headdress top.

Plate M: Uhlan Uniform, Details

1. Uhlanen Regiment Nr. 1, Merveldt; *Gemeiner*, 1799–1804

As for the hussars, the 1798 Regulation established more accurate rules also for uhlan uniform. This included a *meergrün* Polish jacket, the *Kurtka*, **with** ponceau red standing collar, lapels closed to the waist by six buttons forming a 'plastron' front. Pointed cuffs, piping and turnbacks were also in red. Each *Kurtka* required 28 smooth buttons of yellow metal. Laced cuffs were reserved for field officers only. The regulation prescribed no queue of hair, and the hair could be in Polish style; moustaches were obligatory for all ranks, but optional for field officers. The colour of the top section of the *Czapka* identified the regiment: yellow for Regiment Nr. 1, green for Regiment Nr. 2, and black (later red) for Regiment Nr. 3 raised in 1801.

2. *Kurtka* jacket 1799–1808, a: detail of shoulder strap for private and NCO

3. Detail of the Rear of the *Kurtka* Jacket

The uhlan *Kurtka* was the same for all regiments, being the actual facing colour on the top of *Czapka*. The officer's *Kurtka* had the same design and colour but with falling collar.

4. *Kurtka* jacket 1809–11, a: epaulette for *Gemeiner*, b: NCO, c: shoulder strap for *Gemeiner*; d: NCO

In 1809 the *Kurtka* was modified coherently with the change introduced in the uniform of the German cavalry. The major change concerned the new, higher, standing collar introduced for all ranks. After 1811 collar, cuffs, lapels and piping became *carmoisin* red for all regiments.

5. Trousers, a: officer, 1798–1815, b: *Gemeiner*, 1805–1815

Before 1805 trousers for all ranks had two side lace on both sides, but after this date only the officers preserved the double lace. Note the officer's trousers without leather reinforce in the lower section.

6. *Gemeiner*'s *Czapka* 1799–1801

In 1798, the Austrian Uhlans received a new model of *Czapka* with peak. The new headdress measured 21.8cm high and the top square diminished the size to 23cm each side, for 32.5cm of the diagonal. It had a black leather lower section replacing the fur headband and a cloth upper section with a square top covered with the regimental colour: yellow for Nr. 1, green for Nr. 2, and after 1801 black, later red, for the Nr. 3. The new headdress retained the plume, identical to that of the hussars, but usually with richer feathers. In 1803, some coeval pictures show uhlans still retaining a black and yellow pompom as worn by hussars.

7. *Czapka*, a: NCO 1810–1815, b: company officers 1802–1815, late version with reinforced corners, 1812–15, d: cockade pompom for officers of all ranks.

The new higher model of *Czapka* was introduced in 1801, when the 3rd Regiment of Uhlans had been raised, and gradually replaced the older model in the following years in all the regiments. As confirmed by the 1811 Regulation, officers' uniform included the *Czapka* with golden yellow-edged peaks, gilt chains and lion head bosses as for hussars. The leather skull was separated from the cloth by a band of gold lace with two interwoven black stripes. It had yellow/black cords and a 25.5cm upright feather plume of black over yellow, above a gold cockade bearing the Emperor's cipher in the black centre. Before 1810 the senior NCO's *Czapka* had the edge of the square piped in yellow as distinctive rank similar to the hussars, but after this date the golden edging was reserved for field officers only.

8. Field officer's belt, a: detail of the embossed figures.

9. Ammunition Pouch for Uhlan and Hussar Field Officers

10. Uhlan and hussar *Porte-epée* 1792–1815, a: corporal; b: NCO.

Plate N: the Cavalry of the *Reichsarmee*

1. Schwäbischer Kreis Dragoner Regiment Württemberg, 1792
The Swabian Kreis-Regiment of dragoons wore this old-fashioned uniform until the eve of the wars against Revolutionary France. The bulk of the circle contingent was provided by Baden and Württemberg, but also included troops from a large number of small states and Imperial cities such as Ulm and Lindau. Trouble affected the Swabian cavalry in early 1792 when Duke Carl Eugen of Württemberg retired his troops, but shortly the new duke, Ludwig Wilhelm associated them again to the circle contingent. In 1793 the Swabian cavalry numbered about 1,000 troopers in all and were joined to the Austrian army on the Rhine. The uniform is the result of the combined Austrian and Prussian influence, especially for the latter regarding the colour of the coat.

2. Fränkischer Kreis, Cuirassieren Regiment Tresskow, 1792–93

3. Fränkischer Kreis, Dragoner Regiment Anspach, 1792–93
The circle of Franconia still retained one cuirassier and one dragoon regiment, raised in 1681 and 1691 in cooperation among the circle states. The resulting Treskow Cuirassieren Regiment was formed by 20 different territories, with Würzburg, Bamberg, Nurnberg and Ansbach-Bayreuth as major contributors. The Ansbach-Bayreuth Dragoner Regiment had a similar composition. In the spring of 1792 the Franconian cavalry was mobilised, but in March 1793 both regiments were disbanded and replaced as *Kreiskontingent* by five squadrons of the Frankenberg Husaren Regiment provided by Prussia.

All the figures in this plate come form the coeval *Nachricht von den Fränkischer Kraistruppen, nebst einem Anfang von den Schwäbischen Kreisregimentern*, published in Nurnberg in 1782.

Plate O: Austrian Cavalry Ensigns

1. Ordinary Standard Pattern for all Specialties, 1792–1804
After 1771 all Austrian cavalry colours were 80 or 82cm square, with a few exceptions. Each regiment had its own *Leibstandarte*, carried by the *Regiment Estandarte-Führer* attached to the *Regimentsstab*, and one *Ordinärstandarte* for each tactical *Division*. The *Leibstandarte* was white, one

side bearing the image of the Virgin Mary, and the reverse bearing the full Imperial arms upon the breast of the crowned, double-headed, black eagle. The ordinary standard was yellow, bearing the eagle on both sides. There were no differences between one regiment and another, although there were different details such as the distribution of the sword or sceptre in the eagle's legs, the colour of the crown's ribbon, or the flames on the edge. In 1802 the rank of *Regiment Estandarte-Führer* was abolished, and the overall number of standards was established depending the number **of** *Divisionen*, assigning the *Leibstandarte* **to the** *Oberst-Division*. Usually, heavy regiments carried all their standards in the field, but most light regiments did not.

2.Ordinary Standard Pattern for all Specialties, 1805–1815

The main novelty appeared on the Austrian ensigns was the new Imperial monogram in 1805, and the reduction of the Habsburg coat of arms to the new territorial status. Surprisingly, on many flags of this period the crown of the old Roman–German empire has not been removed. From 1806 the regiment's name and number was painted in the top corner on both sides next to the pole. In the same year, the experiences learned in the unsuccessful campaigns of the 1790s and 1805 persuaded the Aulic War Council to reduce the number of ensigns carried by the units on campaign, because they became enemy instruments of propaganda when captured in large quantities. However, on campaign cavalry regiments seem to have used old standards long after they were officially replaced. Four Austrian standards captured by the French at Austerlitz date back to the age of Empress Maria Theresia, and even three cavalry ensigns lost in 1812 by Chevauxlegers Regiment Nr. 3, now preserved in Moscow, seems to have dated between 1711 and 1740, being embroidered with the cipher of Emperor Carl VI. To complicate the matter, the finial bears the monogram of Emperor Franz I.

3. Ordinary Standard, Unknown Hussar Regiment, 1805–15

As with uniforms, the hussars retained several permissions also regarding the ensigns. Among these, each regiment had its own standard, which could differ in size and colour from ordinary ones. Some of these colours are today preserved in the military museums of the country that composed the Habsburg Empire, and the good state of preservation suggests that these ensigns were used on a limited number of occasions.

4. Regimental Standard, Husaren Regiment Nr. 5, 1809–15

This particular ensign, probably a 'Standard of Honour' preserved in the Hungarian Army Museum, is attributed to the 5th Hussars regiment, which probably used it only during ceremonies and parades. Unlike the majority of cavalry standards, which are square, this ensign has a rectangular shape and the background colour represents a significant exception, which confirms the strong sense of identity of the Hungarian subjects.

5. *Ehrestandarte*, 1814

Another 'Standard of Honour' carried by the Austrian hussars was also manufactured following a different pattern. This colour was presented to the Husaren Regiment Nr.4 in 1814 by Pope Pius VII, when one squadron of the regiment had escorted him from Savona. The Pope had been held under house arrest by Napoleon. The reverse carried the Virgin with Child, extending the cloud to the Pope with the inscription *Hungariae Patrona Pium comitatur ad Urbem – O felix tanto Roma sub aupicio.*

6. Standard Finial, 1792–1805

The pole head was a gilt spear with the Imperial cipher or double-headed eagle embossed. The size of the pole was 185–205cm.

7. Ensign Cover

On campaign the standards were preserved inside covers of leather or waxed canvas, with a metal tip corresponding to the standard's spear, and tied with string to secure them to the pole.

Plate P: *Farbtabelle*

The uniform colours table of the Austrian army, after the *Abbildung der K.K. Oesterreichischen Armee durch alle Waffengattungen*, published in Vienna in 1820.

Bibliography

Regulations

Anleitung zum Selbst-Studium der militärischen Dienstwissenschaft für Officiere der k.k. österreichischen Armee, Erster Theil, Waffenlehre (Vienna, 1807)
Generalsreglement (Vienna, 1769)
Dienst-Reglement für die Kaiserlich-Königliche Kavallerie, Part I (Vienna, 1807)
Vorschriften für die kaiserliche Kavallerie (Vienna 1806)

Archive Sources

Österreichisches Staatsarchiv – Kriegsarchiv, Vienna, *Alte Feld Akten, Stand- und Diensttabellen Karton*, 1801–1815

Printed Sources

Angeli Moriz, von, *Erzherzog Carl von Österreich als Feldherr und Heeresorganisator: Im Auftrage seiner Söhne, der Herren Erzherzoge Albrecht und Wilhelm, dann seiner Enkel, der Herren Erzherzoge Friedrich und Eugen; nach österreichischen Original-acten dargestellt*, vol. 5 (Vienna, 1897)
Anger, Gibert, *Illustrierte Geschichte der k. k. Armee*, vols I–III (Vienna, 1886–1887)
Aretin, Karl, *Heiliges Römisches Reich 1776–1806: Reichsverfassung und Staatssouveränität* (Wiesbaden: Franz Steiner Verlag, 1967)
Bancalari, Gustav, *Beiträge zur Geschichte des österreichischen Heerwesens*, vols I-II (Vienna, 1872)
Bergmayr, Ignaz Franz, *Kriegs-und Marine-Verfassung des Kaisertums Österreich* (Vienna, 1842)
Bönninghausen, Klemens von, *Die kriegerische Tätigkeit der münsterschen Truppen, 1651–1800* (Coesfeld: privately printed, 1978)
Bowden, Scott, and Tarbox, Charles, *Armies on the Danube 1809* (Chicago IL: The Emperor's Press, 1981)
Broucek, Peter, Zivkovic, Georg, and Klima, Herbert (eds), *Geschichte der k. u. k. Wehrmacht*, vol. 4: 'Der Allerhochste Oberbefehl, Die Garden', *Militaria Austriaca, Gesellschaft für Österreichische Heereskunde* 1988

Carl, Erzherzog von Habsburg, *Ausgewählte Schriften Weiland seiner kaiserlichen Hoheit des Erzherzogs Carl von Oesterreich* (Vienna: Braumüller, 1894)

Chandler, David G., *The Art of Warfare in the Age of Marlborough* (New York: Hippocrene Books, 1976)

Charry, Sébastien Joseph Baron de Comeau de, *Souvenirs des guerres d'Allemagne pendant la Révolution et l'Empire* (Paris: Plon, 1900)

Criste, Oskar, *Erzherzog Carl von Österreich* (Vienna, Leipzig, 1912), vol. II

Czoernig, Karl, *Ethnographie der oesterreichischen Monarchie*, kaiserlich-koeniglichen Hof- und Staatsdruckerei (Vienna: Kaiserlich-Koenigliche Hof- u. Staatsdr, 1857)

Dedekind, Franz, *Geschichte des k. k. Kaiser Franz Joseph I. Dragoner-Regimentes Nr.11, von seiner Errichtung, 20. Dezember 1688, bis 6. Mai 1879* (Vienna, published by the author, 1879)

Delbrück, Hans, *Geschichte der Kriegskunst*, vol. IV (Berlin: G. Stilke, 1920)

Elting, John, *Swords around a Throne* (Cambridge, MA: Da Capo Press, 1987)

Erdmannsdorff, Georg Anton, *Der Feldzug von 1796 in Italien: nach den besten Quellen bearbeitet* (Magdeburg: Fabricius & Schaefer, 1847)

Gallina, Josef Freiherr von, *Die Armee in der Bewegung: mit 8 Tafeln und Plänen* (Vienna, Verlag des Militär-wissenschaftlichen Vereins in commission bei C. Gerold & Sohn, 1872)

Gallina, Joseph Freiherr von, *Beiträge zur Geschichte des Österreichischen Heerwesens, Erstes Heft: Der Zeitraum von 1757 bis 1814, Mit besonderer Rücksichtnahme auf Organisation, Verpflegung und Taktik* (Vienna: L.W. Seidel & Sohn, 1872)

Gill, John H., *With Eagles to Glory: Napoleon and His German Allies in the 1809 Campaign* (Barnsely: Frontline Books, 2010)

Goetz, Robert E., *1805: Austerlitz* (London: Greenhill Books, 2005)

Gutkas, Karl, *Kaiser Joseph II. Eine Biographie* (Vienna-Darmstadt: Zsolnay, 1989)

Haythornthwaite, Philip J., *Napoleonic Cavalry* (London: Cassell & Co, 2002)

Hayworth, Jordan R., *Revolutionary France's War of Conquest in the Rhineland. Conquering the Natural Frontier, 1792–1797* (Cambridge University Press: Cambridge, 2019)

Heller von Hellewald, Friedrich Anton, *Der Feldzug des Jahres 1809 in Süddeutschland*, vol. II (Vienna: Gerold, 1864)

Hochedlinger, Michael, *Austria's War of Emergence. War, State and Society in the Habsburg Monarchy, 1683–1797* (London and New York: Routledge, 2013)

Hollins, D., and Pavlovic,D., *Hungarian Hussars, 1756–1815* (Oxford: Ospery Publishing, Warrior Series, 2003)

Hornthal, Edler von, Horsetzky, Adolf von, and Gallina, Josef Freiherr von, *Beiträge zum Studium des Feldzuges 1805:* Nach einem Aufsatze des F.-m.-LT. Gallina (Vienna, K.k. Kriegsschule, 1885)

Horstenau, Edmund Glaise von, *Die Tage von Dresden 1813* (Leipzig: Edlinger, 1911)

Hübler Franz, *Militaer Oekonomie-System der kaiserlichen königlichen österreichischen Armee*, vol. 4 (Vienna, 1820–23)

Kählig, E. v. – Jedina, R. Rit. v., *Österreich-Ungarn – Die Heere und Flotten der Gegenwart*, vol IV (Berlin: Schall & Grund, 1898)

Karger, Johann Anton, *Die Entwicklung der Adjustierung, Rüstung und Bewaffnung der österreichische-ungarischen Armee 1700–1809* (printed version of the manuscript dated 1903; Bucholz: LTR, 1998)

Knötel, Richard, and Sieg, Herbert, *Handbuch der Uniformkunde*, vol. 3 (Rathenow, 1956)

Leggiere, Michel V., *The Fall of Napoleon*, vol. I, *The allied Invasion of France, 1813–1814* (Cambridge: Cambridge University Press, 2007)

Ligne, Charles Joseph, Prince de, *Préjugés et fantaisies militaires par un officier autrichien* (A. Kralovelhota, 1783)

Lordick Heiner *Der Feldzug 1809: Truppen und Verbände unter Österreichs Fahnen*; (Elektronische Ressource) CD des Heeresgeschichtlichen Museums, Vienna: 2001, Parts I–IV.

1 – *Namensliste der wichtigsten auf österreichischer Seite beteiligten Personen im Feldzug 1809 unter besonderer Berücksichtigung Tirols*
2 – *Verzeichnis der k. k. Armeen, Armeekorps, Brigaden, selbständigen Abteilungen im Feldzug 1809*
3 – *Verzeichnis der k. k. Regimenter, Bataillone, selbständigen Formationen (bis Kompaniestärke) im Feldzug 1809*
4 – *Verzeichnis der Schützen- und Landsturmeinheiten Österreichs im Jahr 1809*

Lühe, Eggert Willibald von der, *Militair Conversations Lexicon*, vol. IV (Leipzig, 1834)

Mayerhoffer von Vedropolje, Eberhard, and Criste, Oskar, *Der Krieg 1809* (Vienna: L.W. Seidel & Sohn, 1907)

Meynert, Hermann Günther von, *Geschichte der K.k. Österreichischen Armee: Ihrer Heranbildung und organisation, so wie ihrer Schicksale, thaten und Feldzüge* (Vienne: C. Gerold & Sohn, 1852)

Meynert, Hermann Günther von,, *Geschichte des Kriegswesens und der Heeresverfassung in der Österreichischen Monarchie vom Tode des Kaisers Leopold I bis auf die gegenwärtige Zeit* (Vienna: Gerold in Komm., 1854)

Muir, Rory, *Tactics and the Experience of Battle in the Age of Napoleon* (New Haven and London: Yale University Press, 1998)

Müller, Franz, *Die Kaiserliche und Königliche österreichische Armee seit Errichtung der stehenden Kriegsheere bis auf die neueste Zeit: Nebst einer Beigabe: Notizen über die bewaffneten Bürger-Corps der größeren Städte der Monarchie*, vols 1–2 (Prague, 1845)

Nafziger, George, *Imperial Bayonets: Tactics of the Napoleonic Battery, Battalion and Brigade as Found in Contemporary Regulations* (London: Greenhill Books, 1997)

Nafziger, George, and Gioannini, Marco, *The Defense of the Napoleonic Kingdom of Northern Italy 1813–1814* (Westport: Praeger Pub, 2001)

Nagyrévi-Neppel, György, *Huszárok* (Budapest: Corvina, 1973)

Rauch, Josef, *Erinnerungen eines Offiziers aus Altösterreich* (Munich: G. Müller, 1918)

Rauchensteiner Manfried, *Kaiser Franz und Erzherzog Carl: Dynastie und Heerwesen in Österreich 1796–1809* (Vienna: Verlag für Geschichte und Politik, 1972)

Regele, Oskar, *Generalstabschefs aus vier Jahrhunderten das Amt des Chefs des Generalstabes in der Donaumonarchie, seine Träger und Organe von 1529 bis 1918* (Vienna–Munich: Herold, 1966)

Rothenberg, Gunther E., *The Art of Warfare in the Age of Napoleon* (Bloomington: Indiana University Press, 1980)

Rothenberg, Gunther E., *Napoleon's Great Adversary: Archduke Charles and the Austrian Army, 1792–1814* (Bloomington: Indiana University Press, 1982)

Seaton, Albert, *Die österreichisch-ungarische Armee in der Zeit der Napoleonischen Kriege*, vols I–III (Bonn: Wehr und Wissen, 1979)

Schreiber, Georg, *Des Kaisers Reiterei – Österreichische Kavallerie in vier Jahrhunderten* (Vienna: Spiedel, 1967)

Schuster, O., and Franke, F.A., *Geschichte der Sächsischen Armee von deren Errichtung bis auf die neueste Zeit*, vol. II (Dresden: 1885)

Teuber, O., and Ottenfeld, R. v., *Die österreichische Armee von 1700 bis 1867* (Vienna: Berté und Czeiger, 1895)

Thürheim, Andreas Graf von, *Die Reiter-Regimenter der K. K. österreichischen Armee* (Vienna: F.B. Geitler, 1862)

Thürheim, Andreas Graf von, *Gedenkblätter aus der Kriegsgeschichte der k. k. Oesterreichischen Armee*, vols I–II (Wien–Teschen: Buchhandlung für militär-literatur, 1880)

Treuenfest, Gustav Amon von, *Geschichte des k.k. 11. Huszaren-regimentes Herzog Alexander v. Württemberg 1762 bis 1850 Székler Grenz-huszaren* (Vienna: Verlag des Regimentes, 1878)

Treuenfest, Gustav Amon von, *Geschichte des k. k. Dragone-Regimentes Feldmarschall Alfred Fürst zu. Windiscb-Graetz Nr.14* (Vienna: Verlag des Regimentes, 1886)

Treuenfest, Gustav Amon von, *Geschichte des k. und k. Bukowina'schen Dragoner-Regimentes General der Cavallerie Freiherr Piret de Bihain Nr.9 von seiner Errichtung 1682 bis 1892* (Vienna: Verlag des Regimentes, 1892)

Treuenfest, Gustav Amon von, *Geschichte des kaiserl. und königl. Husaren-Regimentes Nr.10 Friedrich Wilhelm III., König von Preussen* (Vienna: Verlag des Regimentes, 1892)

Treuenfest, Gustav Amon von, *Geschichte des k. und k. Husaren-Regimentes Kaiser Nr.1* (Vienna: Verlag des Regimentes, 1898)

Ulmenstein, Christian U. von, *Die Offiziere des Schaumburg-Lippischen Truppenkorps, 1648–1857* (Berlin: Verl. f. Standesamtswesen 1940)

Wagner Walter, *Von Austerlitz bis Königgrätz, Österreichische Kampftaktik im Spiegel des Reglements 1805–1864* (Osnabruck Biblio-Verlag, 1978)

Whaley, Joachim, *Germany and the Holy Roman Empire. Volume II: The Peace of Westphalia to the Dissolution of the Reich, 1648–1806* (New York: Oxford University Press, 2012)

Wilson, Peter, *German Armies, War and German politics,1648–1806* (London: UCL Press, 1998)

Wrede, Alfons Freiherrn von, and Semek, Anton, *Geschichte der K. und K. Wehrmacht: Die Regimenter, Corps, Branchen und Anstalten von 1618 bis Ende des XIX. Jahrhunderts*, vols I–V (Vienna: L.W. Seidel, 1901)

Zeiner, Hubert, *Geschichte des österreichischen Generalstabes* (Vienna, Cologne, Weimar: Bohlau Verlag, 2006)

Articles and Essays

[Author not stated], 'The Armies of Europe', in *Putnam's Monthly*, No. XXXII, 1855

[Author not stated], 'Krieg gegen die Französische Revolution 1792–1797', in *Kriegsgeschichtlichen Abteilung des k. und k. Kriegsarchivs, 1905*, vol. I

[Author not stated], 'Die Kopfbedeckungen der K.K. / K.u.K. Ulanen von 1784–1918', *Militaria Austriaca*, Sonderdruck 3, 1980

Angeli, Moriz von, 'Zur Geschichte des k.k. Generalstabes', in *Österreichisch-ungarische Militär-Zeitung Vedette* (Vienna, 1876), February – N. 25

Breiteneder, Herbert 'Feldzeichen. Ein Begriff aus der osterreichischen Militärsprache bis 1918', in *Militaria Austriaca, Gesellschaft für Österreichische Heereskunde* (Vienna, 1977)

Broucekr, Peter, Zivkovic Georg, and Klima, Herbert, 'Geschichteder k. u. k. Wehrmacht, VI. Band, Der Aller hochste Oberbefehl, Die Garden', *Militaria Austriaca, Gesellschaft für Österreichische Heereskunde* vol. VI (Vienna, 1988)

Gesellschaft für Österreichische Heereskunde (ed.), 'Die Kopfbedeckungen der K.K. / K.u.K. Ulanen von 1784–1918', in *Militaria Austriaca, Gesellschaft für Österreichische Heereskunde*, Sonderdruck, 3-1980

Glover, Michael, 'Jourdan: The True Patriot', in D. Chandler (ed.), *Napoleon's Marshals* (New York: Macmillan, 1987)

Österreichische Militärische Zeitschrift, III (Vienna, 1860)

Peball, Kurt, 'Zum Kriegsbild der österreichischen Armee', in Wolfgang von Groote, Klaus Jürgen Müller (eds), *Napoleon I und das Militärwesen seiner Zeit* (Freiburg: Rombach, 1968), pp.140–185.

Saperstein, Marc, 'In Praise of an Anti-Jewish Empress', in *Shofar*, vol. 6, n. 1 (Purdue University Press, 1987), pp.20–25.

Schels, Johann Baptist, 'Außergewöhnliche Streitkräfte in der österreichischen Armee, in dem Zeitraume von 1792 bis 1815', in *Österreichische Militärische Zeitschrift*, vol. IV (Vienna 1844), pp.70–82

Tessin, Georg, 'Die Inhaber der Fränkischen und Schwäbischen Kreisregimenter', in *Zeitschrift für Heereskunde*, 5–1985, pp.81–83.

Memoirs

Chlapowski, Dezydery, transl. T. Simmons, *Memoirs of a Polish Lancer: The Pamietniki of Dezydery Chlapowski* (Chicago, IL: The Emperor's Press, 2002)

Mensdorf -Pouilly, *Tagebuch des Streifkorps unter Führung des k.k. Oberst Emanuel Grafen von Mensdorf -Pouilly (21. August bis 10. Dezember 1813)*, in HK 14 (1913), pp. 472–473

Saski Commandant, *Campagne de 1809 en Allemagne et en Autriche*, vol. II (Paris–Nancy, 1899–1902)

Rilliet, Constant, 'Tagebuch eines Kürassierenleutnants während des Feldzuges 1813', in G. Kircheisen (ed.), *Napoleons Untergang 1813* (Stuttgart: R. Lutz, 1919), vol. II

Wilson, Sir Robert Thomas, (ed. Rev. Herbert Randolph, 1861), *Private Diary of Travels, Personal Services and Public Events, During Mission and Employment with the European Armies in the Campaigns of 1812 and 1813*, (London, 1814)